Elements of
Microcomputer
Interfacing

Elements of Microcomputer Interfacing

JOSEPH J. CARR

RESTON PUBLISHING COMPANY, INC.
A Prentice-Hall Company
Reston, Virginia

Library of Congress Cataloging in Publication Data
Carr, Joseph J.
    Elements of microcomputer interfacing.

    1. Computer interfaces.   2. Microcomputers.   I. Title.
TK7887.5.C375   1984   001.64'404   83-19122
ISBN 0-8359-1705-3
ISBN 0-8359-1704-5 (pbk.)

© 1984 by Reston Publishing Company, Inc.
A Prentice-Hall Company
Reston, Virginia 22090

1   3   5   7   9   10   8   6   4   2

Printed in the United States of America

Contents

Preface

The programmable digital computer has achieved an almost mystical reputation in the few decades since its invention. Both professionals and laymen alike have stood in awe of the computer's seemingly magical capabilities. But recently, computing has come down to earth and is now a game for all. Schoolchildren can now have their own computers, as can scientists in small laboratories, engineers, and small businesses.

Manipulating, massaging, and designing computer systems was once, and to some extent still is, the domain of a new "priesthood"—programmers, systems analysts, design engineers, operators, and someone called a "computer scientist." But even this situation has changed as more and more people become knowledgeable in this area. The purpose of this book is to provide the reader with the knowledge required to build skills in these areas. At the very least, even if you will have no hands-on experience with computer equipment, you will be able to impress the computer systems salesperson with some measure of expertise.

It is not easy to balance the different interests of the wide variety of people who will need information regarding microcomputer interfacing. On the one hand, we have a small business or professional person who needs a small desktop computer to keep accounts, schedule work, and keep track of inventory that has long since grown too large for the types of management methods that were highly successful only yesterday. On the other hand is the engineer who wants to incorporate a microcomputer into the design of anything from a child's toy to a manufacturing plant process controller. Or, perhaps, the laboratory scientist who wishes to use a microcomputer to control an experiment, collect the data automatically, and then analyze the data so that a human can understand its significance, if any. All these users have different, but overlapping, areas of special interest. In this book I have tried to keep all these needs in focus and, to use photographic terminology, hope that the "depth of field" in each chapter has been carefully controlled for optimal effect.

Some knowledge of basic electronics is assumed in most of the chapters. But, wherever computer jargon is used, it is explained so that a person with less skill can also profit from the book. The book is, first and foremost, a *practical* manual, a "how to" handbook for those who either aspire to the priesthood of the computer subculture, or, who wish to avoid such people by simply performing their function.

JOSEPH J. CARR

Elements of
Microcomputer
Interfacing

1

The Microcomputer:
Its Role in Modern Design

One of the first questions asked by a purchaser of a microcomputer is "what will it do?" This question is exasperating because it has so many *good* answers. Indeed, what *is* the role of a microcomputer? For that matter, what is a microcomputer?

At one time, definitions were simpler. As a freshman engineering student at Old Dominion University in Norfolk, Virginia, I was allowed to use an IBM 1601/1620 machine. *That* was a computer! There was no doubt in anyone's mind about that machine's identity; it took up an entire room on the second floor of the engineering school's building. But, today, an engineering student can sit at a small desk with an Apple II (complete with video CRT display, printer, and two disk drives) that has more computing power than that old 1601. In fact, many engineering school students find that the cost of the typical small system is affordable and now they own their own computer. The cost of the modern microcomputer is less than one-tenth what one of the lesser machines of only a decade ago cost, not counting the fact that 1973 dollars were bigger than today's dollars.

TYPES OF COMPUTERS

Before attempting to define the role of the microcomputer, let's first try to define the microcomputer. Terminology tends to become sloppy both from our own laziness and from the fact that once-genuine distinctions have become blurred

1

as the state-of-the-art advances; terminology in the computer field is often overcome by events. For example, consider the terms *microcomputer* and *minicomputer.* Laziness tends to make some of us use these terms interchangeably, while modern single-chip computers (e.g., the Intel 8048 device) tend to make such usage seem almost reasonable. But, for our purposes, we require sharply focused meanings for these two terms and others: microprocessor, microcomputer, single-chip computer, single-board computer, minicomputer, and mainframe computer.

Microprocessor

The microprocessor is a large-scale-integration (LSI) integrated circuit (IC) that contains the *central processing unit* (CPU) of a programmable digital computer. The CPU section of a computer contains the *arithmetic logic unit* (ALU), which performs the basic computational and logical operations of the computer. The CPU also houses the *control logic* section (which performs housekeeping functions) and may or may not have several *registers* for the temporary storage of data. All CPUs have at least one temporary storage register called the *accumulator,* or *A register.* The principal attribute of a microprocessor is that it will execute instructions sequentially. These instructions are stored in coded binary form in an external *memory.*

Microcomputer

A microcomputer is a full-fledged programmable digital computer that is built around a microprocessor chip (i.e., integrated circuit); the microprocessor acts as the CPU for the computer. In addition to the microprocessor chip, the microcomputer typically will have some additional chips, the number varying from two to hundreds depending upon the design and application. These external chips may provide such functions as memory (both temporary and permanent) and input/output (I/O). The microcomputer may be as simple as a KIM-1 or as complex as a 30-board professional machine with all the electronic data-processing (EDP) options.

Single-Chip Computer

For several years we had no excuse for interchanging the terms *microprocessor* and *microcomputer;* a microprocessor was an LSI chip and a microcomputer was a computing machine. But the 8048 and similar devices began the process of dissolving the previously well defined boundaries because they were both LSI

ICs and a computer. A typical single-chip computer may have a CPU section, two types of internal memory (temporary and long-term permanent storage), and at least two I/O ports. Some machines are even more complex.

The single-chip computer does, however, require some external components before it can do work. By definition, the microcomputer already has at least a minimum of components needed to perform a job.

Single-Board Computer

The single-board computer (SBC) is a programmable digital computer, complete with input and output peripherals, on a single printed circuit board. Popular examples are the KIM-1, SYM-1, AIM-65 and Z80 starter kit machines. The single-board computer might have either a microprocessor or a single-chip computer at its heart.

The peripherals on a single-board computer are usually of the most primitive kind (AIM-65 is a notable exception) consisting of seven-segment LED numerical displays and hexadecimal keypads reminiscent of those on a handheld calculator or Touchtone® telephone. The typical display is capable of showing only hexadecimal numeral characters, and even these are a little optimistic because of the form constraints of using seven-segment LED display devices. The Rockwell International AIM-65, on the other hand, uses a regular ASCII keyboard and a 20-character display made of 5 by 7 dot matrix LEDs. In addition, the AIM-65 has a built-in 20-column dot matrix thermal printer that uses paper similar to calculator and adding machine paper.

Most single-board computers have at least one interface connector that allows either expansion of the computer or interfacing into a system or instrument design. The manufacturers of SBCs, such as the KIM-1 and others, probably did not envision their wide application as a small-scale development system. These computers were primarily touted as trainers, that is, for use in teaching microcomputer technology. But for simple projects such computers also work well as a mini development system. More than a few SBC trainers have been used to develop a microcomputer-based product, only to wind up being specified as a "component" in the production version. In still other cases, the commercially available SBC was used as a component in prototype systems and then, in the production version, a special SBC (lower cost) was either bought or built.

Minicomputer

The minicomputer predates the microcomputer and was originally little more than a scaled-down version of larger data-processing machines. The Digital

Equipment Corporation (DEC) PDP-8 and PDP-11 machines are examples. The minicomputer uses a variety of small-scale (SSI), medium-scale (MSI), and large-scale integration (LSI) chips.

Minicomputers have traditionally been more powerful than microcomputers. For example, they had longer length binary data words (12 to 32 bits instead of 4 or 8 bits found in microcomputers), and operated at faster speeds of 6 to 12 megahertz (mHz) instead of 1 to 3 mHz. But this is an area of fading distinctions. Digital Equipment Corporation, for example, offers the LSI-11 microcomputer that acts like a minicomputer. Similarly, 16-bit microcomputers are available, as are 6-mHz devices. It is sometimes difficult to draw the line of demarcation when a Z80-based microcomputer is in the same-sized cabinet as a minicomputer, and minicomputers can be bought in desk-top configurations.

Mainframe Computer

The large computer that comes to mind when most people think of computers is the *mainframe computer.* These computers are used in large-scale data-processing departments. Microcomputerists who have an elitist mentality sometimes call mainframe computers "dinosaurs." But, unlike their reptilian namesakes, these dinosaurs show no signs of extinction and are, in fact, an evolving species. The IBM 370 and CDC 6600 are examples of mainframe computers.

Advantages of Microcomputers

That microcomputers have certain advantages is attested by the fact that so many are sold. But what are these advantages, and how are they conferred?

The most obvious advantage of the microcomputer is *reduced size;* compared with dinosaurs, microcomputers are mere lizards! An 8-bit microcomputer with 64K bytes of memory can easily fit inside a tabletop cabinet. The Heath/Zenith H89 (Figure 1-1), for example, fits the complete computer (plus one optional disk drive) into the wasted space found inside their H19 video terminal cabinet. Another company packs a computer with 16K of random-access memory (RAM) inside a keyboard housing.

The LSI microcomputer chip is generally more complex than a discrete-components circuit that does the same job. The interconnections between circuit elements, however, are much shorter (micrometers instead of millimeters). Input capacitances are thereby made lower. The metal-oxide semiconductor (MOS) technology used in most of these ICs produces very low current drain; hence the overall power consumption is reduced. A benefit of reduced power requirements is reduced heating. While a minicomputer may require a pair of 100 cubic

Figure 1-1 New Heathkit H89 All-In-One Computer features two Z80 processors, floppy disk storage, smart video terminal, heavy-duty keyboard, numeric keypad and 16K RAM, all in one compact unit. *(Courtesy of Heath/Zenith)*

feet per minute (cfm) blowers to keep the temperature within specifications, a microcomputer may be able to use a single 40-cfm muffin fan or no fan at all.

Another advantage of the LSI circuit is reduced component count. Although this advantage relates directly to reduced size, it also affects reliability. If the LSI IC is just as reliable as any other IC (and so it seems), then the overall reliability of the circuit is increased dramatically. Even if the chip reliability is lower than for lesser ICs, we still achieve superior reliability due to fewer interconnections on the printed circuit board, especially if IC sockets are used on the ICs. Some of the most invideous troubleshooting problems result from defective IC sockets.

MICROCOMPUTER INTERFACING

The design of any device or system in which a microcomputer or microprocessor is used is the art of *defining* the operation of the system or device, *selecting the components* for the device or system, *matching* and *integrating* these components (if necessary), and *constructing* the device or system. These activities are known collectively as *interfacing.*

But let's get down to a more basic level. Most readers of this book are technically minded people with some knowledge of electronics and computer technology. For most readers, therefore, interfacing consists of selecting and matching components and then connecting them into a circuit that does a specific job. These are the matters that are addressed in later chapters.

MICROCOMPUTERS IN INSTRUMENT AND SYSTEM DESIGN

Designers in the past used analog electronic circuits, electromechanical relays (which sometimes precipitate a maintenance nightmare), and other devices in order to design instruments, process controllers, and the like. These circuit techniques had their limitations and produced some irritating results; factors like thermal drift loomed large in some of these circuits. In addition, the design was cast in cement once the final circuit was worked out. Frequently, relatively subtle changes in a specification or requirement produced astonishing changes in the configuration of the instrument; analog circuits are not easily adaptable to new situations in many cases. But, with the advent of the microcomputer, we gained the advantage of flexibility and solved some of the more vexing problems encountered in analog circuit design. The memory of the computer tells it what to do and that can be changed relatively easily. We can, for example, store program code in a *read-only memory* (ROM), which is an integrated-circuit memory. If a change is needed, the software can be modified and a new ROM installed. If the microcomputer was configured in an intelligent manner, it is possible to redesign only certain interface cards (or none at all) to make a new system configuration. An engineer of my acquaintance built an anode heat computer for medical x-ray machines. A microprocessor computed the heating of the anode as the x-ray tube operated and sounded a warning if the limit of safety was exceeded, thus saving the hospital the cost of a $10,000 x-ray tube. But different x-ray machines require different interfacing techniques, a problem that previously had meant a new circuit design for each machine. However, by intelligent engineering planning, the anode heat computer was built with a single interface card that married the "universal" portion of the instrument with each brand of x-ray machine. Thus, the company could configure the instrument uniquely for all customers at a minimum cost.

Another instrument that indicates the universality of the microcomputer is a certain cardiac output computer. This medical device is used by intensive-care physicians to determine the blood-pumping capability of the heart in liters per minute. A bolus of iced or room-temperature saline solution is injected into the patient at the "input" end of the right side of the heart (the heart contains two pumps, a right and left side, with the right side output feeding the left side input via the lungs). The temperature at the output end of the right side is monitored and the time integral of temperature determined. This integral, together with some constants, is used by the computer to calculate the cardiac output. These machines come in two versions, research and clinical. The researcher will take time to enter certain constants (that depend upon the catheter used to inject saline, temperature, and other factors) and will be more vigorous in following the correct procedure. But in the clinical setting, technique suffers owing to the need of caring for the patient, and the result is a perception of "machine error," which is actually operator error. To combat this problem, the manufacturer offers two machines. The research instrument is equipped with front panel controls that allow the operator to select a wide range of options. The clinical model allows no options to the operator and is a "plug and chug" model. The interesting thing about these instruments is that they are *identical* on the inside. All that is different is the front panel and the position of an on-board switch. The manufacturer's program initially interrogates a switch to see if it is open or closed. If it is open, then it "reads" the keyboard to obtain the constants. If, on the other hand, it is closed, the program branches to a subprogram that assumes certain predetermined constants, which are loaded on the buyer's prescription at the time the instrument is delivered. The cost savings of using a single design for both instruments are substantial.

SOME REAL PRODUCTS

The physical machinery that one identifies as a real microcomputer may well depend upon your point of view. Certainly, the Heath H89 machine shown in Figure 1-1 is a microcomputer. It contains a relatively large array of on-board RAM-type memory and can accommodate at least one disk drive right in the same cabinet with the CRT video terminal. But the H89 might not be the computer for all applications. In some cases, other machines will be more appropriate. In this section we will examine some of the different machines that are commonly found on the market. Inclusion in this discussion connotes neither endorsement of the product nor that some other manufacturer's product is not just as good.

Heathkit ET6800

The Heathkit model ET6800 (Figure 1-2) is strictly a student trainer and is probably the lowest-cost computer on the market. It consists of a simple keypad-

Figure 1-2   Small training "computer." *(Courtesy of Heath/Zenith)*

operated computer that is based on the Motorola MC6800 8-bit microprocessor chip. The display consists of a simple array of seven-segment light-emitting diode (LED) numerals, much like those used in calculators and other devices. The cardboard cabinet no doubt contributes immensely to the low cost of the machine. Heath originally designed the ET6800 microcomputer as an aid to their continuing education course on microprocessors (EC-6800), and it is used to learn assembly language programming. The small computer contains a 1K-byte monitor program and permits access to 256 bytes of random-access memory (RAM).

The ET6800 is not a serious microcomputer for most users and is strictly used as a trainer. It is, however, a reasonable beginning for many students, especially in view of its low cost.

Synertek SYM-1

Several years ago, the original manufacturer of the 6502 microprocessor, MOS Technology, Inc., produced a small single-board computer that contained a hexadecimal keyboard and LED readouts. Originally conceived as a trainer, the KIM-1 microcomputer became something of a standard among single-board computers, and its bus is now sometimes referred to as the "KIM-bus." The KIM inspired a large collection of magazine articles and books. For many of today's advanced computer sciences people, the little KIM-1 was their first introduction into the world of microcomputer technology.

Although the SYM-1 microcomputer shown in Figure 1-3 is based on the original KIM-1 machine, it extended the machine and provided more features than the original design. Synertek Systems Corporation of Santa Clara, California, is the manufacturer of the SYM-1 machine.

Probably the principal application for the SYM-1 is training engineers and students in microcomputer interfacing and programming technology, but applications have expanded into engineering laboratory work, prototyping of devices based on the 6502 microprocessor, instrumentation, and conducting both

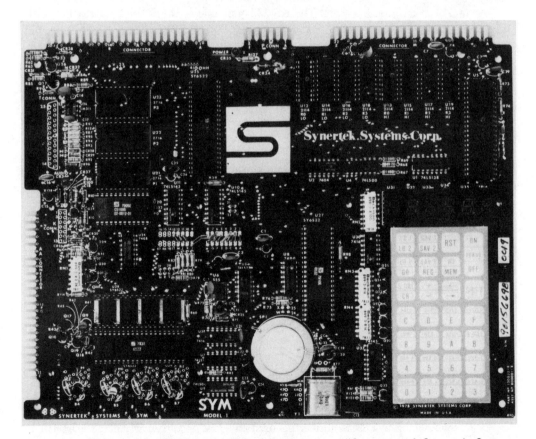

Figure 1-3 SYM-1 single-board computer. *(Courtesy of Synertek Systems Corp.)*

experiments and tests in engineering and scientific laboratories. The SYM-1 uses the identical hardware interface bus as the earlier KIM-1 device, so it may be used in applications previously reserved to the KIM-1 machine.

The SYM-1 device has a 4K-byte on-board monitor program, 1K byte of on-board RAM (expandable to 4K bytes), and provision for up to 28K bytes of on-board ROM or programmable ROM (PROM). The applications port, which, again, is expandable, has 15 bidirectional, TTL-compatible I/O lines. The machine also offers data storage and program storage on audio cassettes (an ordinary cassette tape player, provided that it has both microphone and earphone jacks, can be used), and will accommodate a full-duplex teletypewriter (TTY) 20-milliampere (mA) loop. This last feature makes the SYM-1 compatible not just with TTY machines, but also with a wide variety of hard-copy printers now on the market. The machine includes one other I/O port, the common RS-232 serial interface port. The RS-232 port makes the SYM-1 compatible with a variety of video terminals and other peripherals. An on-board video terminal capability allows you to use either a TV monitor or, if a radio-frequency (RF) modulator is provided, a home TV receiver to receive output data (32-character line of video).

Ohio Scientific Superboard II

The microcomputer in Figure 1-4 solves some of the problems inherent in other single-board designs: inconvenient keyboard format, for one. This machine is also based on the same microprocessor (6502) as the KIM-1 and SYM-1 machines, although it does not use the KIM-1 bus. Programming and data entry are through a full ASCII keyboard like those found on video CRT terminals and larger computers.

The Superboard II can interface with TTY, CRT video terminals, and other peripherals. It is probably one of the simplest of the "advanced" single-board computers and offers much that the lesser machines cannot (e.g., more memory and programming in BASIC).

Heathkit H-8

The model H-8 (Figure 1-5) was the Heath Company's first entry into the microcomputer market, so it has been around a long time. It is basically an 8080A-based machine, but a recent retrofit kit makes the H-8 into a Z80-based machine. The Z80 is still being used in great quantity, while the 8080A has faded somewhat in favor of more sophisticated chips.

The H-8 is a single-board computer, but it comes with a plastic cabinet to make it more attractive. Like other single-board computers, the H-8 uses a hexadecimal keyboard for programming and data entry and a series of LED seven-segment readouts for display.

The H-8 contains a 1K-byte on-board monitor in ROM and comes with 16K bytes of RAM memory. The total memory package is expandable to the

Figure 1-4 Ohio Scientific Superboard II. *(Courtesy of Ohio Scientific)*

(a)

(b)

Figure 1-5   (a) Heath/Zenith H-8 system; (b) internal view. *(Courtesy of Heath/ Zenith)*

full 64K bytes that the 8080A and Z80 chips can accommodate. Extra memory and other features are added with the addition of extra plug-in printed circuit boards. The cabinet contains a total of seven extra PC card-edge connectors for expansion.

With the correct choice of interfacing and memory boards, it is possible to build an H-8 system that has 64K bytes of RAM, a pair of 5.25-inch floppy disk drives, three parallel I/O ports, a 1200-baud serial cassette port, and four RS-232 standard I/O ports (serial). The RS-232 ports make the H-8 compatible with most standard video terminals and other peripherals.

Apple II and III

The Apple II (and its later cousin, the Apple III), shown in Figure 1-6, have become the byword in personal computers, partially through an aggressive advertising campaign and partially because these computers make available a full-service microcomputer in a small package. It is quite possible to make a system that includes 48K bytes of memory, color TV graphics, color TV monitor, a teletypewriter, and two 5.25-inch disk drives and have it take up little more than a tabletop.

The Apple II comes with a plug-in BASIC, with a more extensive version of BASIC available as an option. It also has an assembly language and built-in disassembler capability. The ordinary Apple II is available with an audio cassette interface, although for any serious work it is recommended that at least one disk be acquired.

Also built into the Apple II is a video display circuit that will drive an ordinary television monitor. The regular video format is 40 characters per line, with a total of 24 lines on the CRT screen at any one time. An interesting feature of the Apple II video monitor is that you can use either regular (white characters on black background) or inverse (black characters on white background) modes, and can cause some of the characters to flash on and off. The color graphics video display is capable of 15 different colors on a normal color video monitor.

A high-resolution video display provides 280h $\times$ 192v capability, allowing the programmer to draw graphs and other displays on the CRT screen.

Heath H-11

The Heath H-11 microcomputer is based on the Digital Equipment Corporation LSI-11 16-bit microcomputer board. This machine is fully compatible with the famous DEC PDP-11 series of minicomputers and has a lot more capability than most microcomputers. When interfaced with a disk drive system (see Figure 1-7), the H-11 machine is compatible with the PDP-11/03, although at a much lower cost. In that configuration, the H-11 has 56K bytes of on-board RAM and up to 500K bytes of disk storage in IBM 3740 format.

Figure 1-6 (a) Apple II; (b) Apple III. *(Courtesy of Apple Computers)*

Figure 1-7 Heath H-11 system. *(Courtesy of Heath/Zenith)*

Most users will not need a machine such as the H-11, but it is of immense use to those who have a large number of program packages that are based on the DEC PDP-11 machines (of which there are many in current use). It might be wiser for some users to go ahead and buy the H-11 instead of some lower-cost microcomputer that could also do a limited job, if it would mean that no software rewrite would be necessary. The costs of software in any computer system frequently, in fact usually, exceed the hardware cost; some authorities put the cost of software from commercial sources at $200 per line of working (i.e., debugged) program.

The Heath H-11 has available several different interfacing and accessory options, such as serial interface (serial RS-232 or 20-mA current loop), parallel I/O, hardware multiplication/divide, and a wire-wrapping board for breadboarding circuits.

2
Microprocessor
Fundamentals

The microprocessor chip revolutionized the electronics industry. Although initially thought of as either a small logic controller or as a data-processing machine (depending upon your perspective and the first chip you saw), the microprocessor developed into a major force with hundreds or even thousands of applications in less than a decade.

What is a microprocessor? How does it relate to microcomputers? In this chapter we will explore these questions and give you a good grounding in computer technology basics. But first we will study computers in general by describing a typical programmable digital computer in block diagram form. Second, we will describe two popular microprocessor chips that form the basis for many microcomputers: the Z80 and 6502 devices.

MYTHICAL ANALYTICAL DEVICE

Rather than mold our discussion around any one manufacturer's product, let's make up one that is sufficiently general to cover a large number of actual devices. Our computer will be nicknamed the *mythical analytical device,* or MAD, because the acronym often adequately describes both the emotional state of frustrated programmers and the mental health state of computer science buffs.

Figure 2-1 shows the block diagram of MAD. Let's first describe its parts and then describe a typical program operation.

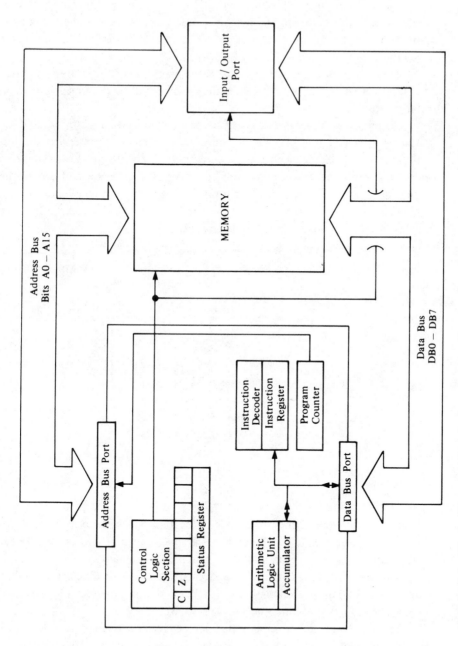

Figure 2-1 Block diagram of typical computer.

17

MAD, like any programmable digital computer, has three main parts: *central processing unit* (CPU), *memory,* and *input/output* (I/O). There are certainly other functions in specific machines, but many of these are either special applications of these main groups or are too unique to be described in a general machine.

The central processing unit controls the operation of the entire computer. It consists of several necessary subsections, which will be described in greater detail later.

Memory can be viewed as an array of cubbyholes such as those used by postal workers (Figure 2-2) to sort mail. Each cubbyhole represents a specific *address* on the letter carrier's route. An address in the array can be uniquely specified (identifying only *one* location) by designating the *row* and *column* in which the cubbyhole is found. If we want to specify the memory location (i.e., cubbyhole) at row 3 and column 2, we could create a *row X column* address number, which, in this example, would be 32..

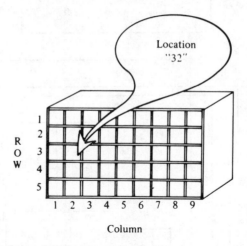

Figure 2-2 Analogy of computer memory.

Each cubbyhole represents a unique location in which to store mail. In the computer, the memory location stores a binary word of information. In an 8-bit computer, each location will store a single 8-bit binary word.

The different types of memory devices are discussed in Chapter 5, so that information will not be given here; to the CPU it does not much matter whether memory at any given location is RAM or ROM.

There are three lines of communication between the memory and the CPU: *address bus, data bus* and *control logic signals.* These avenues of communication control the interaction between memory I/O, on the one hand, and the CPU on the other. Ultimately, therefore, they also control the functioning of the entire computer.

The *address bus* (bits A0 through A15 in Figure 2-1) communicates to the memory bank the address of the exact memory location being called by the CPU, regardless of whether a read or write operation is taking place. The address bus consists of parallel data lines, one for each bit of the binary word that is used to specify the address location. In most 8-bit microcomputers, for example, the address bus consists of 16 bits. A 16-bit address bus can uniquely specify 2^{16} or 65,536 different locations. This size is called "64K," not "65K" as one might expect; the reason is operative. Lowercase "k" represents the metric prefix *kilo,* which denotes 1000. Since 2^{10} is 1024, however, computer users decided that the kilo would be 1024 not 1000. But an uppercase "K" is used, rather than the "k" used for the metric kilo.

The size of memory that can be addressed *doubles* for every bit added to the length of the address bus. Hence, adding 1 bit to our 16-bit address bus creates a 17-bit address bus, which can designate up to 128K locations. Some 8-bit machines that have 16-bit address buses can be made to look like bigger machines by certain tactics that make a longer pseudo-address bus. In those machines, several 64K memory banks are used to simulate continuously addressable 128K, 256K, or 512K memories.

The *data bus* is the communications channel over which data travel between the main register (called the *accumulator* or *A-register*) in the CPU and the memory. The data bus also carries data to and from the various input and/or output ports. If the CPU wants to read the data stored in a particular memory location, those data are passed from the memory location over the data bus to the accumulator register in the CPU. Memory write operations are in exactly the opposite direction, but are otherwise the same.

The size of the data bus is usually cited as the size of the computer. An 8-bit microprocessor/microcomputer, therefore, is one that has an 8-bit data bus; a 16-bit microcomputer will have a 16-bit data bus. Do not be confused by a salesperson who might tell you that a 6502-based machine (8-bit data bus) is "in reality" a 16-bit machine because it has a 16-bit address bus.

The last memory signal is the *control logic* or timing signal. These are one or more binary logic signals that tell memory *if* it is being addressed and whether the request is a read or write operation. The details of control logic signals differ between different microprocessor chips, and so will not be discussed here. Typical signals are those of the 6502 and Z80 machines, which are discussed later in this chapter.

The *input/output* (I/O) section is the means by which the CPU communicates with the outside world. An input port will bring data in from the outside world and then pass them over the data bus to the CPU, where they are stored in the accumulator. An output port reverses that data flow direction.

In some machines, there are separate I/O instructions that are distinct from memory instructions. The Z80 is one such machine. The Z80 will pass the port address over the lower 8 bits of the 16-bit address bus (the 8-bit I/O address used in the Z80 can uniquely address up to 256 different ports). In other machines, such as the 6502, there are no distinct I/O instructions. In those machines, the I/O components are treated as memory locations; this technique is called *memory mapping* or *memory-mapped I/O*. Input and output operations then become memory-read and memory-write operations, respectively. Memory and I/O devices are discussed in Chapters 5 and 6, respectively.

Central Processing Unit (CPU)

The CPU is the heart and brains of any programmable digital computer, including MAD. Although there are some different optional features in certain machines, all will have the features shown in our MAD computer (Figure 2-1). The principal subsections of the CPU include (at least) the following: *accumulator* or *A-register, arithmetic-logic unit* (ALU), *program counter* (PC), *instruction register, status register,* and *control logic section.*

The accumulator is the main register in the CPU and will have the same bit length as the data bus. All instructions executed by the CPU involve data in the accumulator, unless otherwise specified in the description of an instruction. Therefore, an ADD instruction causes an arithmetic addition of the data cited by the instruction to the *contents of the accumulator.*

Although there are often other registers in the CPU, the accumulator is the main register. The main purpose of the accumulator is the *temporary* storage of data being operated on by the instruction being executed. Note that data transfers to and from the accumulator are nondestructive. In other words, data "transfers" are not really transfers at all, but are, instead, *copying* operations. Suppose, for example, the hexadecimal number $8F_{16}$ is stored in the accumulator when an instruction is encountered requiring that the contents of the accumulator be stored at memory location $A008_{16}$. After the instruction is executed, we will find $8F_{16}$ both in memory location A008 *and* in the accumulator. If we have the opposite operation (i.e., transfer contents of accumulator to location $A008_{16}$), then we will see the same situation; after the transfer, the data will be in both locations. Since the accumulator contents change every time an instruction is executed, we will have to use such transfers to hold critical data someplace in memory.

The arithmetic-logic unit (ALU) contains the circuitry that performs the arithmetic operations of addition and (sometimes) subtraction, plus the logical operations of AND, OR, and XOR.

The program counter (PC) contains the address of the next instruction to be executed. The secret to the success of a programmable digital computer is its ability to *fetch and execute instructions sequentially.* Normally, the PC will increment appropriately (1, 2, 3, or 4) while executing each instruction: 1 for 1-byte instructions, 2 for 2-byte instructions, and so on. For example, the instruction LDA,n is a 6502 instruction mnemonic that loads the accumulator with the number *n*. In a program, we will find the code for LDA,n followed by *n*.

Location	Code	Mnemonic
0100		LDA,n
0101	*n*	*n*
0102	(next instruction)	

At the beginning of this operation, PC = 0100, but after execution it will be PC = 0102 because LDA,n is a 2-byte instruction.

There are other ways to modify the program counter. Executing any form of JUMP instruction, for example, modifies the contents of the PC to contain the address of the jumped-to location. Another way to modify the PC contents is to activate the *reset* line. The computer sees reset as a hard-wired JUMP to location 0000.

The *instruction register* (IR) is the temporary storage location for instruction codes stored in memory. When the instruction is fetched from memory by the CPU, it will reside in the instruction register until the next instruction is fetched.

The *instruction decoder* is a logic circuit that reads the instruction register contents and then carries out the intended operation.

The *control logic section* takes care of housekeeping chores within the CPU and issues or responds to control signals from the outside world. These signals are not universally defined (which is one reason why we will consider two chips later in this chapter), but control such functions as memory requests, I/O requests, read/write signaling, interrupts, and so forth.

The *status register,* also sometimes called *status flags,* is used to indicate to the program and (sometimes) to the outside world the status of the CPU at any given instant. Each bit of the status register represents a different function. Different microprocessor chips use slightly different status register architectures, but all will have a *carry flag* (C) to indicate when an instruction execution caused a carry, and a *zero flag* (Z) to indicate when an arithmetic or logic instruction resulted in zero or nonzero in the accumulator (typically, $Z = 1$ when the result is zero).

We have now developed the CPU for our MAD computer. This discussion in general terms also describes a typical microprocessor chip; a microprocessor (as opposed to a single-chip computer) is essentially the CPU portion of a MAD.

Operation of MAD

A programmable digital computer such as MAD operates by sequentially fetching, decoding, and then executing instructions stored in memory. These instructions are stored in the form of *binary numbers*. In some early machines there were two memories, one each for program instructions and data. The modern method, however, uses the same memory for both data and instructions.

How, one might ask, does the computer know whether the binary number stored in any particular location is an instruction, data, or an alphanumeric character representation (e.g., ASCII or BAUDOT codes)? The answer to this important question is the key to the operation of MAD: *cycles.*

The MAD operates in cycles. A computer will have at least two cycles: *instruction fetch* and *execution,* and these are often broken into several subcycles. The details differ even though general methods are similar.

Instructions are stored in memory as binary numbers called *operation codes* (op-codes, for short). During the instruction fetch cycle, an op-code will be retrieved from the memory location specified by the program counter and stuffed into the instruction register. The CPU assumes that the programmer was smart enough to arrange things such that an op-code will be stored at that location when the PC increments to that address.

During the first cycle, an instruction is fetched and stored in the instruction register. During the second cycle, the instruction decoder will read the IR and then carry out the indicated operation. When these two cycles are completed, an instruction will have been fetched and executed, the program counter incremented to reflect the memory location that will contain the next instruction, and the CPU made ready for the next instruction. The CPU will then enter the next instruction fetch cycle and the process repeats itself. This process continues over and over again as long as the MAD is working. Each step is synchronized by a train of clock pulses so that events remain rational.

From our description you might be able to glean a truth concerning what a computer can or cannot do. The CPU can shift data around, perform logical operations (e.g., AND, OR, XOR), and add two *N*-bit numbers (sometimes subtract as well), all in accordance with a limited repertoire of binary word instructions. These chores are performed *sequentially* through a series of discrete steps. The secret to whether a problem is amenable to computer solution depends upon whether a plan of action (called an *algorithm*) can be written that will lead to a solution by a sequentially executed series of steps. Most practical instrumentation, control, or data-processing chores can be so solved, a factor that accounts for the meteoric rise of the microprocessor. The field of endeavor that studies sequential solutions to practical (and some not so practical) problems is called *numerical methods.*

EXAMINATION OF TWO POPULAR MICROPROCESSOR CHIPS

There are numerous microprocessor chips on the market. The 6502 and Z80 devices were selected for comparison because they represent two different basic philosophies in design and they are both immensely popular. There is a lot of available hardware and software for both Z80 and 6502 systems, which might not be the case for some other selections.

The Zilog Z80

The Z80 is an integrated-circuit microprocessor designed and manufactured by Zilog, Inc. (10460 Bubb Road, Cupertino, California 95014), and second-sourced by Mostek, Inc. (1215 West Crosby Rd., Carrollton, Texas 75006). The Z80 is similar to, but an advancement over, the Intel 8080 microprocessor.

If you are familiar with the 8080 device, making the switchover to the Z80 will be very easy. The Z80 instruction set contains all the 8080 instructions, plus a few more. It is usually claimed that the Z80 device has 158 different instructions, as opposed to only 78 for the 8080.

In general, any program that will run on an 8080 system, with the exception of those dependent upon timing loops, will also run on a Z80 system. There are differences in the clock timing, so those programs that create, or are dependent upon, specific 8080 timing will not usually run properly on the Z80.

Besides the different instruction set sizes, there are other differences between the Z80 and the 8080. The programmer of the Z80 device can use more internal registers and has more addressing modes than does the 8080 programmer.

In addition, there are several hardware differences. For one, the Z80 does away with the two-phase clock of the 8080. In the Z80, then, only a single-

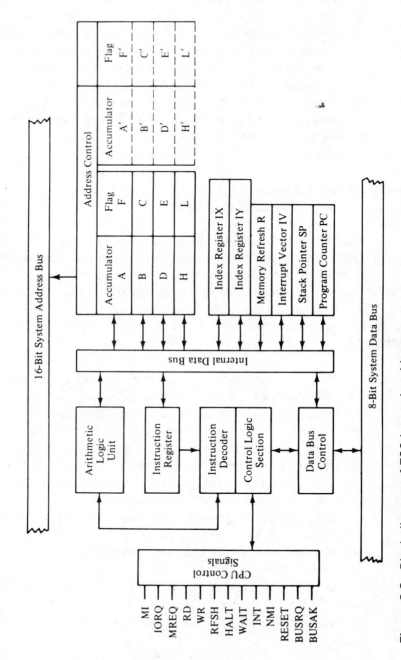

Figure 2-3 Block diagram of Z80 internal architecture.

24

phase clock is used. The Z80 clock operates at 2.5 mHz, while the faster Z80A device will accept clock speeds to 4 mHz. The Z80 also differs from the 8080 in that it will operate from a single + 5-volt (V) power supply. The 8080 devices require, in addition to the + 5-V supply, a − 5-V supply and a + 12-V supply.

The Z80 also provides an additional interrupt and the logic required to refresh dynamic memory. The Z80 uses n-channel MOS technology, so it must be handled with care in order to avoid damage from static electricity discharge.

Figure 2-3 shows the block diagram for the internal circuitry of the Z80 device. Note that the Z80 contains the following sections: arithmetic logic unit (ALU), CPU registers, and instruction register, plus sections to decode the instructions received and control the address placed on the address bus.

The Z80 uses an 8-bit data bus and a 16-bit address bus. The use of 16 bits on the address bus means that the Z80 can address up to 65,536 different memory locations.

The internal registers of the Z80 represent 208 bits of read/write memory that can be accessed by the programmer. These bits are arranged in the form of eighteen 8-bit registers and four 16-bit registers. Figure 2-4 shows the organization of the Z80 register set.

The main register set consists of an accumulator (register A) and a flag register (register F), plus six general-purpose registers (B, C, D, E, H, and L).

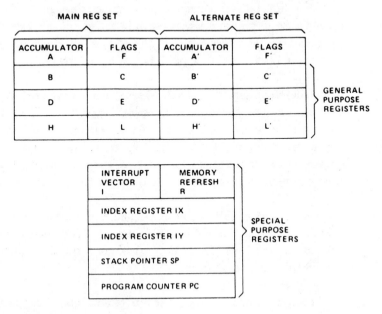

Figure 2-4   Register organization.

An alternate set of registers is provided that duplicates these registers: accumulator (A') and flag register (F'), plus the general-purpose registers B', C', D', E', H', and L'. Only one set of these registers can be active at any one time. One cannot, for example, use the B and B' registers without first using one of the instructions that interchanges the register sets.

The general-purpose registers can be paired to form three register pairs of 16 bits each: BC, DE, and HL. The alternate registers are also paired to allow 16-bit register pairs: BC', DE', and HL'.

The Z80 special-purpose registers include interrupt vector I and memory fresh R (both 8-bit registers) and four 16-bit registers: index register IX, index register IY, stack pointer SP, and program counter PC.

Interrupt Vector I.   The I register is used to service interrupts originated by a peripheral device. The CPU will jump to a memory location containing the subroutine that services the interrupting device. The device will supply the lower-order 8 bits of the 16-bit address, while the I register will contain the high-order 8 bits of the address.

Memory Refresh R.   This register is used to refresh dynamic memory during the time when the CPU is decoding and executing the instruction fetched from memory. Seven bits of the R register are incremented after each instruction fetch, but the eighth bit remains as programmed through an LD R,A instruction. During refresh, a refresh signal becomes active, the contents of the R register are placed on the lower 8 bits of the address bus, and the contents of the I register are placed on the upper 8 bits of the address bus.

Index Registers IX and IY.   These registers are used to point to external memory locations in indirect addressing instructions. The actual memory location addressed will be the sum of the contents of an index register and a displacement integer d (or, alternatively, some instructions use the two's complement of d). Both IX and IY index registers are independent of each other. Note that many microprocessor chips do not have index registers at all.

Stack Pointer (SP).   The stack pointer is a 2-byte register that is used to hold the 16-bit address of a last-in, first-out (LIFO) stack in external memory. The data to and from the memory stack are handled through the PUSH and POP instructions, respectively.

Program Counter (PC).   The program counter in any computer holds the address of the instruction being fetched from memory. In the Z80, the program counter is a 16-bit register. The PC will be automatically incremented the correct number of digits after each instruction (e.g., 1-byte instructions increment PC + 1, 2-byte instructions PC + 2). When a JUMP operation occurs, the program counter will contain the address of the location to which the program jumped. When it is RETURNED, the PC will contain the address of the next sequential instruction that would have been fetched if no jump had occurred.

Figure 2-5 shows how the program counter would work on a jump operation. Let us say that we have a program that starts at location 02 00 (hex) and finishes at location 02 06. But when it encounters the instruction at 02 02, it is an unconditional jump to location 06 12. Now, for the purposes of illustration, our subroutine at 06 12 is a RETurn instruction (useless in the real world, perhaps, but useful for illustration). It then jumps back to the next sequential location 02 05. Note that the next sequential location from 02 02 in this case is not 02 03, but 02 05. This is due to the fact that the jump instruction was a 3-byte instruction. We had to give it the instruction (02 02), the low-order byte of the memory location to jump to (02 03), and the high-order byte of the memory location (02 04).

Arithmetic Logic Unit (ALU). The heart of any computer or microprocessor, and the factor that distinguishes it from all other digital electronic circuits, is the arithmetic logic unit, or ALU. This circuit performs the data manipulation for the device. The functions possible in the Z80 microprocessor are add, subtract, compare, logical AND, logical OR, logical exclusive-OR

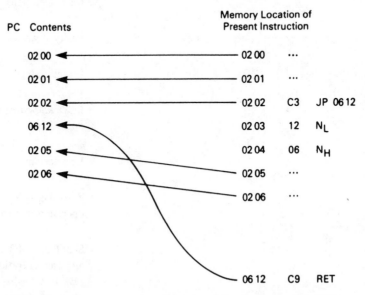

Figure 2-5 How the program counter works on a jump operation.

(XOR), left shift (logical), left shift (arithmetic), right shift (logical), right shift (arithmetic), increment, decrement, set a bit (i.e., make it 1), reset a bit (make it 0), and test a bit to see whether it is 1 or 0.

Flag Registers (F and F'). The Z80 provides two status registers: F and F'. Only one is active at any one time, depending upon whether the programmer has selected the main register bank or the alternative register bank. These registers are each 8 bits long, and each bit is used to denote a different status condition. As a result, these bits of the F and F' register are also called *condition bits.*

The flags in the F and F' register are SET or RESET after certain arithmetic or other operations upon data. The program can then tell something about the result of the operation. The allocations are shown in Table 2-1.

TABLE 2-1

Bit (F/F')	Designation	Meaning
0	C	Carry flag; indicates a carry from the high-order bit of the accumulator (B7)
1	N	Subtraction flag used in BCD subtract operations
2	P/V	Parity/overflow
3	X	Undetermined
4	H	BCD *half-carry* flag (bit 4 in BCD operations)
5	X	Undetermined
6	Z	Zero flag is SET if the result of an operation is zero
7	S	Sign flag is SET if the sign of a result after an operation is negative; RESET if it is zero or positive

Z80 Pinouts

The Z80 device is constructed in a standard 40-pin DIP integrated circuit package. Since the Z80 uses NMOS technology, one is cautioned to become familiar with the rules for handling such devices before trying to handle the Z80 device. Those rules are actually very simple, so failing to follow them will net you what you deserve—a destroyed IC.

Figure 2-6 shows the Z80 pinouts and package configuration. The definitions of the pinouts are as follows:

A0–A15	Address bus (16 bits). Permits addressing up to 64K (i.e., 65,536 bytes) of memory, plus 256 different I/O ports. The address bus is active when HIGH, and has tristate outputs. The entire 16 bits are used to address memory, while only the low-order byte (A0–A7) is used to address I/O ports.
D0–D7	Eight-bit data bus terminals. The data bus is, like the address bus, active high and uses tristate outputs.
$\overline{M1}$	Machine cycle 1. When this terminal is LOW, the CPU is in the op-code fetch portion of the instruction/execution cycle.
$\overline{MREQ}$	Memory request signal. Is active low, and is an active low output. When this terminal goes low, the address on the address bus is valid for a memory operation (read or write).
$\overline{IORQ}$	Input/output request. This active low tristate output indicates that an I/O operation is to take place. The low-order byte of the address bus (A0–A7) contains the address (0–255) of the selected port. The contents of the accu-

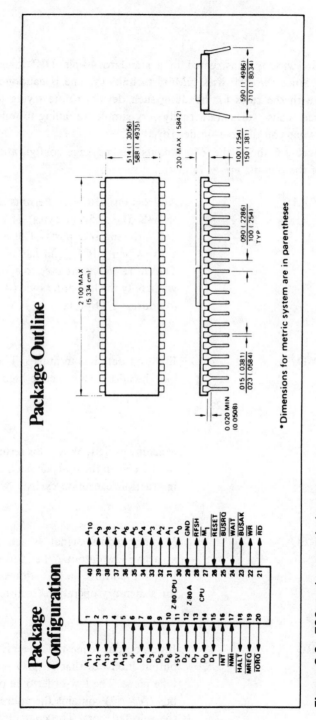

Figure 2-6 Z80 package and pinouts.

mulator may be placed on the high-order byte of the address bus during this period. The $\overline{\text{IORQ}}$ is also generated to acknowledge an interrupt request, and tells the interrupting device to place the interrupt vector word on the data bus (i.e., low-order byte of the address of the interrupt service program).

$\overline{\text{RD}}$ This is an active low tristate output that indicates when a read operation from memory, or an I/O device, to the CPU is taking place.

$\overline{\text{WR}}$ Tristate active low output that indicates when a write operation from the CPU to a memory location, or I/O device, is taking place. Tells the memory or I/O device that the data on the data bus are currently valid.

$\overline{\text{RFSH}}$ Refresh signal. This is an active low output that indicates that the lower 7 bits of the address bus contain a refresh address for the dynamic memory.

$\overline{\text{HALT}}$ Active low output that indicates that a halt instruction is being executed. The CPU executes NOPs while in the halt state and is awaiting the receipt of an interrupt signal.

$\overline{\text{WAIT}}$ Active low input that indicates that the addressed memory, or I/O device, is not yet ready to transfer data to the data bus.

$\overline{\text{INT}}$ Active low input that tells the CPU that an external device has requested an interrupt. The

CPU will honor the request at the end of the current instruction cycle if the interrupt flip-flop (software controlled) is SET.

$\overline{\text{NMI}}$

Active low input for nonmaskable interrupt operation. This line will cause the CPU to honor the interrupt at the end of the current instruction cycle, regardless of the state of the interrupt flip-flop. Forces automatic restart at location 00 66 (hex).

$\overline{\text{RESET}}$

Active low input that enables the interrupt flip-flop, clears the program counter (i.e., loads PC with 00 00), and clears I and R registers. This terminal can serve as a hardware jump-to-00-00 control.

$\overline{\text{BUSRQ}}$

Active low input that requests that the CPU address bus, data bus, and the control signals go to the high impedance (tristate) state so that some other device can obtain control of these buses. The $\overline{\text{BUSRQ}}$ has a higher priority than $\overline{\text{NMI}}$ and is always honored at the end of the present instruction.

$\overline{\text{BUSAK}}$

Active low output that is used with the bus request signal and tells the request device that the CPU buses are now in the high-impedance state. When $\overline{\text{BUSAK}}$ drops low, the requesting device may take control of the buses.

Φ

Clock signal input. Wants to see TTL level at 2 mHz or 4 mHz (Z80A) maximum.

GND   DC and signal ground terminal.

+5   Power supply terminal, to which is applied
                             +5 V dc from a regulated power supply.

The 6502

The 6502 microprocessor chip is available from the originator, MOS Technology, Inc., and more than 15 secondary sources. Among the secondary sources are Synertek and Rockwell International, who make the SYM-1 and AIM-65 microcomputers, respectively. The 6502 device is widely used in microcomputer systems as well as in small-scale process controllers and other similar applications. Figure 2-7 shows the block diagram of the 6502 architecture, while Figure 2-8 shows the pinouts.

That there are certain similarities between the Z80 and 6502 devices testifies

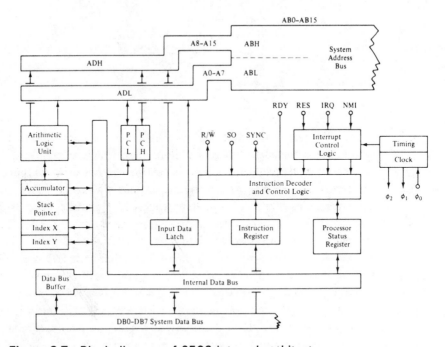

Figure 2-7 Block diagram of 6502 internal architecture.

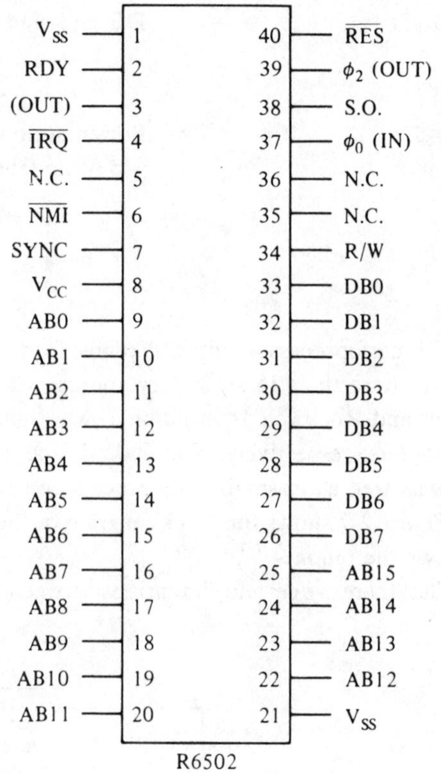

```
        V_SS  ——| 1          40 |—— RES
        RDY   ——| 2          39 |—— φ₂ (OUT)
     φ₁ (OUT) ——| 3          38 |—— S.O.
        IRQ   ——| 4          37 |—— φ₀ (IN)
       N.C.   ——| 5          36 |—— N.C.
        NMI   ——| 6          35 |—— N.C.
       SYNC   ——| 7          34 |—— R/W
        V_CC  ——| 8          33 |—— DB0
        AB0   ——| 9          32 |—— DB1
        AB1   ——| 10         31 |—— DB2
        AB2   ——| 11         30 |—— DB3
        AB3   ——| 12         29 |—— DB4
        AB4   ——| 13         28 |—— DB5
        AB5   ——| 14         27 |—— DB6
        AB6   ——| 15         26 |—— DB7
        AB7   ——| 16         25 |—— AB15
        AB8   ——| 17         24 |—— AB14
        AB9   ——| 18         23 |—— AB13
        AB10  ——| 19         22 |—— AB12
        AB11  ——| 20         21 |—— V_SS
                    R6502
```

Figure 2-8   6502 pinouts.

only to the fact that they are both microprocessor chips. The Z80 and 6502 devices are designed to different philosophies, which are reflected in their respective internal architectures. The Z80 allows separate input/output commands. The lower-order byte of the address bus will carry the port number (256 different ports numbered 000 to 255) address, while the high-order byte of the address bus carries the contents of the accumulator that is to be output. The I/O data are fed to and from the accumulator over the data bus. The 6502, on the other hand, uses a memory-mapping technique in which each I/O port is designated as a separate location in memory. We can then read or write to that memory location, depending upon whether the operation is an input or an output. The 6502 also lacks the multiple internal registers of the Z80. But this feature, like the lack of discrete I/O ports, does not hinder most microcomputer designs. Very few microcomputers will need more than a total of a dozen or so I/O ports and/or registers. Also, very few microcomputers will need the entire 64K (i.e., 65,536 bytes) of available memory addresses. In fact, most systems have less than 48K of memory. This allotment of memory would leave all locations above 48K for "firmware" (i.e., ROM) programs and I/O port or register selection.

Blocks in Figure 2-7 that have names similar to blocks in the Z80 diagram perform roughly similar (sometimes exactly identical) jobs for the 6502 device. Note, however, that the program counter (PC) is divided into two 8-bit (1 byte) registers called PCL (for low-order byte) and PCH (for high-order byte of 16-bit address). Similarly, the address bus is divided into low (ADL) and high (ADH) order segments. Unlike the Z80, the 6502 uses a multiphase clock for timing of the operations.

The 6502 pinouts are shown in Figure 2-8 and are defined next. Some are similar to Z80 pinouts, while others are unique to the 6502.

DB0–DB7	Eight-bit data bus.
AB0–AB15	Sixteen-bit address bus.
Φ_0	CPU clock.
Φ_1, Φ_2	System clocks.
R/$\overline{\text{W}}$	Indicates a *read* operation when HIGH, and a *write* operation when LOW. The normal inactive condition is read (i.e., HIGH). The CPU is writing data to the data bus (DB0–DB7) when this terminal is LOW.
$\overline{\text{IRQ}}$	*Interrupt request.* This active-low input is used to interrupt the program being executed so that a subroutine can be executed instead. This interrupt line is maskable so it will respond only if the internal interrupt FF is enabled.

NMI

Nonmaskable interrupt. Similar to the interrupt request, except that this active-low input cannot be disabled by the programmer.

RESET

Active-low *reset.* Essentially a hardware jump to location 0000_{16} instruction. If this terminal is brought LOW, then the PC is loaded with the address 0000_{16} and program execution starts from there. Can be used for manual or power-on reset operations, and does not alter the contents of the accumulator.

RDY

The *ready* signal is an input that will insert a wait state into the normal machine-cycle sequence. The RDY line must make a negative-going (i.e., HIGH-to-LOW) transition during the Φ_1-HIGH clock cycle during any operation other than a *write.*

SO

Set overflow flag. This input will set the overflow flag *if* it makes a negative-going (i.e., HIGH-to-LOW) transition during the trailing edge of the Φ_1 clock cycle.

SYNC

Active-high output that is used to indicate the *instruction fetch* machine cycle.

Status Register (6502).   Like the F and F′ registers in the Z80, the 6502 device has a status register that can be used by the programmer in a number of important ways. The status register can be read by the program during certain operations, but is inaccessible to external hardware. The register has 8 bits defined as follows:

TABLE 2-2

Bit	Use
0	C, carry. Indicates that a carry occurred from the accumulator on the last instruction executed; active HIGH (logical 1).
1	Z, zero. Indicates that the last operation performed resulted in a zero (if Z = HIGH) or nonzero (if Z = LOW).
2	(unused)
3	D, decimal mode. When this bit is HIGH, it causes a decimal add with a carry or subtract with borrow for BCD operations.
4	B, break. HIGH when an interrupt is executed.
5	(blank)
6	O, overflow.
7	S, sign. Indicates positive or negative results.

Z80 TIMING AND INTERFACE CONTROL SIGNALS

If you are planning to use a ready-built computer containing a Z80 micro-processor chip, it is not likely that you will need to know much about the chip-level interface and timing signals of the chip. Languages like BASIC, and even some assemblers, will not require that you know much at all about these signals. But if you are doing machine-level programming, using most assemblers, or are trying to interface some other instrument to the Z80 directly, or to the bus of a Z80 computer, it is necessary for you to know and understand the timing structure.

Earlier we discussed the definitions of the Z80 pins. Among the pins discussed were the interface and timing signals. For emphasis, let us reiterate this discussion here, but grouping the signals according to use.

Data/Address Buses

There are two buses in the Z80: a 16-bit address bus and an 8-bit data bus. The address bus pinouts are labeled A0–A15, while the data bus terminals are designated B0–B7. In both cases, the 0 bit is the least significant bit, while the highest numbered bit (7 on the data bus, 15 on the address bus) is the most significant bit.

Both address and data buses are designed to be tristate outputs. This means that there are the HIGH and LOW states for logical 1 and 0, respectively, plus a third high-impedance state that can be used to effectively disconnect the Z80 CPU chip from the external bus lines. In some cases, a bus request signal (discussed later) will cause the data and address buses to go into the tristate condition so that an external device can control the buses. Also, both address and data buses are active when HIGH.

The data bus is used to pass data to and from the CPU chip. Unless one knows the status of the control signals and the word applied to the address bus, however, one does not know what is taking place on the data bus.

The address bus does several things. In the memory address mode, for example, the 16-bit address bus will be capable of designating 2^{16}, or 65,536, different memory locations. This size is usually called 64K.

The address bus is also used in the control of input/output operations. When an I/O command is being executed, the lower byte of the address bus holds the address of the I/O port designated in the instruction. The upper byte contains the accumulator data, repeated on the data bus.

The lower byte of the address bus is also used in the memory refresh operation. During the period of the machine cycle in which the refresh operation is to take place, as indicated by a LOW condition on the $\overline{\text{RFSH}}$ output terminal, the lower 7 bits (A0–A6) of the address bus contain the refresh address.

Input/Output (I/O) Operations

The Z80 design philosophy is a little different from the philosophy of its direct ancestor, the 8080 device. This is especially noticeable in the I/O operations. In the Z80, an *input/output request* $(\overline{\text{IORQ}})$ signal is available. This is a tristate, active low output that is used to tell external devices and memory that an input or output operation is taking place.

The $\overline{\text{IORQ}}$ signal will go LOW when (1) an input or output operation is taking place, and (2) when an interrupt is being acknowledged. In the latter case, an $\overline{\text{M1}}$ signal is also generated during interrupts. This combination of signals is used to tell the interrupting device to place the address vector pointing to the interrupt service subroutine. These two types of operation can be distinguished from each other because interrupt acknowledgments always occur during the M1 period (discussed later), and I/O operations never occur during the M1 period.

It is not possible to use just one signal for I/O control, because there are three possible states: no I/O operation, input, and output. In the first case, the $\overline{\text{IORQ}}$ line would be HIGH, but it will be LOW for both of the other possible conditions. In the Z80 device, the input and output states are distinguished by the condition of the $\overline{\text{WR}}$ and $\overline{\text{RD}}$ control signal. These are also used in memory operations, and are the *write* ($\overline{\text{WR}}$) and *read* ($\overline{\text{RD}}$) signals. If the I/O operation is an input (i.e., read), then the $\overline{\text{RD}}$ line goes LOW along with $\overline{\text{IORQ}}$. But if the I/O operation is an output, then the $\overline{\text{WR}}$ control signal goes LOW along with $\overline{\text{IORQ}}$.

Memory Control Signals

Control of memory operations requires the same $\overline{\text{WR}}$ and $\overline{\text{RD}}$ signals as used in the I/O operations. But instead of the $\overline{\text{IORQ}}$ signals, a *memory request* ($\overline{\text{MREQ}}$) is used. This signal is an active low tristate output that is used to indicate that the address bus contains a valid memory location address. Whether the CPU is reading from memory or writing to memory is indicated by the coincidence of the $\overline{\text{MREQ}}$ and $\overline{\text{RD}}$ (memory read) or $\overline{\text{MREQ}}$ and $\overline{\text{WR}}$. Address decoders in memory, then, must take note of these signals in order to determine whether a read or write operation is taking place.

A *refresh* ($\overline{\text{RFSH}}$) signal is used to control dynamic memories. Unlike static memory devices, dynamic memory often requires a refresh operation or the data stored will be lost. $\overline{\text{RFSH}}$ is an active low tristate output, and is active once during each instruction fetch operation. When the $\overline{\text{RFSH}}$ and $\overline{\text{MREQ}}$ are both low, a memory refresh can take place. The contents of the R register are loaded onto the lower 7 bits of the address bus to address the memory to be refreshed. The R register is incremented after each operation, so all memory will eventually be refreshed.

CPU Control Signals

There are four basic CPU control signals: $\overline{\text{M1}}$, $\overline{\text{RESET}}$, $\overline{\text{WAIT}}$, and $\overline{\text{HALT}}$. The $\overline{\text{M1}}$ signal is used to indicate that an M1 instruction fetch period is in effect. The M1 machine cycle occurs when an instruction is being fetched from memory. If the instruction being fetched is a 2-byte instruction, then an $\overline{\text{M1}}$ signal is generated as each op-code is being fetched.

The $\overline{\text{M1}}$ signal is also generated during interrupt acknowledgments, in conjunction with an $\overline{\text{IORQ}}$ signal. This combination allows the interrupting device to place the address vector of the memory location containing the interrupt service subroutine.

The $\overline{\text{RESET}}$ signal is an active low input. When this terminal is brought low, the CPU does the following: disables the interrupt flip-flop; sets the I register to 00 (hex); sets the R register to 00 (hex); sets interrupt mode 0. In effect, the $\overline{\text{RESET}}$ is a *hardware* jump to 00 00 instruction.

The $\overline{\text{WAIT}}$ terminal is an active low input that can be used to tell the CPU that an addressed I/O device is not ready to transfer data. The CPU keeps entering wait states until this signal goes high again. This signal is needed because many types of I/O device are not as fast as the CPU.

The $\overline{\text{HALT}}$ signal is an active low output that indicates that a halt instruction is being executed. The CPU will execute no-ops (NOP) until an interrupt is received.

Interrupt Signals

The principal interrupt signals are the $\overline{\text{INT}}$ and $\overline{\text{NMI}}$. The regular *interrupt request* signal is the $\overline{\text{INT}}$. It is an active low input. The interrupt request signal is generated by the interrupting I/O device, and will be honored at the end of the present instruction cycle. There are three modes of response by the CPU: mode 0, 1, or 2.

The nonmaskable interrupt ($\overline{\text{NMI}}$) signal is used to allow interrupts that *must* be serviced at the end of the current instruction cycle.

BUSRQ and BUSAK

These signals are used to allow access to the memory by external devices, without the use of the CPU. The $\overline{\text{BUSRQ}}$ is an active low input. When the $\overline{\text{BUSRQ}}$ line goes low, the CPU outputs (address and data buses) go tristate at the end of the current instruction cycle.

The $\overline{\text{BUSAK}}$ is an active low output that tells the external device that the CPU is in the high-impedance tristate condition. When this signal goes low, the external device knows that it now has control of the data and address buses.

Basic CPU Timing

All instructions in any programmable digital computer are merely a series of certain basic operations. In discussing the timing of the CPU, we must determine how these operations occur. The clock produces periods called T cycles (see Figure 2-9). There are also three different M cycles for each instruction cycle. M cycles are machine cycles, while the T cycles are clock cycles.

In the paragraphs to follow, we will discuss the op-code instruction fetch, memory data read/write, I/O read/write, bus request/acknowledge, interrupt request, nonmaskable interrupt request, and exit from HALT instruction cycles.

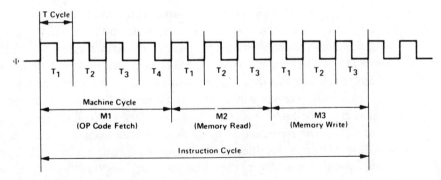

Figure 2-9 Timing diagram for instruction cycle.

Op-code Instruction Fetch.   Figure 2-10 shows the CPU timing during the M1 op-code instruction fetch cycle of the Z80 CPU. The program counter (PC) contains the address of the next instruction. The contents of the PC are placed on the address bus (A0–A15) during the first half of the M1 cycle.

Since we are trying to fetch (i.e., *read*) an instruction from some location in memory, the $\overline{\text{MREQ}}$ and $\overline{\text{RD}}$ signals are also placed low. This tells the memory that a read operation is taking place from a location whose address is found on the address bus.

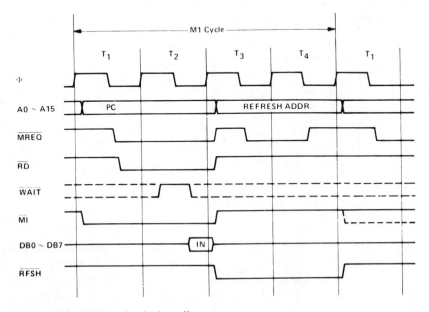

Figure 2-10 M1 cycle timing diagram.

The $\overline{\text{WAIT}}$ line is sampled during this period. If the memory device is slow, it may generate a wait signal to slow down the operation. If a wait signal is found during each sample (i.e., once during each T cycle), the CPU will enter another wait state. When the device is ready to transfer data, the wait signal disappears, and the data bus contains the data from that memory location.

During the last half of the M1 cycle (i.e., T3/T4), the refresh address is placed on the lower 7 bits of the address bus, and a $\overline{\text{RFSH}}$ is generated. This will allow the refreshing of dynamic solid-state memories. During the portion of the M1 cycle that the program counter contents are on the address bus, the $\overline{\text{M1}}$ signal is low. The M1 machine cycle will lengthen for as long as there is a wait signal present. Using the $\overline{\text{WAIT}}$ line permits us to synchronize the CPU and an external device.

Memory Data Read/Write.   The M2 and M3 machine cycles are used to read to, or write from, memory locations. Figure 2-11 shows the CPU timing during these operations. The principal signals used in this type of operation are the $\overline{\text{MREQ}}$, $\overline{\text{WR}}$, and $\overline{\text{RD}}$.

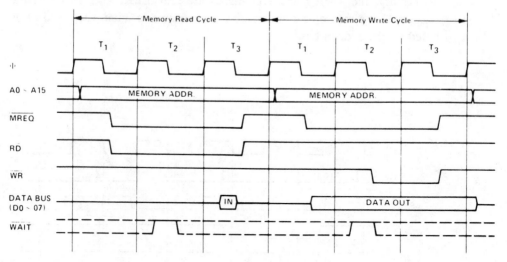

Figure 2-11   Memory read/write cycle timing.

If a memory read operation is needed, an address is placed on the address bus (A0–A15) during the M2 machine cycle. During this period, the $\overline{\text{MREQ}}$ (memory request) and $\overline{\text{RD}}$ lines coincidentally go low. The $\overline{\text{MREQ}}$ signal does not become active until the data on the address bus are stable.

Memory write operations cause data from the CPU to be written into specified locations in memory. This occurs during the M3 machine cycle. In this operation, the $\overline{\text{MREQ}}$ and $\overline{\text{WR}}$ signals become active. The $\overline{\text{MREQ}}$ signal, however, does not become active until the data on the data bus are stable (i.e., valid) so that semiconductor memory can be accommodated. Again, the address of the specified location is applied to the address bus (A0–A15).

As in the instruction fetch cycle, a wait state can be created. If the $\overline{\text{WAIT}}$ signal is low, the CPU continues to enter wait states until the signal becomes inactive. The $\overline{\text{WAIT}}$ signal can be used to synchronize the CPU to memory sources.

I/O Read/Write.   Figure 2-12 shows the CPU timing during input and output cycles. During each of these types of operation, the $\overline{\text{IORQ}}$ request line becomes active (i.e., goes low). If the operation is a read cycle, the $\overline{\text{RD}}$ signal will also go low. But if the operation is a write cycle (i.e., an output), the $\overline{\text{WR}}$ signal goes low coincidentally with $\overline{\text{IORQ}}$.

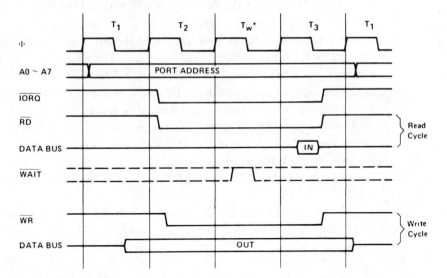

Figure 2-12 I/O timing diagram.

I/O Read/Write.   Figure 2-12 shows the CPU timing during input and output cycles. During each of these types of operation, the $\overline{\text{IORQ}}$ request line becomes active (i.e., goes low). If the operation is a read cycle, the $\overline{\text{RD}}$ signal will also go low. But if the operation is a write cycle (i.e., an output), the $\overline{\text{WR}}$ signal goes low coincidentally with $\overline{\text{IORQ}}$.

In both input and output cycles, the address of the designated port is placed on the lower byte of the address bus (A0–A7). Since this is an 8-bit address, we can specify up to 256 different addresses from 000–255 (decimal).

During an input (i.e., I/O read) operation, the $\overline{IORQ}$ and $\overline{WR}$ signals are low during T2 and T3, and data from the input port are passed along the data bus.

During an output (i.e., I/O write) operation, the $\overline{IORQ}$ and $\overline{WR}$ signals are low during T2 and T3. Data from the accumulator are passed over the data bus to the output port whose address is contained on the lower byte of the address bus. But note that the $\overline{IORQ}$ signal does not become active immediately, allowing the data on the data bus to stabilize before the operation is consummated.

Bus Request/Acknowledge.   The bus request signal ($\overline{BUSRQ}$) is used to allow external devices to gain control of the CPU control lines, the address bus, and the data bus. This allows direct access to memory for the external device.

The CPU samples the $\overline{BUSRQ}$ input during the last T cycle of any given M cycle. If the bus request is active, the CPU will complete the current instruction and then service the request. Following the last T cycle of the last M cycle, the CPU will go into a high-impedance state. The address bus lines, the data bus lines, and the control lines ($\overline{MREQ}$, $\overline{RD}$, $\overline{WR}$, $\overline{IORQ}$, $\overline{RFSH}$) are placed in the high-impedance condition, effectively disconnecting them from the external circuits. This will allow the external device to gain control of the lines to directly input data to memory locations without going through the CPU. When the CPU lines are in the high-impedance state, the CPU generates a $\overline{BUSAK}$ (bus acknowledge) signal that tells the requesting device that the buses are available for its use. The timing for this type of operation is shown in Figure 2-13.

When the external device is finished with the memory, it will deactivate (i.e., make high) the $\overline{BUSRQ}$ signal, thus telling the CPU that it can have control again.

Interrupt Request.   The ability to service interrupts allows the CPU to use certain types of external device more efficiently. The CPU can do other chores while the slower external device is working, or it may perform other chores while awaiting rarely occurring situations to develop. The $\overline{INT}$ signal is the interrupt request. This line is sampled by the CPU on the rising edge of the last T state of each M cycle. See Figure 2-14.

These interrupts can be masked in software because the CPU will not accept the request unless an internal CPU flip-flop is set. This interrupt flip-

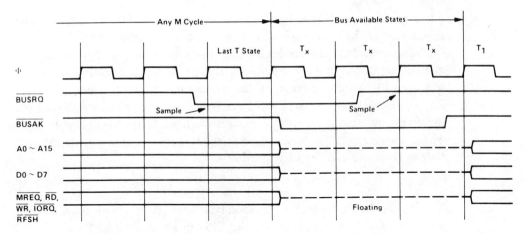

Figure 2-13 Bus request timing diagram.

flop is controlled by software commands. Interrupts are also ignored if the bus request ($\overline{\text{BUSRQ}}$) line is active (i.e., low).

If the CPU accepts the interrupt request, a special M1 state is generated, so the $\overline{\text{M1}}$ line goes low. The address bus receives the contents of the program counter (PC) so that the CPU can return to the original program after the

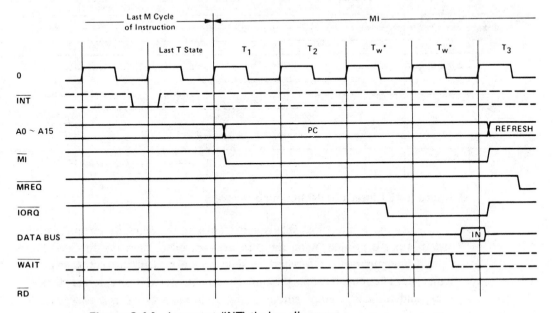

Figure 2-14 Interrupt (INT) timing diagram.

interrupt is serviced. The address of the next instruction to be executed following termination of the interrupt is stored on an external memory stack.

Once the PC contents are stored, the $\overline{\text{IORQ}}$ line goes low, telling the interrupting device that it can place an address vector on the data bus, which tells the CPU where the program that services the interrupt is located.

As in the previous conditions, the $\overline{\text{WAIT}}$ signal can be used to lengthen the timing by causing the CPU to enter wait states. If the $\overline{\text{WAIT}}$ line is active when sampled, the CPU enters the wait state. If the signal is inactive, no wait state is generated and the CPU continues.

Nonmaskable Interrupts.   Certain types of interrupt situations cannot wait for the software being executed by the CPU to set an internal flip-flop. Such interrupts might be an alarm condition in the process or factory or in a medical computer. These situations require a nonmaskable interrupt. Figure 2-15 shows the CPU timing for the nonmaskable interrupt in the Z80.

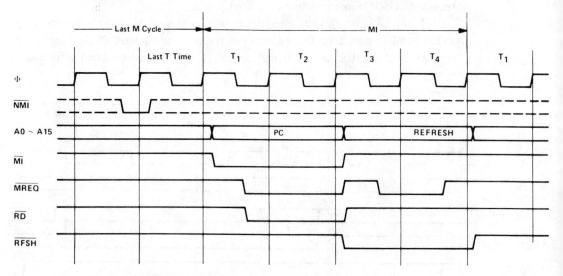

Figure 2-15   Interrupt (NMI) timing diagram.

This type of interrupt cycle is very similar to the regular interrupt, except that it is not dependent upon the software-controlled interrupt flip-flop. This type of interrupt will be serviced as soon as the present instruction cycle is completed. The contents of the program counter are stored in an external memory stack, and the CPU jumps automatically to location 00 66 (hex) to find the interrupt service program.

Exit From a HALT.   If a software HALT instruction is encountered, the CPU will sit there executing no-ops (NOP) until one of two situations occurs: (1) a nonmaskable interrupt is received, or (2) a maskable interrupt is received and the internal interrupt flip-flop is SET.

If the interrupt lines ($\overline{\text{INT}}$ or $\overline{\text{NMI}}$) are active when sampled during the T4 portion of the M1 cycle, the HALT condition is terminated following T4. The $\overline{\text{HALT}}$ line then goes inactive (high). The CPU timing for the exit from halt operation is shown in Figure 2-16.

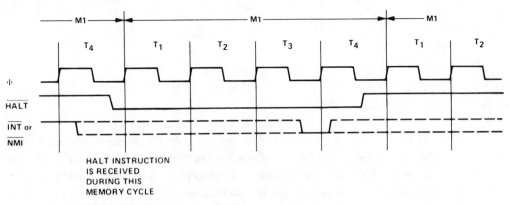

Figure 2-16 Halt timing diagram.

3
Selecting the Right Microprocessor/ Microcomputer

The terms microcomputer and microprocessor cover a variety of different devices that have different capabilities. There is no such thing as a "universal" computer that is all things to all applications. Matters to consider when buying a microcomputer/microprocessor are the architecture of the machine (i.e., register, memory, or I/O oriented), the instruction set (computationally strong or I/O operations strong), and the associated hardware requirements.

A large variety of hardware is available under the rubric "microcomputer." A full-sized system involving several CRT terminals and hard-disk drives may properly be called a microcomputer if the CPU is a microprocessor chip (and such elaborate microcomputers are available). The Heath Model H89 with its built-in disk and CRT monitor is also a microcomputer. So is a little single-board trainer such as the KIM-1, SYM-1, and AIM-65 machines. The Radio Shack TRS-80, Apple II, and IBM Personal Computer are all properly called microcomputers. On the low end of the scale we have single-board computers that are intended as Original Equipment Manufacturer (OEM) components to be used inside some other product almost as if it were a piece part. Pro-Log, Wintek, and John Bell Engineering make such products. We also have single-chip computers (e.g., the 8048 family) that contain everything we need on one chip.

Which of these do you select for *your* application? All are microcomputers, yet they have vastly different properties. Obviously, one would not use the same machine for such vastly different chores as data processing and, say, burglar alarm or environmental systems monitoring.

It is, therefore, essential that you evaluate the task to be performed and also discern any *reasonable* future accretions to the system. Keep in mind that all projects tend to grow in scope as time passes. Some of this growth is legitimate; some growth occurs because people tend to enlarge a project into additional functions that were neither intended nor are advisable; some growth is due to *your* poor evaluation in the early stages of the project. Try to anticipate future needs and plan for them. A more or less valid rule of thumb is to follow the 50 percent rule regarding initial capacity: the current requirements should occupy only *one-half* of the machine resources (memory size, processing time, and number of I/O ports).

It is claimed that a smart designer will provide twice or three times the memory actually required for the presently specified chore, but will not under any circumstances tell the programmer. Programmers tend to use up all the memory available. Perhaps, if they think there is somewhat less available to them, they can find more efficient means to solve their problems.

The decisions made during planning phases of a project will affect future capabilities in large measure. If adequate means for expansion are not provided, extraordinary problems will surface later. One sure sign of poor planning in a microprocessor-based instrument is the use of extra "kluge boards" hanging onto the main printed circuit board.

The key to good planning is evaluation of system requirements. How many I/O ports are needed? How much memory (guess and then double the figure if cost will allow)? How fast will the processor have to operate? What kind of displays and/or input devices are needed? How many? What size of power supply is needed? In a small system, a bank of seven-segment LED numerical readouts can draw as much current as the rest of the computer.

Perhaps one of the earliest hardware decisions regards the microprocessor chip that will be selected. You will find such decisions are often made more or less on emotional grounds rather than technical; one gets attached to a type, often the first type you learned to program. Just as it is in photography and high fidelity equipment, microprocessors and microcomputers attract "true believers." Sometimes, however, an emotionally satisfying choice made turns out later to have been utterly stupid for the need at hand.

Typical of the factors that must be considered, especially if the microcomputer is being used as a part of another instrument, are the following: power consumption, speed–power product, size, cost, reliability, and maintainability. These factors are not here arranged in any hierarchy, but they should be ranked by importance in your design planning. For example, if you are designing a computerized bedside patient monitor for a hospital, power consumption and speed–power product assume less important roles than in, say, a space shuttle computer where available power is limited, heat dissipation tightly controlled, and data rates extremely high. Similarly, in the bedside monitor we can tolerate lower-reliability (hence lower cost) equipment because repair service is readily available, and replacement units can be procured and stocked against the possibility of a failed unit. For a NASA satellite, on the other hand, once launched there is no possibility of repair. For that computer, it might be worthwhile to build according to high-reliability specifications. Maintainability is less important to the satellite, but of critical importance to the hospital's biomedical equipment technician or clinical engineer. Cost, of course, is also very important to the hospital user.

Speed–power product can become important in many applications. Processing speed, as measured by system clock frequency, is usually related to power consumption. In most semiconductor devices, the operating speed relates to internal resistances and capacitances that form frequency-limiting RC time constants. Reducing internal resistances in order to increase operating speed (i.e., a short RC time constant) also causes increased power consumption.

Processing speed as measured from program execution time, however, is another matter. This time limitation depends upon the efficiency of instruction execution and the nature of the instructions available to the programmer. There are cases, for example, where the 1-mHz 6502 device will execute a program slightly faster than the 2-mHz Z80 machine.

A measure of programming speed is the *benchmark program.* Such a program attempts to standardize evaluation comparisons by having the different microcomputers under test perform some standard task and noting amount of time required. There are numerous pitfalls in this approach, however, because the selection of the task and the programming approach used to solve the problem or task can significantly affect results through bias in favor of one machine over another. The benchmark program should, therefore, be representative of the tasks to be performed by the end product.

Factors that can seriously affect processing speed are the nature of the instruction set and the architecture of the microcomputer. If the task is heavy on I/O operations, for example, it may be wise to use a microprocessor with a good repertoire of input/output instructions. A number-crunching data-processing task, on the other hand, requires strong shift-left and shift-right instructions. Also, some microcomputers have hardware multiply and divide capability that is much faster than software implementations of these functions. Since these arithmetic functions tend to be time consuming in software, they are a major consideration if your computer will have to make many such computations.

If the program will require numerous subroutines, especially if several subroutines are nested within others, the computer should have a good *stack* capacity. Also, the bit size of the computer can be important. If the application requires a 16-bit word (or anything greater than the 8 bits normally found on "traditional" microprocessors), the computer will have to be either a 16-bit machine or be programmed to process 16 bits by sequentially grabbing 2 bytes at a time.

Support can also be a driving factor in the selection of the microcomputer. First, there is the matter of software and/or hardware available on the open market for that microcomputer. Both the Z80 and 6502 machines, for example, have immense amounts of software available. The CP/M operating system, as a single example, works on Z80 machines. It may or may not be the best operating system for your case, but it is extensively used and almost every dealer stocks CP/M-compatible programs. Machines like the TRS-80, Apple II, S-100 (of which many exist), and certain others offer many software and hardware options, and many of these are offered by vendors other than the original manufacturer. It is not really a bargain to buy a little-known machine for which little software is available if you are going to have to develop your own software; software costs often outstrip hardware costs by a considerable margin.

If you are going to include either a microcomputer or microprocessor in the design of a product, be sure to consider second sourcing. Most major microprocessor chips are now second sourced. The Z80, for example, is available from both Zilog, Inc. (its inventor) and Mostek. The reason for requiring a second source is that all companies from time to time have problems that prevent timely deliveries. If you are locked into a source that is a sole source, and they should have such problems, you will be in a bind that is difficult to resolve. Your own production will be brought to a halt by someone else's problems.

It is often more difficult to obtain single-board computers that are second sourced. These products are often highly unique in their design, so only one company will make them. There are options, however, and these should be considered. Some standard bus single-board computers are made by several companies, so even if the products are not exactly interchangeable, they are close enough to make conversion less damaging to your schedules. Also, some single-board OEM manufacturers advertise that they will give you the drawings to allow you to become your own second source once you purchase a minimum number of machines (usually 100 to 200).

4
Generating
Device-Select Pulses

One aspect of any programmable digital computer is the use of a main data bus operated in a synchronous manner. In this type of arrangement, the data bus is common to a large variety of devices and is shared in common. The data bus, for example, services the computer memory, all input/output (I/O) ports, and many peripherals that may be connected directly to the computer as if they were either memory or I/O ports in their own right.

The secret to the operation of any bus system is *synchronization*. The central-processing unit will designate the I/O port or the memory location as well as the type of operation that is to take place. During the period the operation is being executed, only the affected device is actively connected to the data bus. For example, let's assume that an I/O port is being designated. On the output side, we want it to accept data to be sent out to the peripheral connected to it only when the computer is executing a pertinent instruction. We would not want the port to be active at all other times, because not everything that passes along the data bus is intended for that output port. Indeed, only a few pieces of data will be destined for any one port in most cases. We want that output port to accept data only when commanded to do so.

On the other hand, we would not want the input side of the I/O port to be active except when commanded. Not only do we wish to avoid sending inappropriate data into the computer, we also want to avoid having a constantly active port from capturing the data bus and thereby distorting the data transmitted over the bus.

The answer to the problem of synchronization is the generation of device-select pulses to designate and turn on the memory location, I/O port, or peripheral designated by the computer CPU chip.

All microcomputers generate several control signals that are used to synchronize operations. In the Z80 microprocessor[1] for instance, we have the $\overline{\text{WR}}$, $\overline{\text{RD}}$, $\overline{\text{IORQ}}$, and $\overline{\text{MREQ}}$ signals, which are detailed next:

$\overline{\text{WR}}$ Active-low output signal that indicates a *write* operation is taking place.

$\overline{\text{RD}}$ Active-low output that indicates that a read operation is taking place. Neither $\overline{\text{RD}}$ or $\overline{\text{WR}}$ tell whether the operation is an I/O operation or a memory operation. At least one additional signal is needed.

$\overline{\text{IORQ}}$ Input/output request. This active-low output indicates when an I/O operation is taking place.

$\overline{\text{MREQ}}$ Memory request. This active-low output indicates that a memory operation is taking place.

In the Z80 microprocessor, two signals are needed to define fully the type of operation that is taking place, while one additional signal (valid address) is needed to designate the specific port or memory location. For memory operations, the coincidence of $\overline{\text{MREQ}}$ and $\overline{\text{WR}}$ indicates a *write operation to memory* (all directional designations in microcomputers are from the CPU point of view, not that of the outside observer). Similarly, an $\overline{\text{MREQ}}$ and $\overline{\text{RD}}$ indicates that a *read from memory* is taking place. The two different types of I/O operation are, of course, *input* and *output*. These operations are denoted by the coincidence

---

[1]For additional details, see Joseph J. Carr, *Z80 User's Manual*, Reston Publishing Co., Reston, Va., 1981.

of $\overline{\text{IORQ}/\text{RD}}$ and $\overline{\text{IORQ}/\text{WR}}$, respectively. We may, therefore, use these signals and the address but to specify uniquely a particular memory location or I/O port.

Each microprocessor chip has its own particular set of control signals, and it is necessary for the designer to learn and understand their use in order to generate correctly the device-select signals. In some systems, there will be no discrete I/O ports, but, rather, memory locations are designated as I/O ports. Such systems are called memory-mapped I/O computers. Other devices, such as the Z80 microprocessor, use a separate I/O structure. Since this is the more complex of the two schemes, we will construct our examples principally around the Z80 device.

In the Z80 microprocessor there is a 16-bit address bus, allowing a total of 65,536 (i.e., 64K) different memory locations to be addressed. In addition, during I/O operations the unique "address" of the I/O port is passed along the lower 8 bits of the address bus (A0–A7), while the data in the accumulator at that instant are passed along the higher 8 bits (A8–A15). Since 8 bits are used to designate the I/O ports, we may specify a total of 256 different discrete ports numbered from 000 to 255. Figure 4-1 shows the structure of the Z80 micro-computer as needed to generate the device-select signals.

ADDRESS DECODING

The microcomputer uses a 16-bit binary word passed along the 16-bit parallel address bus to indicate memory locations. In the Z80, 8 of these bits are also used to designate I/O port addresses. The problem for the designer is to create a circuit that will uniquely decode the required address, that is, generate a signal that exists if and only if the correct address is passed along the bus.

Several different techniques may be used for the decoding of the address bus. One method that is based on the properties of the NAND gate is shown in Figure 4-1. Recall the properties of the NAND gate: (1) if any *one* input is LOW, then the output is HIGH; and (2) all inputs must be HIGH for the output to be LOW.

We must, therefore, create a situation in which *all* inputs of the NAND gate are HIGH when the correct address is passed along the bus. At all other times at least one NAND gate input will be LOW, thereby forcing the output HIGH. The correct indication of the proper address will be a LOW on the output of the NAND gate.

In most 8-bit microcomputers we will have to decode either 8 bits or 16

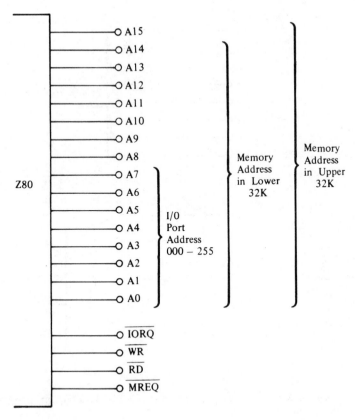

Figure 4-1 Z80 pinouts.

bits of the address bus. The TTL 7430 device is an 8-bit NAND gate and so is almost ideally suited to this type of service.

In the circuit of Figure 4-2a, we are attempting to decode the address 11110010. Five bits of the address bus will naturally be HIGH when the correct address is present and so require no additional treatment. There are, however, 3 bits that will be LOW when the correct address is present: A0, A2, and A3. The lines for these bits are not connected directly to the address bus, but are first *inverted*. By connecting an inverter in each of these three lines, the input to the NAND gate will be 11111111 when the data word on the address bus is 11110010.

Hardwiring the inverters into the circuit sometimes unnecessarily limits our selection to the addresses selected in advance. We can, however, take one of several tacts that overcome this problem. We could, for example, place an

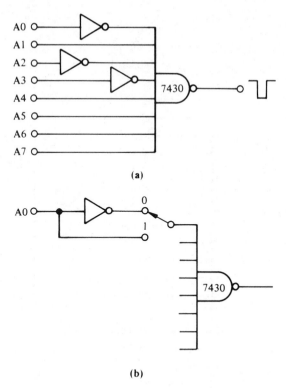

Figure 4-2   (a) Address decoder for 11110010_2; (b) programmable address decoder.

inverter in each input line and then use either a switch or movable jumpers to determine whether a 1 or 0 on the particular address bus will generate the required HIGH on the NAND gate input. This method is shown in Figure 4-2b.

We can also select I/O port numbers that require fewer inverters. If we select port 0, then we must decode 00000000, which requires eight inverters. If, on the other hand, we select port 255, we need no inverters because the correct code will be 11111111 (FF in hex). Any address in the higher end of the permissible range will require substantially fewer inverters if the scheme of Figure 4-2 is used.

The key to making our decoder work on all locations or addresses other than FF_{16} is the use of inverters. We must, however, sometimes use a certain economy of design in order to achieve a lower cost or, perhaps, a lower components count. The most obvious option is to use one or more hex inverter IC devices to get the inverters that we need. Each hex inverter contains six independent inverter stages. To get eight inverters, then, we must use all six stages from one hex inverter IC and two stages from a second hex inverter IC. This means a potential waste of four inverter stages. The key to our design economy may well be the use of wasted sections of various ICs to gain the inverters that we need. Unless some printed writing board layout problem prevents it, we can use unused inverter stages from other ICs or make inverters from NAND, NOR, and exclusive-OR (XOR) gates that may be left over when the IC was only partially used elsewhere in the circuit. Figure 4-3 shows the use of NAND, NOR, and XOR gates. In the TTL line, we find the 7400 NAND gate contains four independent two-input NAND gates; the 7402 contains four independent NOR gates; the 7486 device contains four independent XOR gates.

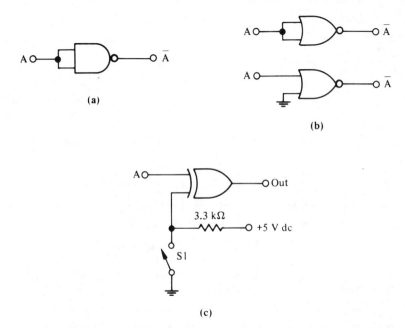

Figure 4-3 (a) NAND inverter; (b) NOR inverters; (c) XOR inverter or buffer.

There are two tactics that will result in making either a NAND gate or a NOR gate into an inverter. For both types of gate, we can connect both inputs together to make an inverter. We can also make the NAND gate into an inverter by connecting one input permanently HIGH (i.e., tie it to +5 V dc through a 1- to 5-kilohm (kΩ) resistor. The resistor effectively disables that particular input. The other input follows the normal rules for NAND gates: when the other input is LOW, then the output is HIGH; when the other input is HIGH, the output is LOW.

The NOR gate function is exactly the opposite of the NAND gate function. As might be suspected in such a case, therefore, we can make the NOR gate into an inverter by permanently grounding one input. Recall the rules for the operation of the NOR gate: (1) if either input is HIGH, then the output is LOW; (2) if both inputs are LOW, then the output is HIGH. When one input is permanently LOW, therefore, the NOR gate will operate as an inverter.

The exclusive-OR (XOR) gate is a little different from the other types. The output of the XOR gate will be HIGH only when the data applied to the two inputs are *different*. In other words, the output is HIGH if either input is HIGH or LOW, but not when both are at the same level at the same time. The truth table for the XOR gate is as follows:

Input		Output
A	*B*	
0	0	0
0	1	1
1	0	1
1	1	0

Figure 4-3c shows the use of an XOR gate as either an inverter or a noninverting buffer, depending on the setting of switch S1. When the switch is open, one input is held HIGH. In this case, a LOW on the other input means that the two inputs are different, so the output is HIGH: it is inverted. When switch S1 is closed, however, that input is held LOW. A LOW on the other input will produce a LOW output, and a HIGH on that input will produce a HIGH output: no inversion takes place. We can use the XOR gate version to replace the switches used in Figure 4-2b. Connecting the control input to ground will pass the 1 on the data bus on to the NAND gate decoder input. Similarly, holding the control input HIGH will cause an inversion of the address bit. This method will be used in another illustration shortly.

We do not always need all 8 bits of an address to specify an I/O port. The Z80 microprocessor can uniquely address 256 different ports. While that may sound impressive, we will very rarely actually use that many ports. In most projects, the designer will find no more than one or two different ports (e.g., a keyboard and a teletypewriter or printer). In those cases, we can often achieve economy of design by ignoring most of the higher-order ports and only worry about a few. We can replace the eight-input NAND gate with a simpler four- or two-input NAND gate that may be a wasted section of an IC that is already in the design.

Figure 4-4a shows the binary codes for the four lowest-order addresses. Note that only 2 bits are needed to uniquely decode these addresses: A0 and A1. Bits A2 and A3 are always LOW. As long as we are not going to use any higher numbered ports, only these 2 bits are needed.

Figure 4-4b shows the use of a multi-input NAND gate to decode the first few addresses within the permissible range. The 7430 is an 8-bit device, so we can tie four to six inputs permanently HIGH and only use the required inputs. For the circuit shown, the code 0000 will cause the output of the NAND gate to drop LOW. We can delete or keep each inverter as needed. With four address lines, up to 16 devices can be selected with this circuit. The simplest case is shown in Figure 4-4c in which a simple two-input NAND gate is used. This circuit will decode all four lower-order I/O ports. For the circuit as shown, with both inverters wired into place, the output of the 7400 will drop LOW only for port 0 (for which the code is 00). With two inputs, we can decode up to four ports (ports 0 through 3), depending upon whether or not the inverter is wired into the circuit.

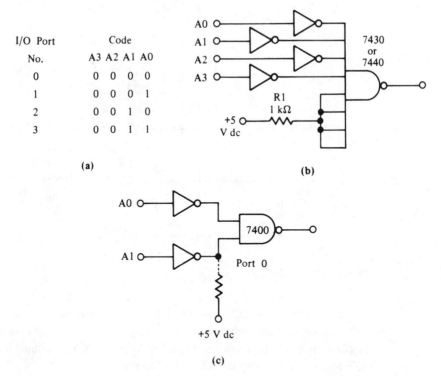

Figure 4-4 (a) Address decoder (4-bit) for I/O ports; (b) port address-select codes; (c) 2-bit decoding.

In a further simplification, port 0 and port 1 can be decoded with only one input, the other input being wired permanently HIGH. In that case, we would use the inverter for port 0 and delete the inverter (or wire around it) for port 1.

Figure 4-5 shows a circuit that can be switch selected to decode any port from port 0 to port 15. Since 16 different ports are possible, a total of 4 bits are needed: A0–A3.

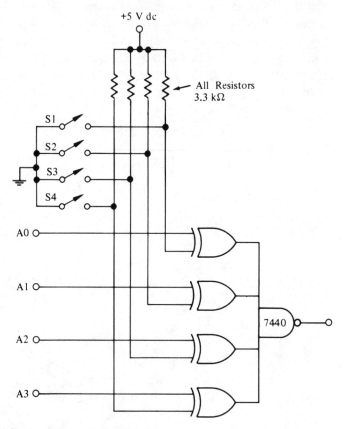

Figure 4-5   Programmable decoder.

The circuit uses XOR gates (see Figure 4-3c) as either inverters or non-inverting followers depending upon the setting of the respective bit-select switches (S1 through S4). The rules for Figure 4-3c apply in this circuit as well. The 7440 device is a four-input TTL NAND gate.

Thus far, all our address decoders have involved the use of NAND gates and inverters to generate a signal that is unique to the selected address. This method is not always the most viable, especially where lower-order addresses are called out. The circuit in Figure 4-6 is based on a differnt type of TTL integrated circuit, the 7442 *BCD-to-1-of-10 decoder* .

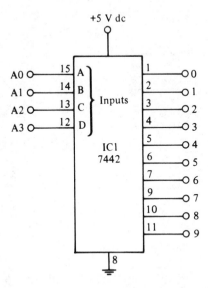

Figure 4-6   The 7442 used as a decoder.

The 7442 device is not specifically intended as an address decoder, despite the use of the word "decoder" in its type designation. Originally, it was intended to drive decimal numerical readout devices. In older types of digital decimal counters, the readout display would be either a column of ten incandescent lamps or a ten-digit Nixie[R] tube. In either case, the binary word from the counter would be in the 8-4-2-1 binary coded decimal (BCD) format. BCD is a limited version of 4-bit binary in which only the first ten states are allowed. The 7442 decodes the BCD word at the 4-bit input and issues an output that uniquely specifies the decimal value of the BCD word. The active output will drop LOW when its BCD word is applied. We can, therefore, use the 7442 device to select any of ten discrete addresses or I/O port numbers, as shown in Figure 4-6.

In Figure 4-6, the first 4 bits of the address bus are connected to the BCD inputs of the 7442 device. Any correct address from 0 to 9 can be decoded by this circuit. The selection is made by connecting the enable line of the selected address to the 7442 output terminal that corresponds to its address. A 16-line decoder can be made with the 74154 device, which will be discussed in the next section.

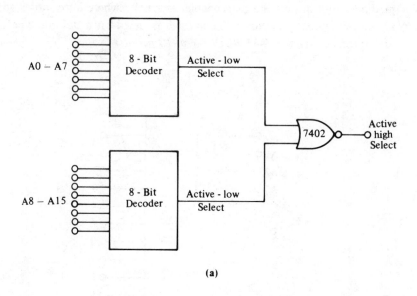

(a)

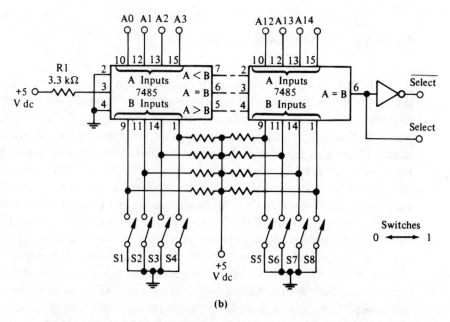

(b)

Figure 4-7 (a) Sixteen-bit decoder using 7430 and other chips; (b) N-bit decoder (4-bit increments) using 7485.

Sixteen-Bit Decoders

The decoder circuits presented thus far have been 8-bit designs. They are, therefore, limited to 256 different combinations. Only a few microcomputers will use only 256 bytes of memory, so the 8-bit decoder will be insufficient for that purpose. We will have to be able to decode up to 16 bits in order to uniquely address all 64K memory locations. Figure 4-7 shows two methods for decoding up to 16 bits of address bus.

The first method, shown in Figure 4-7a, uses two of the circuits shown earlier; two 8-bit decoders will select from 16 bits. The active-low outputs are connected to the two inputs of a 7402 NOR gate. According to the rules of the NOR gate, both inputs must be LOW for the output to be HIGH. Since each 8-bit decoder output is an active-low select signal, we will achieve the NOR-gate input condition needed to create a HIGH output only when the correct address is present on bits A0–A15 of the address bus.

A second method is shown in Figure 4-7b. This circuit uses the 7485 *4-bit binary word comparator* integrated circuit. This device compares two 4-bit binary words, designated word A and word B, and issues outputs that indicate whether A = B, A is greater than B, or A is less than B. In addition, cascading inputs and outputs allows using additional 7485 devices to make 8-, 12-, or 16-bit comparators. If we apply the lines of the address bus to one set of 7485 inputs and program the alternate inputs for required address, the output (pin 6) of the most significant 7485 will go HIGH only when the correct address is present.

A number of different switch options are available to make the address selection. The cheapest is to use jumper wires. When the jumper wire is in place, the 7485 input is permanently LOW. If, on the other hand, the jumper is left out, the input is permanently LOW. Alternatively, we may use either thumbwheel or binary DIP switches mounted on the printed circuit board, or even on the front panel if some pressing design reason indicates such an arrangement.

Additional information on address decoding is given in Chapter 5 when we discuss memory interfacing. Given in that discussion are methods for minimizing the component count by selecting memory in banks rather than having a large (impossibly large) array of decoder circuits.

GENERATING *IN* and *OUT* SIGNALS

The IN and OUT signals are generated by the proper convergence of control signals and the correct address. For example, let's assume that we want to generate an IN1 signal (i.e., a signal to indicate that input port 1 is to be activated). In the Z80 chip, this signal would require the IORQ and $\overline{RD}$ signals to be LOW, as well as an address decoder SELECT output to indicate that address 1 (i.e., 00000001 on the lower 8 bits of the address bus) is present.

In some rare cases, we might want to generate an IN or OUT signal that is not dependent upon the address bus. In those cases, the signal would be active whenever the correct operation, an input or output, is taking place. Figure 4-8 shows several circuits for generating such signals. Again, the Z80 control signal system is used. In Figure 4-8a, we see the method used to generate a *data direction* signal that is HIGH for the OUT condition and LOW for the IN condition. Recall that the $\overline{IORQ}$ and $\overline{WR}$ signals must both be LOW for the OUT condition. In this situation, the two inputs of the 7402 NOR gate are LOW, so the output will be HIGH. This signal, however, is not unambiguous because it does not really tell us when an IN operation is being executed because we do not have an $\overline{RD}$ (read) signal in the picture. The IN status is implied because no output operation is taking place, and that is not always a safe way to proceed.

Figure 4-8b shows the same sort of idea using a pair of open-collector output inverters to make a single two-input NOR gate. The open-collector outputs are connected in a hardwired-OR configuration in which a LOW on either output forces the combination to be LOW. It requires both outputs to be HIGH in order for the combination to be HIGH. In other words, for the circuit as shown, both $\overline{IORQ}$ and $\overline{WR}$ must be LOW in order for the combination output to be HIGH. Again, the same ambiguity regarding the input operation exists as in the NOR gate version of Figure 4-8a.

To create a truly unambiguous control signal for IN and OUT operations, we must have two independent circuits as shown in Figure 4-8c. Here we combine the $\overline{IORQ}$ signal with $\overline{WR}$ and $\overline{RD}$ signals in a pair of NOR gates in order to create a pair of unambiguous data direction signals. NOR gate G1 is connected exactly as in Figure 4-8a and creates an active-high signal that denotes an output operation (OUT). If both $\overline{IORQ}$ and $\overline{WR}$ are LOW, indicating that a write operation is taking place, the output of G1 will be HIGH. If we want an active-low OUT signal (i.e., $\overline{OUT}$), it will be necessary to place an inverter at the output of G1.

Similarly, gate G2 is connected to denote a read operation to the Z80 microprocessor. The two inputs of the G2 NOR gate are connected to the $\overline{IORQ}$ and $\overline{RD}$ signals and so will produce an active-high IN signal. Again, an inverter is required for an $\overline{IN}$ signal.

The only truly unambiguous signal that will command one and only one device or port to turn on is that which takes into account the address of the

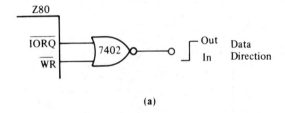

(a)

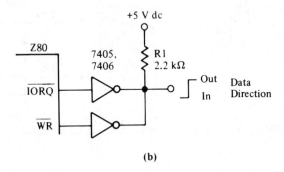

(b)

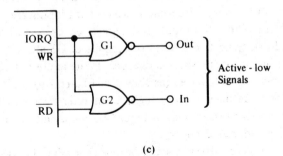

(c)

Figure 4-8 (a) 7402 data direction selector; (b) open-collector inverters used as data direction selector; (c) NOR gate IN and OUT data direction selectors.

device. Figure 4-9 shows the previous circuits combined with an address decoder to perform as a unique OUT/IN signal generator. Gates G1 and G2 are exactly as shown in Figure 4-8c and require no further discussion except to relabel their respective output signals. To avoid confusion, we will label the output of G1 (OUT) and that of G1 (IN) in order to indicate that these signals do not account for the port/device address, but only that an output or input operation is taking place, respectively.

Gates G3 and G4 are NAND gates. They produce a HIGH output whenever either input is LOW, and a LOW output if and only if both inputs are

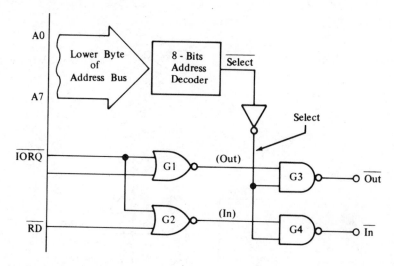

Figure 4-9 Complete data direction decoders.

HIGH. To generate active-low output ($\overline{\text{OUT}}$) and input ($\overline{\text{IN}}$) signals, therefore, we must create a situation in which both inputs are HIGH only at the correct instant. The (OUT) and (IN) signals are connected to one input each for G3 and G4, respectively. The other inputs of G3 and G4 are connected together at the output of the address decoder. If the address decoder output is active-low, an inverter is required (as shown in Figure 4-9). If, however, the output of the address decoder is active-high, no inverter is needed. The $\overline{\text{OUT}}$ and $\overline{\text{IN}}$ signals generated by the circuit of Figure 4-9 are unique to only one port, that selected by the address decoder.

Figure 4-10 shows a technique that might be used as an economy measure in some designs. Here we are decoding a specific port (port 1) to perform an output operation. Open-collector inverters are used to create an (OUT) signal at their mutual wire-OR output terminal. If we also wire-OR an output from an address decoder to the same point, however, the OUT signal will be unique to that one port. In this case, we can wire in the output an open-collector noninverting buffer to denote port 1. In the case of port 1, we would require a HIGH on address bus line A0 plus a LOW on both $\overline{\text{IORQ}}$ and $\overline{\text{WR}}$ lines in order to create a HIGH at the output of the wired-OR connections.

There is a limitation to this method. Can you spot it? If we use only 1 bit of the address bus, we must be absolutely certain that the program written for the computer does not call for any other ports than that allowed by the design. In the case of port 1, bit A0 will be HIGH. However, it will *also* be HIGH if

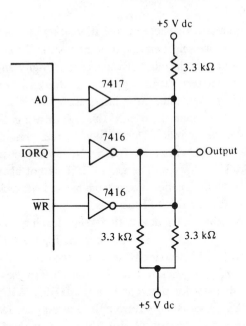

Figure 4-10   Wired-OR inverters using data direction selectors.

the programmer calls up port 3 (0011), port 5 (0101), port 7 (0111), and so forth. As long as we are certain that no ambiguity can be created by the programming of the microprocessor, this method is valid. In some small instrumentation or control systems, therefore, it is a valid technique. In those cases, it is unlikely that someone will want to add a port at some later time. If they do, we can use another bit of the address bus for that port and program accordingly. On a 16-bit address bus, we can accommodate up to 16 different ports if we consider them to be memory-mapped I/O ports. On the Z80, which uses discrete I/O commands in the instruction set, the lower 8 bits of the address bus contain the address of the I/O port, and using a system like Figure 4-10 we can make up to eight discrete I/O ports that are indicated by only 1 bit each. This system is used in many smaller control and instrumentation computers that will never have the full 64K complement of memory. Most such computers use 1K, 2K, 4K, or 8K of memory. A popular tactic is to make a memory-mapped port for a device at the 32K boundary. If there will be no address higher than 32K, we can connect bit A15 of the address bus to denote the device in question. It has been popular in data-converter applications to use A15 to turn on the data device. Bit A15 combined with an OUT signal will turn on a digital-to-analog converter, while bit A15 and an IN signal will turn on an analog-to-digital converter.

Numerous devices on the IC market can be pressed into service to make make a device-select signal. It is interesting, however, that certain devices tend to be used even in more recent designs. Many engineers are sensitive to using the most modern technology possible for each job, but that is not always the best policy. Remember, the important thing is to get the job done in a timely and *economic* manner, even if this means using devices that have been around for a decade or more. Don't listen to the admonishments of those who think that newest is always best. The NAND and NOR gates described in this chapter are old TTL devices. The use of TTL is not always mandated, however, and NAND/NOR function blocks from newer logic technologies will perform exactly as indicated for the TTL devices.

Another older device that keeps finding its way into new designs is the 7442 described earlier in this chapter. Figure 4-11 shows the use of the 7442 BCD-to-1-of-10 decoder IC as a device-select pulse generator. In the circuit as shown, we can generate both $\overline{IN}$ and $\overline{OUT}$ pulses.

The basis for this circuit is the $\overline{IORQ}$, $\overline{WR}$, and $\overline{RD}$ control signals and the $\overline{SELECT}$ signal output from the address decoder. These signals are connected to form a 4-bit binary word at the input of the 7442 device. In this case, we connect $\overline{IORQ}$ to the A input, $\overline{RD}$ to the B input, $\overline{WR}$ to the C input, and $\overline{SELECT}$ to the D input (weighting A = 1, B = 2, C = 4, and D = 8). Using this connection scheme, considering that these are active-low outputs, we find that the input condition is represented by binary word 0100 (see the table in Figure 4-11) and the output by 0010; these are 4_{10} and 2_{10} in the decimal system, respectively. We can, therefore, use the 4 output (pin 5) for the $\overline{IN}$ signal and the 2 output (pin 3) for the $\overline{OUT}$ signal. The only time that these respective output terminals on the 7442 are LOW is when the correct port is selected.

MULTIPLE DEVICE-SELECT PULSES

The 7442 and other devices may also be used to select multiple devices in larger systems. We can use the 7442 to select from ten different devices if the correct connection is used. Similarly, a 74154 device can select up to 16 devices. The 74154 device is a *4-bit-binary-to-1-of-16 decoder,* also called a *4-line-to-16-line decoder* in some manuals and a *data distributor* in others. The latter name is derived from the fact that the data applied to pin 19 (DS) will be transferred to the output line that is selected by the 4-bit word applied to the ABCD inputs. In Figure 4-12 we use this feature to determine whether the outputs are active high or active low. The level that is applied to DS will be transmitted to the active output. For example, if the switch is open, the level applied to DS will be HIGH. The selected output will then be HIGH and all others will be LOW.

	D	C	B	A	
	Address $\overline{\text{Select}}$	$\overline{\text{WR}}$	$\overline{\text{RD}}$	$\overline{\text{IORQ}}$	
In	0	1	0	0	4_{10}
Out	0	0	1	0	2_{10}

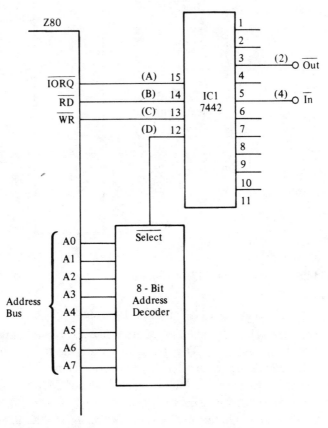

Figure 4-11 IN/OUT signal generation using 7442.

If, on the other hand, the switch is LOW, the active output will be LOW and all others will be HIGH.

The $\overline{\text{CE}}$ terminal (pin 18) is used to turn on the selected output. When this terminal is LOW, the selected terminal will be at the data level that is selected by DS. We use in the $\overline{\text{IN}}$ or $\overline{\text{OUT}}$ terminals to drive this terminal.

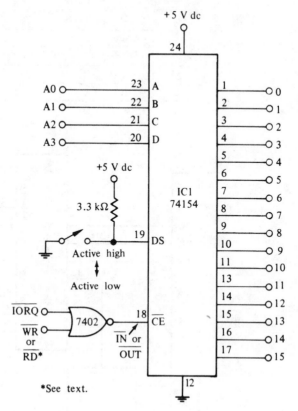

Figure 4-12   The 74154 decoder.

The input word for the 74154 is a 4-bit binary word made up of 4 bits of the address bus. In this case, we have selected bits A0 through A15, so that the first 16 permissible I/O port addresses are the ports addressed. The selection code follows the ordinary binary numbering system. This same system, however, might be used for any four sequential sets of address lines within the system. In some cases, for example, we might wish to use A0, A1, A2, and A15 to locate the ports in the first locations of the upper 32K. In at least one 16-channel A/D–D/A converter on the market, the user can program the most significant bit in the address code by connecting it to one particular address bus bit (usually A15 or one of the other high-order bits). The others are connected to the lower-order bits of the address bus, thereby forcing the correct address to be the first 16 sequential addresses from the programmed memory page boundary address.

Both 7442 and 74154 devices can be combined in circuits to provide a large number of discrete device-select signals. In Figure 4-13, for example, we see seventeen 74154 devices connected to form 256 device-select pulses labeled

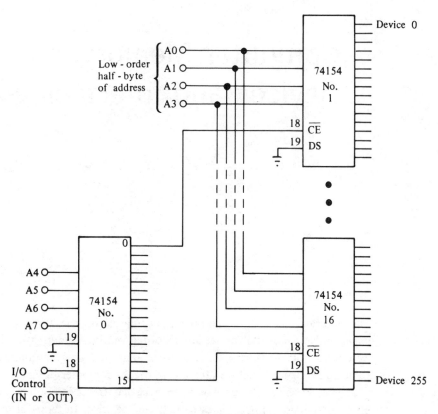

Figure 4-13 Multiple decoding using 74154 devices.

device 0 (or port 0) up to device 255 (or port 255). In this case, the lower-order 4 bits of the address bus are connected to the 4-bit inputs of 74154s 1 through 16. The next higher-order 4 bits (A4–A7) are connected to the 4-bit input of 74154 no. 0. The 16 active-low outputs from this 74154 are connected to the $\overline{CE}$ lines of the 16 other 74154 devices. A particular 74154 will, therefore, be activated only when its turn comes. Let's examine an example. Suppose we wanted to activate device 24. Decimal 24 is hexadecimal (base 16) 18, so we find that the most significant digit (74154 no. 0) must be 1, while the 4-bit code placed over the A0–A3 lines must be that for 8, or 1000. We must, therefore, transmit the binary word 00011000 over A0–A7. When this happens, the 1 output of 74154 no. 0 will drop LOW, thereby enabling 74154 no. 2, which will also respond to the 8 on A0–A3 by causing line 24 to drop LOW. This particular scheme can be carried out almost indefinitely provided that you have sufficient address line bits to accommodate the number of devices and the address bus power capacity or drive all the TTL inputs hanging on the line.

5
Computer Memory: Devices and Interfacing

The programmable digital computer, no matter how large or small, requires *memory*. No sequential or serial processing machine could work unless there were some way to store (i.e., remember) data and programming instructions. Hence, memory devices are inherent in digital computer design.

The principal difference between large mainframe computers and the smallest single-board computer is essentially one of scale. In terms of memory, this difference translates into certain restrictions on the microcomputer regarding the types of memory devices that are used. The generally slower 8-bit microcomputer, for example, has little need for 20-nanosecond (ns) ECL memory elements because the CPU will never operate fast enough to make either efficient or cost-effective use of such memory.

Similarly, the microcomputer probably has no need for multiple disk packs such as are found in almost all large mainframe computer installations. For most microcomputers, the floppy disk (*diskette*) is sufficient. As the lines blur between classes of computer, however, the situation may radically change. There are already multimegabyte large single-disk drives on the market made especially for microcomputers. Several manufacturers offer microcomputers in upright 19-inch racks that look like minicomputers of not long ago, and these are equipped with hard-disk drives. One wonders whether the traditional definitions that distinguish between minicomputers and microcomputers are still valid. This industry moves too fast for tradition to have much meaning, as reality keeps changing.

MEMORY HIERARCHY

Various types of memory are available, and they differ markedly as to the time required to read or write data. We can classify memory into several very broad categories according to approximate access times: *cache memory, short-term* or *working store memory, medium-term memory,* and *long-term memory.*

A cache memory operates at ultrahigh speeds and is used when the memory must keep up with a high-speed central processor. Typical technologies used to form semiconductor cache memories are all high-frequency devices: *emitter-coupled logic* (ECL), *high-speed TTL,* and *current injection logic* (IIL or I²L). As with any circuit that operates in ultrashort periods of time (i.e., 5 to 100 ns), cache memory designers must be aware of such matters as VHF/UHF circuit layout practices, matching of input and output impedances, and the transmission-line properties of electrical conductors. Cache memories are usually limited to a small portion of a mainframe computer's total memory array. Data are transferred in and out of the small cache as needed.

Short-term memory is the main volatile memory of a microcomputer and consists mostly of semiconductor *random-access memory* (RAM) chips. Short-term memory devices usually operate with access times on the order of 100 ns to 5 microseconds (μs).

The *working store* of most microcomputers consists of an array of high-speed short-term devices comprising as few as 32 bytes and as much as hundreds of kilobytes.

The "typical" (if that word really has meaning in this context) 8-bit microcomputer has a 16-bit address bus and so can access 2^{16} or 65,536 different 1-byte (i.e., 8 bits) memory locations. In the microcomputer, the memory size designation advertised for a particular machine (e.g., 24K, 48K, 64K) refers to the short-term storage in some type of volatile semiconductor RAM array.

Some microcomputers do not have the entire 64K of short-term memory available for programmer use. In some machines, this may be due to economic considerations. Small single-board computers such as KIM-1 and AIM-65 come with either 1K or 4K, even though the 6502 microprocessor chip used in those machines is capable of supporting up to the full 64K. Although some programmers will object if a computer is limited in memory, the 1K or 4K is not necessarily a tight limiting factor. For users who are developing software for small microprocessor-based instruments (scientific, medical, engineering, factor process control, etc.), it has been found by a survey that most applications programs, some 70 percent, require less than 2K of RAM. For those applications, a versatile, low-cost SBC such as Rockwell's AIM-65 makes good sense.

In some other machines, some of the available memory is taken up by overhead software such as the built-in monitor, peripheral drivers and display generators. There seem to be two philosophies regarding the basal program of a computer. In some machines, an entire monitor and operating system are stored in permanently programmed *read-only memory* (ROM), which includes software drivers for all peripherals, video display, and other features. In the Apple II, for example, overhead programs are stored in the upper 16K of memory, so only 48K is available for the user.

The alternate method is to store a tiny "bootstrapping" program, or mini-monitor, somewhere in memory, often in the lowest-order page (256 bytes). By selecting the zero page for the bootstrap program, a situation is created where both the *power-on reset pulse* circuit and the manual *reset* button (if any) will cause the computer to automatically enter the program. The reset function is nothing but a hardware JUMP to 00 instruction. When it is activated, the computer program counter is set to zero, so the next instruction to be executed will be found at location 0000 (hex). When the power is applied to the machine or when the operator presses the *reset* button, the computer will jump to the beginning of the program. The use of the manual reset button allows us a "panic button" to escape from a program when a programming error causes unexpected results.

The main purpose of the bootstrap system is to allow maximum use of 64K memory size. The bootstrap program will contain only enough instructions to load a program from an external long-term storage device such as a magnetic tape, floppy disk, or other such media. The medium-term RAM resident in the computer will be essentially tabula rasa (except for the bootstrap program in page 0) until an operating program is input from some external device.

The alternative to bootstrapping is to use a front panel or other circuit to individually step and load program into memory *by hand*. This tedious process is called "finger-boning" for good reason and is extremely time consuming.

Short-term memory is often reserved for data or instructions that are needed imminently. Data that are not needed immediately may be held in longer-term storage media such as medium-term or long-term memory.

Medium-term memory includes floppy disks (which come in 5¼- and 8-in. sizes), magnetic drum memory, and bubble memory (a semiconductor process). Some people would also include larger-capacity hard disks in this category, especially when housed in a single-disk drive.

Long-term memory media consists of reel-to-reel magnetic tape, assorted forms of magnetic tape cassettes, multiple hard disk drives, punched paper tape, and punched paper cards.

Microcomputers tend to use magnetic floppy disks, magnetic tape in the standard Phillips-style cassettes (i.e., the familiar audio cassette), and punched paper tape. The latter is not very popular, but it is still seen in some cases. Computer magazines still carry advertisements for paper tape supplies and the machinery to support tape.

The read-only memory (ROM) is a device that will store a permanent program, even though it is a semiconductor product similar to RAM. In this sense, the ROM would have to be considered long-term storage despite its close similarity to RAM semiconductor devices. It is often the case that RAM and ROM devices are mixed together on the same board with each other, and ROM is assigned some of the available 64K addresses. We will consider specific ROM devices later in this chapter, but first we must examine a few other topics.

Virtual Memory

Virtual memory permits the programmer/user to see all memory (short, medium, or long term) as if it were readily available short-term memory. As such, the programmer can think almost in terms of an "infinite" working store. Virtual memory is realized by making the hardware responsible for controlling paging and transfers to and from medium-term memory. In nonvirtual memory machines, the programmer must continuously be aware of the location of data or programming and perform periodic data transfers between short- and medium-term memory. Virtual memory is a function of hardware and is found in larger computers rather than microcomputers.

Single Memory Versus Dual Memory

Some older computers used two memories, one for program instructions and one for data. This technique is no longer used in most computer designs because the currently favored approach is the single-memory design. In this type of memory, the same memory bank will serve for both program instructions and data. The memory bank might be broken into zones reserved for one purpose or another, but it constitutes a single memory array in which each address designates but a single location.

In dual-memory systems, the two banks of memory may contain repeated addresses. Hence, the program memory addresses might run from 0000 to FFFF (hex) for a 64K system, and the data addresses will also run from 0000 to FFFF (hex) but in another bank.

A similar if not identical scheme is found in certain single-chip computers that contain built-in ROM. Some of these will have a *memory bank select* instruction that the programmer can use to switch between the internal 0 to 2K ROM and 0 to 2K external RAM.

Not to be confused with dual memory are the schemes that permit multiple banks of 64K memory to be selected. Some 128K and larger microcomputers are nothing more than 64K microprocessor chips (with 16-bit address buses) with clever designs that appear to extend the address bus. Such systems provide a means for selecting from two or more 64K banks of memory. Each 1-bit extension of the address bus will double the addressing capacity; hence, a 17-bit address bus will address 128K of RAM or ROM.

If we designate an 8-bit output port as a bank-select point, we create a system that allows multiple-64K banks to be used. For example, if each bit selects a different bank, we will have $8 \times 64K$, or 512K, of memory. Up to $256 \times 64K$ can be accommodated if we provide decoding to allow full use of the 256 different states of an 8-bit word. Such a computer would have 16,384K, at which point the cost of RAM/ROM chips and supporting circuitry becomes prohibitively high and disk or tape is more reasonable.

RANDOM-ACCESS MEMORY

The invention of low-cost semiconductor RAM more than any other factor made the microcomputer revolution possible. The older technology for memory used doughnut-shaped ferrite cores arranged in an XY matrix of rows and columns. Figure 5-1 shows core memory. Although this form of memory is by and large obsolete, there are still some applications where it is the memory of choice. Figure 5-1a shows the core and its approximate dimensions; Figure 5-1b shows the manner in which it is used. The direction of the magnetic flux is used to determine whether the core stores a logical 1 or logical 0. The magnetism is caused by currents flowing in perpendicular lines, each of which carries half the total magnetization current. Figure 5-1c shows how the cores are arranged in an XY matrix of rows and columns. Since only half of the needed magnetization current flows in each wire, we can arrange them in this row–column plane. Passing currents down a single row and a single column will cause sufficient current for magnetization only at one specific core at the point where the row and column cross.

Although ferrite-core memory is still used in some special applications, it has been totally supplanted by semiconductor memory in all microcomputer and most minicomputer applications. Ordinary core memory is simply too costly,

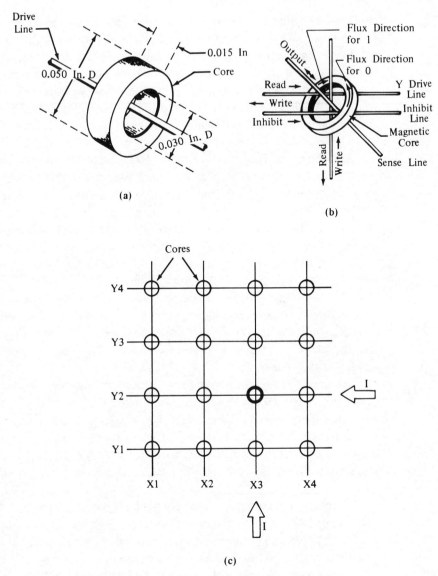

Figure 5-1 (a) Ferrite core memory; (b) ferrite code wiring; (c) matrix connections for ferrite cores.

requires substantial read–write overhead circuitry, and takes up too much space. Core is also relatively slow because the magnetization–demagnetization phenomenon on which it works is not instantaneous.

Semiconductor memory solves many of the problems that make core memory unsuitable for microcomputer applications. Remember that a binary digit (bit) must be either 1 or 0. We can implement these digits by using a transistor (saturated or off) or a flip-flop (set or reset), and both are used.

Semiconductor memory chips contain arrays of memory elements (called *cells*) arranged in an *XY* matrix of rows and columns. The memory is said to be *cell addressable,* which means that a cell may be accessed from the outside world by applying a unique code to the address pins. When the CPU issues an appropriate address, the cell which corresponds to that address will be turned on to either receive or send a data bit.

There are two basic kinds of RAM device: *static* and *dynamic.* Both types are used extensively and both will be considered here. There are reasons and trade-offs to be made when selecting one type over another, so general guidelines will be provided.

The *static memory* device consists of an array of bistable flip-flops that are made from pairs of cross-coupled bipolar transistors. When the flip-flop is in the *set* condition, the cell contains a 1 (i.e., HIGH), and when it is *reset,* the cell contains a 0 (i.e., LOW). Figure 5-2a shows such a flip-flop.

The advantage of static memory is that data, once written to a cell, will remain there permanently unless power is removed from the device or the processor writes a new bit to that same location. The disadvantages of static memory include a relatively large power dissipation that increases the heat buildup in the system.

Dynamic memory can be modeled as a leaky capacitor isolated from the outside world by MOS or bipolar transistor buffer amplifiers. Figure 5-2b shows a dynamic memory cell. The capacitor is not a genuine discrete capacitor, but the base-junction capacitance of a bipolar transistor. Charge is stored in the form of a current injected into the base region of the transistor. The 1 state exists when the transistor is *on,* while the 0 state exists when the transistor is *off.*

Dynamic random-access memory (DRAM) would seem to have all the advantages: less chip area, greater cell density, lower power dissipation (hence less heat buildup and greater reliability), and lower cost (dollars/bit). Why, one might reasonably ask, are not all RAMs dynamic?

The reason why DRAMs are not universally used is that they must be periodically *refreshed.* The base of a bipolar transistor can only maintain an injected charge for approximately 2 to 4 milliseconds (ms) before the charge will begin to decay. Hence, data stored in the form of a base charge will automatically decay and disappear unless some means is provided for the DRAM to sense whether a 1 or 0 is stored and renew the charge as appropriate. The leakage resistance across the capacitor in Figure 5-2b represents the charge decay

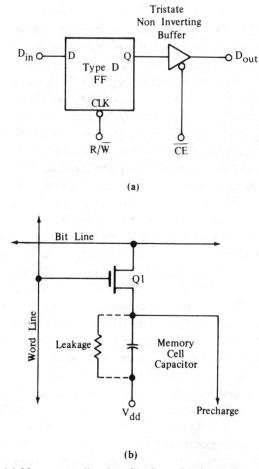

Figure 5-2 (a) Memory cell using flip-flop; (b) dynamic memory cell.

phenomenon. The charge decay present in the **DRAM** makes it necessary to rewrite the data into the cell every 2 ms (now every 4 ms in some devices). This process is called *refreshing* the memory. The DRAM chip must, therefore, contain built-in *refresh circuitry*.

Fortunately, clever design keeps us from having to independently refresh each cell sequentially. Let's suppose that we have a memory of 65,536 bytes (i.e., 8-bit arrays to store one 8-bit data word). If each took 10 μs to refresh (not unreasonable at typical microcomputer CPU clock speeds), then 655.36 ms are needed to refresh, which is excessive given that the entire job must be done within 2 ms in order to avoid data loss.

The solution to the problem is to refresh many cells at one time. A popular 16K-bit DRAM, for example, is arranged in an array of 128 × 128 cells (i.e., rows and columns). By using row addressing, we can refresh every cell in a given row at one time. This operation requires only 128 steps instead of 16,384.

We will discuss refresh strategies further when we discuss individual memory chips. For the present, however, we will content ourselves with the two main macro-philosophies: *burst* and *distributed* refreshing.

If at least one cell in any given row is addressed normally in the programming not less than once every 2 ms, then all is well, and all elements in that row can be refreshed within the specified time. But this does not occur very often, so we must provide time for refresh operation. In the *burst refresh* method, all memory cells are refreshed at once. Burst refreshing requires either that (1) software executed by the CPU perform the operation, or (2) hardware perform the operation, during which time the CPU will be held in a *wait* state.

Distributed refresh provides refresh operations distributed (from whence it gets its name) throughout the 2-ms period. This method is particularly handy when "stolen" CPU time can be used for refresh operations.

The Z80 microprocessor has provision for DRAM refreshing. An active-low refresh control signal ($\overline{\text{RFSH}}$) is provided to tell memory when a refresh is taking place. The Z80 contains a refresh register (R) that outputs over bits A0 through A6 of the address bus (bit A7 is kept permanently LOW) during the third and fourth clock periods of the *instruction-fetch* cycle. The combination of $\overline{\text{MREQ}}$, $\overline{\text{RFSH}}$, and A0–A6 will cause refresh operation to occur. The contents of the R register are incremented one step during each instruction-fetch cycle. As a result, all 128 possible combinations of A0–A6 will come up periodically during program execution (even if the CPU is idling in NOP status). This feature of the Z80 makes it very easy to use with dynamic memory devices.

In the sections to follow we will discuss several popular semiconductor memory devices of both static and dynamic varieties. The first such memory devices were very small arrays by today's standards and were made using bipolar transistor technology. Those devices consisted of a 16 × 16 cell array that formed a 256 × 1-bit memory; eight connected together formed a 256-byte memory, so a total of 2048 chips were required to provide a 64K memory in a microcomputer.

When MOS technology came along, we saw the first 1024 × 1-bit arrays (e.g., the 2101A/8102A devices). Eight 1024 × 1-bit devices will form a 1K-byte memory, so 64 such devices will make 8K bytes, and 512 are required to make up the full 64K memory. The 1024 × 1-bit chips are, therefore, approximately four times as dense as the 256 × 1-bit devices that they replaced and thus consume less electrical power.

The 2102A Static RAM

The 2102A device is a 1024 × 1-bit NMOS device housed in a 16-pin DIP integrated circuit package (see Figure 5-3). The 2102A operates from a single +5-V dc power supply, and the input/output/control lines are TTL compatible. The power consumption is typically 150 milliwatts (mW) per chip, so one can expect a 64K memory to use more than 75 W of electrical power. At +5 V dc, then, 15 amperes (A) of current is needed just for the memory. This is one reason why early microcomputers tended to have 20- to 30-A power supplies and is the most powerful reason for using DRAM devices in large arrays.

The *data out* (D_{out}) line is tristate, which means that it will be disconnected from the output terminal when the $\overline{CE}$ pin is HIGH (the D_{out} will see a high impedance to both V+ and ground). This feature makes it possible to connect several 2102A outputs together in the wired-OR connection needed to form a bus. Any one 2102A will be turned on only when its $\overline{CE}$ line is LOW, and it is off line all other times.

When the $\overline{CE}$ line is HIGH, the 2102A is not selected and will not respond to either read or write requests from the CPU. The R/$\overline{W}$ line determines whether a *read* (R) or *write* (W) will take place. The line is HIGH to denote a read operation and LOW to denote a write operation. A truth table showing 2102A control options is shown in Figure 5-3b. When $\overline{CE}$ and R/$\overline{W}$ are both LOW, data on the *data in* (D_{in}) line will be written to the memory cell designated by the address pins (A0–A9). Note that terms line "read" and "write" are always taken to mean from the CPU point of view. When data flow from the CPU *to* memory, it is a *write,* and when data flow *from* memory to CPU, it is a *read.*

There are 1024 one-bit cells in the 2102A device, so we need a 10-bit address bus (2^{10} = 1024) to uniquely designate each location. These address bits are provided to pins A0 through A9, which are usually connected to like-numbered pins on the system address bus.

Figure 5-3 also shows the internal block diagram of the 2102A memory device. The memory cells are arranged in an *XY* array consisting of 32 rows by 32 columns. Address bits A0 through A4 select the row, while A5 through A9 select the column. Row and column addresses taken together uniquely designate a single cell in a manner not dissimilar to crosspoint (mechanical) switching.

Static RAM devices have relatively easy timing requirements since there are neither clock nor refresh requirements. There are some time delays associated with the device, but it operates only in response to control signals (i.e., it is asynchronous with respect to the system clock).

The read cycle (see Figure 5-3c) outputs data from pin D_{out} of the 2102A to the system data bus. There is a certain *access time* (T_A) required to read data.

Pin Configuration   Logic Symbol

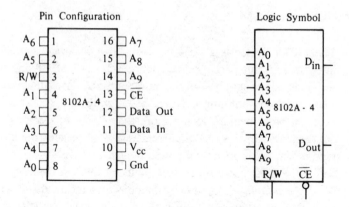

Pin Names

D_{in}	Data Input	$\overline{CE}$	Chip Enable
$A_0 - A_9$	Address Inputs	D_{out}	Data Output
R/W	Read/Write Input	V_{cc}	Power (+5V)

Block Diagram

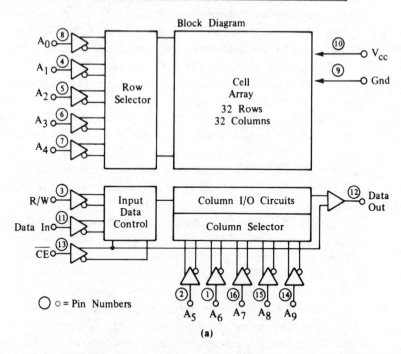

(a)

Figure 5-3 (a) 2102/8102 memory chip (1024 × 1); (b) control logic for 2102; (c) read-cycle wave forms; (d) write-cycle wave forms. *(Parts a, c, and d copyright 1977 by Intel Corporation)*

2102A Truth Table

$\overline{CE}$	$R/\overline{W}$	D_{in}	D_{out}	Mode
H	X	X	Hi - Z	(Device not selected)
L	L	L	L	Write 0
L	L	H	H	Write 1
L	H	X	D_{out}	Read

H = High
L = Low
X = Don't Care

(b)

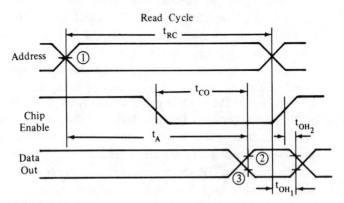

Read Cycle

(c)

1   1.5 Volts
2   2.0 Volts
3   0.8 Volts

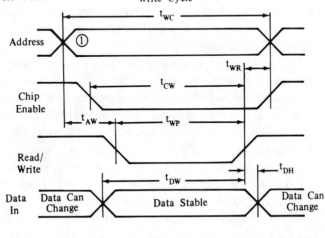

Write Cycle

(d)

Figure 5-3   *continued*

The read cycle must be at least this long or data will be lost. For 2102A devices, the nominal T_A is 450 ns; selected devices are available with 250-ns capability. The 450-ns devices cannot be operated with microprocessor chips whose read cycle is of less than 450-ns duration, a very real possibility given the clock speeds of some modern CPU chips. For those cases, faster chips are mandatory.

4116 16K × 1-Bit Dynamic RAM

Dynamic RAM provides certain advantages over static RAM, especially in systems with large RAM arrays. For small systems (i.e., those of only a few thousand bytes of memory), static RAM is probably most economical. The DRAM device usually has a density of at least 4 to 1 over the static versions, so it can be configured in a large array that occupies little space. This factor makes it possible to make small desk-top computers that do not generate so much heat that the room temperature is raised. The reliability of the computer is also improved when DRAM devices replace static memory in large arrays. The lower heat generation has a lot to do with reduction in failures, as does the lower parts count (there are fewer components to fail). As a result of these factors, the use of DRAM devices permits a lower cost, more reliable unit when large arrays are used. The extra cost of the external refresh circuitry does not increase proportionally with memory size and so is distributed over the entire 64K, which makes the DRAM more economical in higher-order arrays.

Although we are going to discuss one of the most popular 16K DRAM devices, be aware that there are many that offer greater than 16K size. The Fairchild 4164 device is a 64K single-chip DRAM, as is the MCM6664A by Motorola Semiconductor, Inc.

The 4116 device is shown in Figure 5-4. The block diagram of the internal circuitry is shown in Figure 5-4a, the logic symbol used in schematics is shown in Figure 5-4b, and the pinouts and pin names are shown in Figure 5-4c. Note that the 4116 device only has seven address bits (A0–A6). The 16K memory contained within the chip, however, would normally require 14 bits on the address bus. The 4116 overcomes this seeming problem by using a multiplexed addressing scheme in which a *row address select* ($\overline{RAS}$) and a *column address select* ($\overline{CAS}$) alternately select half the total address bits required. When the $\overline{RAS}$ line is LOW, the seven address lines input the lower-order 7 bits into a special 7-bit latch (that holds the data). Similarly, when the $\overline{CAS}$ is made LOW, the high-order 7 bits are input to another 7-bit register. Of course, the microcomputer must be designed to connect bits A0 through A6 of the system address bus to the A0 through A6 lines of the 4116 on one cycle, and A7 through A13 of the address bus to A0 through A6 of the 4116 on the next cycle.

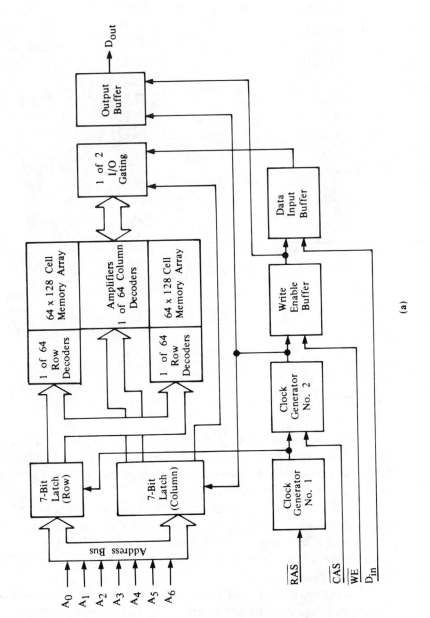

Figure 5-4 (a) 16K $\times$ 1 MOS dynamic memory cell; (b) 4116 chip; (c) 4116 pinouts.

(a)

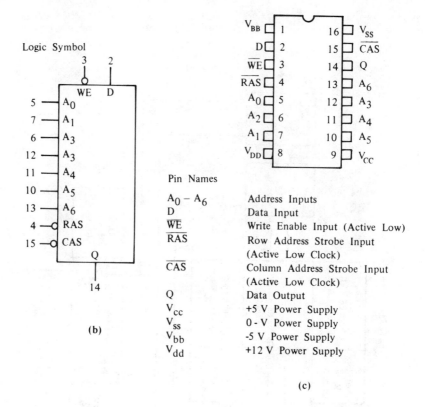

Pin Names

$A_0 - A_6$	Address Inputs
D	Data Input
$\overline{WE}$	Write Enable Input (Active Low)
$\overline{RAS}$	Row Address Strobe Input (Active Low Clock)
$\overline{CAS}$	Column Address Strobe Input (Active Low Clock)
Q	Data Output
V_{cc}	+5 V Power Supply
V_{ss}	0 - V Power Supply
V_{bb}	-5 V Power Supply
V_{dd}	+12 V Power Supply

(b)

(c)

Figure 5-4 *continued*

The organization of the 4116 device is an *XY* matrix in which a storage array of 128 horizontal rows contains 128 memory cells each. Each cell in any given row is connected to its own vertical column (or "bit line") that serves to connect it to a sense amplifier (Figure 5-5).

The DRAM read cycle is shown in Figure 5-6. The operation of $\overline{RAS}$ and $\overline{CAS}$ with respect to the address data passed to the 4116 is shown. The *write enable* ($\overline{WE}$) is an active-low input that must be kept HIGH during the read operation. After all these timing actions take place, the *data out* line will contain a valid data signal.

The refresh cycle for the 4116 is shown in Figure 5-7. The arrangement of this chip allows us to refresh all cells using only the row address line. Either the CPU (e.g., in the case of the Z80), the program (in almost any other microprocessor), or an in-memory counter will supply a row address to A0 through A6 at the same time that an $\overline{RAS}$ signal is generated. During this

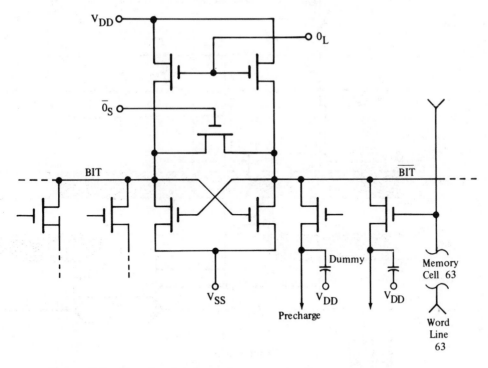

Figure 5-5 Circuitry for dynamic memory cell.

period, the *data out* line is open (i.e., tristated). This process must be accomplished not less often than every 2 ms.

READ-ONLY MEMORY (ROM) DEVICES

The read-only memory is a semiconductor device that will store a program or data and may be treated in the circuit as if it were a semiconductor RAM device. The difference is that the ROM will not accept data from the CPU during write operations; it allows only read operations (hence the name). The *write-only memory* (WOM) is a joke that made the rounds of the microcomputer/semiconductor industries a few years ago and referred to an imaginary device that will accept data and never give it up again (of course, an open conductor accomplishes the same trick).

There are several different types of ROM on the market. Some are permanently programmed and cannot be reprogrammed. These devices use internal fuse links that are either left intact or blown with a high-current input from the

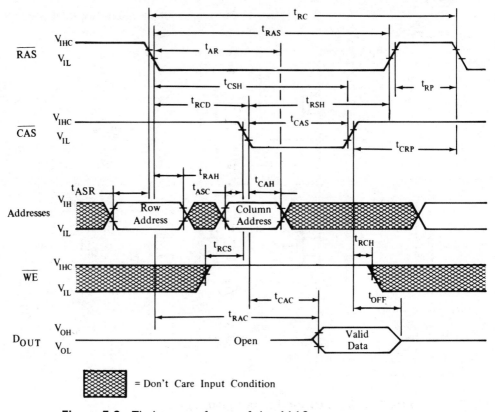

Figure 5-6 Timing waveforms of the 4116.

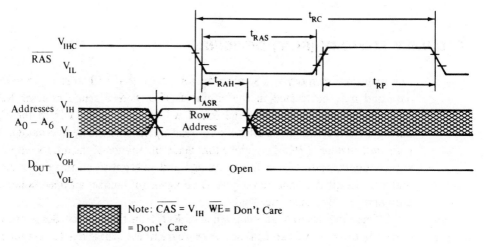

Note: $\overline{CAS} = V_{IH}$ $\overline{WE}$= Don't Care

= Dont' Care

Figure 5-7 RAS cycle for the 4116.

external world. In one condition, the internal transistor is made LOW, whereas in the other the transistor is HIGH. Another type of ROM is the *erasable programmable read-only memory* (EPROM). This device is programmed in a manner similar to the other type, except the internal mechanism is different and allows the device to be reprogrammed. There is a quartz window in the top of the IC package that allows the chip to be exposed to an ultraviolet light source that will erase (i.e., set to HIGH) the EPROM.

INTERFACING MEMORY

The typical microprocessor chip uses a 16-bit address bus, so it is able to directly address up to 2^{16}, or 65,536 memory locations. The data bus uses 1 byte (8 bits), so each memory location can store a single 8-bit word.

The mixture of possible memory devices used with the microprocessor includes static random-access memory (RAM), dynamic RAM, read-only memory (ROM), programmable read-only memory (PROM), erasable PROM (EPROM), plus a number of devices such as analog-to-digital converters (ADC) and digital-to-analog converters (DAC), which are sometimes treated as memory. This technique, called *memory mapping,* makes some data-acquisition chores easier (or at least faster).

Control Signals for Memory Operations

Let us consider the Z80 as our interfacing example. We must be cognizant of the basic control signals that apply to memory operations: $\overline{\text{MREQ}}$, $\overline{\text{WR}}$, and $\overline{\text{RD}}$. These signals are the memory request, write, and read, respectively. The memory request signal will drop LOW whenever the CPU is executing either a memory read or memory write operation. It tells the system that the data on the bus are memory data. If a memory write operation is taking place, then the *write* ($\overline{\text{WR}}$) signal will also go LOW. If, on the other hand, it is a memory read, then the *read* ($\overline{\text{RD}}$) signal will go LOW. All memory operations, therefore, will generate a LOW on two control pins of the Z80: $\overline{\text{MREQ}}/\overline{\text{WR}}$ for memory write operations and $\overline{\text{MREQ}}/\overline{\text{RD}}$ for memory read operations.

Most integrated circuit memory devices have at least one chip enable (CE) pin, and some have two chip enable pins (labeled CE1 and CE2). There also may be a *read/write* (R/W) pin to instruct the device whether the desired operation is a memory read or a memory write.

One of the simplest cases is shown in Figure 5-8. Here we see 1024 bytes of *read-only memory* (ROM) interfaced directly to the Z80. In this case, we

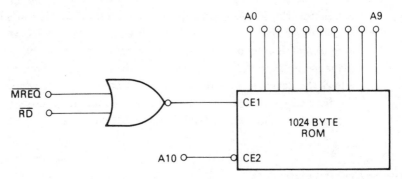

Figure 5-8 Operating CE of memory from MREQ and RD.

have assigned the ROM to the lower 1K of the memory address range. The locations available, then, are 00 00 (H) to 03 FF (H). Since we are dealing with the lower 1K, we need only the lower-order byte of the address bus, A0–A7, plus the two least significant bits of the upper-order byte (A8 and A9).

Two chip enable (CE) terminals are available. We use one of them (CE2) to make sure that the ROM will respond only to addresses in the lower 1K of memory. Address bus bit A10 will always remain LOW when the CPU is addressing a location in the lower 1K, but will go HIGH when an address greater than 03 FF (H) is selected. The ROM, therefore, is enabled only when the address on the address bus is less than 03 FF (H).

The second chip enable pin (CE1) is used to turn on the ROM only when the memory read operation is taking place. This CE pin wants to see a HIGH for turn on of the ROM. Recall that a NOR gate will output a HIGH only when both inputs are LOW. We can, therefore, create a device-select command for CE1 by applying the $\overline{\text{MREQ}}$ and $\overline{\text{RD}}$ control signals from the CPU to the inputs of a NOR gate. CE1 will go HIGH, then, only when a memory read operation takes place.

At least two of the more popular ROM chips require only a single chip enable command. In the example shown in Figure 5-9a, the chip enable is an active-low input (so is designated $\overline{\text{CE}}$). This terminal is brought LOW whenever we want to read the contents of one of the locations in the chip.

The example shown in Figure 5-9a is a 256-byte ROM, with a single $\overline{\text{CE}}$ terminal. We must, therefore, construct external circuitry that will bring the chip enable terminal LOW when we want to perform the read operation. The simplest way is to use a three-input NOR gate and an inverter. The output of the NOR gate will go HIGH only when all three of the inputs are LOW. We connect the $\overline{\text{MREQ}}$, $\overline{\text{RD}}$, and bit A8 of the address bus to the respective inputs

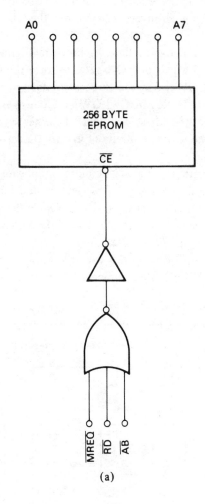

(a)

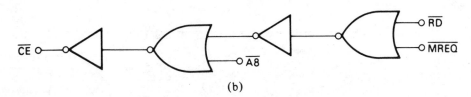

(b)

Figure 5-9 (a) Enabling EPROM from MREQ/RD/A8; (c) same function accomplished with two-input gates.

of the NOR gate. When the conditions are met, the output of the gate snaps HIGH and is then inverted to become the $\overline{\text{CE}}$ signal required by the EPROM chip.

An alternative method is shown in Figure 5-9b. Here we are using two inverters and a pair of NOR gates to form the $\overline{\text{CE}}$ signal. The idea is to cause $\overline{\text{CE}}$ to go LOW when the three conditions are met. To do this, we must see both inputs of NOR gate G2 LOW simultaneously. One of the inputs is connected to bit A8 of the address bus, while the other is connected to the inverted output of NOR gate G1. The inputs of G1 are, in turn, connected to the $\overline{\text{MREQ}}$ and $\overline{\text{RD}}$ signals.

A situation that is a little more complicated is shown in Figure 5-10. Here we are interfacing static RAM devices that have a chip enable and an $\overline{\text{R/W}}$ terminal. This latter terminal will cause the device to read out data when LOW and allow writing in data when HIGH. We connect the $\overline{\text{R/W}}$ terminal, then, to the $\overline{\text{RD}}$ signal of the Z80 CPU.

The chip enable in this example wants to see a HIGH in order to turn on the device. We can, then, connect CE to the output of a NOR gate. The $\overline{\text{MREQ}}$

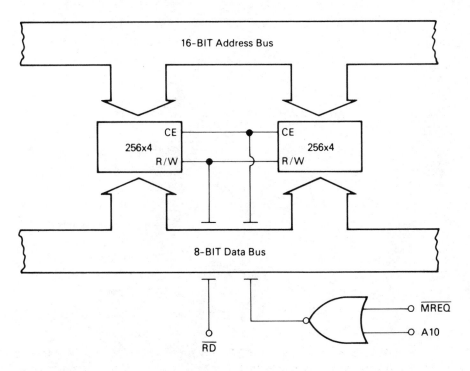

Figure 5-10   Interfacing RAM.

and $\overline{A8}$ signals are connected to the two inputs of the NOR gate. If both of these signals go LOW simultaneously, and the $\overline{RD}$ is also LOW, a memory read operation takes place from the location addressed by A0–A7. Alternatively, if the $\overline{MREQ}$ and $\overline{A7}$ signals are LOW, and the $\overline{RD}$ signal is HIGH, a memory write operation will take place.

Note in Figure 5-10 that two chips are used to form a 256-byte static RAM memory. Most memories require more than a single chip in order to form a complete byte array. In this case, each memory chip contains a 256 $\times$ 4-bit array, so two connected together will form a 256 $\times$ 8-bit array (i.e., 256 bytes of memory). The popular 2102 device is listed as a 1024 $\times$ 1-bit device. Connecting eight of these devices into an array will result in a 1024-byte memory.

Dynamic Memory

Dynamic memory (RAM) will not hold its data for an indefinite length of time unless a refresh operation is performed. The refresh operation is a function of the CPU in most cases, although some non-CPU examples exist. Although the use of static RAM will eliminate this problem, it will do so only at the cost of a higher power consumption. The Z80A device provides for refresh of the dynamic memory by adding a refresh segment to the M1 (instruction fetch) machine cycle.

During clock periods T3 and T4 of the M1 cycle, used by the Z80 for the decoding of the instructions fetched in the earlier T periods, a refresh signal is generated. The $\overline{RFSH}$ terminal (pin 28) of the Z80 will go LOW during this period. Note that this signal must be used in conjunction with the $\overline{MREQ}$ (memory request) signal, because the $\overline{RFSH}$ is guaranteed to be stable only when the $\overline{MREQ}$ is also active.

During the refresh period, the lower portion of the address of a refresh location is placed on the lower 7 bits (A0–A6) of the address bus (A7 is 0). The data on A0–A6 are from the R register in the Z80, which is incremented after each instruction fetch. The upper 8 bits of the address bus carry the contents of the I register. Figure 5-11 shows an example of an 8K dynamic RAM interfaced to a Z80. In this particular case, 4K $\times$ 8-bit dynamic RAMs are used. If no other RAM is used, we may use bit A12 of the address bus as a chip-select line.

Adding Wait States

All solid-state memory chips require a certain minimum period of time to write data into, or read data from, any given location. Many such devices are graded

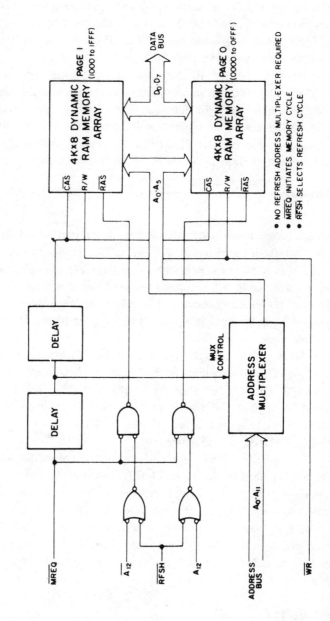

Figure 5-11 An 8K dynamic RAM interfaced to a Z80.

94

(and priced) according to memory speed. The popular 2102 device, a 1K × 1-bit IC, is available in 250-, 400-, and 500-ns versions. The cost per chip rises with the speed.

Since the Z80A can operate at speeds up to 4 mHz, we sometimes find the cycle (M1 or memory) over before the data have settled to, or from, memory. This problem can be overcome by adding the circuitry shown in Figure 5-12. Both of these circuits generate a $\overline{\text{WAIT}}$ input (pin 24 of the Z80) equal to the period of one clock pulse.

The circuit in Figure 5-12 uses both sections of a TTL 7474 dual type-D flip-flop. The 7474 is a positive-edge triggered device, which means that data on the D input are transferred to the Q output *only* during the positive-going transitions of the clock pulse.

Immediately after the onset of clock pulse T1, the $\overline{\text{M1}}$ line goes LOW, forcing the D input of FF1 LOW. When clock pulse T2 snaps HIGH, this LOW is transferred to the Q output of FF1. This signal becomes the $\overline{\text{WAIT}}$ signal for the CPU and inserts one additional clock period (T_w) into the M1 cycle.

At the onset of clock period T_w, then, FF2 sees a LOW (i.e., the $\overline{\text{WAIT}}$ signal) on its D input. This LOW is transferred to the Q output of FF2. The Q_2 terminal (FF2) is connected to the *set* input of FF1, so this condition forces the Q_1 (FF1) HIGH again, thereby terminating the action.

A similar circuit, also shown in Figure 5-12, is used to add a wait state to any memory cycle. When the first clock pulse (T1) arrives, the $\overline{\text{MREQ}}$ line goes LOW, forcing the D input of FF1 LOW. At the onset of clock pulse T2, this LOW is transferred to the Q output of FF1. At this time Q_1 is HIGH and Q_2 is HIGH, so the output of the NAND gate drops LOW. (Both NAND inputs must be HIGH for the output to be LOW.) This causes the $\overline{\text{WAIT}}$ input of the CPU to become active. But at the onset of T_w, the added clock period, the LOW on Q_1 is transferred to Q_2. This forces one input of the NAND gate HIGH, thereby canceling the $\overline{\text{WAIT}}$ signal.

Memory-Mapped Devices

Some peripheral devices used with microcomputers can be more efficiently employed if they are treated as a memory location, instead of an I/O device. An example might be a *digital-to-analog converter* (DAC), which is a device that creates an analog output voltage (or current) that is proportional to a binary digital word applied to its input.

Figure 5-13 shows how an 8-bit DAC can be interfaced with a Z80 *as if the DAC were a memory location*. The DAC requires stable input data, but the

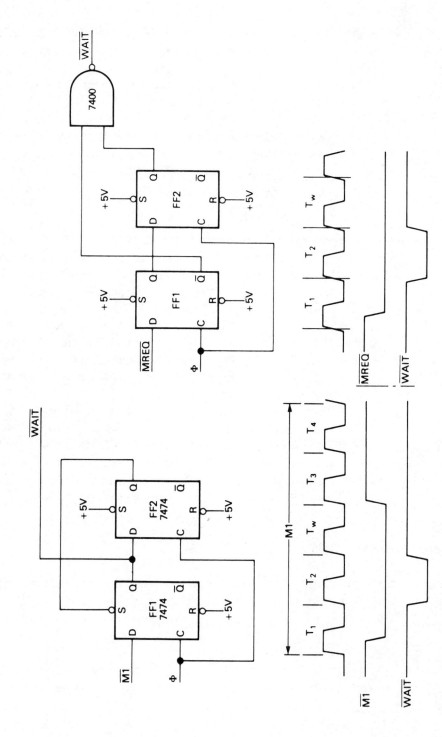

Figure 5-12 Adding a wait state to the M1 cycle.

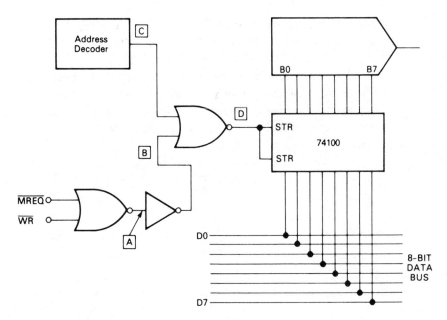

Figure 5-13 Using a device such as a DAC as a piece of memory.

data on the bus are transitory. Therefore, we need a *data latch* between the 8-bit data bus and the DAC inputs. There are a number of interface chips that will perform this job, but most of these special-purpose devices are costly. A low-cost solution, which works just as well, is to use a 74100 TTL dual quad-latch. The two 4-bit sections of the 74100 become an 8-bit latch when the *strobe* terminals are tied together.

The 74100 latch transfers the information on the data bus to the DAC when the strobe line is HIGH. The 74100 outputs, connected to the DAC inputs, will retain these data when the strobe line again goes LOW. The idea is to make the 74100 strobe line HIGH during the period when the desired DAC input data are present on the data bus.

Three criteria must be met before the data on the bus can be input to the DAC: (1) the write signal ($\overline{\text{WR}}$) must be active; (2) the memory request ($\overline{\text{MREQ}}$) must be active; (3) the correct address (the address of the location assigned to the DAC) must be present on the address bus. The first two criteria are examined by a single NOR gate. When both $\overline{\text{WR}}$ and $\overline{\text{MREQ}}$ are LOW (i.e., active), we are producing a memory write operation. This will cause point A to go HIGH and point B to go LOW. We do not want the DAC to respond, however, unless point C is LOW at the same time. When point C is LOW, we know that the address for the DAC is being sent over the address bus. When all three criteria are met, the strobe input of the 74100 (point D) will go HIGH. This will allow transfer of data from the data bus into the DAC.

Most microcomputers have less than the full 64K complement of memory. This is why most memory-mapped devices tend to be allocated addresses in the upper 32K of memory. This, incidentally, allows us to use bit A15 of the address bus to discriminate between the various addresses.

6
Input/Output: Components and Programming

The topic of input and output devices, components, and circuits is often overlooked in texts and articles on microcomputers because they are not quite as exotic and interesting as some microprocessor chips. But the I/O section of the computer is vitally important to the overall functioning of the machine because it determines how data are transferred in and out of the machine. The utility of a device is often determined, or more often limited, by the structure of the I/O circuitry used. After you purchase a microcomputer and decide to expand its capability, it is almost inevitable that the question of I/O ports will come up: there will probably be too few to support the extra peripherals and devices that you want to add.

The input and output functions are operated by the control signals of the microcomputer and may take either of two forms, *direct I/O* or *memory mapped*. Some microprocessor chips provide for direct I/O in the form of I/O instructions; the Z80 is one such machine.[1] In the Z80 device, the address of the port will be passed over the lower-order 8 bits (A0–A7) of the address bus, while the data from the accumulator is passed simultaneously over both the data bus (DB0–DB7) and the high-order 8 bits of the address bus (A8–A15). The 8-bit memory address will support up to 256 different I/O ports, which can be numbered 0 through 255. The Z80 device control signals allow for I/O operations and are combined in such a way as to produce unique IN and OUT commands to the I/O devices (see Chapter 4).

---

[1]See Joseph J. Carr, *Z80 Users Manual,* Reston Publishing Co., Reston, Va., 1981.

Other microprocessor chips do not provide input and output commands in the instruction set and thus will not have the control signals and capabilities for direct I/O. In those machines, the input and output ports are treated as if they were memory locations; such ports are called memory-mapped I/O ports.

Although I/O may not necessarily be the most interesting aspect of microprocessor technology, we must nevertheless study some of these mundane details in order to gain an understanding of how the microcomputer deals with the outside world. To begin this study, we will consider some elementary digital electronics theory and some of the devices used to form I/O ports. From an understanding of these topics, you should be able to progress to designing I/O ports and interfacing techniques.

LOGIC FAMILIES

Digital electronic circuits use assorted *logic blocks* such as gates (AND, OR, NOT, NAND, NOR, XOR, etc.) and flip-flops to perform the various circuit functions. On initial inspection, it seems that digital logic circuit design is made simpler because all the logic blocks are available in integrated circuit form and can be simply connected together with seeming impunity. The reason this situation exists is that the IC logic devices are part of various *families* of similar devices. A digital logic family will use standardized input and output circuits that are designed to work with each other, use the same voltage levels for both power supply and logical signals, and generally use the same technology in construction of the devices. Common logic families in current use are TTL, CMOS, NMOS, PMOS, and MOS, with certain subgroups within each of these. Obsolete forms, such as RTL and DTL, although interesting to the owner of older equipment, are of too little interest to justify inclusion here. There are also certain devices that will mix technologies (e.g., an NMOS microprocessor chip that uses TTL input and output circuits) in order to gain some of the advantages of both families.

Transistor–Transistor Logic

Transistor–transistor logic (TTL; also called T^2L) is probably the oldest of the currently used IC logic families and is based on bipolar transistor technology. Bipolar transistors are the ordinary PNP and NPN types, as distinguished from the field-effect transistors.

The TTL logic family uses power supply potentials of 0 and $+5$ V dc, and the $+5$-V potential must be regulated for proper operation of the device.

Most specifications for TTL devices require the voltage to be between +4.5 and 5.2 V dc, although there appear to be practical limitations on even these values. Some complex function ICs, for example, will not operate properly at potentials below +4.75 V, despite the manufacturer's statements to the contrary. Also, at potentials above 5.0 V, even though less than the +5.2-V maximum potential "allowed," there seems to be an excess failure rate that is probably due to the higher temperatures generated inside the ICs. The best rule of thumb is to keep the potential of the power supply between +4.75 and +5.0 V; furthermore, the potential must be regulated.

Figure 6-1 shows the voltage levels used in the TTL family of devices to represent logical 1 and logical 0. The logical 1, or HIGH, condition is represented by a potential of +2.4 V or more (+5 V maximum). The device must be capable of recognizing any input potential over +2.4 V as a HIGH condition. The logical 0, or LOW, condition is supposedly 0 V, but most TTL devices define any potential from 0 to 0.8 V as logical 0. The voltage region between +0.8 and +2.4 V is undefined; the operation of a TTL device in this region is not predictable. Care must be exercised to keep the TTL logical signals outside the undefined zone, which can be a source of problems in some circuits that are not properly designed.

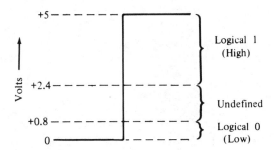

Figure 6-1 TTL logic levels.

The inverter, or NOT gate, is the simplest form of digital logic element and contains all the essential elements required to discuss the characteristics of the family. Figure 6-2a shows the internal circuit of a typical TTL inverter. The output circuit consists of a pair of NPN transistors connected in the "totem pole" configuration in which the transistors form a series circuit across the power supply. The output terminal is taken at the junction between the two transistors.

The HIGH state on the output terminal will find transistor Q4 turned off and Q3 turned on. The output terminal sees a low impedance (approximately

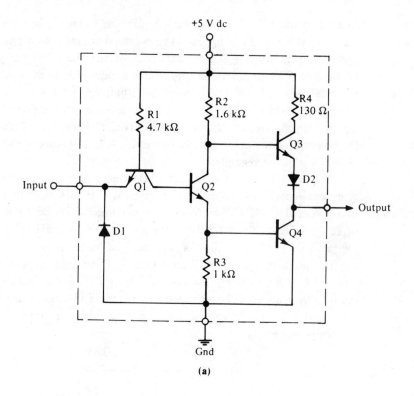

(a)

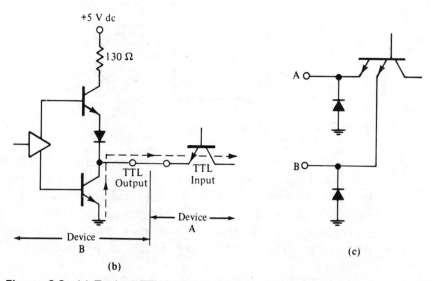

(b)

(c)

Figure 6-2 (a) Typical TTL inverter; (b) TTL output–input interface; (c) TTL input configuration.

130 Ω) to the +5-V line. In the LOW output state, exactly the opposite situation exists: Q4 is turned on and Q3 is turned off. In that condition, the output terminal sees a very low impedance to ground.

The input terminal of the TTL inverter is a transistor emitter (Q1). When the input is LOW, the emitter of Q1 is grounded. The transistor is forward biased by resistor R1 so the collector of Q1 is made LOW also. This condition causes transistor Q2 to be turned off, so the voltage on its emitter is zero and the voltage on its collector is HIGH. In this situation, we have the conditions required for a HIGH output: Q4 is turned off and Q3 is forward biased, thereby connecting the output terminal through the 130-Ω resistor to the +5-V dc power supply terminal.

Exactly the opposite situation obtains when the input terminal is HIGH. In that case, we find transistor Q1 turned off and the voltage applied to the base of Q2 is HIGH. Under this condition, the collector voltage of Q2 drops and its emitter voltage rises. Transistor Q4 is turned on, grounding the output terminal, and transistor Q3 is turned off. In other words, a HIGH on the input terminal produces a LOW on the output terminal.

Figure 6-2b shows the current path when two TTL devices are connected together in cascade. The emitter of device A input is connected to the output terminal of device B. The *input* of a TTL device is a current *source* that provides 1.6 mA at TTL voltage levels. The *output* transistors are capable of *sinking* up to 16 mA. We may conclude, therefore, that for regular TTL devices the output terminal will provide current sinking capability to accommodate up to 10 TTL input loads. Some special buffer devices will accommodate up to 30 TTL input loads.

The input and output capabilities of TTL devices are generally defined in terms of *fan-in* and *fan-out*. The fan-in is standardized in a unit, or standard, input load rather than current and voltage levels. This convention allows us to interconnect TTL devices simply without being concerned with matters such as impedance matching. In interfacing TTL devices it is merely necessary to make sure that the number of TTL input loads does not exceed the fan-out of the driving device. In brief, the fan-in is one unit TTL input load, whereas the fan-out is the output capacity expressed in the number of standard input loads that a device will drive. In the case of the regular TTL devices, the output current capacity is 16 mA, while the standard input load is 1.6 mA; so a fan-out of 16/1.6, or 10, exists.

Asking a TTL device to drive a number of TTL loads in excess of the rated fan-out will result in reduced noise margin and the possibility that the logic levels will be insufficient to reliably drive the inputs connected to the output. Some devices will provide a fan-out margin, but most will not. When it is necessary to drive a large number of TTL loads, it is wise to use a high fan-out buffer.

Multiple TTL inputs are formed by adding extra emitters to the input transistor (see Figure 6-2b). This type of circuit is used on multiple input devices such as NAND gates; each emitter is capable of sourcing 1.6 mA of current and represents a fan-in of one standard TTL load.

Open-Collector Output.   The standard TTL output circuit shown in Figure 6-2a must be connected to a standard TTL input in order to work properly. At times, however, it becomes necessary to interface the TTL device with a device other than a TTL. In some cases, the external load will be at the same voltage level as TTL, but in others the voltage level might be considerably higher than +5 V. The open-collector circuit of Figure 6-3 will accommodate such loads.

Figure 6-3 shows only the output stage of the open-collector device; all the other circuitry will be as in Figure 6-2a. Transistor Q1 is arranged so that its collector is brought out to the output terminal of the device. Since there is no current path to the V+ terminal of the power supply, an external load must be provided for the device to work. In the case of the situation shown, an external *pull-up resistor* is connected between the output terminal (i.e., Q1 collector) and +5 V dc; for most TTL open-collector devices the value of the pull-up resistor is 2 to 4 kΩ. Other loads and higher voltages can be accommodated provided that the dc resistance of the load is sufficient to keep the collector current in Q1 within specified limits.

Speed Versus Power.   The TTL logic family is known for its relatively fast operating speeds. Most devices will operate to 18 to 20 MHz, and some

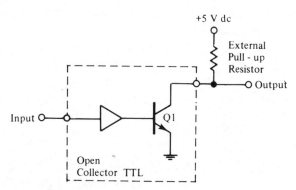

Figure 6-3 Open-collector TTL output.

selected devices operate to well over 30 MHz. But the operating speed is not without a concomitant trade-off: increased operating power. Unfortunately, higher speed means higher power dissipation. The problem is the internal resistances and capacitances of the devices. The operating speed is set in part by the *RC* time constants of the internal circuitry. To reduce the time constant and thereby increase the operating speed, it is necessary to reduce the resistances and that will necessarily increase current drain and power consumption.

TTL Nomenclature.   Each logic family uses a unique series of type numbers for the member devices so that users can identify the technology being used from the number. With very few "house number" exceptions, TTL type numbers will have either four or five digits beginning with the numbers 54 or 74. The normal devices found most commonly are numbered in the 74xx and 74xxx series, while higher-grade military specification devices carry 54xx and 54xxx numbers. The 54 and 74 series retain the same xx or xxx suffix for identical devices. For example, the popular NOR gate will be numbered 7402 in commercial grade components and 5402 in military grade. In general use, we can substitute the more reliable 54xx devices for the identical 74xx devices.

TTL Subfamilies.   Certain specialized TTL devices are used for certain purposes, such as increased operating speed and lower power consumption. These family subgroups include (in addition to regular TTL) low-power (74Lxx), high-speed (74Hxx), Schottky (74Sxx), and low-power Schottky (74LSxx) devices. A principal difference between these groups that must be addressed by the circuit designer or interfacer is the input and output current requirements. In most cases, the levels shown in Table 6-1 apply.

TABLE 6-1

Subfamily	Input Current, mA	Output Current, mA
74××	1.6	16
74L××	0.18	3.6
74H××	2.0	20
74Sxx	2.0	20
74Sxx	0.4	8.0

Complementary Metal Oxide Semiconductor

The complementary metal oxide semiconductor, or CMOS, digital IC logic family is based on the metal oxide semiconductor field-effect transistor (MOSFET). In general, CMOS devices are slower in operating speed than TTL devices, but they have one immensely valuable property: low power dissipation. The nature of the CMOS device is such that it presents a high impedance across the dc power supply at all times except when the output is undergoing transition from one state to the other. At all other times, the CMOS device draws only a few microamperes of electrical current, which makes it an excellent choice for large systems where speed of operation is not the most important specification.

Figure 6-4 shows two CMOS devices that are representative of the larger family of related logic elements. In Figure 6-4a is a simple CMOS inverter. Note that it consists of an N-channel and a P-channel MOSFET connected such that their respective source–drain paths are in series, while the gate terminals are in parallel. This arrangement is reminiscent of push–pull operation because the N-channel and P-channel devices turn on and off with opposite polarity signals. As a result, one of these two transistors will have a low channel resistance with the input LOW, while the other will offer a very high resistance (megohms). When the input is made HIGH, the role of the two transistors is reversed: the one with the low channel resistance becomes high resistance, while that with the high resistance goes LOW. This operation has the effect of connecting the output terminal to either V_{dd} or V_{ss} depending upon whether the input is HIGH or LOW. Since, in both cases, one of the series pair is high resistance, the total resistance across the V_{dd}–V_{ss} power supply is high. Only during the transition period, when both transistors have a medium-range source–drain resistance, will there be any appreciable load in the power supply. The output terminal will not deliver any current because it will be connected to another CMOS input, which is a very high impedance. As a result, there is never any time when the CMOS IC, operated only in conjunction with other CMOS devices, will draw any appreciable current. An example of the difference between TTL and CMOS current levels is seen by comparing the specs for a common quad two-input NAND gate in both families. The TTL version needs 25 mA, whereas the CMOS device requires only 15 μA.

Figure 6-4b shows a typical CMOS AND gate. The two inputs are connected to independent inputs of a pair of series-connected N-channel MOSFETs. The output of this stage will not change state unless both inputs are active, a result of the series connection.

The operating speed of typical CMOS devices is limited to 4 to 5 MHz,

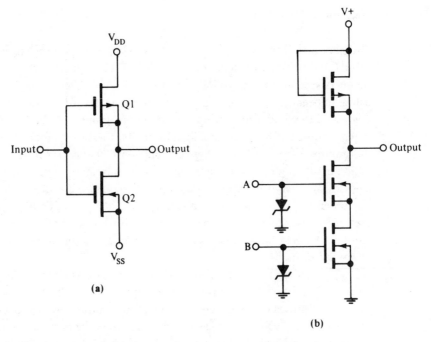

Figure 6-4   (a) Typical CMOS inverter; (b) typical CMOS AND gate.

although some 10- to 15-MHz devices are known. The speed is the principal disadvantage to the CMOS line; typical TTL devices operate to 20 MHz but require a lot more current.

Another problem with the CMOS device is sensitivity to static electricity. The typically very thin insulating layer of oxide between the gate element and the channel has a breakdown voltage of 80 to 100 V. Static electricity, on the other hand, can easily reach values of 1000 V or more. Whenever the static is sufficient to cause a biting spark when you touch a grounded object, it is generated by a potential of 1000 V or more. This potential is sufficient to destroy CMOS devices. This problem is especially critical in dry climates or during the low-humidity portions of the year. There are, however, methods of working with a CMOS that allow us to minimize damage to the device. In general, the CMOS working rules require use of a grounded working environment, grounded tools, and avoidance of certain wool or artificial fiber garments. Also, the B series (e.g., CA-4001B) has built-in zener diodes to protect the delicate gate structure by shunting dangerous potentials around the gate.

Tristate Devices

Ordinary digital IC logic devices are allowed only two permissible output states: HIGH and LOW, corresponding to TRUE–FALSE logic or 1–0 of the binary numbers system. In the HIGH state, the output is typically connected through a low impedance to a positive power supply; in the LOW state the output is connected to either a negative power supply or ground. Although this arrangement is sufficient for ordinary digital circuits, there is a problem when two or more outputs are connected together but must operate separately. Such a situation exists in a microcomputer on the data bus. If any one device on the bus stays LOW, then it more or less commands the entire bus: no other changes on any other device will be able to affect the bus, so the result will be chaos. Also, even if we could conspire to make all bits HIGH when not in use, there would still be a loading factor and also an ambiguity as to which device is turned on at any given time.

The answer to the problem is in *tristate logic,* as shown schematically in Figure 6-5. Tristate devices, as the name implies, have a third permissible output state. This third state effectively disconnects the output terminal from the workings of the IC. In Figure 6-5, switch S1 represents the normal operating modes of the device. When the input is LOW, switch S1 is connected to R1, so the output will be HIGH. Similarly, when the input is HIGH, switch S1 is connected to R2, so the output is LOW. The third state is generated by switch S2. When the active-low *chip enable* ($\overline{\text{CE}}$) terminal is made LOW, switch S2 is closed and the output terminal is connected to the "output" of S1. When the $\overline{\text{CE}}$ terminal is HIGH, however, switch S2 is open, so the output floats at a high impedance (represented by R3). Because of this operation, the tristate device can be con-

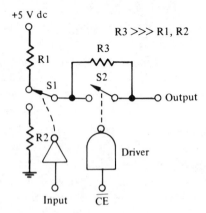

Figure 6-5 Model of tristate logic circuit.

nected across a data bus line and will not load the line except when $\overline{CE}$ is made LOW.

An advantage of tristate digital devices is that the chip enable terminals can be driven by device-select pulses, thus creating a unique connection to the data bus that is not ambiguous to the microcomputer. In other words, the computer will "know" that only the data from the affected input port or device are on the bus whenever that $\overline{CE}$ is made LOW.

INTERFACING LOGIC FAMILIES

One of the defining characteristics of a logic family is that the inputs and outputs of the devices within the family can be interconnected with no regard to interfacing. A TTL output can always drive a TTL input, and a CMOS output can always drive a CMOS input without any external circuitry other than a conductor. But when we want to interconnect logic elements of different families, some consideration must be given to proper methods. In some cases, it will suffice to simply connect the output of one device to the input of the other; in other cases some external circuitry is needed.

Figure 6-6a shows a series of cascade inverters. The CMOS device is not comfortable driving the TTL input, and the TTL input is not happy with the CMOS output. As a result, we must use a special CMOS device that will behave as if it has a TTL output while retaining its CMOS input: 4050 and 4049. The 4049 device is a hex inverting buffer, while the 4050 is the same in noninverting configuration. The special character of these devices is the bipolar transistor output that will mimic the TTL output *if* the package V+ potential is limited to +5 V dc. The 4049/4050 will operate to potentials up to +15 V, but it is TTL compatible *only* at a V+ potential of +5 V dc, with the other side of the device power supply grounded. The input of the 4049/4050 is CMOS, so it is compatible with all CMOS outputs.

The TTL input is a current source, so the TTL output depends for proper operation on driving a current source. The CMOS input, however, is a very high impedance because the CMOS family is voltage driven. If we want to interface an ordinary TTL output to a CMOS input (see Figure 6-6b), we must provide a pull-up resistor between the TTL output terminal and the +5-V dc power supply. A value between 2 and 4 kΩ is selected to make the current source mimic a TTL input current level.

The method of Figure 6-6b works well in circuits where both CMOS and TTL devices operate from a +5-V dc power supply. While this is the usual situation in most circuits, there are occasions where the TTL and CMOS devices

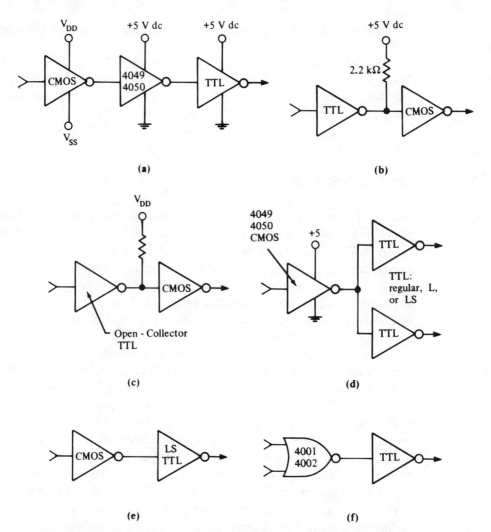

Figure 6-6 (a) CMOS-to-TTL interfacing using 4049 and 4050 devices; (b) TTL–CMOS interfacing; (c) open-collector TTL device interfacing higher-voltage CMOS; (d) 4049 and 4050 devices will drive two TTL loads; (e) CMOS outputs will drive one LS-series TTL input; (f) 4001 and 4002 devices will drive one standard TTL load.

operate from different potentials, and the correct interfacing method is shown in Figure 6-6c. Here we use an open-collector TTL output with a resistance to the V_{dd} power supply (used by the CMOS device) that is sufficiently high to keep the current flowing in the TTL output at a level within tolerable limits.

We can use a single 4049/4050 device to drive up to two regular TTL inputs (Figure 6-6d), and an ordinary CMOS device will drive a single LS series TTL input (Figure 6-6d). The 4001 and 4002 CMOS devices are capable of directly driving a single regular TTL input. With the exception of the 4049/4050 device just discussed, these methods depend upon the CMOS and TTL devices operating from a common +5-V dc power supply. If the CMOS devices are operated at higher potentials, we will be forced into using the 4049/4050 method given earlier in order to prevent burnout of the TTL input.

Most microprocessor chips have limited output line capacity; most are limited to one or two TTL inputs load. Most MOS series microprocessor chips use MOS logic internally, but have TTL-compatible output lines. In the case of a two loads output, the total allowable output current is 3.2 mA. There may be, however, many TTL-compatible inputs connected to the data bus or address bus of the microcomputer. We need a high-current bus driver on each line of the bus in order to accommodate these higher current requirements. Figure 6-7 shows a series of eight noninverting bus drivers interfacing the data bus of a microcomputer (DB0–DB7) with the data bus outputs of the microprocessor chip (B0–B7). This circuit will increase the drive capacity of the microcomputer from a fan-out of 2 to a fan-out of 30 or even 100, depending upon the bus driver selected.

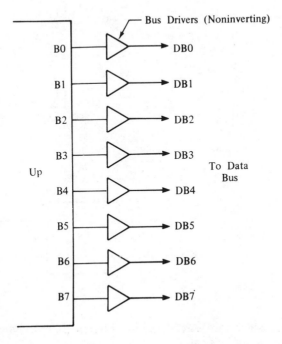

Figure 6-7   Bus driver buffering.

FLIP-FLOPS

All the gates used in digital electronics are transient devices. In other words, the output state disappears when the input stimulus disappears; the gate has no *memory*. A flip-flop, on the other hand, is a circuit that is capable of storing a single bit, one binary digit, of data. An array of flip-flops, called a *register*, can be used to store entire binary words in the computer. In this section, we will examine some of the common flip-flops used in digital circuits. All these circuits can be built with discrete digital gates, even though few modern designers would do so because the various forms of flip-flop are available as discrete units in their own right.

Figure 6-8 shows the basic *reset–set*, or RS, flip-flop. There are two versions, based on the NOR and NAND gates, respectively. An RS flip-flop has two inputs, S and R (for set and reset). When the S input is momentarily made active, the output terminals go to the state in which Q = HIGH and NOT-Q = LOW. The R input causes just the opposite reaction: Q = LOW and NOT-Q = HIGH. A rule that must be followed is that these inputs must not be made active simultaneously, or an unpredictable output state will result.

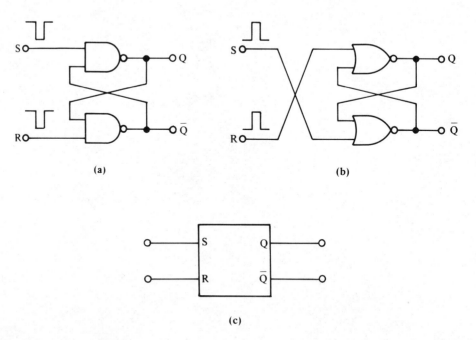

(a)   (b)

(c)

Figure 6-8   (a) NAND-logic RS flip-flop; (b) NOR-logic RS flip-flop; (c) RS flip-flop circuit symbol.

Figure 6-8a shows the RS flip-flop made from a pair of two-input NAND gates. In each case, the output of one gate drives one input of the other; the gates are said to be cross-coupled. The alternate inputs of each gate form the input terminals of the flip-flop.

The inputs of the NAND gate version of the RS flip-flop are active low. This means that a momentary LOW on either input will cause the output action. For this reason, the NAND gate version is sometimes designated as $\overline{RS}$ FF, and the inputs designated $\overline{S}$ and $\overline{R}$, respectively.

The NOR gate version of the RS flip-flop is shown in Figure 6-8b. In this circuit, the inputs are active-high, so the output states change by applying a HIGH pulse momentarily. The circuit symbol for the RS flip-flop is shown in Figure 6-8c. In some instances, the NAND version will be indicated by the same circuit, while in others there will be either $\overline{R}$ and $\overline{S}$ indications for the inputs or circles indicating inversion at each input terminal.

The RS flip-flop operates in an asynchronous manner (i.e., the outputs will change any time an appropriate input signal appears). Synchronous operation, which is required in most computer-oriented circuits, requires that output states change only coincident with a system clock pulse. The circuit in Figure 6-9 is a clocked RS flip-flop. Gates G3 and G4 form a normal NOR-based RS flip-flop. Control via a clock pulse is provided by gates G1 and G2. One input of each is connected to the clock line. These two gates will not pass the R and S pulses unless the clock line is HIGH. The input lines can change all they want between clock pulses, but an output change is affected *only* when the clock pulse is HIGH.

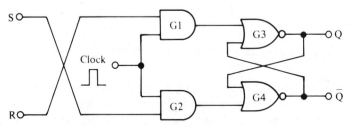

Figure 6-9   Clocked RS flip-flop.

A type D flip-flop is made by using an inverter to ensure that the S and R inputs of a clocked RS flip-flop are always complementary. The S input of the RS flip-flop and the input of the inverter that drives the R input of the RS FF are connected in parallel. When the S input is made HIGH, therefore, the R input will be LOW. Similarly, a LOW on the S input will place a HIGH on the R input. The circuit symbol for the type D FF is shown in Figure 6-10b.

The rule for the operation of the type D flip-flop is as follows: The input data applied to the D terminal will be transferred to the outputs *only* when the clock line is active. Figure 6-10c shows a typical timing diagram for a level-triggered type D flip-flop that has an active-high clock. The output line of this flip-flop will follow the input line only when the clock line is HIGH. Trace D shows the data at the D input, while trace Q shows the output data; CLK shows the clock line, which is presented with a series of regular pulses.

At time T_0, the data line goes HIGH, but the clock line is LOW, so no change will occur at output Q. At time T_1, however, the clock line goes HIGH and the data line is still HIGH, so the output goes HIGH. Note that the Q output remains HIGH after pulse T1 passes and will continue to remain HIGH even when the data input drops LOW again. In other words, the Q output of the type D flip-flop will remember the last valid data present on the D input at the time the clock pulse went inactive. At time T_2, we find another clock pulse, but this time the D input is LOW. As a result, the Q output drops LOW. The process continues for times T_3 and T_4. Note that in each case the output terminal follows the data applied to the input *only* when the clock pulse is present.

The example shown is for a level-triggered type D flip-flop. This type of flip-flop will allow continuous output changes all the while the clock line is HIGH. An edge-triggered type D flip-flop timing diagram is shown in Figure 6-10d. In this case, the data on the outputs will change only during either a rising edge of the clock pulse (positive edge triggered) or on the falling edge of the clock pulse (negative edge triggered). The flip-flop will respond only during a very narrow period of time.

I/O PORTS: DEVICES AND COMPONENTS

There are a number of devices on the market that can be used for input and output circuitry in microcomputers. Some devices are merely ordinary TTL or CMOS digital integrated circuits that are adaptable to I/O service. Still others are special-purpose integrated circuits that were intended from their inception as I/O port devices. Most of the microprocessor chip families contain at least one general-purpose I/O companion chip that is specially designed to interface with that particular chip. In this section, we will study some of the more common I/O components. Keep in mind, however, that many alternatives may be better than those shown here. You are advised to keep abreast of the integrated circuits that are available from various manufacturers.

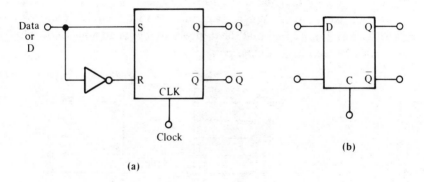

(a)

(b)

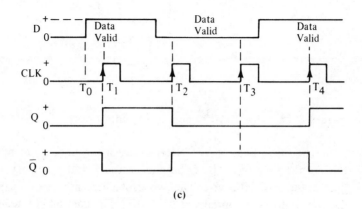

(c)

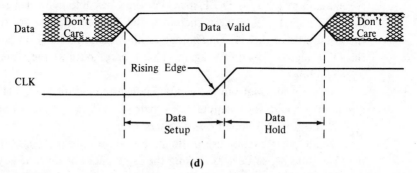

(d)

Figure 6-10 Type D flip-flop: (a) circuit using RS FF, and (b) circuit symbol; (c) timing wave form showing type D FF operation; (d) timing wave form.

Figure 6-11 shows the TTL 74100 device. This integrated circuit is a dual 4-bit latch circuit. When we connect the latch strobe terminals together (pins 12 and 23), we find that the device is usable as an 8-bit latch. The 74100 device can be used as an *output port.*

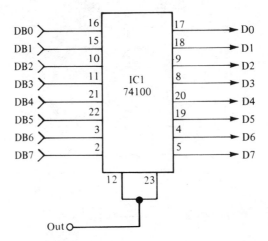

Figure 6-11 The 74100 used as an output port.

The input lines of the 74100 device are connected to bits DB0 through DB7 of the data bus. The Q outputs of the 74100 are being used as the data lines to the external device. The two strobe lines are used to gate data from the data bus onto the Q outputs of the 74100. The data latch (including the 74100) will transfer data at the D inputs to the Q outputs when the strobe line is HIGH. (Note the similarity to the operation of the type D flip-flop; the data latch is a special case of the type D FF in which the *clock* line is labeled *strobe.*) When the OUT signal goes HIGH, therefore, the data on the bus are transferred to the Q outputs of the 74100. The data will remain on the Q outputs even after the OUT signal goes LOW again. This type of output, therefore, is called a *latched output.*

It is not necessary to use a single integrated circuit for the latched output circuit. We could, for example, use a pair of 7475 devices or an array of eight type D flip-flops (although one wonders why).

Input ports cannot use ordinary two-state output devices because there may be a number of devices sharing the same data bus lines. If any one device, whether active or not, develops a short to ground, that bit will be permanently LOW regardless of what other data are supposed to be on the line. In addition, it is possible that some other device will output a HIGH onto the permanently

LOW line and thereby cause a burnout of another IC. Similarly, a short circuit of any given output to the V+ line will place a permanent HIGH on that line. Regardless of the case, placing a permanent data bit onto a given line of the data bus always causes a malfunction of the computer or its resident program. To keep the input ports "floating" harmlessly across the data bus lines, we must use *tristate output* components for the input ports; such components were discussed earlier in this chapter (see Figure 6-5).

A number of 4- and 8-bit tristate devices on the market can be used for input port duty. Figure 6-12a shows the internal block diagram for the 74125 TTL device. This device is a quad noninverting buffer with tristate outputs. A companion device (74126) is also useful for input port service if we want or need an inverted data signal. The 74126 device is a quad inverter with tristate outputs. Each stage in the 74125/74126 devices has its own *enable* terminal ($\overline{C1}$–$\overline{C4}$) that is active low. When the enable terminal is made LOW, therefore, the stage will pass input data to the output and operate in the manner normal to TTL devices. If the enable terminal is HIGH, however, the output floats at a high impedance and so will not load the data line to which it is connected.

Figure 6-12b shows a pair of 74125 devices connected to form a single 8-bit input port. The output lines from each 74125 (i.e., pins 3, 6, 8, and 11) are

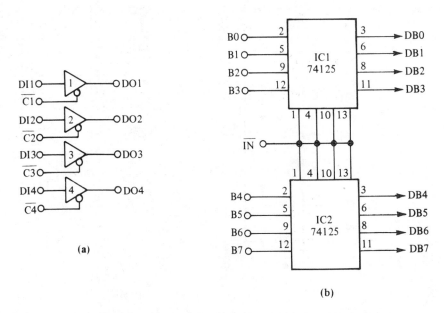

(a)

(b)

Figure 6-12   (a) 74125 device; (b) 74125 devices used as an 8-bit input port.

connected to lines DB0 through DB7 of the data bus. The input pins of the 74125 (pins 2, 5, 9, and 12) are used to accept data from the outside world.

The $\overline{IN}$ signal generated by the microrprocessor chip and the device-select circuits is used to turn on the 74125 devices. Note that all four enable lines of each 74125 device are parallel connected so that all stages will turn on at the same time.

The output lines of the input port are *not* latched. The data will, therefore, disappear when the $\overline{IN}$ signal becomes inactive, exactly the requirements of an input port on a shared bus.

Another useful input port device is the 74LS244 TTL integrated circuit. Like the 74125 device, the 74LS244 has tristate outputs. The 74LS244 is an array of eight noninverting buffer stages arranged in a *two-by-four* arrangement in which four devices share a common enable terminal. In the case of Figure 6-13a, we find that stages A1 through A4 are driven by chip enable input $\overline{CE1}$

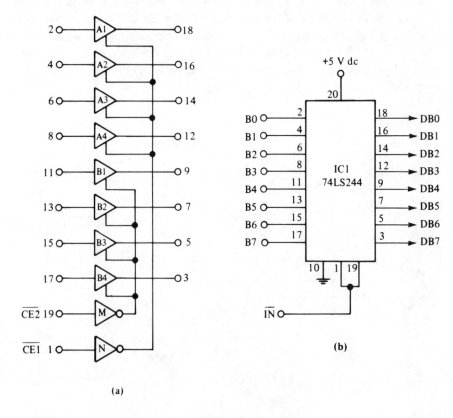

(a)

(b)

Figure 6-13   (a) 74LS244 device; (b) 74LS244 input port.

(i.e., pin 1), while B1 through B4 are driven by chip enable input $\overline{CE2}$ (i.e., pin 19). In the circuit of Figure 6-13b, we strap the two chip enable terminals together to force the 74LS244 device to operate as a single 8-bit input port. The eight input lines are connected to the respective input terminals of the 74LS244, while the output lines are connected to their respective data bus lines. When the $\overline{IN}$ signal becomes active (i.e., LOW), data on B0 through B7 will be gated onto data bus lines DB0 through DB7.

The techniques used thus far in this chapter require separate integrated circuits for input and output functions. While this is often satisfactory, it involves an excessive number of chips for some applications. We can, however, make use of combination chips in which the input and output functions are combined. Several devices on the market are classified as *bidirectional bus drivers*. These devices will pass data in either direction depending upon which is selected by the control signals. Typical devices used for several years in microcomputer designs are the 4-bit 8216/8226 devices and the 8-bit 8212 device, all from Intel. Originally, these devices were intended for use in the 8080A microprocessor circuit. Even though the 8080A has been long since superseded by newer and more powerful microprocessors, some of the support chips still find wide application.

Figure 6-14 shows the internal structure (simplified) for the 8216 and 8226

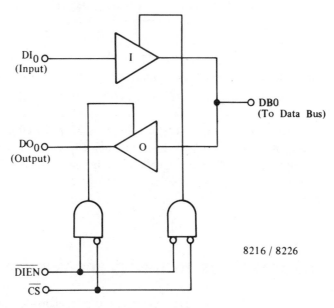

Figure 6-14   Intel 8216 and 8226 I/O chips.

devices. The principal difference between the 8216 and the 8226 is that the 8216 uses noninverting stages whereas the 8226 uses inverting stages. Note that the two buffers in each stage are facing in opposite directions with respect to the data bus line (i.e., DB0). In other words, the output line of I is connected to the data bus, so stage I can be used as an input port line. Similarly, the input of O is connected to the data bus, thereby allowing us to use O as an output line. The DI and DO lines are for input and output, respectively.

Control of the 8216 and 8226 devices is through the $\overline{\text{DIEN}}$ and $\overline{\text{CS}}$ inputs. Figure 6-15 shows the truth table that applies to these chips. The *chip select* line ($\overline{\text{CS}}$) is active low, so we find that the output will be in the high impedance state if $\overline{\text{CS}}$ is made HIGH. The $\overline{\text{CS}}$ line must be LOW in order for the device to operate. The data direction ($\overline{\text{DIEN}}$) line will connect the input lines (DI) to the data bus (DB) when the $\overline{\text{DIEN}}$ is LOW and connect the data bus lines to the output lines (DO) when $\overline{\text{DIEN}}$ is HIGH.

8216 / 8226

$\overline{\text{CS}}$	$\overline{\text{DIEN}}$	State	
0	0	DI	DB
0	1	DB	DO
1	X	High - Z	
1	X	output	
0 = Low, 1 = High, X = Either			

Figure 6-15   Control logic signals for 8216/26 in truth table form.

Figure 6-16 shows two alternate plans for connecting the 8216 and 8226 devices into actual microprocessor circuits. Figure 6-16a shows the basic connections to make these devices work properly, while Figure 6-16b shows a method for using a pair of 8216 devices with an 8080A microprocessor chip. The control signals from the microprocessor chip are specifically designed for use with the 8216/8226 devices.

INTERFACING KEYBOARDS TO THE MICROCOMPUTER

The microcomputer is able to communicate to humans through means of various displays (e.g., video CRT, strip-chart recorder, and seven-segment LEDs). The

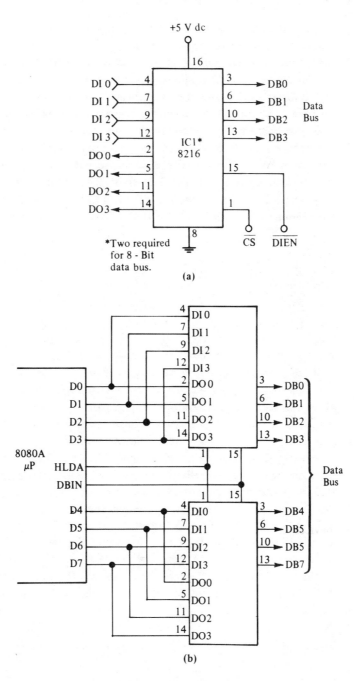

Figure 6-16 (a) 8216 pinouts; (b) 8216 devices used in microcomputer control.

real world can communicate to the computer through transducers and data converters. But humans have to communicate to the computer through a device like a keyboard. The purpose of the keyboard is to allow the human operator to send uniquely encoded binary representations of alphanumeric characters or special symbols that denote special functions to the computer. If the computer has been programmed to recognize these special codes, the human operator can direct the operation of the computer, feed it data, and so forth.

There are at least three general types of keyboard. First, there is the simple hexadecimal keypad. This type of keyboard will have 16 keys that are labeled 0 through 9 and A through F. The "hex" keypad will produce either the 4-bit binary representations of the hex numbers (0000 through 1111) or the ASCII representation (note that the ASCII is a 7-bit code of which the lowest-order 4 bits are the same as the binary code for hexadecimal). The second form of general keyboard is the full ASCII keyboard that contains all the alphanumeric characters and outputs unique 7-bit ASCII binary codes representing those characters. There are several different forms of this type of keyboard and they offer 56, 64, or 128 characters (the maximum number allowable with 7-bit codes). The 7-bit ASCII code is ideal for 8-bit microcomputers because the binary word length of the character code is only 1 bit less than the word length of the microprocessor. When the *strobe* or *data valid* bit is added to the code bits, a single 8-bit word is totally filled and there is no wasted bits.

The third type of keyboard is the custom or special-purpose keyboard. These are used on electronic instrument panels for point-of-sale terminals designed to be operated by quickly trained Christmas and summer replacement clerks, and in certain other cases. The custom keyboard may be merely a series of switches that set some input port bits HIGH or LOW depending upon the situation, or it may be a general-purpose or hexadecimal keyboard with special keycaps that denote special functions. The computer would be programmed in that case to look for the special symbol and then jump to the program that performs the requisite function when it is received.

Figure 6-17 shows the circuit for a typical type of keyboard that is based on a *read-only memory*. Addressing the locations of the memory IC (*IC1*) is accomplished by shorting together specific row (*X*) and column (*Y*) input pins. When the @ key is pressed, for example, the key switch that denotes @ is used to short together row *X*0 and column *Y*8 (see character table in Figure 6-17). This combination uniquely addresses the memory location inside of IC1 that contains the binary code that represents the ASCII character @.

Lines DB0 through DB6 are the data lines for the ASCII code, and DB7 is the strobe line. The strobe line is used to tell the outside world that the data on the other seven lines are valid. Normally, there will be "trash" signals on

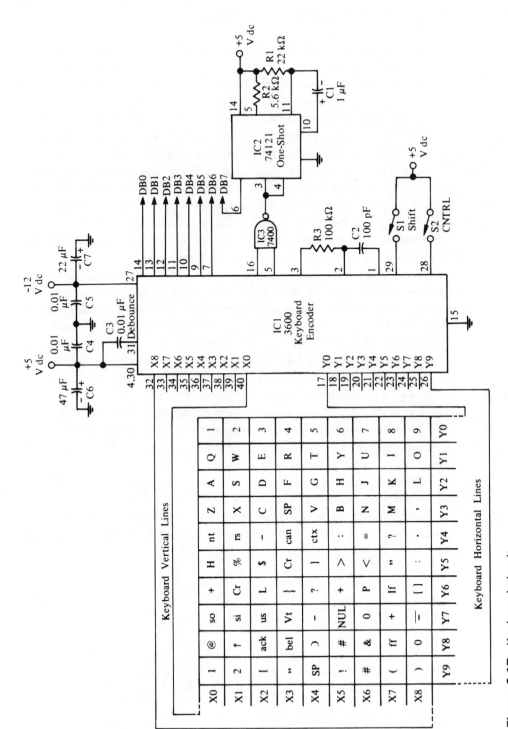

Figure 6-17 Keyboard circuit.

those other lines until a key is pressed and the ASCII code appears. By using the strobe line judiciously, we can create a signal that tells the computer when to believe the DB0 to DB6 data. In the case of Figure 6-17, the strobe is a pulse that is created by a monostable multivibrator (i.e., one-shot) IC2.

There are two different types of strobe signal, as shown in Figure 6-18. The level type of signal is simply a voltage level that becomes active when the key is closed and remains active until the key is released. In the case of Figure 6-18a, the signal is active high and thus pops HIGH when key closure occurs and drops LOW again when the key is released. The alternate form of strobe signal is the pulse as shown in Figure 6-18b. This signal will snap HIGH only for a brief period (often measured in microseconds) and then go LOW again. By the time the operator releases the key (i.e., after dozens of milliseconds), the computer has input the data and gone on to other things.

It is important to make sure that the type of strobe signal matches the computer and the software being used. There are problems that can make an otherwise normal keyboard appear to malfunction. Examples of typical problems involve the duration of the strobe pulse, software that expects to find one type of strobe signal but the keyboard supplies the other, and inverted strobe signals (i.e., the keyboard is active low and the program wants to see active high, so no data-valid strobe signal is received, except when the data are trash). We will shortly deal with possible solutions for these problems.

The keyboard is most easily interfaced to the microcomputer that has a spare input port to accommodate it. We can then connect DB0 to DB6 to the low-order 7 bits of the input port and the strobe signal to the highest-order bit of the port. A program is then written to continuously examine that high-order bit and branch to the input routine when it sees an active strobe signal. In that case, simple interconnection is all that is needed.

When there is no available input port, we may create one using one of the methods shown earlier or some special function I/O port IC device. The

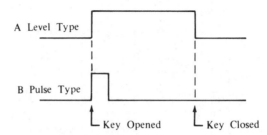

Figure 6-18   (a) Level-type strobe; (b) pulse-type strobe.

I/O port circuitry could then be used to input data from the keyboard directly to the data bus.

Most methods for interfacing keyboards will work fast enough so that the computer can pick up the valid data each and every time a key is pressed. But at times we will want the computer to come back later and pick up the data (note that "later" could mean 500 ms, but the key would have been released by that time) so that some other program task is not interrupted. In that case, we would want a latched-output keyboard. If the output data on any given keyboard are not latched, a circuit such as Figure 6-19 may be used. Here we see the use of another 74100 8-bit data latch. Seven of the latch inputs are used to accommodate the ASCII data lines, and the eighth is not connected. The ASCII strobe signal is used to activate the 74100 strobe lines and will transfer valid ASCII data from the inputs to the outputs of the 74100 so that the computer always sees a valid data signal.

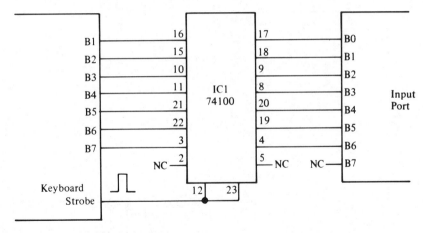

Figure 6-19   Data latching keyboard output using 74100.

In the case shown in Figure 6-19, the computer must periodically interrogate the input port and take the data each time. Unless there is some reason why the computer has to know that the data are new, there is no reason for the strobe. We could, however, add a flip-flop that changes state when the strobe signal is received and is then reset when the computer takes the data. In that case, the IN signal generated to activate the input port could also be used to deactivate the strobe FF, provided that the timing could be worked out.

Figure 6-20 shows the solutions for several problems. When the strobe signal is of the wrong polarity, we can interpose an inverter between the strobe

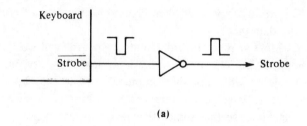

(a)

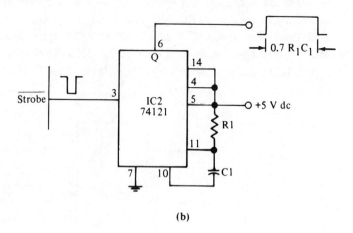

(b)

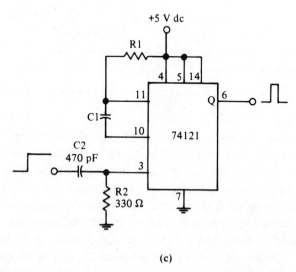

(c)

Figure 6-20 (a) Inverting strobe pulse; (b) stretching strobe pulse (negative-going pulse); (c) stretching strobe pulse (positive-going pulse).

output of the keyboard and the strobe line of the computer input port (Figure 6-20a).

The same basic idea is used when the voltage levels from the keyboard are not compatible with the input level requirements of the microcomputer. It is almost universally true that microcomputers want to see TTL-compatible voltage levels for all signals (i.e., 0 V and 2.4 to 5.2 V for LOW and HIGH, respectively). If the keyboard produces something else, for example a CMOS logic level, some form of level translation must be used. The interface device in that case could be a CMOS 4049 or 4050 (depending upon whether inversion is desired) operated from a $+5$-V power supply. When the IC is operated from $+5$ V dc, the output lines are TTL-compatible while the input will still accommodate CMOS levels.

Figure 6-20b shows one solution for the situation when the keyboard strobe signal is too short for the microcomputer being used. In many cases, the keyboard used on a microcomputer will seem to malfunction intermittently. The operator will notice that keyboard instructions will not always be picked up by the computer. The problem in that case may well be that the strobe pulse is too short. Microcomputer programs typically loop through several steps that input the data at the port, mask all bits but the strobe, test the strobe for either 1 or 0, depending upon whether active high or active low is desired, and then act accordingly. If the strobe is active, the program jumps to the input subroutine that will accept the data and place them somewhere. If, on the other hand, the strobe test shows that it is inactive, the program branches back to the beginning and inputs the data to test again. It will continue this looping and testing until valid data are received. The problem is that the looping requires a finite period of time to execute, not much time, but still finite. If the strobe pulse comes alive and disappears while the loop program is in another phase than input data, it will be lost forever. To the operator, it will appear that the computer ignored the keystroke, and service technicians may be called in. An example of such a situation would be when the computer requires 22 μs to execute the loop program, and the keyboard has a 500-ns strobe (they exist). In such a case, we can use the pulse stretcher circuit of Figure 6-20b. The circuit is merely a one-shot, and does not actually stretch anything; it only looks that way to the naive. What happens is that the circuit uses the strobe pulse from the keyboard as the trigger signal for the one-shot, and then the output of the one-shot becomes the new, longer, and presumedly "stretched" strobe pulse that is sent to the computer. The duration of the pulse is given approximately by $0.7R_1C_1$, and these values can be any normal values under 10 MΩ and 10 microfarads (μF). Select values that will make the strobe pulse duration at least long enough that the loop program will catch it, but not so long as to require several loops to outrun it.

When a low-cost keyboard outputs a *level* strobe signal, and the computer wants to see a *pulse* strobe signal, use an arrangement such as Figure 6-20c. Here we have a 74121 one-shot similar to that used previously. The difference is that the trigger input is connected to the keyboard strobe line through an RC differentiator (R2 and C2). The purpose of the differentiator is to produce a pulse signal when the level becomes active. Note that sometimes one-shot devices will respond to both rising and falling edges, so some sort of diode suppression might be needed in the differentiator output (i.e., trigger input) to eliminate the unwanted version of the signal.

CUSTOM KEYBOARDS, SWITCHES, AND LED DISPLAYS

Custom keyboards may be ordinary keyboards with special keycaps, or they may be specially designed sets of switches that tell the computer to do some particular thing or another. In this section we will consider some of the techniques used to interface and construct these keyboards.

Perhaps the simplest method is that shown in Figure 6-21a. The active element of the keyboard is an input port with switches connected to set each bit either HIGH or LOW. In some cases, especially when a special-purpose I/O port IC is used, the bits of the port might be ordinarily maintained HIGH by internal pull-up resistors to +5 V dc, but in most cases we will have to supply the pull-up resistors externally. The resistors are designed to ensure that the open bit of the input port remains HIGH and is not erroneously driven LOW by noise or other factors. The switches will produce a HIGH on the bit line when they are open and a LOW when they are closed.

When there is no available input port, we can create one by using a 74LS244 or some similar device to interface the switches to the data bus line. An $\overline{IN1}$ signal is used to turn on the 74LS244 when the computer wants to read the setting of the switches. The read operation can be either periodic, as in the case of the previous keyboards, or it may occur just once when the computer is first turned on or the program first begins execution. In the latter case, the computer is asking the "keyboard" what modes are selected or some similar question.

Some designers use this same method to tell the computer which options the customer has purchased. Suppose we have a scientific or medical instrument that has, for example, eight optional modes that the customer must pay for separately from the main instrument. The designer might put a circuit such as Figure 6-21b on the printed circuit board (the switches being DIP switches) so that the customer's engineer or production people can set them according to the options purchased. The program to support these options could already be

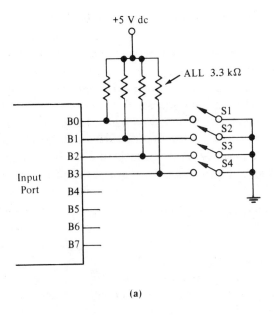

(a)

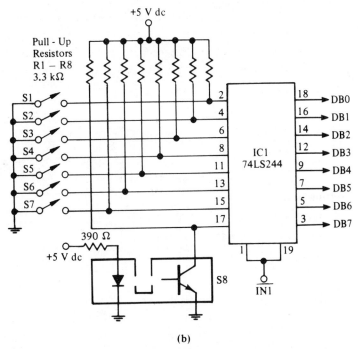

(b)

Figure 6-21 (a) Interfacing switches to input port; (b) making a switch-interface input port.

built into the software supplied via ROM to the customer, but it only becomes activated when the switch is set to the correct position. Of course, the setting protocol of these switches would have to be kept confidential lest the customer set them himself, thereby avoiding payment of the license fee.

The example of Figure 6-21b also shows an optoisolator switch. These are sometimes used to indicate the position of some object. In a popular printer, for example, there is a little metal flange on the print head assembly that will fit into the space between the LED and the phototransistor, thereby blinding the transistor when the print head assembly is at the end of its travel. As long as the transistor sees light, it will be turned on and the state of DB7 will remain LOW. When the print head assembly reaches the limit of travel, however, it will blind the transistor, causing it to turn off, and DB7 goes HIGH. The microprocessor used to control the printer carriage will then know to issue the signal that returns the carriage to the left side of the page and issue a line feed signal to advance the paper.

Switches do not make and break in a clean manner; there is almost always some *contact bounce* to contend with. In the case of toggle switches that we set and forget, this bounce is not too much of a problem. But in the case of push-button switches that are operated regularly, contact bounce will produce spurious signals that may erroneously tell the computer to do something besides what the operator intended. The two circuits in Figure 6-22 can be used to "debounce" the push-button switches. Figure 6-22a is the *half-monostable* circuit and will produce an output pulse with a duration set by R1 and C1 every time the push-

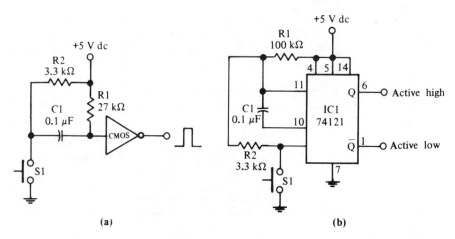

Figure 6-22   (a) Half-monostable and (b) Monostable circuit for switch debouncing.

button switch is operated. The inverter is CMOS type, such as the 4049 or 4050 devices (again, depending upon the desired polarity of the signal). The alternate circuit (Figure 6-22b) is merely the one-shot circuit used earlier but with a push-button switch and pull-up resistor forming the trigger input network. In either case, the output will be a pulse with a duration long enough to allow the bounce signals to die out.

Figure 6-23 shows methods for interfacing LEDs and LED seven-segment displays to the microcomputer. In both cases an output port is needed. If none exists, use a 74100 or some other device to form an output port. In the case of Figure 6-23, a single output port is used. Figure 6-23a shows the method for interfacing individual LEDs to the port. Each light-emitting diode is driven by an open-collector TTL inverter. The LED and a current-limiting resistor are used to form the collector load for the inverters. Note that the value of the resistor is selected to limit the current to a level that is compatible with the limits of the LED *and* the output of the inverter. With the value shown, the current is limited to 15 mA, which is within the capability of most of the available open-collector TTL inverters on the market and will provide most LEDs with sufficient brightness to be seen in a well-lighted room (although not outdoors in direct sunlight).

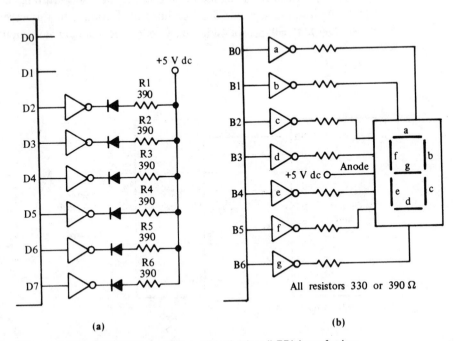

(a)   (b)

Figure 6-23   (a) LED interfacing; (b) display (LED) interfacing.

When the input signal of the inverter in Figure 6-23a is HIGH, the output is LOW, thereby grounding the cathode of the LED. This condition will turn on the LED. Alternatively, when the input of the inverter is LOW, its output will be HIGH, so the cathode of the LED will be at the same potential as the anode and no current will flow. The LED will therefore be off.

Figure 6-23b shows a similar method for interfacing seven-segment LEDs to the microcomputer output port. Here we drive the seven segments of the LED numerical display device with open-collector TTL inverters in exactly the same manner as was done previously with the individual LEDs. This method assumes that the LED numerical display is of the common anode variety with the anode connected to the +5-V dc power supply.

A constraint on this method is that the computer must generate via a software method the seven-segment code. For example, when the number to be displayed is 4, we will want to light up the following segments: f, g, b, and c. These segments are controlled by bits B5, B6, B1, and B2, respectively. Since the segment is turned on when the output port level is HIGH (as in the previous case), we will want to output the binary word 01100110 in order to turn on the segments that indicate 4. In this case, the decoding of the number 4 into seven-segment code is performed in software, probably using a *look-up table*.

Figure 6-24 shows a method for interfacing the display through an ordinary TTL BCD-to-seven-segment decoder integrated circuit, in this case the 7447 device. The 7447 will accept 4-bit binary coded decimal data at its inputs, decode

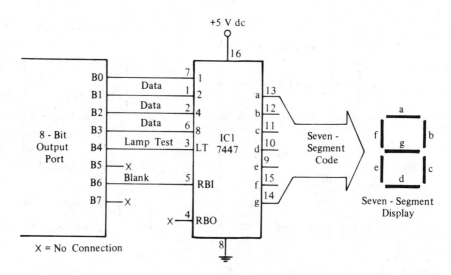

Figure 6-24 Interfacing with LED display via 7447 decoder.

the data, and turn on the segments of the LED display as needed to properly display that digit. The 7447 outputs are active low, which means that they drop LOW when a segment is to be turned on, and are HIGH at all other times. We therefore would use a common-anode seven-segment LED display for this application.

The BCD code applied to the inputs is weighted in the popular 8-4-2-1 method, and according to our connection scheme shown in Figure 6-24: B0 = 1, B1 = 2, B2 = 4 and B3 = 8.

Three control terminals are available on the 7447 device. We have a *lamp test* (LT, pin 3) that will turn on all seven segments when it is LOW; at all other times LT is kept HIGH. One function of this terminal is to provide a test of the LED readout to ensure that no burned out segments exist. Because of the nature of seven-segment readouts, erroneous readout can occur if one or more segments are burned out or otherwise inoperative. For example, if segment g is defective, an 8 output will read 0. There may be no way for a user to find this defect unless a lamp test is performed. In some cases the LT is performed on demand by the user: a push-button switch grounds pin 3 and the user notes whether or not an 8 appears. Of course, all LT terminals of the entire multidigit display can be connected together in one bus in order to light up all at the same time. In a six-digit display, grounding the common LT line would produce 888888. The other alternative is to connect the LT line(s) to an output bit of the microcomputer. The program would then display all 8s for a few seconds when the computer or instrument is first turned on so that the user will observe any defective segments. Be careful when connecting the LT terminals to the output port lest the drive capability of the port bit be exceeded. Most computer output port lines will drive no more than two or three TTL loads, and the LT input represents one such load. When more drive is needed, use a noninverting buffer with an appropriate fan-out.

The RBI input is for *ripple blanking*. If the RBI input is LOW, the display will turn off *if* the BCD word applied to the data inputs is zero (i.e., 0000). The purpose of this is to blank leading zeros. In other words, without ripple blanking the number 432 displayed on a six-digit display would read "000432." If we used ripple blanking, however, the three leading zeros would be extinguished and the display would read 432. Complementary to the RBI is the *ripple blanking output* (RBO), which tells the next display that zero blanking is desired. Note that the RBO being grounded will turn off the display, so it can be used in multiplexing applications.

When using the display of Figure 6-24, a program will have to load the accumulator with the correct binary coded decimal representation for that digit and then output it to the port that controls the display. Since microcomputer data words (hence accumulator registers) tend to be 8 bits or longer, it will be necessary to mask the data to provide zeros in the high-order half-byte of the word. By eliminating the lamp test and blanking features, we can pack the bits to make a single 8-bit word contain two BCD digits or up to four BCD digits in a 16-bit word. In the case of the 8-bit accumulator, we could pack the least significant digit (in BCD form) into B0 to B3 and the most significant digit into B4 to B7 of the 8-bit word. Most common microprocessors have the instructions to automatically accomplish the packing and unpacking of BCD data.

As long as only one or two digits are required or sufficient output ports are available, the preceding method will be satisfactory. But when one has to create output ports or there are a large number of digits, we might want to consider multiplexing the displays. In a multiplexed (MUX) display, each digit is turned on in sequence and no two digits are on at the same time. If the multiplexed rate is rapid enough, the human eye will blend the on–off transitions and will not notice the flicker. Human vision has a persistence of approximately 1/13 second (i.e., 80 ms), so we will want to switch through the displays at a rate that allows each digit to be turned back on before the image persistence gives it a chance to be recognized. In the case of a six-digit display, therefore, we would want to switch at a rate faster than 80 ms/6, or 12.8 ms. If we take the reciprocal of time, we will find the switching frequency, which in this case would be 1/0.0128 s, or 78 Hz. We can, therefore, apply an 80-Hz or higher clock and still meet the persistence requirements of the eye. In most cases, however, faster clock rates are used with the attendant smoothing of the display.

Besides the reduced complexity and chip count of the circuit (hence, improved reliability), multiplexing provides the advantage of improved current drain requirements. A typical LED device wants to see 15 mA per segment. If the digit 8 is displayed, with all seven segments lit, the current per digit would be 15 mA $\times$ 7, or 105 mA. In the case of our hypothetical six-digit display, we would need 6 $\times$ 105 mA, or 630 mA, for the display alone. That is more than a half-ampere in order to light display segments and may well be greater than the allowable current budget in many applications (hand-held instruments, such as calculators, need to MUX the display in order to have a battery life that is even reasonable).

Figure 6-25 shows a method of using a single 7447 device to drive a larger number of seven-segment readouts. The a to g segment lines are bussed together in such a way that all a lines, all b lines, and so on, are connected into a single line. Therefore, seven lines will be feeding the seven segments of all digits. In the case shown, we would need 21 lines to individually address all seven segments of all three digits. In this arrangement, only seven lines are used, and the anodes of each digit are connected to the power through transistor switches that are turned on sequentially.

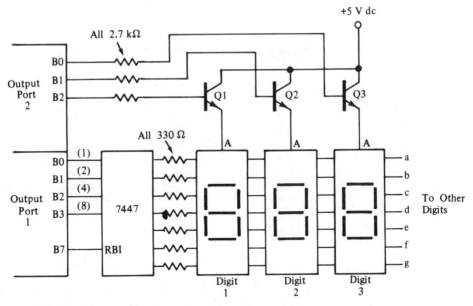

Figure 6-25 Multiplexing LED displays.

The BCD data is fed to the 7447 through output port 1, while the MUX information is fed to the bases of the control transistors (Q1–Q3) through output port 2. If four or less digits are used, we can conspire to use only one output port, with the BCD data supplied through B0 to B3 and the control bits through B4 to B7. Alternatively, we could also add a 7442 BCD-to-1-of-10 decoder to control up to ten digits, thereby making fuller use of the binary nature of the output port. In that case, the low-order 4 bits (B0–B3) would contain the BCD code, while B4 to B7 would contain a BCD word that sequences 0000 through 1001. Let's see what would be needed to make Figure 6-25 display the number 432. We know that the port 2 bits must be HIGH in order to turn on a digit, so the sequence will be as shown in Table 6-2.

Figure 6-26a shows a method for connecting the display/decoder circuits to a single output port. In the case shown here, the display/decoder might be an old-fashioned combination of 7447 and an LED display or one of the new combination units that contain both the decoder and the seven-segment LED in a single DIP integrated circuit package (e.g., the Hewlett-Packard units). The four BCD lines of all displays are connected to a common 4-bit BCD data bus formed from the 4 low-order bits of the output port. The high 3 bits of the port are used as the MUX control signals. The displays are turned on by an active-low chip enable ($\overline{\text{CE}}$) line, so the control bits are required to be LOW when the digit is turned on and HIGH at all other times.

TABLE 6-2

Decimal No.	Port 1[a]	Port 2[b]
4	0100	001
3	0011	010
2	0010	100
4	1000	001
3	0011	010
2	0010	100
4	1000	001
3	0011	010
2	0010	100

[a]Bits B4 to B7 = 0.
[b]Bits B3 to B7 = 0.

The timing diagram for the multiplex display is shown in Figure 6-26b. Note that the chip enable lines $\overline{CE1}$ through $\overline{CE3}$ are active low and so will each be LOW one-third of the time, in sequence.

SERIAL DIGITAL COMMUNICATIONS

The interchange of data between machines requires some means of data communications. Parallel communications are probably the fastest method, but can be too expensive for practical applications. In parallel communications systems there will be at least one line for each bit plus a common. For an 8-bit microcomputer, therefore, not less than nine lines are required. In some cases, especially in noisy environments or where the data rate is very high, it may also be necessary to add additional lines for control or synchronization purposes. A parallel system is practical over only a few meters distance and is the method generally used in small computer systems for intermachine local connections. But where the distance is increased beyond a few meters, or where it becomes necessary to use a transmission medium other than hard wire (e.g., radio or telephone channels), another means of transmission may be required. For the 8-bit system, for example, we would require not less than eight separate radio or telephone transmission links between sending and receiving units. That is very expensive. The solution is to use one communications link and then transmit the bits of the data signal *serially* (i.e., one after another in time) rather than simultaneously.

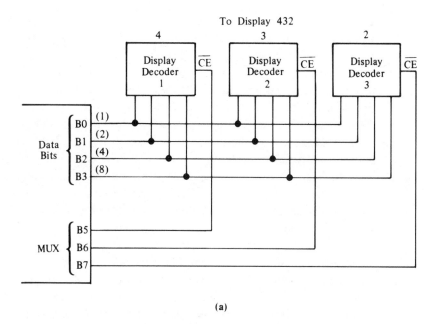

(a)

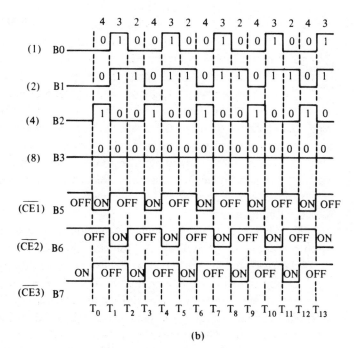

(b)

Figure 6-26 (a) Multiplexing LED displays; (b) timing wave form.

There are two forms of serial data communications, *synchronous* and *non-synchronous;* both are diagrammed in Figure 6-27. The efficacy of serial communications depends upon the ability of the receiver to remain synchronized with the transmitter. Otherwise, if they are out of sync, the receiver merely sees a series of high and low shifts of the voltage level and cannot make any sense out of them. The principal difference between the synchronous and asynchronous methods is in the manner that the receiver stays in step with the transmitter. In the synchronous method, shown in Figure 6-27a, a separate signal is transmitted to initialize the receiver register and let it know that the data word is being transmitted. In some cases, the second transmission medium path will be used to send a constant stream of clock pulses that will allow operation of the receiver register only at certain times. These times correspond to the time of arrival of the data signals. Each bit will be sent simultaneously with a clock pulse. If the incoming signal is LOW when the clock pulse is active, the receiver knows that a LOW is to be entered into the register, and so forth.

The problem with the synchronous method is that it requires a second transmission medium path, which can be expensive in radio and telephone systems. The solution to this problem is to use an asynchronous transmission system such as shown in Figure 6-27b. In this system, only one transmission channel is required. The synchronization is provided by transmitting some initial start bits that tell the receiver that the following bits are valid data bits. In most systems, the data line will remain HIGH when inert and will signal the intent to transmit a binary word by dropping LOW.

There are two ways to keep the clock of the receiver in synchrony with the transmitter. In one case, an occasional sync signal will be transmitted that keeps the clock on the correct frequency. In most modern systems, however, the receiver clock and the transmitter clock are both kept very accurate. Most small computer standards call for the receiver clock frequency to be within either 1 or 2 percent of the transmitter frequency. As a result, it is typical to find either crystal clocks or RC clocks made with precision low-temperature coefficient components.

The design of serial transmission circuits requires the construction of parallel in, serial out (PISO) registers for the transmitter, and a serial in, parallel out (SIPO) register for the receiver. Each register is designed from arrays of flip-flops and so can be quite complex. Fortunately, we can also make use of a large scale integration (LSI) integrated circuit called a UART (universal asynchronous receiver/transmitter). Figure 6-28 shows the block diagram for a popular UART IC. The transmitter section has two registers: the *transmitter hold register* and the *transmitter register*. The transmitter hold register is used as a buffer to the outside world and is a parallel input circuit. The data bit lines

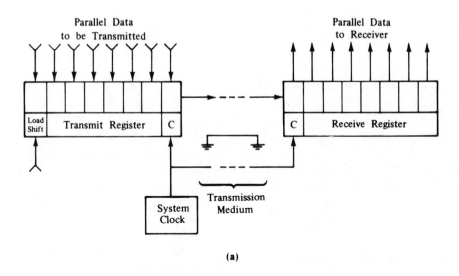

(a)

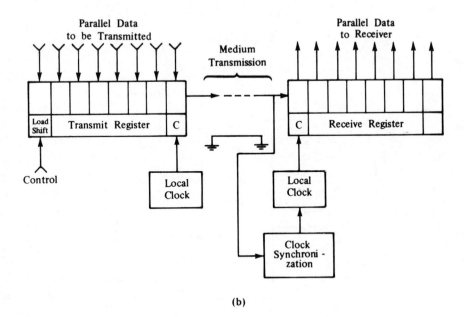

(b)

Figure 6-27 (a) Asynchronous data communications; (b) synchronous data communications.

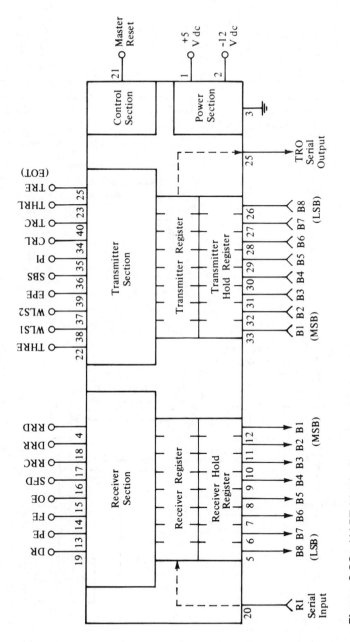

Figure 6-28 UART block diagram.

from outside the UART input the data to this register. The output lines of the transmitter hold register go directly to the transmitter register internally and are not accessible to the outside world. The transmitter register is of the PISO design and is used to actually transmit the data bits. The operation of the transmitter side of the UART is controlled by the *transmitter register clock* (TRC) input. The frequency of the clock signal applied to the TRC terminal must be 16 times the data transmission rate desired.

The receiver section is a mirror image of the transmitter section. The input is a serial line that feeds a *receiver register* (a SIPO type). The output register *(receiver hold register)* is used to buffer the UART receiver section to the outside world. In both cases, the hold registers operate semi-independently of the other registers and thus can perform certain handshaking routines with other circuits in order to ensure that they are ready to participate in the process.

Like the transmitter, the receiver is controlled by a clock that must operate at a frequency of 16 times the received data rate. The receiver clock (RRC) is separate from the transmitter clock (indeed, the entire receiver and transmitter circuits are separate from each other), so the same UART IC can be used independently at the same time. Most common systems will use the UART in a half-duplex or full-duplex manner so the receiver and transmitter clock lines will be tied together on the same 16x clock line.

The modes of transmission are *simplex, half-duplex,* and *full-duplex.* The simplex method can transmit data in only one direction. A single UART will be used at the transmit end with the receiver section disabled, while at the receive end another UART is required with an active receive section and a disabled transmit section. In half-duplex transmission, both sections of both UARTs will be used. The half-duplex system is one that has the ability to transmit data in both directions, but only in one direction at a time. The full-duplex method allows the transmission of data in both directions at the same time. With proper external circuit configuration, most UARTs will support full-duplex communications.

Several control terminals and signals are available on the UART, and these aid in operation of the circuit. Some of them, however, may be inactive in any given communications system. The *master reset* terminal is used to set all registers to zero and return all signals to their inert state. Table 6-3 shows the other signals and control inputs. Figure 6-29 shows a typical design for a UART interface with a microcomputer/microprocessor; here we will define only those terminals used in that application.

Data received (DR). A HIGH on this terminal indicates that the data have been received and are ready for the outside world to accept.

TABLE 6-3 *Continued*

PIN NO.	MNEMONIC	FUNCTION
1	V$_{CC}$	+5 volts dc power supply.
2	V$_{EE}$	−12 volts dc power supply.
3	GND	Ground.
4	RRD	Receiver Register Disconnect. A high on this pin disconnects (i.e., places at high impedance) the receiver data output pins (5 through 12). A low on this pin connects the receiver data output lines to output pins 5 through 12.
5	RB$_6$	LSB ⎫
6	RB$_7$	⎪
7	RB$_6$	⎪
8	RB$_5$	⎬ Receiver data output lines
9	RB$_4$	⎪
10	RB$_3$	⎪
11	RB$_2$	⎪
12	RB$_1$	MSB ⎭
13	PE	Parity Error. A high on this pin indicates that the parity of the received data does not match the parity programmed at pin 39.
14	FE	Framing Error. A high on this line indicates that no valid stop bits were received.
15	OE	Overrun Error. A high on this pin indicates that an overrun condition has occurred, which is defined as not having the DR flag (pin 19) reset before the next character is received by the internal receiver holding register.
16	SFD	Status Flag Disconnect. A high on this pin will disconnect (i.e., set to

TABLE 6-3 *Continued*

PIN NO.	MNEMONIC	FUNCTION
		high impedance) the PE, FE, OE, DR, and THRE status flags. This feature allows the status flags from several UARTs to be bus-connected together.
17	RRC	$16 \times$ Receiver Clock. A clock signal is applied to this pin, and should have a frequency that is 16 times the desired baud rate (i.e., for 110 baud standard it is 16×110 baud, or 1760 hertz).
18	DRR	Data Receive Reset. Bringing this line low resets the data received (DR, pin 19) flag.
19	DR	Data Received. A high on this pin indicates that the entire character is received, and is in the receiver holding register.
20	RI	Receiver Serial Input. All serial input data bits are applied to this pin. Pin 20 must be forced high when no data is being received.
21	MR	Master Reset. A short pulse (i.e., a strobe pulse) applied to this pin will reset (i.e., force low) both receiver and transmitter registers, as well as the FE, OE, PE, and DRR flags. It also sets the TRO, THRE, and TRE flags (i.e., makes them high).
22	THRE	Transmitter Holding Register Empty. A high on this pin means that the data in the transmitter input buffer has been transferred to the transmitter register, and allows a new character to be loaded.

TABLE 6-3   *Continued*

PIN NO.	MNEMONIC	FUNCTION
23	THRL	Transmitter Holding Register Load. A low applied to this pin enters the word applied to TB1 through TB8 (pins 26 through 33, respectively) into the transmitter holding register (THR). A positive-going level applied to this pin transfers the contents of the THR into the transmit register (TR), unless the TR is currently sending the previous word. When the transmission is finished the THR→TR transfer will take place automatically even if the pin 25 level transition is completed.
24	TRE	Transmit Register Empty. Remains high unless a transmission is taking place in which case the TRE pin drops low.
25	TRO	Transmitter (Serial) Output. All data and control bits in the transmit register are output on this line. The TRO terminal stays high when no transmission is taking place, so the beginning of a transmission is always indicated by the first negative-going transition of the TRO terminal.
26	TB_8	LSB ⎫
27	TB_7	⎪
28	TB_6	⎪
29	TB_5	⎬ Transmitter input word.
30	TB_4	⎪
31	TB_3	⎪
32	TB_2	⎪
33	TB_1	MSB ⎭

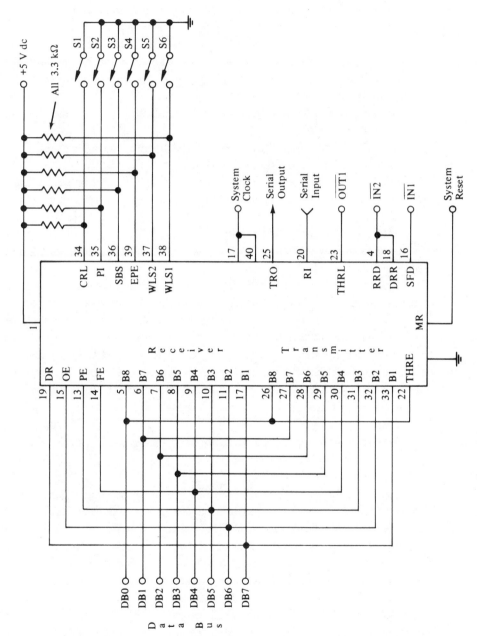

Figure 6-29 UART connection to a computer data bus.

Overrun error (OE). A HIGH on this terminal tells the world that the data reset (DR) flag has not been reset prior to the next character coming into the internal receive hold register.

Parity error (PE). A parity error signal indicates that the parity (odd or even) of the received data does not agree with the condition of the parity bit transmitted with that data. A lack of such match indicates a problem in the transmission path.

Framing error (FE). A HIGH on this line indicates that no valid stop bits were received.

B1 to B8 receiver. Eight-bit parallel output from receiver (tristate).

B1 to B8 transmitter. Eight-bit parallel input to transmitter.

Transmitter hold register empty (THRE). A HIGH on this pin indicates that the data in the transmitter hold register have been transferred to the transmitter register and that a new character may be loaded from the outside world into the transmitter hold register.

Data receive reset (DRR). Dropping this line LOW causes reset of the data received (DR) flag, pin 19.

Receiver register disconnect (RRD). A HIGH applied to this pin disconnects (causes to go tristate) the B1 through B8 receiver data output lines.

Transmitter hold register load (THRL). A LOW applied to this pin causes the data applied to the B1 to B8 transmitter input lines to be loaded into the transmitter hold register. A positive-going transition on THRL will cause the data in the transmitter hold register to be transferred to the transmitter register, unless a data word is being transmitted at the same time. In that case, the new word will be transmitted automatically as soon as the previous word is completely transmitted.

Receiver (serial) input (RI). Data input to the receiver section.

Transmitter register (serial) output (TRO). Serial data output from the transmitter section of the UART.

Word length select (WLS1 and WLS2). Sets the word length of the UART data word to 5, 6, 7, or 8 bits according to the protocol given in Table 6-3.

Even parity enable (EPE). A HIGH applied to this line selects even parity for the transmitted word and causes the receiver to look for even parity in the received data word. A LOW applied to this line selects odd parity.

Stop bits select (SBS). Selects the number of stop bits to be added to the end of the data word. A LOW on SBS causes the UART to generate only 1 stop bit regardless of the data word length selected by WLS1/2. If SBS is HIGH, however, the UART will generate 2 stop bits for word lengths of 6, 7, or 8 bits and 1.5 stop bits if a word length of 5 bits is selected by WLS1/2.

Parity inhibit (PI). Disables the parity function of both receiver and transmitter and forces PE LOW if PI is HIGH.

Control register load (CRL). A HIGH on this terminal causes the control signals (WLS1/2, EPE, PI, and SBS) to be transferred into the control register inside the UART. This terminal can be treated in one of three ways: strobe, hardwired, or switch controlled. The strobed method uses a system pulse to make the transfer and is used if the parameters either change frequently or are under program control. If the parameters never change, this terminal can be hardwired HIGH. But if changes are made occasionally, the control lines and CRL can be switch controlled as in Figure 6-29.

Figure 6-29 shows a method for connecting the UART to a common 8-bit data bus in a microcomputer. Lines DB0 through DB7 are the lines of the data bus. Since the flag signals (DR, PE, FE, and OE) are tristate logic, they may also be connected in parallel across the bus and will become active only when commanded.

The actual transmission medium used for most data communications will be either hardwire telephone lines or radio links. In either case, the HIGH and LOW signals of the data word must be converted into audio tones that have a frequency within the modulation bandwidth of the communications medium. It is typical to assign one tone for HIGH and another for LOW. Filters or PLL circuits at the receiver end will reconvert the tones back to HIGH and LOW designations. This must be done prior to the UART receiver input terminal, since the UART is strictly a digital device.

7

Special Interface Chips

To make most microprocessor chips perform as a microcomputer, it is necessary to provide external circuitry that will permit the computer to communicate with memory, the external world, or special devices. In some digital devices, including many computers, this circuitry takes the form of TTL and CMOS chips connected together to perform the desired logic function. But some companies make it easier to use their microprocessor chips by providing special-purpose interface chips. Although these chips were usually designed with a particular microprocessor chip in mind, they are often used with other chips, and sometimes in noncomputer digital circuits as well.

A host of devices fall under the rubric used as the chapter title, but we have space to consider only some of the more popular. In keeping with the Z80/6502 examples used in this book, we will describe the special-purpose interface chips intended for these microprocessors. Keep in mind, however, that the sampling selected here is merely representative. There are many other chips on the market, and the fast-moving semiconductor industry will generate even more wonderful devices in the future. Therefore, the reader is admonished to consult the product literature of semiconductor houses prior to making a definite commitment to any one device.

Since special-purpose chips are often considerably more expensive than ordinary TTL and CMOS chips, why do we use them? If all you need are simple I/O ports, it would probably be wiser to use chips such as the 74LS244 for input port duty and the 74100 for output port duty. But if you need more complex I/O functions, or the ability to designate under program control whether a port will be input or output, or if you want to save a lot of space on the printed circuit board, the special-purpose chip may not only be more attractive, but it will be the economically more viable solution to your design problem.

In this chapter we will consider the 6522 peripheral interface adapter (PIA) used with 6502 microprocessors and the Z80-family devices designated as Z80-SIO, Z80-PIO, Z80-CTC, and Z80-DMA.

6522 PERIPHERAL INTERFACE ADAPTER

The 6522 PIA is a 40-pin DIP integrated circuit that contains all the logic to implement I/O functions, with complex handshaking routines, and timer functions. In addition to the standard pair of 8-bit I/O ports, the 6522 also offers a pair of interval timers, a shift register that is useful for serial-to-parallel and parallel-to-serial data conversions.

The 6522 is designed to operate with the 6502 microprocessor, so it is often encountered in microcomputers from small single-board OEM models

TABLE 7-1

Address					
RS3	RS2	RS1	RS0	Register Designation	Comments
0	0	0	0	ORB	
0	0	0	1	ORA	Controls handshaking
0	0	1	0	DDRB	
0	0	1	1	DDRA	
0	1	0	0	T1L-L, T1C-L	Timer 1 write latch and read counter
0	1	0	1	T1C-H	Trigger T1L-L/T1C-L transfer
0	1	1	0	T1L-L	
0	1	1	1	T1L-H	
1	0	0	0	T2L-L/T2C-L	Timer 2 write latch and read counter
1	0	0	1	T2C-H	Triggers T2L-L/T2C-L transfer
1	0	1	0	SR	
1	0	1	1	ACR	
1	1	0	0	PCR	
1	1	0	1	IFR	
1	1	1	0	IER	
1	1	1	1	ORA	No effect on handshake

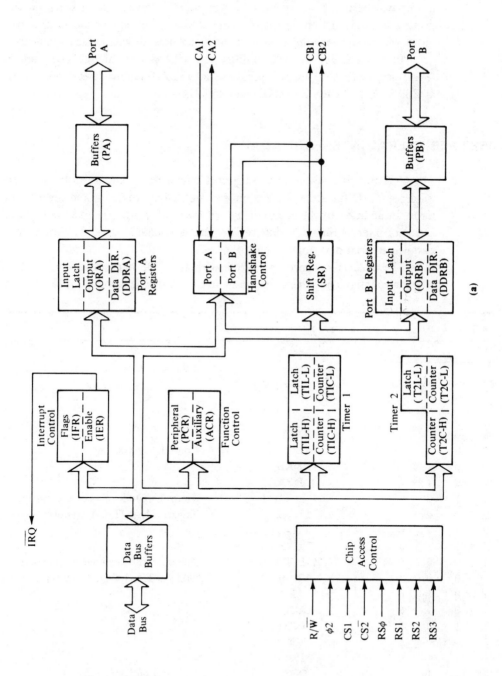

(a)

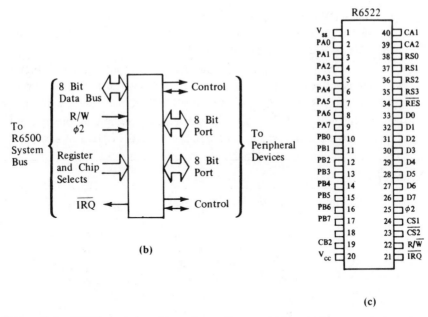

Figure 7-1   6522 peripheral interface adapter: (a) block diagram; (b) interface diagram; (c) pinout designations.

intended to be installed in larger instruments to full-scale microcomputers with the regular complement of peripheral devices. As a 6502 adjunct, the 6522 is intended for memory-mapped operation. There are four address lines on the 6522, identified in Figure 7-1 as RS0 through RS3. These lines form a 4-bit address that is capable of uniquely addressing up to 16 different internal memory-mapped functions. The 6522 functions are located at the internal addresses shown in Table 7-1.

The 6522 is memory mapped, so it will be treated by the microprocessor chip as if it were a bank of 16 bytes of memory. In the AIM-65 microcomputer, for example, the 6522 is memory mapped at locations A000 through A00F (hex addresses). If we want to write a word to port A, we would want to address ORA at location 0001, which in the AIM-65 is A001H.

The configuration of the 6522 ports is interesting and most useful. The port registers are designated ORA (port A) and ORB (port B). These *output registers* can be configured as either input or output, on a bit-by-bit basis, under program control. The control mechanism resides in the related *data direction registers* A and B (DDRA and DDRB). If we want to make all bits of either register an output, we will write a 1 to the corresponding DDR. Similarly, if we want the register to act as an input, a 0 is written to the DDR. Thus, to make ORA an output port, we will write FFH to location 0011 (DDRA) of the 6522. If we wanted the port to be an input port, we would have written 00H to location 0011H instead of FFH.

The interesting thing about the 6522 output registers is that we may make the ports either inputs or outputs on a bit-for-bit basis. Thus, we can make B0 an input, B1 an output, and so forth. All we need do is write the correct word to the selected DDR that will configure the individual bits as needed. Suppose, for example, we wanted to configure the bits of ORB as shown in Table 7-2.

TABLE 7-2

ORB Bit No.	Function	DDRB State
PB7	Input	0
PB6	Input	0
PB5	Output	1
PB4	Input	0
PB3	Output	1
PB2	Output	1
PB1	Output	1
PB0	Input	0

Thus, if we write the binary word 00101110_2 (i.e., 2EH) to DDRB at location 0010H of the 6522, ORB will be configured as shown. We can also configure ORA as needed using a similar scheme modified to meet the needs of the user. This is done under program control. If the function of each bit of both ports remains immutable, the programming chores can be accomplished once when the computer is first turned on or reset. The initial program steps will be housekeeping in nature and may well include setting up ORA and ORB by programming DDRA and DDRB.

The 6522 pinouts are shown in Table 7-3.

TABLE 7-3

Designation	Pin No(s).	Description
ϕ_2	25	Phase 2 clock input. This clock regulates the transfer of data between the PIA and the system (transfer on ϕ_2 = HIGH), and serves as the timer base for on-chip timers and shift registers (SR).

TABLE 7-3   *Continued*

Designation	*Pin No(s).*	*Description*
CS1, $\overline{CS2}$	24, 23	Chip-select lines. CS1 is active high; $\overline{CS2}$ is active low. Both lines must be active for chip to be on.
RS0–RS3	38–35	Register-select lines. These lines address the internal functions of the 6522 and are normally connected to bits of the address bus as dictated by system memory map.
R/$\overline{W}$	22	Read/write line. A HIGH indicates that data are being transferred out of the 6522 to the system; a LOW indicates data will be transferred into the system. This line is a control input and will not affect the 6522 unless CS1 is HIGH and $\overline{CS2}$ is LOW.
D0–D7	33–26	Data bus lines. Data will be transferred to and from the 6522 over these lines if the chip select, R/$\overline{W}$, and ϕ_2 = HIGH criteria are met.
$\overline{RES}$	34	Reset. Active-low input that will clear (i.e., set = 0) all registers except T1, T2, and SR.
$\overline{IRQ}$	21	Interrupt request. This active-low output will go LOW when both the interrupt enable bit and interrupt flags of the 6522 are set (i.e., equals 1). This pin is used for such purposes as signaling the processor that a timer interval has expired.
PA0–PA7	2–9	Peripheral interface for port A. The input and/or output pins for port A.
PB0–PB7	10–17	Peripheral interface for port B. The input and/or output pins for port B.

TABLE 7-3   *Continued*

Designation	Pin No(s).	Description
CA1, CA2	40, 39	Peripheral control lines for port A. These lines act as either interrupt lines or handshaking lines. Operation is controlled through the internal control register (ICR).
CB1, CB2	18, 19	Peripheral control lines for port B (see CA1, CA2). In addition, these lines act as the serial port for the shift register (SR).

Z80 DEVICES

Two special-function devices are used to provide serial and parallel input/output capability for the Z80. The Z80-SIO device is a serial I/O chip, while the Z80-PIO is a parallel I/O port. These devices are second sourced by Mostek under the type numbers MK3884 (Z80-SIO) and MK3381 (Z80-PIO).

There is also a direct-memory access device called the Z80-DMA (Mostek MK3883). Direct-memory access in a computer allows the external memory to be written to, or read from, by a peripheral device without first going through the CPU. This allows the operation to be performed much more rapidly and is conservative of CPU time, a precious commodity in some applications.

The Z80-CTC (Mostek MK3882) is a four-channel, multimode counter/timer circuit. It provides counter and timer capability in Z80-based microcomputer systems.

Z80-PIO

The Zilog Z80-PIO (Mostek MK3881) is used as a parallel I/O port controller. It contains two ports and is user programmable. The Z80-PIO contains two completely independent, 8-bit bidirectional ports. Complete handshaking capability is permitted, so the device can be used for synchronous transfers.

The Z80-PIO can be programmed to operate in four different modes: *byte output, byte input, byte bidirectional bus* (port A only), and *bit control.*

The *byte output mode,* also called mode 0, is used to allow the CPU to write data to the peripheral via the CPU data bus. If mode 0 is selected, a *data write* operation causes a handshake signal (*ready*) to be generated. This signal is used to let the peripheral know that the data are available and valid. Note that the data remain available and the *ready* signal remains HIGH until a strobe is received back from the peripheral.

The *byte input mode,* also called mode 1, allows the selected port to behave as an input port only. When a *data read* operation is performed by the CPU, the PIO will issue a *ready* signal to the peripheral. This tells the peripheral that the Z80 CPU is now in a condition to receive the input data. The peripheral responds by issuing a strobe that causes the data to be transferred to the data input register of the PIO.

The *byte bidirectional mode,* also called mode 2, uses the port as a bidirectional, 8-bit I/O port. Mode 2 uses all four possible handshake lines. Because of this restriction, only port A can be used in the bidirectional mode.

The *bit control mode,* also called mode 3, is used for status and control applications. Mode 3 does not make use of the handshake signals. This mode is used to define which port data bus lines will be inputs and which will be outputs. The next word fed to the PIO after mode 3 is selected must define these conditions.

Figure 7-2 shows the pinouts for the Z80-PIO; the different types of pins are defined as follows:

D0–D7	These pins connect to the Z80 CPU data bus and are both bidirectional and tristate. All command signals and data passed between the CPU and the PIO, in either direction, must be passed over these lines.
B/A SEL	This active-high input will select either port A or port B. A LOW on B/A SEL will select port A, whereas a HIGH will select port A.
C/D SEL	This active-high input selects the type of data transfer to take place between the CPU and PIO. A LOW on this line tells the PIO that the data on the Z80 data bus are I/O data. But a HIGH will tell the PIO that the data being transferred are a command for the port selected by B/A SEL.

$\overline{\text{CE}}$ Active-low input that acts as a chip enable. A LOW on this terminal allows the PIO to accept command/data inputs from the Z80 CPU during any write cycle or to send data to the Z80 CPU during any read cycle.

$\overline{\text{M1}}$ This terminal synchronizes the PIO to the CPU and is generally connected to the similarly named terminal on the CPU chip, Indicates that an M1 machine cycle is in progress.

$\overline{\text{IORQ}}$ Input/output request line from the Z80 CPU chip that is part of the sync system. Usually connected to the similarly named terminal on the Z80 device.

$\overline{\text{RD}}$ Active-low input that detects the read cycle of the Z80.

IEI   Interrupt enable input. This is an active-high input.

A0–A7   Tristate, bidirectional address bus for port A.

$\overline{\text{A STB}}$ Active-low input that strobes port A from peripheral device.

A RDY   Active-high output signals that the A register is ready.

B0–B7   Tristate, bidirectional address bus for port B.

$\overline{\text{B STB}}$ Active-low input that allows peripheral device to strobe port B.

B RDY   Active-high output that signals that the B register is ready.

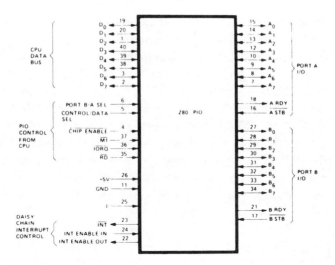

Figure 7-2   Z80-PIO pinouts.

Z80-SIO

The Z80-SIO device is a serial I/O chip that interfaces directly with the Z80 CPU chip. It is similar to the Z80-PIO in that it is a programmable two-channel device. The SIO, however, transmits the data in a *serial* stream (i.e., 1 bit at a time). Parallel transfer is, of course, faster in most cases. But often a serial transfer is preferred because it reduces the hardware overhead between the computer and the peripheral with which it is communicating. Even when the "run" is only a short distance, it is often much less costly to use a serial data transfer because only one pair of wires, one telephone line, or one radio communications channel is required. The Z80-SIO is designed to handle just about any reasonable serial bit protocol. Like the other chips of the Z80 family, it is operated from a single +5-V dc supply and uses only a single-phase clock.

The two channels (also labeled A and B, as in the PIO device) are totally independent of each other, except for power supply and CPU bus connections. The SIO channels are full duplex, so data can be transmitted and received simultaneously. The Z80-SIO allows data rates from zero to 550,000 bits per second.

Both receiver and transmitter registers are fully buffered. But in the case of the transmitter section, the registers are doubly buffered. The receiver registers, on the other hand, are quadruply buffered.

The Z80-SIO is capable of *asynchronous* operation (in which it behaves much like an ordinary UART, but with a Z80-system flavor), *synchronous binary* operation, and HDLC/IBM-SDLC operation. The SIO provides eight MODEM control input/outputs, allows daisy chain priority interrupt logic to automatically provide the vector word, and permits both CRC-16 and CRC-CCIT $(-0/-1)$.

The SIO looks very much like the ordinary UART in its asynchronous mode. It can be programmed for 5, 6, 7, or 8 eight-bit words. Like the UART, it will provide 1, 1.5, or 2 stop bits at the end of each transmitted word. The CPU, incidentally, need not provide these bits; the SIO adds them to the word received from the CPU before the word is transmitted. Also, like the UART, the SIO will provide parity bits (even, odd, none) and detection of parity, framing errors, and overrun. Unlike most UARTs, however, the SIO also provides for the generation and detection of breaks. Clock rates of $1\times$, $16\times$, $32\times$, and $64\times$ the data rate are permitted.

Figure 7-3 shows the organization of the Z80-PIO device. In Figure 7-3a we see the overall block diagram of the device, while Figure 7-3b shows the block diagram for the channels. The input section from the CPU receives eight data bus lines and six control signal lines. Once inside, the device operates from an internal bus not accessible to the outside world. There are two sections for channels A and B, some internal control logic, the interrupt section, and a discrete control section (used with MODEMs and other controlling devices).

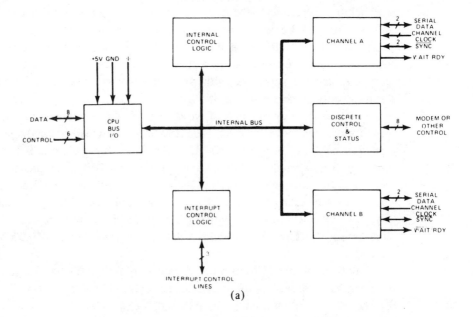

(a)

Figure 7-3   Z80-PIO organization: (a) overall internal block diagram;

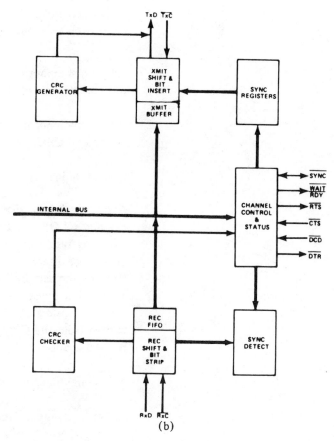

Figure 7-3 *continued:* (b) channel block diagram.

The pinouts for the Z80-SIO are shown in Figure 7-4 and are defined as follows:

D0–D7   Tristate, bidirectional data bus to/from Z80-CPU and rest of Z80 system.

B/A   Channel A/B select. Channel A is selected when this pin is LOW, and channel B is selected when it is HIGH.

C/D   Control/data select. If this input is HIGH, the control mode is selected, but if it is LOW, the data mode is selected.

$\overline{M1}$	Active-low input that detects the M1 machine cycle in Z80.
$\overline{IORQ}$	Active-low input that detects the input/output request state of the Z80 CPU.
$\overline{RD}$	Active-low input that detects the read cycle of the Z80 CPU.
Φ	Clock terminal.
$\overline{RESET}$	Active-low input that resets the system. Placing a LOW on this terminal has the following results: both receivers and transmitters are disabled, TDA/TDB are forced marking, modem controls are forced HIGH, and all interrupts are disabled. *Note:* The control registers of the SIO *must* be rewritten from the CPU before the SIO can be used again.
IEI	Active-high interrupt enable input.
IEO	Active-high output. Note that IEI/IEO are used together to form a daisy-chain priority interrupt control function.
$\overline{INT}$	Active-low output to the interrupt request line of the Z80. Note that this terminal is an open-drain type.
$\overline{WAIT}$ READY A WAIT/ READY B	These lines, one for each channel, have two principal functions, In one case, they can be used as ready lines for the Z80 DMA (direct-memory access) controller. In another, they can be used to synchronize the Z80 CPU to the Z80-SIO (i.e., to sync the data rate between CPU and SIO).

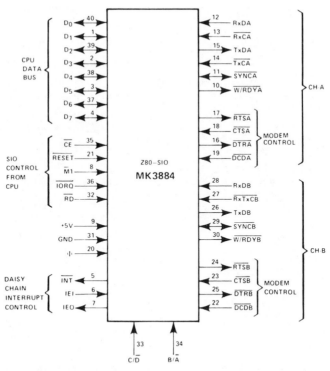

Figure 7-4 Z80-SIO pinouts.

CTSA
CTSB

These lines, one for each channel, provide a *clear to send* function. Both are active-low inputs. If programmed for *auto enable,* these pins will act as transmitter enable controls. But when not programmed for auto enable, they can be programmed for general control purposes. *Note:* These pins are buffered through Schmitt-trigger circuits, thereby allowing slow rise-time signals.

DCDA
DCDB

Data carrier detect. These two active-low inputs serve as receiver enable control signals.

RDA/RDB

Active-high receiver data inputs.

TDA/TDB	Active-high transmit data outputs.
$\overline{\text{RCA}}/\overline{\text{RCB}}$	Schmitt-trigger buffered, active-low receiver clock inputs.
TCA/TCB	Same as preceding, but transmitter clocks.
$\overline{\text{RTSA}}/$ $\overline{\text{RTSB}}$	Active-low outputs providing *request-to-send* signals.
$\overline{\text{DTRB}}$ $\overline{\text{DTRA}}/$	Active-low outputs providing *data-terminal-ready* signals.
$\overline{\text{SYNCA}}/$ $\overline{\text{SYNCB}}$	Used for synchronization of external characters.

Z80-DMA

The Z80-DMA (Mostek MK3883) is a *direct-memory access* controller. This type of operation is very useful in a computer. It speeds up direct transfers between an external device, or peripheral, and the memory because it allows bypassing of the CPU. Ordinarily, if you wanted to transfer a data word from some peripheral device and a specific memory location, you would have to execute an input instruction to move the data into the accumulator first. Then a second instruction would be required in order to move the data from the CPU to the desired memory location. Unless the data are to be used immediately after input, this would be a waste of valuable time. DMA allows the data to be placed directly into the desired location from the peripheral.

The DMA chip allows three modes, or classes, of operation: *transfer only, search only,* and *search–transfer.* There are also four types of operation: *single byte at a time, continuous burst* (as long as ports are ready), *continuous* (CPU locked out), and *transparent* (i.e., it steals time from refresh cycles).

Three types of interrupt are allowed. In one case, the DMA chip will interrupt the CPU only when a match to a desired word is found. It will also interrupt on *end-of-block* or *ready.* The DMA can be enabled, disabled, or reset totally under software control.

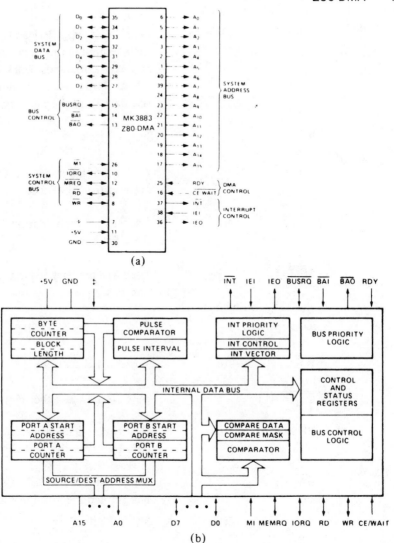

Figure 7-5 (a) Z80-DMA pinouts; (b) Z80-DMA block diagram.

Figure 7-5a shows the pinouts for the Z80-DMA; Figure 7-5b shows the internal block diagram. The pinout functions are defined as follows:

A0–A15   System address bus (from Z80 and mem-
                                ory). This 16-bit address bus can, like the
                                Z80 bus, address all 64K of allowed mem-
                                ory.

| D0–D7 | Data bus from CPU and memory. These tristate input/output pins carry three types of data: commands from the Z80 CPU, DMA status (from memory/peripherals), and data from the memory/peripherals. |

Φ System clock.

$\overline{M1}$ Active-low input detects the M1 machine cycle in the Z80 CPU.

$\overline{IORQ}$ Used as an input/output request to/from the CPU bus.

$\overline{MREQ}$ Used as a memory request to/from Z80 system bus.

$\overline{RD}$ Read to/from Z80 CPU bus.

$\overline{WR}$ Write signal to/from Z80 CPU bus.

$\overline{CE/WAIT}$ May be used as either chip enable or $\overline{wait}$.

$\overline{BUSRQ}$ Bus request is used to request control of the data bus from the Z80 CPU.

$\overline{BAI}$ Input that tells the Z80-DMA that the CPU has granted it control of the bus. It is a bus acknowledge input.

$\overline{BAO}$ Bus acknowledge output that allows daisy chain connection of DMA-requesting peripherals.

$\overline{INT}$ Active-low output that tells the Z80 CPU that an interrupt is requested.

IEI   Active-high interrupt enable input.

IEO	Active-high interrupt enable output. Forms ability to daisy chain when used in conjunction with IEI.
RDY	Active-high/low (i.e., programmable) input that tells the Z80-DMA when a peripheral device is ready for a write/read operation.

Z80-CTC

The Z80-CTC (Mostek MK3882) is a universal counter-timer chip that can provide all the counter and timer requirements for a Z80-based computer. There are four independent channels in the Z80-CTC. Consistent with the design of the rest of the Z80 family, this device requires only a single +5-V dc power supply and a single-phase clock. Each of the four channels can operate as either a counter or a timer.

The Z80-CTC pinouts are shown in Figure 7-6, and their respective descriptions are as follows:

D0–D7	Bidirectional tristate data bus to/from CPU.
CS0–CS1	Active-high channel select inputs.
$\overline{CE}$	Active-low chip enable input.
Φ	System clock.
$\overline{M1}$	Active-low input from CPU that detects the M1 machine cycle.
$\overline{IORQ}$	Active-low input that detects the input/output request state of the CPU.
$\overline{RD}$	Active-low input that detects the Z80-CPU read cycle.
IEI	Active-high interrupt enable input.

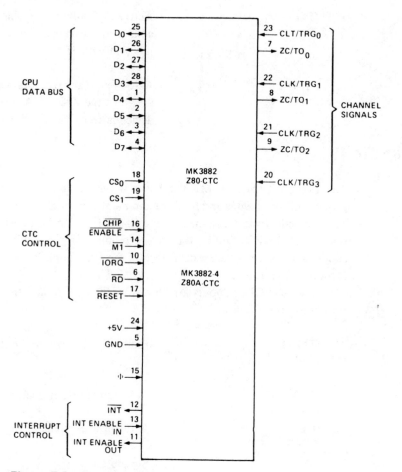

Figure 7-6 Z80-CTC pinouts.

IEO	Active-high interrupt enable output. Used with IEI to permit daisy chaining.
$\overline{\text{INT}}$	Active-low, open-drain output to the Z80-CPU interrupt request input.
$\overline{\text{RESET}}$	Active-low reset input.

8
Using the Standard Buses

A standard bus is an arrangement of printed wiring board pinouts that obey a fixed protocol as to pin and signal designations, voltage levels, and connector styles. Only a few of the standard buses in the microcomputer market are, in fact, national or internationally recognized standards, in the accepted sense of the term; they have become "standards" through vigorous promotion by the inventing company. Hence, a protocol made by, say, the XYZ corporation may well become the "XYZ bus" and be widely imitated. Other companies will note the success of the XYZ bus and will offer either second-source computer boards or peripheral/accessory boards for the XYZ bus.

A disadvantage of such uncontrolled buses comes in the matter of copycat designation of undesignated pins on the connectors. There may be several unreserved pins on any given bus, and some accessory manufacturers may designate them for some special purpose without consulting the originator of the bus. A problem arises when the user attempts to insert two different accessory cards into the computer each of which designates an unreserved pin for some special purpose. Everything would be all right if no such conflict exists, but it does happen. Perhaps the greatest offender is the S-100 bus (properly called the *Altair* bus after the originator), which is now the subject of an IEEE standard. So many manufacturers have made plug-in S-100 cards for special purposes that the conflict discussed becomes especially likely. Careful attention to the quirks of the special cards is necessary.

An advantage of the standard bus is the ability to easily interface various elements to form a computer or a computer-based instrument or machine. We can assemble a collection of CPU, memory, and assorted I/O and/or interface cards that are custom configured to perform some specific purpose that may or may not look like a traditional data-processing or other "computer"chore.

Several buses have more or less become "standards," if not by formal action by some authoritative group, then by common usage. Some are more widely used than others, but one must not assume that popularity denotes either a logical, well thought out design, or usefulness for any given application. Indeed, engineering opinion generally holds that one of the most popular buses is actually among the least professional and least useful on the market.

The concept of "buses" refers to situations in which a mother board contains sockets into which CPU, memory, I/O, interface, and other cards plug. Such a bus will typically have tracks on the mother board for all bits of the data bus, all bits of the address bus, CPU and or system control signals, possibly some I/O lines, and, finally, dc power distribution. All these features are needed to make the plug-in cards work together.

Another type of bus is the I/O-oriented form. One would suppose the 20-mA current loop and RS-232 serial I/O ports could qualify for the designation as "I/O-oriented buses," but that requires the definition to be loose, which it often is. It is better to consider those "buses" as merely serial I/O ports, which they are, and only designate as I/O-oriented buses those that offer certain CPU control signal and addressing capabilities. The general-purpose interface bus (GPIB) would certainly qualify under this criterion.

Certain problems with microcomputer buses tend to limit or constrain the designer. One such problem is the drive capability of devices connected to the bus. A typical microprocessor chip output pin (e.g., on the data bus) will only drive two TTL loads (3.2 mA); that is, it has a TTL fan-out of 2. A bus line may represent a much heavier load; in fact, it almost always requires a fan-out much larger than 2. There are at least two reasons why this is true. First, there are *many* TTL inputs connected across each line of the data and address buses in a typical microcomputer, even one that is relatively simple. The load presented by such a situation to each line can be estimated by adding up the total number of devices hanging on each line and then multiplying by 1.6 mA. The second reason is that the multiple parallel bus lines form capacitive loads that the microprocessor chip outputs simply cannot handle. The solution in both cases is to use high-power bus driver or buffer ICs to interface the bus with its drive sources.

Another problem seen occasionally is bus *ringing*. The long bus line represents a complex reactive network of distributed capacitances and inductances, which combine to make the bus act exactly like a high-frequency antenna transmission line. When fast risetime, high-repetition-rate signals are applied to the line, as they are in digital circuits, the result is exactly as if pulses were applied to a length of coaxial cable transmission line. The pulse will travel the length of the line, where it will be *reflected* unless the line is properly terminated. The reflected pulses can raise havoc by changing data values or instructions or can cause timing problems that are difficult to deal with.

Improper termination was a problem on certain early S-100 bus computers. Very soon after their introduction, however, companies began to offer both active and passive terminator kits to solve the problem. Some had to be wried into the S-100 mother board from the underside. Others were mounted on a shortened S-100 card and so could be plugged into a mother-board socket; usually an end socket was selected.

One final constraint is the number of sockets on the bus mother board. The S-100 bus, for example, might have anywhere from five to thirty 100-pin sockets. Obviously, if expansion or a large number of optional cards is needed, one must select a mother board with sufficient sockets to do the job. In this same vein, some thought needs to be given to later expansion; rare is the computer system that does not expand as the owner becomes more enthusiastic or proficient, or both!

The type of bus required, as well as its size, depends much on the type of applications. A quite different machine is required for a number-crunching data-processing chore than for a controller of small scientific experiments.

When a standard-bus microcomputer is used, we can often obtain a computer-based instrument by designing only an interface board. Let's consider a simple example, an evoked potentials computer for studying the human electroencephalograph response to specified stimulii, such as audio clicks or a flash of light.

Evoked potentials are a means of recording the minute component of the electroencephalograph (EEG) signal. The EEG is a record of the brain's minute electrical activity as acquired from a set of differential scalp electrodes. Normally, the scalp surface EEG signal is the summation of many dozens of signals from throughout the brain, only one component of which is due to the specified stimulus. In other words, the surface EEG potential is the algebraic sum of many time-varying signals. The analogy would be the situation of trying to discern one voice from the crowd by lowering a microphone ten feet inside the Houston Astrodome during a football game. The problem is one of too much signal to discern the minute contribution of one small voice. The solution to the problem used in evoked potentials work is to repeat the stimulus many times, and then coherently average the EEG signal in a digital computer. *Coherent averaging* means that many samples are taken following the stimulus, but they are only compared with the signal taken at the same poststimulus time as

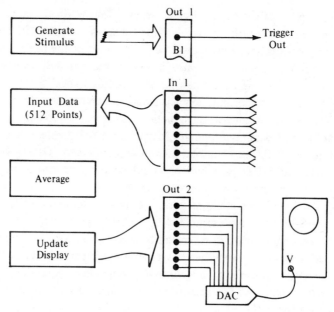

Figure 8-1 Evoked potentials routine.

previous trials. For example, all signals taken 100 ms after the stimulus will be averaged together, and all signals taken 101 ms after the stimulus are averaged together independently. If this is done properly, the component due to the stimulus will be enhanced, while the rest of the signals will tend to zero because of randomness. The result is that the signal remaining will represent the brain-wave component caused by the stimulus.

Typical stimulii tested by this method have included lights (the most common form of stimulus because of the ease of acquiring the relevant EEG potentials), sound, touch, and smell. Coherent signal averaging requires either that the computer be synchronized to the stimulator or that it synchronize the stimulus; both methods are used.

Figure 8-1 shows the basic solution to the problem. We will select a computer system that has (in addition to a CPU) enough read-only memory (ROM) to contain the program, plus 25 to 50 percent reserve capacity, enough random-access memory (RAM) for the data points plus expansion reserve (2K to 4K are probably sufficient), and I/O capability. For the I/O function, we might use either an I/O card (or existing ports) or build I/O ports onto each interface card.

Figure 8-2 shows in block diagram form a suitable interface card to plug into one standard slot of a bus-organized microcomputer. The card may be

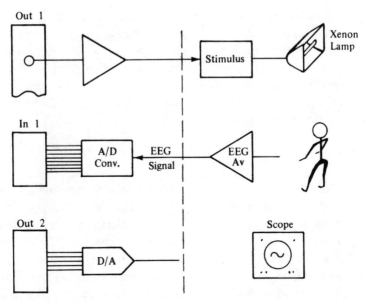

Figure 8-2   Hardware configuration.

acquired under any of several options. First, the computer manufacturer may build suitable blank interface cards or I/O cards as one of the standard system accessories (available at extra cost, of course). Second, you could design a suitable printed circuit wiring board from scratch. Such a card would have to adhere to the computer maker's specifications regarding pinouts, card-edge connectors, size, shape, and voltage levels if it is to be successful. Finally, you could purchase a *prototyping card.* These cards are of the correct size and shape and contain an appropriate card-edge connector suitable for the computer on hand. The card may also contain power distribution tracks and printed circuit IC pads (usually for DIP ICs). Otherwise, however, they are blank. The user adds components and point-to-point wiring (which may be either solder or wire-wrap).

In the simplest case, the interface card simply plugs into a mother-board slot, and analog signals are brought via connectors to the interface card from the outside world. We can, therefore, build other computer-based instruments by changing only the interface card and panel connectors and/or designations.

STANDARD BUSES

There are several "standard" microcomputer buses on the market. Some are very good, others are not; some become very popular, while others have disappeared; some offer extensive optional accessories, while others have none. Oddly, popularity does not guarantee either proper or even acceptable design.

In the remainder of this chapter we will discuss several popular microcomputer buses. Space limits both the depth and scope of the discussions. Many perfectly valid systems are not covered for lack of space. It is not proper for you to construe either endorsement or condemnation of any bus from its exclusion or inclusion here.

S-100 Bus

The S-100 bus is probably the oldest popular microcomputer bus still in existence. It was introduced in 1975 by MITS, Inc., in their Altair microcomputer. The original Altair was based on the Intel 8080a microprocessor chip, although many modern S-100 computers use the more powerful Z80 device instead. The Z80 was designed by Zilog, Inc., and is more or less compatible with the 8080a system. The two chips are not pin-for-pin compatible, and the Z80 contains a larger instruction set. Most programs designed for 8080a will also run on the Z80 machine, except for those that are dependent upon certain timing relationships.

To date, there are more than 350 boards available from a variety of manufacturers that are allegedly compatible with the S-100 bus. There are literally dozens of memory boards, I/O boards (serial, parallel, 20 mA, RS-232, etc.), video boards, disk controllers, cassette tape controllers, speech synthesizers, and other special accessories. Unfortunately, many companies have taken it upon themselves to designate certain of the unreserved lines on the S-100 bus for some special purpose of their own. If two different boards try to use these lines for their own purpose, a confict will arise that will lead to strange results.

The S-100 connector consists of two rows of 50 pins (100 all together) spaced 0.125 in. apart. The S-100 standard configuration calls for the lower 50 (1 through 50) pins to be on the component side, while the upper 50 are on the foil side of the board. The connector is offset along the 10-in. side of the 5.3 × 10 in. S-100 printed circuit board so that it is impossible to insert the card incorrectly. Otherwise, catastrophic failure will result. Pins 55 to 67 and 12 to 17 are unreserved in the standard, but are often designated for special purposes by S-100 computer manufacturers or accessory makers.

Power supply for the S-100 bus microcomputer consists of three lines: an +8-V unregulated line with high current capacity and positive 16-V and negative 16-V low-current lines. The circuits on each card usually want to see +5 V regulated for the digital circuitry, and either ±12 or ±15 V for the analog circuitry and some digital devices such as EPROMs; the 8080a microprocessor required -12 V for proper operation. In the S-100 scheme, each circuit card contains its own voltage regulators. There are some cards available with three independent $+5$ -V (1 or 3 A) voltage regulators. This *distributed regulation* scheme accomplishes several goals. For one thing, it all but eliminates the problem of voltage drop in the high-current lines. Ordinarily, a high-current regulated voltage line will see a voltage drop. In some computers, there will be a *sense* line from the voltage regulator that is attached to the printed circuit board at the point where the regulated voltage value must be precise. This approach does not work well in some digital equipments where there are plug-in printed circuit cards. After all, at which card can you accept a voltage error? The second advantage of distributed voltage regulation is that a failure in the regulator will not wipe out the entire computer, but only that fraction of the circuit served by the smaller regulator. In most S-100 cards, the voltage regulation is provided by three-terminal IC voltage regulators in TO-3 or TO-220 power transistor packages; examples are the LM-309K, LM-340K-05, and 7805.

The S-100 pinouts and signals are given in Table 8-1. Note that not all pinouts are found in all systems. The originally unreserved pins are specified in this table.

TABLE 8-1   S-100 Bus

Pin No.	Designation	Function
1	$+8$ V	Main power line for digital circuits; $+8$ V is supplied to the $+5$-V regulators on the cards.
2	$+16$ V	Unregulated voltage to the $+12$-V regulators on the circuit cards.
3	$\overline{\text{XRDY}}$	External ready.
4	VI0	Vectored interrupt 0. Main vectored interrupt.
5	VI1	
6	VI2	
7	VI3	
8	VI4	Lower-priority vectored interrupts.
9	VI5	
10	VI6	
11	VI7	
12–17	Undesignated	

TABLE 8-1   S-100 Bus—*Continued*

Pin No.	Designation	Function
18	$\overline{\text{STATDSB}}$	Status disable. Active-low input that will force SINP, SMI, SMEMR, SOUT, SHLTA, and SSTACK into the high-impedance output state (i.e., disconnected).
19	$\overline{\text{CCDSB}}$	Command and control disable. Active-low input that will force PDBIN, PSYNC, PHLDA, PINTE, Not-PWR, and PWAIT into the high-impedance output state (disconnected).
20	UNPRO	Unprotect line. An active-high input that will reset the protect flip-flop on the board addressed so that board can become active. See also pins 69 and 70.
21	SS or SSO	Single-step operation. Used by the front panel in S-100 computers equipped with such a panel, and will disable the bus buffer so that the front panel can drive the bus instead. Active-high.
22	$\overline{\text{ADDDSB}}$ or $\overline{\text{ADRDSB}}$	Address bus disable. Active-low input that forces the 16-bit address bus into the high-impedance output state (disabled).
23	$\overline{\text{DODSB}}$ or $\overline{\text{DBDSB}}$	Data bus disable. Active-low input that forces 8-bit data bus into the high-impedance output state (disabled).
24	ϕ-2	Phase 2 clock
25	ϕ-1	Phase 1 clock (not used on Z80 systems)

TABLE 8-1 S-100 Bus—*Continued*

Pin No.	Designation	Function
26	PHLDA	HALT acknowledgment. Active-high output that indicates a HOLD signal is received. The CPU will go into the dormant high-impedance output (disabled) state after execution of the current instruction cycle.
27	PWAIT	Wait. Active-high output that indicates the CPU is in the wait state.
28	PINTE	Interrupt enable flag. An active-high output that indicates the CPU will respond to interrupts (i.e., when PINTE is HIGH). The internal interrupt flip-flop that controls this signal is under program control, not hardware control.
29	A5	Address bus bit 5
30	A4	Address bus bit 4
31	A3	Address bus bit 3
32	A15	Address bus bit 15
33	A12	Address bus bit 12
34	A9	Address bus bit 9
35	DO1	Data bus bit 1 output
36	DO0	Data bus bit 0 output
37	A10	Address bus bit 10
38	DO4	Data bus bit 4 output
39	DO5	Data bus bit 5 output
40	DO6	Data bus bit 6 output
41	DI2	Data bus bit 2 input
42	DI3	Data bus bit 3 input
43	DI7	Data bus bit 7 input
44	SM1	Machine cycle 1. Active-high output that indicates CPU is in instruction op-code fetch cycle.

TABLE 8-1   S-100 Bus—*Continued*

Pin No.	Designation	Function
45	SOUT	Active-high output that, in conjunction with $\overline{\text{PWR}}$, indicates when the address bus data is valid for an output device.
46	SINP	Input status line. Active-high output that, in conjunction with PDBIN, indicates when the address bus data are valid for an input device. Tells a peripheral when data should be put on the data bus.
47	SMEMR	Active-high output indicating a memory read operation.
48	SHLTA	Active-high output signal that indicates execution of a HALT command.
49	$\overline{\text{CLOCK}}$	Complement of ϕ-2 main system clock.
50	GND	Ground for digital signals and power supply.
51	+8 V	Same as +8 V on pin 1 and occupies the space on the other side of the PC board, opposite pin 1, so that pins 1 and 51 can be connected in parallel to the +8-V unregulated power supply.
52	−16 V	Unregulated negative 16 V used to supply −12-V regulators.
53	$\overline{\text{SSWDSB}}$	Sense switch disable. An active-low input that permits sense switches on front panel to input data.
54	$\overline{\text{EXTCLR}}$	Signal from front panel that resets all I/O devices.
55	RTC	Real time clock line, if used.
56–67	Undesignated	
68	MWRITE	Active-high output that indicates contents of the data out bus (DO0–

TABLE 8-1   S-100 Bus—*Continued*

Pin No.	Designation	Function
		DO7) are being written into memory at the location specified by A0–A15 of the address bus.
69	$\overline{PS}$	Protect status line. Active-low output indicates the status of the protect flip-flop on the plug-in card.
70	PROT	Active-high line resets protection flip-flop (see pin 20 for both pins 69 and 70).
71	RUN	Active-high signal that indicates that the front panel RUN/STOP flip-flop is in the *set* condition.
72	$\overline{PRDY}$	Ready
73	$\overline{PINT}$	Active-low interrupt request input will cause the CPU to recognize the interrupt line unless the interrupt enable flip-flop is reset (see pin 28) or if the CPU is in HOLD status.
74	$\overline{PHOLD}$	Active-low input that requests the CPU to go to the HOLD state at the end of the current instruction execution.
75	$\overline{PRESET}$	Active-low reset line. This line is essentially a "hardware jump to location 00000000" instruction, and will reset (clear) the contents of the program counter when made LOW.
76	PSYNC	Active-high output that indicates the onset of a machine cycle.
77	$\overline{PWR}$	Active-low write output indicates that a white operation to either memory or output port is taking place.
78	PDBIN	Active-high read output signal indicates a request from the CPU to either memory or input to place data on the data in (DI0–DI7) bus.

TABLE 8-1   S-100 Bus—*Continued*

Pin No.	Designation	Function
79	A0	Address bus bit 0
80	A1	Address bus bit 1
81	A2	Address bus bit 2
82	A6	Address bus bit 6
83	A7	Address bus bit 7
84	A8	Address bus bit 8
85	A13	Address bus bit 13
86	A14	Address bus bit 14
87	A11	Address bus bit 11
88	DO2	Data bus bit 2 output
89	DO3	Data bus bit 3 output
90	DO7	Data bus bit 7 output
91	DI4	Data bus bit 4 input
92	DI5	Data bus bit 5 input
93	DI6	Data bus bit 6 input
94	DI1	Data bus bit 1 input
95	DI0	Data bus bit 0 input
96	SINTA	Active-high output that indicates acknowledgment of an interrupt request. See pin 73.
97	$\overline{\text{SWO}}$	Active-low signal indicating data transfer from CPU to either memory or I/O.
98	SSTACK	Active-high output signal indicating that the address of a push-down stack is on the address bus.
99	POC	Hardware jump to location 00000000 instruction that clears the program counter on either power on or PRESET.
100	GND	Ground. Opposite side of board from pin 50 so that grounds may be connected together.

Radio Shack TRS-80® Bus

The TRS-80® bus was developed by the Tandy Corporation for use in their Z80-based Radio Shack computers. With the possible exception of the Apple II bus, the TRS-80 bus has become the most popular with the general public. This popularity is not only because of the Radio Shack marketing organization, which consists of many thousands of local company-owned and franchise stores, but also because the machine is easy for the nonexpert to learn to operate.

Unlike the S-100 and Apple II buses, the TRS-80 bus does not permit plug-in accessories within the mainframe. There is, however, an interface bus that may be used to good advantage. The pinouts and signal definitions are given in Table 8-2.

TABLE 8-2   TRS-80 Bus

Pin No.	Designation	Function
1	$\overline{RAS}$	Active-low row address select. This signal is used in the refresh operation of dynamic random-access memory devices used in the TRS-80. See also pins 3 and 16.
2	SYSRES	Active-low reset output goes LOW when the main system reset line is operated internal to the computer. This output may be used to reset peripherals and other devices interfaced with the TRS-80. The $\overline{SYSRES}$ line will go LOW whenever the reset button is pressed or when power is applied to the TRS-80 (i.e., the power-on reset circuit is operated). The effect of the reset is to load the program counter register of the Z80 with 00H, so the reset is basically a hardware JUMP to 00H instruction.
3	$\overline{CAS}$	Active-low column address select signal used in the refresh operation of dynamic RAM memory used in the TRS-80. See pins 1 and 16 also.

TABLE 8-2   TRS-80 Bus—*Continued*

Pin No.	Designation	Function
4	A10	Address bus bit 10
5	A12	Address bus bit 12
6	A13	Address bus bit 13
7	A15	Address bus bit 15
8	GND	Ground
9	A11	Address bus bit 11
10	A14	Address bus bit 14
11	A8	Address bus bit 8
12	$\overline{OUT}$	System output. This active-low output denotes an output operation being executed by the Z80 microprocessor used in TRS-80. This device-select pulse is generated by applying the $\overline{IORQ}$ and $\overline{WR}$ control signals of the Z80 to an OR gate.
13	$\overline{WR}$	Active-low output that goes LOW during a memory write operation. This signal is not to be confused with the Z80 $\overline{WR}$ signal, even though it is the product of ORing $\overline{WR}$ and $\overline{MREQ}$ Z80 control signals. The Z80 write signal is also used in output operations (see pin 12).
14	$\overline{INTAK}$	Interrupt acknowledge. This active-low signal tells the outside world that an interrupt subroutine is beginning. In modes 0 and 2, this signal can be used to signal the peripheral to place the interrupt vector address onto the data bus.
15	$\overline{RD}$	Active-low output that tells the outside world that a memory read operation is taking place. This signal is not to be confused with the Z80 control signal using the same mnemonic.

TABLE 8-2   TRS-80 Bus—*Continued*

Pin No.	Designation	Function
		The $\overline{RD}$ signal on the TRS-80 bus indicates only memory read, while the $\overline{RD}$ Z80 control signal is also used for input operations. In the TRS-80, $\overline{RD}$ is generated by ORing $\overline{MREQ}$ and $\overline{RD}$. See also pin 13.
16	MUX	Active-high signal that controls internal data multiplexers used in memory refresh operations.
17	A9	Address bus bit 9
18	D4	Data bus bit 4
19	$\overline{IN}$	Active-low output that tells the outside world that an input operation is taking place. See also pin 12.
20	D7	Data bus bit 7
21	$\overline{INT}$	Active-low interrupt request line. May be used by external devices to interrupt the CPU. See Chapter 10 of this book, or Joseph J. Carr, *Z80 User's Manual,* Reston Publishing Co., Reston, Va. for description of Z80 interrupt protocols.
22	D1	Data bus bit 1
23	$\overline{TEST}$	Active-low input that will allow external devices interfaced with the TRS-80 to gain control of the data bus.
24	D6	Data bus bit 6
25	A0	Address bus bit 0
26	D3	Data bus bit 3
27	A1	Address bus bit 1
28	D5	Data bus bit 5
29	GND	Ground
30	D0	Data bus bit 0

TABLE 8-2   TRS-80 Bus—*Continued*

Pin No.	Designation	Function
31	A4	Address bus bit 4
32	D2	Data bus bit 2
33	$\overline{\text{WAIT}}$	Active-low input that forces Z80 microprocessor used in TRS-80 to go into the wait state. This signal is used to allow the Z80 to work with slow memory and peripherals, and will continue to insert wait states into the CPU cycles until $\overline{\text{WAIT}}$ is HIGH again.
34	A3	Address bus bit 3
35	A5	Address bus bit 5
36	A7	Address bus bit 7
37	GND	Ground
38	A6	Address bus bit 6
39	(see text)	This pin is designated +5 V dc on level I TRS-80 machines and GND on level II machines.
40	A2	Address bus bit 2

The Radio Shack TRS-80 microcomputers are a wise selection for many users. The interface connector pinouts described in Table 8-2 allow wide latitude for interfacing chores, despite the lack of plug-in capability inside the machine. The TRS-80 has a wide variety of software written for it, both by Radio Shack (Tandy Corporation) and independent vendors.

Apple II Bus

It is probably a toss-up whether the TRS-80 computer or the ubiquitous Apple II is the most popular personal microcomputer. The Apple II is found almost everywhere, and there seems to be about as many retail outlets for this machine as for any other personal microcomputer. The Apple II is based on the 6502 microprocessor chip. The Apple II is so popular that it has spawned not only imitators (some of which use seemingly exact copies of the Apple II printed wiring board layout), but also *counterfeits*. Some unscrupulous manufacturers in Southeast Asia have offered for sale exact duplicates of the Apple II without bothering to obtain a license from the U.S. manufacturer.

The Apple II is a single-board computer housed in a small case about the size of an inexpensive typewriter. There are eight slots on the mother board that will accommodate accessories and interface devices. The basic computer comes with 16K of memory, but we can configure it with up to 48K of 8-bit memory by replacing the 4K memory chips with 16K memory chips.

A feature of the Apple II is the use of software to replace hardware complexity. The memory allocations above the 48K boundary are used for the monitor program and for housekeeping functions like driving the disk system.

The connectors for each of the plug-in cards have 50 pins, with pins 1 through 25 on the component side of the inserted printed wiring boards and 26 through 50 on the foil side of the card. Several companies offer either plug-in accessory cards (e.g., I/O cards or A/D converter cards) or blank interfacing cards on which you may build your own circuitry. The Apple II plug-in card pinouts are described in Table 8-3.

TABLE 8-3   APPLE-II BUS

Pin No.	Designation	Function
1	I/O SELECT	This active-low signal is LOW if and only if one of the 16 addresses assigned to that particular connector is called for in the program. The 6502 used in the Apple II uses memory-mapped I/O, so each I/O port number is represented by a memory location in the range from C800H and C8FFH. Reference the Apple II memory map in the manual for specific locations.
2	A0	Address bus bit 0
3	A1	Address bus bit 1
4	A2	Address bus bit 2
5	A3	Address bus bit 3
6	A4	Address bus bit 4
7	A5	Address bus bit 5

TABLE 8-3   APPLE-II BUS—*Continued*

Pin No.	Designation	Function
8	A6	Address bus bit 6
9	A7	Address bus bit 7
10	A8	Address bus bit 8
11	A9	Address bus bit 9
12	A10	Address bus bit 10
13	A11	Address bus bit 11
14	A12	Address bus bit 12
15	A13	Address bus bit 13
16	A14	Address bus bit 14
17	A15	Address bus bit 15
18	R/$\overline{\text{W}}$	Control signal from 6502 microprocessor is HIGH during read operations and LOW during write operations.
19	(NC)	No connection.
20	$\overline{\text{I/O STR}}$	Active-low signal that lets the outside world know that an input or output operation is taking place. This line will go LOW whenever an address in the range C800H to C8FFH is on the address bus.
21	$\overline{\text{RDY}}$	Active-low input. If this line is LOW during the phase 1 clock period, the CPU will halt (i.e., enter a wait state) during the following phase 1 clock period. If $\overline{\text{RDY}}$ remains HIGH, normal instruction execution will occur on the following phase 2 clock signal.
22	$\overline{\text{DMA}}$	Active-low direct memory access line allows external devices to gain access to the data bus and apply an 8-bit data word to the address it places on the address bus.

TABLE 8-3   Apple-II Bus—*Continued*

Pin No.	Designation	Function
23	INTOUT	Interrupt output. Signal that allows prioritizing of interrupts from one plug-in card to another. The INTOUT line of each lower-order card runs to the INTIN pin of the next card in sequence. See pin 28.
24	DMAOUT	Direct-memory access version of INTOUT.
25	+5	+5-V dc power supply available from main board to plug-in card.
26	GND	Ground
27	DMAIN	Direct-memory input; signal that allows prioritizing DMA functions.
28	INTIN	Interrupt input. See DMAOUT (pin 24).
29	$\overline{\text{NMI}}$	Active-low nonmaskable interrupt line. When brought LOW, this line will cause the CPU to be interrupted at the completion of the present instruction cycle. This interrupt is not dependent upon the state of the CPU's interrupt flip-flop flag.
30	$\overline{\text{IRQ}}$	Interrupt request. This active-low input will cause the CPU to interrupt at the end of the present instruction cycle, provided that interrupt flip-flop is reset.
31	$\overline{\text{RES}}$	Reset line. This active-low input will cause the program to return to the Apple II monitor program.
32	$\overline{\text{INH}}$	Active-low input that disconnects the ROMs of the monitor in order to permit custom software stored in ROMs on the plug-in board to be executed.

TABLE 8-3   APPLE-II BUS—*Continued*

Pin No.	Designation	Function
33	−12	−12-V dc power from main board to plug-in board.
34	−5V	−5-V dc power from main board to plug-in board.
35	(NC)	No connection.
36	7M	7-mHz clock signal
37	Q3	2-mHz clock signal
38	01	Phase 1 clock signal
39	USER1	Similar to $\overline{\text{INH}}$ except that it disables all ROMs, including C800H to C8FFH, used for I/O functions.
40	02	Phase 2 clock signal
41	$\overline{\text{DEVICESEL}}$	Active-low signal that indicates one of the 16 addresses assigned to that connector is being selected.
42	D7	Data bus bit 7
43	D6	Data bus bit 6
44	D5	Data bus bit 5
45	D4	Data bus bit 4
46	D3	Data bus bit 3
47	D2	Data bus bit 2
48	D1	Data bus bit 1
49	D0	Data bus bit 0
50	+12	+12-V power from main board to plug-in boards.

KIM-1 (SYM-1 and AIM-65) Bus

The KIM-1 microcomputer was a single-board trainer that was introduced by MOS Technology, Inc., of Norristown, Pennsylvania, the originator of the 6502 microprocessor chip. It was apparently intended as a means of introducing the world of microprocessing to engineers who would incorporate the 6502 into their instrument and computer designs. The KIM-1 computer, however, developed into a popular starter computer as well as a trainer. Many current computer experts began their careers with a KIM-1 device.

The KIM-1 was a single-board computer that contained 1K of 8-bit memory, a 6522 versatile interface adapter (VIA), a 20-mA TTY current loop for making hard copies, and a cassette (audio) interface to allow storage of programs on ordinary audio tape. One feature of the KIM-1 tape interface not found on others of the era is the ability to search for programs on the tape by a designator applied to the beginning of the program on the cassette.

The SYM-1 is a more recent single-board trainer computer that uses the KIM-1 bus. The SYM-1, however, is still easily obtained and contains more features than the original KIM-1. For the *aficionado* of the KIM-1, the SYM-1 is a good substitute.

The AIM-65 (Rockwell Microelectronics, Inc.) is a more advanced microcomputer based on the KIM bus. The AIM-65 computer uses a standard ASCII typewriter keyboard instead of the hexadecimal pad of the KIM-1. It also has a 20-character 5 × 7 dot matrix LED display and a 20-column 5 × 7 dot matrix thermal printer instead of the standard seven-segment LED readouts of the KIM-1 (which require some training to read hexadecimal digits above 9). The printer uses standard calculator printer paper, which is available at stationery stores.

The AIM-65 also has a sophisticated monitor program stored in ROM and the ability to incorporate BASIC and a 6502 assembler into other on-board ROMs. In contrast, the KIM-1 originally used a relatively simple monitor. To write and input programs, one had to fingerbone instructions into the computer on a step-by-step basis. The AIM-65 comes with a text editor. Also, the AIM-65 can be configured with either 1K or 4K of memory, and external memory to 48K can be added if desired.

Two interfacing connectors are etched onto the boards of the KIM-1, SYM-1, and AIM-65 computers. The *applications connector* is basically an I/O connector, while the *expansion connector* is more similar to a genuine bus connector. Both are of primary interest to microprocessor users who must interface the computer with an external device. Pinouts are described in Table 8-4 for the applications connector and in Table 8-5 for the expansion connector.

TABLE 8-4   KIM-1/SYM-1/AIM-65 APPLICATIONS CONNECTOR

Pin No.[a]	Designation	Function
1	GND	Ground
2	PA3	Port A, bit 3

TABLE 8-4   KIM-1/SYM-1/AIM-65 Applications Connector—*Continued*

Pin No.[a]	Designation	Function
3	PA2	Port A, bit 2
4	PA1	Port A, bit 1
5	PA4	Port A, bit 4
6	PA5	Port A, bit 5
7	PA6	Port A, bit 6
8	PA7	Port A, bit 7
9	PB0	Port B, bit 0
10	PB1	Port B, bit 1
11	PB2	Port B, bit 2
12	PB3	Port B, bit 3
13	PB4	Port B, bit 4
14	PA0	Port A, bit 0
15	PB7	Port B, bit 7
16	PB5	Port B, bit 5
17	KB RO	Keyboard row 0
18	KB CF	Keyboard column F
19	KB CB	Keyboard column B
20	KB CE	Keyboard column E
21	KB CA	Keyboard column A
22	KB CD	Keyboard column D
A	+5	+5-V dc from main board power supply.
B	K0	
C	K1	
D	K2	
E	K3	Memory-bank select signals (active-low).
F	K4	
H	K5	
J	K7	

TABLE 8-4   KIM-1/SYM-1/AIM-65 APPLICATIONS CONNECTOR—*Continued*

Pin No.[a]	Designation	Function
K	Decode	Memory decode signal. Used to increase memory capacity with off-board memory devices.
L	AUD IN	Audio input from cassette.
M	AUDOUTL	Low-level audio output to cassette with "microphone" input.
N	+12	+12-V dc power from main board.
P	AUDOUTH	High-level audio output to cassette player with "line" input.
R	TTYKBD+	Positive terminal of 20-mA teletype keyboard loop.
S	TTYPNT+	Positive terminal of 20-mA teletypewriter printer loop.
T	TTYKBD−	Negative terminal of 20-mA teletypewriter keyboard loop.
U	TTYPNT−	Negative terminal of 20-mA teletypewriter printer loop.
V	KB R3	Keyboard row 3
W	KB CG	Keyboard column G
X	KB R2	Keyboard row 2
Y	KB CC	Keyboard column C
Z	KB R1	Keyboard row 1

[a]Numbered connector pins are on the top or component side of the printed wiring board; alphabetic pins are on the bottom or foil side of the board.

The KIM-1 and related computers use the 6522 VIA device. The 6522 contains two 8-bit I/O ports, designated ports A and B. These ports are represented by bits PA0 to PA7 and PB0 to PB7. Both ports can be configured under software control for either input or output port service on a bit-by-bit basis. In other words, PA0 might be an input bit, while PA1 is an output port bit. Or we can configure all 8 bits of either or both ports as either input or output.

TABLE 8-5 KIM-1/SYM-1/AIM-65 EXPANSION CONNECTOR

Pin No.	Designation	Function
1	SYNC	Active-high output line that goes HIGH during the phase 1 clock signal during instruction fetch operations. This line is used to allow the 6502 to operate with slow memory, dynamic memory, or in the direct-memory access mode.
2	$\overline{RDY}$	Has the effect of inserting a wait state into the CPU operating cycle. See similar description for same signal in Apple II discussion.
3	01	Phase 1 clock signal
4	$\overline{IRQ}$	Maskable interrupt request line. Active-low.
5	RO	Reset overflow input. A negative-edge triggered input that will reset the overflow flip-flop in the CPU.
6	$\overline{NMI}$	Active-low nonmaskable interrupt input line. This interrupt line cannot be masked by the internal interrupt flip-flop.
7	$\overline{RST}$	In parallel with the reset line on the 6502 and on the microcomputer. When brought LOW, this line will cause the program counter inside of the 6502 to be loaded with 00H. The effect of this line is to form a hardware "JUMP to 00H" instruction.
8	DB7	Data bus bit 7
9	DB6	Data bus bit 6
10	DB5	Data bus bit 5
11	DB4	Data bus bit 4
12	DB3	Data bus bit 3
13	DB2	Data bus bit 2
14	DB1	Data bus bit 1

TABLE 8-5   KIM-1/SYM-1/AIM-65 EXPANSION CONNECTOR—*Continued*

Pin No.	Designation	Function
15	DB0	Data bus bit 0
16	K6	Address decoder output that goes HIGH whenever the CPU addresses a location from 1800H to 1BFFH.
17	SSTOUT	Single-step output
18	(NC)	No connection
19	(NC)	No connection
20	(NC)	No connection
21	+5	+5-V dc power supply from main board.
22	GND	Ground
A	AB0	Address bus bit 0
B	AB1	Address bus bit 1
C	AB2	Address bus bit 2
D	AB3	Address bus bit 3
E	AB4	Address bus bit 4
F	AB5	Address bus bit 5
H	AB6	Address bus bit 6
J	AB7	Address bus bit 7
K	AB8	Address bus bit 8
L	AB9	Address bus bit 9
M	AB10	Address bus bit 10
N	AB11	Address bus bit 11
P	AB12	Address bus bit 12
R	AB13	Address bus bit 13
S	AB14	Address bus bit 14
T	AB15	Address bus bit 15
U	02	Phase 2 block signal
V	R/$\overline{W}$	Read/write line is HIGH during read operations and LOW during write operations.

TABLE 8-5   KIM-1/SYM-1/AIM-65 EXPANSION CONNECTOR—*Continued*

Pin No.	Designation	Function
W	R/$\overline{\text{W}}$	Complement of the R/$\overline{\text{W}}$ line. This line is LOW for read operations and HIGH for write operations.
X	PLLTST	Phase-locked-loop test. This line is used in testing and adjusting the PLL that operates the audio cassette tape recorder audio FM signal.
Y	$\overline{02}$	Complement of phase-2 clock signal.
Z	RAMRW	Line turns on RAM during read/write operations during phase-2 clock periods.

9
Interfacing Standard Peripherals

Rarely will a computer stand alone for long. It is almost certain that the owner will want to add capability by incorporating peripherals into the system. There is an almost endless variety of peripherals that perform a large assortment of different jobs. The strong desire for hardcopy readouts instead of volatile video prints will likely cause the microcomputer owner to buy a printer or teletypewriter. Other peripherals include remote CRT/video terminals, device controllers or sensors, other computers in remote locations, and assorted forms of display.

Figure 9-1 shows two popular printers. The low-cost Heath/Zenith H14 device shown in Figure 9-1a is built from a kit (although it may also be purchased ready built). This printer uses a 5 × 7 dot matrix impact printer head. Because of this head the H14 does not produce letter-grade readouts, but is more than sufficient for copy that need not be sent to someone else. At the price, it is difficult to beat the H14, provided that you do not need the quality of higher-priced devices. The Heath/Zenith H14 can be user wired to interface with two popular serial data communications system, which we will discuss in this chapter: the 20-milliampere current loop and the RS-232 voltage-oriented interface.

The Diablo printer shown in Figure 9-1b is also available from Heath/Zenith, as well as a number of other sources. This printer uses a daisy-wheel print mechanism that produces letter-grade print. Like the H14, this printer will respond to either 20-mA or RS-232 systems, as specified by the buyer.

Figure 9-1   (a) Heath H14 dot matrix printer; (b) Diablo Daisy Wheel Printer (*Courtesy Heath/Zenith*)

SERIAL VERSUS PARALLEL COMMUNICATIONS

Most microcomputer internal data buses are configured in a parallel format in which all 8 (or 16) bits are transmitted simultaneously. This method is an example of *parallel* data transmission and is used internally because it is the fastest method available. The disadvantage of parallel data transmission, however, is that it requires one or more separate lines for each bit of the data word. This presents little problem inside the computer where these parallel data lines are merely a few centimeters of copper track laid side by side on a small printed circuit board. But when we go outside the computer, the situation changes. For short runs, say across a table or within an equipment rack, parallel transmission is still economical, but the situation changes rapidly as distance increases. Even a few yards of wire might provide enough problems to make it worthwhile to convert to serial transmission, where a single pair of conductors carries all data. If the data have to be transmitted through media other than wire, say telephones lines or radio channels, it is extremely costly to use parallel transmission. For sending data across the country we would need the equivalent of eight telephone circuits in order to send an 8-bit data word asynchronously. But if we use serial transmission, the number of channels reduces to one.

The key to serial data transmission is a serial input/output port for the computer (see Chapter 6). There are several ways to accomplish a serial I/O port: discrete hardware, IC UART, and software UART. The discrete hardware method requires a shift register with a length equal to the number of bits in the data word. The proper form of shift register is *parallel in, serial out* (PISO). Data from the parallel data bus are input to the PISO shift register and then clocked out through the serial output one by one. This requires at least one operation for each bit of the shift register and so will take a fair amount of time. The IC UART, or universal asynchronous receiver/transmitter, is a special device that makes *parallel-to-serial* conversions for the transmitter section and *serial-to-parallel* conversions for the receiver section. These devices were discussed in detail in Chapter 6. Finally, we have the software implementation. In this type of UART the data word to be transmitted is loaded into the accumulator of the CPU, then shifted one place right or left, and output one time for each bit of the word. All three methods are used in various computers, although the discrete logic method is probably used least.

SERIAL DATA COMMUNICATION STANDARDS

The two major serial data communication standards are the 20-mA current loop and RS-232. The 20-mA current loop uses an electrical current to carry the data; the RS-232 uses voltage levels. The RS-232 is a standard of the Electronic Industries Association (EIA) and is extensively used throughout the computer industry. There are two extant RS-232 versions, the older RS-232B and the more recent (and current) RS-232C.

The RS-232 Standard

The RS-232B/C standard was issued by the EIA in an attempt to make it possible to interface equipment made by wide variety of manufacturers without the need for special engineering for each case. The idea is to use the same electrical connector (i.e., the DB-25 family of D-shell connectors) wired in the same manner all the time, and to use the same voltage levels for the binary digits 1 and 0 all the time. Supposedly, if everyone interprets the standard the same way, it should be possible to connect together any two devices with RS-232 ports without any problem, and it usually does work that way. Modems (modulator/demodulators), CRT video terminals, printers, and other devices all come with RS-232 connectors, at least as options. Some computers provide RS-232 serial output ports, and almost all have RS-232 capability available as an option from either the original computer manufacturer or a specialty house.

It is relatively easy to design an RS-232 port, especially if the application will operate asynchronously at a low data rate such as 110 baud. RS-232C receiver and transmitter integrated circuits are available from various manufacturers (e.g., Motorola). The RS-232 transmitter/buffer chip will accept TTL-level inputs and convert them to the appropriate RS-232C level for transmission. The RS-232 receiver works exactly the opposite: it will accept RS-232 input signals and convert them to equivalent TTL levels.

The RS-232 is a very old standard and predates TTL standards. As a result, the RS-232 standards use what appear to younger eyes as very odd voltage levels to recognize logical 0 and logical 1 levels. Besides voltage levels, the standard also fixes load impedances presented to the bus by receivers and the output impedances of transmitter/drivers.

There are basically two RS-232 standards (RS-232B and RS-232C), both of which are depicted in Figure 9-2. In the older version, RS-232B, logical 1 is any potential in the range from −5 to −25 V, while logical 0 is anything from +5 to +25 V. The voltages in the −3 to +3-V range are a transition state, while the ranges from ±3 to ±5 V are undefined and will produce unpredictable results if used (a situation that can occur in poorly designed systems).

The RS-232C standard uses narrower limits between logical 0 and logical 1 in order to make the data transmission speedier. The upper limits for the logical 0 and logical 1 levels are ±15 V, rather than ±25 V as in the RS-232B standard. In addition to narrowing the voltage ranges, the newer RS-232C

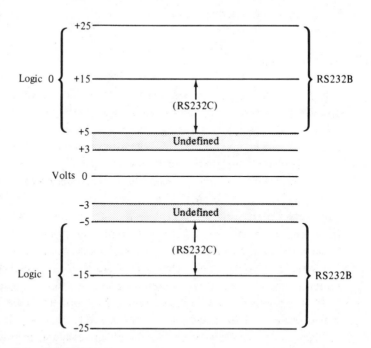

Figure 9-2 RS-232C voltage levels versus logic levels.

standard fixes the load impedance to 3000 to 7000 Ω, and the driver output impedance is lower than previously. Also, the driver must provide a slew rate of 30 volts per microsecond (30 V/μs). The Motorola MC1488 and MC1489 meet these specifications.

The RS-232 standard specifies a standard connector so that all products will be compatible. The DB-25 (i.e., the male DBM-25 and female DBF-25) D-shell connector is used for this purpose and is the identifying feature of an RS-232 equipped piece of equipment. Figure 9-3 shows the pinout designations for the RS-232C connector.

Pin No.	RS232 Name	Function
1	AA	Chassis Ground
2	BA	Data from Terminal
3	BB	Data Received from Modem
4	CA	Request to Send
5	CB	Clear to Send
6	CC	Data Set Ready
7	AB	Signal Ground
8	CF	Carrier Detection
9	undef	
10	undef	
11	undef	
12	undef	
13	undef	
14	undef	
15	DB	Transmitted Bit Clock, Internal
16	undef	
17	DD	Received Bit Clock
18	undef	
19	undef	
20	CD	Data Terminal Ready
21	undef	
22	CE	Ring Indicator
23	undef	
24	DA	Transmitted Bit Clock, External
25	undef	

Figure 9-3 EIA RS-232C DB-25 connector designations.

The electrical requirements for the RS-232C standard are as follows:

1. The *mark* (logical 1) level shall be −3 to −15 V; the *space* (logical 0) level shall be +3 to +15 V.
2. Load impedances on the receiver side of the circuit shall be greater than 3000 Ω, but less than 7000 Ω.
3. The maximum data rate is 20 kilobits/second.
4. Inputs for receivers must have a capacitance of less than 2500 picofarads (pF).
5. There should be not more than 50 feet of hardwire between inputs and outputs without an audio modem (modulator/demodulator) at each end of the circuit.
6. Standard data rates are 50, 75, 110, 150, 300, 600, 1200, 2400, 4800, 9600, and 19,200 baud.

Current Loop Transmission

The current loop form of data communications system was derived from the standard method used on teletypewriter equipment. These electromechanical typewriters were popularized in the late 1930s with equipment from companies such as Kleinschmitt and The Teletype Corporation (Skokie, Illinois). The word Teletype is a registered trademark of The Teletype Corporation, even though it is frequently used erroneously as a generic term for all teletypewriter equipments. Such use is improper, however, unless the machine being discussed was manufactured by The Teletype Corporation.

There are actually two different current loop standards: 60-mA and 20-mA. The 60-mA standard is now obsolete, but is covered here because two groups of users still occasionally use Model 15, Model 19, and Model 28 Teletypes: amateur hobbiests who buy old surplus equipment and professionals who are attempting to interface a computer with older equipment that uses 60-mA teletypewriters.

The reason why current loops became popular for teletypewriters is that the characters are selected by five or seven electrical solenoids that activate the mechanical selector bars inside the machine. These solenoids are connected in series banks of differing numbers depending upon the character being formed. As a result, voltage transmission is not as effective as current loop transmission.

There are at least three different types of current loop device: *printer only,* *keyboard only,* and *keyboard/printer combinations.* The printer-only type contains the solenoids and typing mechanism and will print the characters transmitted over the current loop. There is no method for sending data back from the printer-only machine. The keyboard-only device is exactly the opposite: it contains the encoder and keyboard but is incapable of printing. Such machines are rare and are used primarily for remote entry of data.The keyboard/printer combination machine contains both the receiver and sender sections in one cabinet. Figure 9-4 shows the circuit for a 20-mA current loop keyboard/printer teletypewriter unit. The transmitter consists of a keyboard and an encoder (that forms the data word) that can be modeled as a simple electrical switch. When the switch is closed, the circuit passes current down the 20-mA loop and to its own printer. Similarly, when the 20-mA loop is active from the other end, the current will flow in the solenoid, causing the remote print operation. Since the keyboard switch is in series with the circuit, some means must be provided to close the printer circuit during receive operations. This function is provided by switch S1, labeled in Figure 9-4 as *send-receive*.

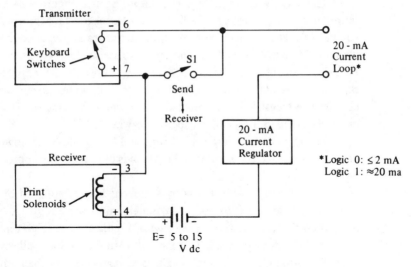

Figure 9-4 A 20-mA current loop system.

Three modes of communication are used with current-loop systems: *simplex, half-duplex* and *full-duplex*. The simplex system allows communication in one direction only. There will be a dedicated receiver and a dedicated transmitter that never change roles; data flow is always in one direction only. The half-duplex system allows two-way communications, but only in one direction at a time. We can send data from, say, A to B one time, and then reverse the situation and transmit from B to A; we may never, however, simultaneously send data from A to B and from B to A. Simplex and half-duplex current loops require only one pair of wires, while full-duplex normally requires two pairs of wires (one for each direction). Note, however, that full duplex operation over a single pair of wires is possible if the data levels are first converted to audio tones. In that case, the system will use different pairs of tones to represent *mark* and *space,* one pair for each direction.

60-Milliampere Current Loops. The 60-mA current loop is now obsolete and is no longer found except in the case of old installations or where old surplus equipment is used. The 60-mA system shown in Figure 9-5 shows how one of these teletypewriters can be interfaced to the TTL-compatible serial output port. In many cases, one bit of a parallel output port will be configured as a serial port through either software or hardware implementation. In Figure 9-5, the least significant bit (LSB) of the parallel output port is designated as the serial output.

The TTL level from the serial output port in Figure 9-5a drives the base terminal of a high-voltage, NPN power transistor (a Motorola MJE-340 or equivalent). The collector-emitter path of the transistor is connected in series with the 60-mA current loop and so acts as a switch. When the TTL level is HIGH, transistor Q1 is turned on and current flows in the loop. However, when the TTL bit is LOW, the transistor is turned off, so no current will flow in the circuit. The transistor therefore provides a *mark* (i.e., logical 1) when the TTL bit is HIGH, and a *space* (i.e., logical 0) when LOW.

The current loop is powered from a 120- to 140-V dc power supply that has a series-connected rheostat (R2), which is used to set the approximate current level.

The current level in the 60-mA current loop is adjusted by breaking the loop and inserting a 0 to 100 milliammeter into the circuit. A key should be pressed on the keyboard, or in the case of Figure 9-5a, a HIGH must be written to the serial output port. That action will turn on the loop, allowing current to flow. Potentiometer R2, which is rheostat connected, is then adjusted for approximately 60-mA current flow.

The circuit in Figure 9-5a suffers from a problem. When the 60-mA current flows in the solenoids, a magnetic field is built up around each coil. Abruptly interrupting the current (i.e., going to a space bit) will cause the field to collapse, giving rise to a high voltage spike created by the *inductive kick* phenomenon. As a result of this spike, which can damage semiconductor devices, we must provide some means of suppression. This function is provided by diode D1, a 1000-V PIV, 1-A rectifier-type diode. Diode D1 is normally reverse biased,

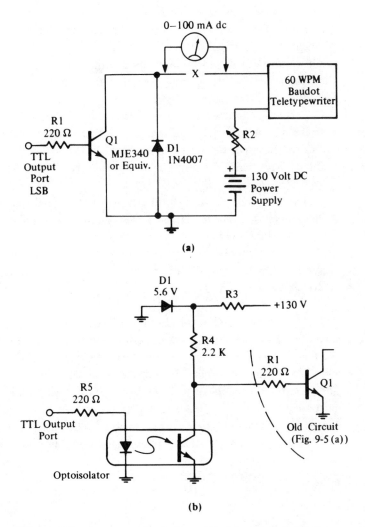

Figure 9-5 A 60-mA current-loop for teletypewriters (obsolete models): (a) regular circuit; (b) isolated circuit.

except when the spike is present, so it will clip off the spike before it has the chance to do any damage.

There is a further problem: *isolation.* High-voltage, high-current circuits can cause "glitches" in the computer that alter data and interrupt the process. In fact, this problem is one of the worst defects in some types of computer. The solution is to completely isolate the current loop from the computer through a device called an *optoisolator.*

Figure 9-5b shows the use of an optoisolator between the computer and the current-loop peripehral. An optoisolator is an IC-like device that contains a light-emitting diode (LED) juxtaposed with a phototransistor. When the LED illuminates the phototransistor, the transistor is turned on; when the LED is dark, the phototransistor is off.

If the TTL output port has sufficient drive and will source current, we may use the circuit as shown. If, on the other hand, a normal open-collector output port is used, we must connect the 220-Ω resistor in Figure 9-5b to +5 V and connect the TTL output bit to the cathode of the LED (which is shown as grounded in Figure 9-5b).

The transistor in the optoisolator will not normally operate from a 130-V dc source, so a lower voltage power supply must be provided. We could provide a separate low-voltage power supply or derive a low voltage from the +130-V power supply. In Figure 9-5b we use a 5.6-V zener diode (D1) and a current-limiting resistor (R3) to provide a low-voltage consistent with the needs of the phototransistor.

20-Milliampere Current Loops.   The newer current-loop standard uses a current of 20 mA for the mark condition and a current of 0 to 2 mA for the space condition. The 20-mA current loop was used on the Model 33 Teletype and all subsequent models. There was also a code change with these models. The older 60-mA machines used the 5-bit Baudot Code, while 20-mA machines most frequently use the modern ASCII (American Standard Code for Information Interchange) code: keep that in mind when using older machines.

Figure 9-6 shows a simple method for using an optoisolator to interface

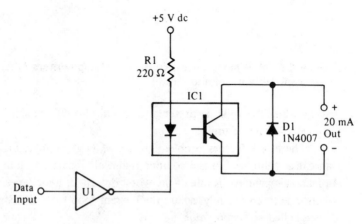

Figure 9-6   Isolated 20-mA current loop connection to computer output bit.

a computer serial output port with a 20-mA current loop. The operation of this circuit is exactly like that of Figure 9-5b. When the data input is HIGH, indicating a mark or logical 1 condition, the output of the open-collector inverter (U1) will go LOW, thereby grounding the cathode of the LED. This will turn on the transistor, which allows current to flow in the circuit. Again, a reverse-biased diode is used to prevent damage and other troubles caused by the inductive spike generated when the solenoids are de-energized.

A transmitting version is shown in Figure 9-7. Here we have a keyboard or 20-mA transmitter sending data to a computer that has a TTL-compatible input. A dc power supply (+5 to +15 V) and a pair of series resistors are selected to provide a current of 20-mA or so when switch S1 is closed. We must assume that R1 is much greater than R2. When switch S1 is open, there is no current flow, so the voltage at point A will be HIGH. A double inverter sequence makes the output of the circuit HIGH also. If, however, the switch is closed, current flows in the circuit, so a voltage drop is created across R1 and R2. If R1 is much greater than R2, the input of U1 sees a LOW condition.

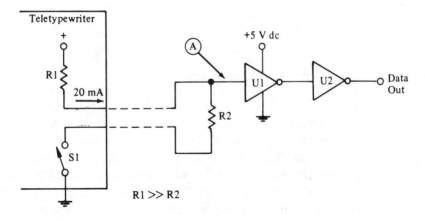

Figure 9-7 Keyboard (20 mA) interface for computer.

A somewhat more satisfying circuit is shown in Figure 9-8. This circuit uses an optoisolator with the LED in series with the current loop to interface with the computer. When the current flows in the loop, the LED is turned on, so the phototransistor is illuminated and turned on. When the transistor is on, the resistance from collector to emitter is very low, so the input of the inverter (IC2) sees a LOW. If the LED is off, indicating a space, the transistor is off. This condition makes the collector-emitter resistance high, so the voltage applied to the input is also high; the input of IC2 is HIGH. The values of resistor R1 and the supply voltage (shown in Figure 9-8 as +5 V) can be varied to other values if TTL-compatibility is not needed. Of course, IC2 cannot be a TTL inverter in that case; a CMOS 4049 or 4050 is recommended.

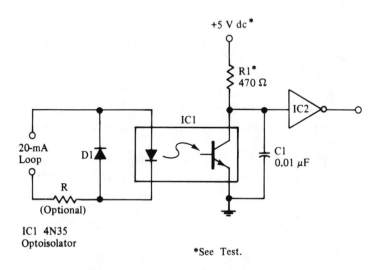

Figure 9-8   Isolated 20-mA loop interface.

Figure 9-9a shows the connections to the popular Model-33 Teletype. The terminal strip shown in this figure is normally found on the right-rear panel (viewed from the operator's seat) under a cover. Be careful to unplug the teletypewriter from the 110-V ac when accessing this terminal strip because that potential is found on pins 1 and 2 of the strip. Isolated versions of the receive and transmit circuits are shown in Figures 9-9b and 9-9c, respectively.

Handshaking

Most peripherals can operate in an asynchronous manner only at slower data rates (e.g., 300 baud and less). Once the speed becomes greater than 300 baud or when there is a tremendous difference in speed between the two devices, we must use synchronous operation. This method of interfacing generally requires a system called *handshaking,* which is a system of interrogation and acknowledgment of readiness to send or receive data. A sender unit will send a signal to the receiver when data are available. The receiver, in turn, will acknowledge that it is taking the data by sending a second signal back to the transmitter,

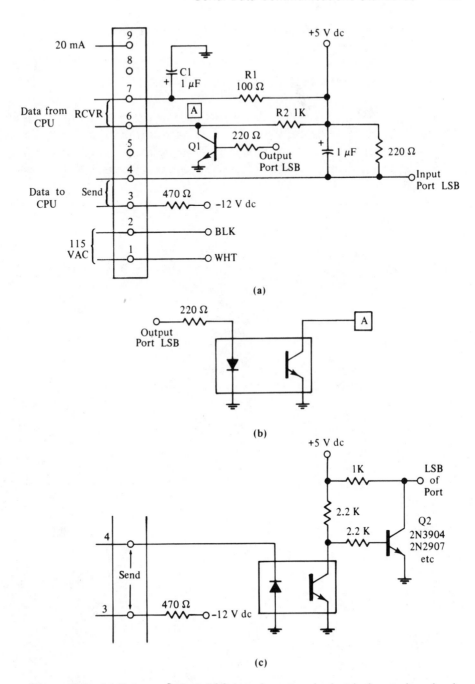

Figure 9-9 (a) Teletype^R Model-33 interface terminal strip located on back of machine; (b) isolation modification; (c) keyboard interface to microcomputer input port.

thereby resetting the data ready signal. Some devices will provide two-way handshaking.

General Purpose Interface Bus: GPIB, IEEE-488

The GPIB is a system that allows interconnection of up to 15 electronic instruments or devices so that they can interact with each other. There are three categories of device on the GPIB: talkers, listeners, and controllers. The system is programmable and so can form the basis of automatic test equipment systems.

10
Interface Software Methods

The art of interfacing with microcomputers and microprocessors is essentially an exercise in input/output strategies. Although memory interfacing chores have basically the same requirements as other interfacing, most microcomputers come with either a full set of memory or the provision to easily add extra memory. We have discussed I/O hardware in Chapter 6, so we will now confine our discussion to I/O software methods.

Two different situations may be faced by various readers. In one case, it will be necessary to generate a device-select pulse to select an I/O port or some peripheral device that connects to the data bus. In other cases, it might be necessary to execute a simple I/O operation and then do something with the data besides leaving it in the accumulator.

Different microprocessor chips handle I/O operations differently. In some, like the Z80, there will be a set of specific I/O instructions. In the Z80, the 8-bit I/O port address selects 256 different I/O ports (0 to 255). During the execution of I/O instructions, the 8-bit port address appears on the lower-order byte (A0–A7) of the address bus. If the instruction is an output operation, the contents of the accumulator pass over the high-order byte of the address bus (A8–A15). The main data channel to and from the accumulator for both input and output operations is the 8-bit *data bus*.

Other microprocessor chips, like the 6502, use memory-mapped I/O. In this type of system, I/O functions are allocated to locations in memory. I/O components are wired into the circuit as if they were memory components. Software strategies will differ slightly for this type of device.

We find that there are three different strategies for handling interface input. In all three, we assume that an outside device is either turned on or off by the computer or wants to send or receive data to the computer. One method requires the microcomputer to *continuously* poll an I/O port looking for new data. The second method calls for the microcomputer to *periodically* poll an input port for new data. During the rest of the time it is free to perform other chores. Finally, we have the interrupt method. In this type of operation, the CPU executes the main program until an external device activates the CPU interrupt line. After the interrupt signal is received, the CPU will complete the operation currently being executed and then jump to an interrupt subroutine. Later in this chapter we will examine interrupt functions and hardware to facilitate the interrupt capabilities of the microprocessor; the Z80 will be used as the example, but other microprocessors have similar functions.

GENERATING TIMING LOOPS

Unless a system has a built-in hardware timer (many do), it may sometimes be necessary to generate timing loops in software. There are several instructions in both 6502 and Z80 machines that will facilitate this type of operation. But before examining actual microprocessor instructions, let's consider the overall software strategy.

Figures 10-1 and 10-2 give flow diagrams for typical timing loop subroutines. It is assumed that the microprocessor contains X and Y index registers, although the technique will work on any register or memory location that can be either decremented or incremented (the former is preferred) by software instructions. In fact, there is one instruction in the Z80 repertoire that makes it desirable on that chip to use the B register for timing subroutines.

Both subroutines (Figures 10-1 and 10-2) depend upon the system clock to set the time duration. Every subroutine requires a certain number of clock cycles to execute. A typical subroutine for Figure 10-1 in 6502 language may require five clock cycles. At a system clock rate of 1 mHz, each cycle will require one microsecond (1 μs), so the time to complete each loop is 5 μs.

The basic technique is to load index register X (or whichever location is selected) with the number of times the loop must be exercised, less the time required to enter and exit the subroutine (i.e., JSR, LDX, and RTS instructions) to form the desired duration. The X register is then decremented and tested for the condition X = 0. As long as X $\neq$ 0, the program will branch backward

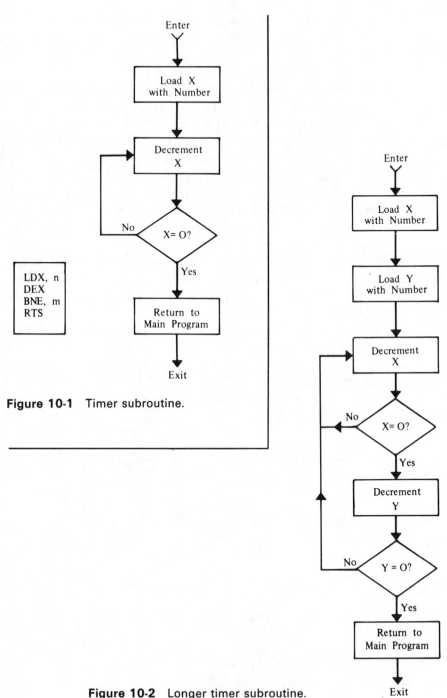

Figure 10-1   Timer subroutine.

Figure 10-2   Longer timer subroutine.

and decrement X one more time. When the required number of iterations has expired, X will be zero and the program can exit the loop to return to the main program.

Using the 6502 example, we know that each loop requires 5 μs. In addition, there is the overhead of 8 μs internally and 6 μs for the JSR instruction. Suppose we want to generate a 0.5-ms (i.e., 500 μs) time delay. We have an 8-μs overhead, so the loop time is (500 $-$ 8) or 492 μs. To find the number of loops required, we must divide the total loop time by the time required to execute each loop: (492 μs/5μs) $= 98_{10}$ executions of the loop. Since $98_{10} = 52H$ (hexadecimal), we will load 52H into the X register.

The instructions required for execution of the timing loop in 6502 language are LDX,n (load X with number n), DEX (decrement X), BNE,aa (branch forward or backward by displacement aa on result equal to nonzero), and, of course, RTS (return from subroutine).

Let's look at a typical 6502 program to generate a 500-μs time delay. We will locate the subroutine at memory location 0F00H. To call this subroutine, thereby creating our 500-μs delay, we would use the JSR 0F00H (jump to subroutine at location 0F00H) instruction.

Table 10-1 shows a sample program in 6502 language. This subroutine can be changed for any time delay from 13 to 1275 μs (i.e., 1.275 ms) by changing the index stored in the X register to a hexadecimal number from 01H to FFH, respectively.

TABLE 10-1   PROGRAM LISTING

Step No.	Memory Location	Mnemonic	Code	No. Cycles	Remarks
1	0F00H	LDX,52H	A2	2	
	0F01	(data)	62	—	
2	0F02	DEX	CA	2	Decrement X register
	0F03	BNE	D0	2	Branch to 0F03 on X $\neq$ 0
	0F04	(data)	FD	—	Two's complement of -3
3	0F05	RST	60	6	Return to main program

A Z80 implementation of Figure 10-1 may well use the B register because there is a single 3-bit instruction that handles all of step 2: DJNZ (decrement B and jump on nonzero).

Figure 10-2 shows an extension of the concept of Figure 10-1. In this example, both X and Y registers are used such that the loop containing X is nested within the loop containing Y. Like the previous example, a minimum time delay is associated with the overhead. In this case, the internal overhead is 20 μs, with a 6-μs offset due to the JSR instruction (affects both Figures 10-1 and 10-2), for a total overhead of 26 μs. The minimum duration occurs with 01H loaded into both X and Y registers. As with the previous example, the minimum resolution is 5 μs (the 1-LSB value of X). Thus, we can generate timing delays of 26 μs (X = Y = 01H) to 325,125 μs (X = Y = FFH).

GENERATING SOFTWARE PERIPHERAL/ DEVICE-SELECT PULSES

In Chapter 6 we discussed hardware-generated device-select pulses. These pulses are generated by combining certain control and address signals to turn on I/O ports. But we also sometimes use bits of existing I/O ports to provide device selection, which is the subject of this section.

Figure 10-3a shows a hypothetical situation in which up to eight peripherals can be signaled without the need for decoding. A single output port, which we see here as memory-mapped at location A003, serves the signaling function. All bits of port 2 are normally kept LOW (i.e., 00H), so the bit line connected to the desired device is brought HIGH for a time T when that device is commanded by the computer to turn on. In the example shown, peripheral 4 is connected to bit B3 of port 2, so to turn on only that one device we would write 00001000_2 (or 08H) to location A003.

Note that adding 8-bit decoding to each peripheral will permit us to uniquely address up to 255 devices with one *all-off* state, or 256 devices if there is no all-off state. If we designate 00H as the all-off signal, the 255 codes from 01H to FFH will each be available to turn on one device. Such an application, incidentally, requires all 8-bits of the output port to be connected to all peripherals and probably necessitates using a high-power 8-bit line driver or buffer for the output port.

A typical program flow for this application is shown in Figure 10-3b. We are assuming here that output port 2 is memory-mapped to location A003, and its companion input port 2 is at A004. The input port receives the data that

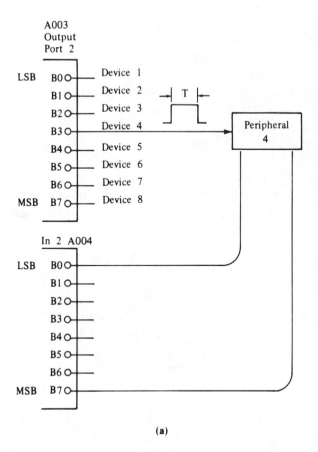

(a)

Figure 10-3 Peripheral control via 1 bit of output port; (b) subroutine operation.

the peripheral wants to deliver. If there is no need for data from the peripheral, input port 2 is not used. Such an application might make use of the computer to turn on lights, certain other devices, and so forth.

The program also assumes that a time-delay subroutine (Table 10-1) is stored at location 0F00H. Peripheral 3 requires a turn-on pulse of not less than 250 μs. If the time-delay routine loads the X register with 32H, the time delay will be 264 μs, providing a margin of error. (*Note:* 32H $=$ 50$_{10}$; 50$_{10}$ $\times$ 5 μs $=$ 250 μs; 250 μs $+6$ μs for JSR $+$ 8 μs internal delay yields 264 μs.)

When executing the main program, the computer comes across the device-select segment at location 0300H. The first instruction (LDA #08H) loads into the accumulator the binary number 00001000$_2$, or 08H. This number will form

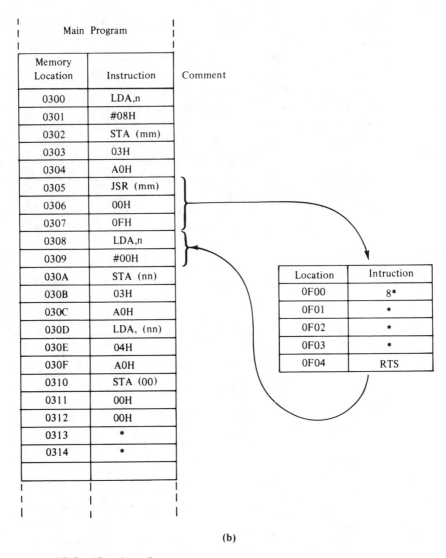

Memory Location	Instruction	Comment
0300	LDA,n	
0301	#08H	
0302	STA (mm)	
0303	03H	
0304	A0H	
0305	JSR (mm)	
0306	00H	
0307	0FH	
0308	LDA,n	
0309	#00H	
030A	STA (nn)	
030B	03H	
030C	A0H	
030D	LDA, (nn)	
030E	04H	
030F	A0H	
0310	STA (00)	
0311	00H	
0312	00H	
0313	*	
0314	*	

Main Program

Location	Intruction
0F00	8*
0F01	*
0F02	*
0F03	*
0F04	RTS

(b)

Figure 10-3 *(Continued)*

the bit pattern on part 2 that will make B3 HIGH (turning on device 4) and all others LOW. The following instruction (STA A003) stores #08H from the accumulator in location A003, which is the memory location allocated to port 2. The program will then jump to the 264-μs subroutine located at 0F00H. Since port 2 is a latching-type circuit, bit B3 remains HIGH for 264 μs. When program control returns to the main program at location 0306H, the instruction sequence requires #00H to be loaded into port 2 at A003. This sequence returns all bits of port 2 to LOW.

If the external device is to input data to the computer, a simple instruction sequence must be followed. In our example of Figure 10-3b, we will input data from port 2 at A004 and then store it at location 0500H.

In some cases, the program will, like the example, operate asynchronously. This protocol assumes that the data at the peripheral will be ready and valid at the end of the 264-μs period of the device-select pulse. If this is not the case, some sort of scheme must be provided to have the CPU wait until the peripheral indicates that it is ready to transmit data. Such schemes are sometimes called *handshaking* routines. In the simplest case, the computer just loops, doing nothing until a *data ready* signal is received. The computer will then input the data and, sometimes, send a *data received* signal back to the peripheral.

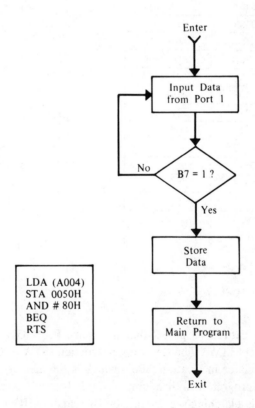

Figure 10-4   Keyboard data input routine.

SAMPLE KEYBOARD ROUTINE

Most microcomputers use the American Standard Code for Information Interchange (ASCII) encoded keyboards, which use 7 bits to represent 128 different alphanumeric symbols and control signals. We can apply the seven parallel ASCII lines to the lower 7 bits of a computer input port.

The eighth bit of the input port is reserved for the *strobe* signal generated by the keyboard. This bit is a *data ready* signal that tells the computer that the data on B0 to B6 are valid. Prior to an active strobe being received, the keyboard data would be either 00H, 7FH, or trash (the usual case), depending upon design.

In the example of Figure 10-4, it is assumed that the strobe signal is active high. The program inputs data from the port located at A004 and then stores it in memory (this is done to save the data). We must then test the data (which are still in the accumulator) to determine if the most significant bit (B7) is 1 or 0.

The strategy for ascertaining the state of B7 is to perform a logical-AND operation between the data in the accumulator and a binary number that will yield a 1 only when the tested bit is also a 1. Let's review the rules for logical-AND:

0 AND 0 = 0

1 AND 0 = 0

0 AND 1 = 0

1 AND 1 = 1

If we wish to mask an 8-bit word stored in the accumulator to find B7 = 1, we would AND the accumulator with 10000000_2 (i.e., 80H). If B7 is LOW (i.e., 0), the AND instruction will yield 00000000_2 (00H), no matter what state the other bits take on. If the result is 00H, therefore, we will branch back to the instruction that inputs data from A004. The program will loop through this program until a valid word is received, as indicated by B7 = 1. In that case, the program will exit the keyboard subroutine and return to the main program with the keyboard data stored in 0050H (or whatever other location that the programmer selected; there is nothing special about 0050H).

INTERRUPTS

One very useful feature of most (perhaps all) computers is *interrupt* capability. An interrupt permits the CPU to occupy itself with other more profitable chores than looping while some sluggish peripheral makes up its mind to transmit data. The interrupt capability may also be used for alarms and other applications. In other words, an *interrupt* is a process in which a computer stops executing the main program and begins executing another program located somewhere else in memory. This is not a mere "jump" or "call" operation, but a response to an external stimulus.

There are several reasons why an interrupt capability may be required. One of these is the case of an *alarm* condition. We could, for example, use a computer in an environmental control system, and use the interrupt capability to allow response to alarm situations (e.g., smoke detector, liquid level, burglar alarm, overtemperature). The computer would ordinarily go about some other chore, perhaps the business of controlling the system. But once during the execution of each instruction of the program, the CPU will interrogate the interrupt system. It is thus monitoring the alarm status while executing some unrelated program. When an interrupt is received, indicating an alarm status, the computer would jump immediately to the program that *services* the interrupt—rings a bell, calls the fire department, turns on a light, and the like.

Another application is to input data that occur only occasionally or whose periodicity is so long as to force the computer to do nothing for an inordinate amount of time. A real-time clock, or timer, for example, might want to update its input to the computer only once per second or once per minute. An analog-to-digital converter (ADC) might have a 20-ms conversion time. Even the slower version of the Z80 CPU chip (using a 2.5-mHz clock) can perform hundreds of thousands of operations while waiting for the ADC to complete its conversion job. Since the ADC will not provide valid data until after the conversion time expires, waiting for those data would be a tremendous waste of CPU time.

Another use is to input or output data to or from a peripheral device such as a line printer, teletypewriter, keyboard, or terminal. These electromechanical devices are notoriously slow to operate. Even so-called "high-speed" line printers are considerably slower than the Z80 CPU. A classic example is the "standard" 100-word-per-minute teletypewriter. A "word," in this case, is five ASCII characters, so we have to output 500 characters per minute to operate at top speed. This is a rate of 8 characters per second, so each character requires 1/8 of a second, or 125 ms, to print. The CPU, on the other hand, is considerably faster. It can output the character to the input buffer of the teletypewriter in something like 3 μs. The Z80 can execute almost 42,000 outputs in the time it takes the teletypewriter to print just one character.

There are at least two ways to handle this situation, and both involve having the peripheral device signal the CPU when it is ready to accept another character. This is done by using a strobe pulse from the peripheral, issued when it is ready to receive (or deliver) another data byte. One way to handle this problem is to have the programmer write in a periodic poll of the peripheral. The strobe pulse is applied to 1 bit of an input port. A program is written that periodically examines that bit to see if it is HIGH. If it is found to be HIGH, the program control will jump to a subroutine that services the peripheral. But this approach is still wasteful of CPU time, and places undue constraint on the programmer's freedom.

A superior method is to use the computer's interrupt capability. The peripheral strobe pulse becomes an *interrupt request.* When the CPU recognizes the interrupt request, it transfers program control to an interrupt service sub-routine (i.e., a program that performs some function required for the operation of the peripheral that generates the interrupt). When the service program is completed, control is transferred back to the main program at the point where it left off. Note that the CPU does not recognize an interrupt request until after it has finished executing the current instruction. Program control then returns to the *next* instruction in the main program that would have been executed had no interrupt occurred.

Types of Z80 Interrupt

There are two basic types of interrupt recognized by the Z80 CPU; *nonmaskable* and *maskable.* The nonmaskable interrupt is executed next in sequence regardless of any other considerations. Maskable interrupts, however, depend upon the condition of an interrupt flip-flop inside of the Z80. If the programmer wishes to mask (i.e., ignore) an interrupt, the appropriate flip-flip is turned off. There are three distinct forms of maskable interrupt in the Z80, and these take the designations *mode 0, mode 1,* and *mode 2.*

There are two interrupt input terminals on the Z80 chip. The $\overline{\text{NMI}}$ (pin 17) is for the nonmaskable interrupt, while the $\overline{\text{INT}}$ is for the maskable interrupts.

The nonmaskable interrupt ($\overline{\text{NMI}}$) is much like a *restart* instruction, except that it automatically causes program control to jump to memory location 00 66 (hex), instead of to one of the eight standard restart addresses. Location 00 66 (hex) must be reserved by the programmer for some instruction in the interrupt service program, very often an unconditional jump to some other location higher in memory.

The mode 0 maskable interrupt causes the Z80 to pretend that it is an 8080A, preserving some of the software compatibility between the two CPUs. During a mode 0 interrupt, the interrupting device places any valid instruction on the CPU data bus, and the CPU executes this instruction. The time of execution will be the normal time period for that type of instruction, plus two clock pulses. In most cases, the interrupting device will place a *restart* instruction on the data bus, because all of these are 1-byte instructions. The restart instructions transfer program control to one of eight page 0 locations.

Any time that a $\overline{\text{RESET}}$ pulse is applied (i.e., pin 26 of the Z80 is brought LOW), the CPU automatically goes to the mode 0 condition. This interrupt mode, like the other two maskable interrupt modes, can be set from software by executing the appropriate instruction (in this case, an IM0 instruction).

The mode 1 interrupt is selected by execution of an IM1 instruction. Mode 1 is totally under software control and cannot be accessed by using a hardware action. Once set, the mode 1 interrupt is actuated by bringing the $\overline{\text{INT}}$ line LOW momentarily. In mode 1, the Z80 will execute a restart to location 00 38 (hex).

The mode 2 interrupt is, perhaps, the most powerful of the Z80 interrupts. It allows an *indirect* call to any location in memory. The 8080A device (and the Z80 operating in mode 0) permits only eight interrupt lines. But in mode 2, the Z80 can respond to as many as 128 different interrupt lines.

Mode 2 interrupts are said to be *vectored,* because they can be made to jump to any location in the 65,536 bytes of memory.

INTERRUPT HARDWARE

In this section we will discuss some of the circuitry needed to support the Z80 interrupt capability. Note that the primary emphasis will be on low-cost circuits not necessarily intended originally for use with the Z80. Keep in mind, however, that Zilog, Mostek, and others manufacture sophisticated interrupt controller devices or build into PIO and SIO chips the ability to control interrupts.

Interrupt Requests

In the simplest cases, interrupt request lines can be built simply by extending the $\overline{\text{INT}}$ and/or $\overline{\text{NMI}}$ lines to the peripheral device. This assumes a very simple arrangement in which only one peripheral is to be serviced. Figure 10-5 shows

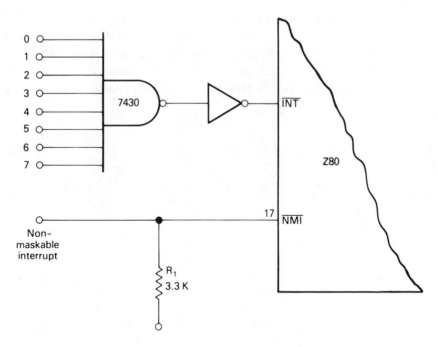

Figure 10-5 Interrupt interfacing.

how this might be accomplished. The $\overline{\text{NMI}}$ line (pin 17) is brought out as a nonmaskable interrupt line. The optional pull-up resistor (R1) is used to ensure that pin 17 remains at the **HIGH** condition, and thereby helps reduce noise response.

The $\overline{\text{INT}}$ line can be treated in exactly the same manner if there is to be but one interrupting peripheral. But in this case, we have demonstrated how the same pin might be used to recognize up to eight interrupts. This arrangement can be used if only mode 0 is anticipated. The peripheral that generates the interrupt then places the correct restart instruction on the data bus. The specific restart instruction received tells the **CPU** which peripheral initiated the interrupt. The key to this $\overline{\text{INT}}$ circuit is the eight-input TTL NAND gate (i.e., a 7430 IC). If any one of its inputs, which form $\overline{\text{INTERRUPT REQUEST}}$ lines, goes **LOW**, the 7430 output goes **HIGH**. This forces the output of the inverter **LOW**, which creates the needed $\overline{\text{INT}}$ signal at pin 16 of the Z80.

Interrupt Acknowledge

The CPU will always finish executing the current instruction before recognizing an interrupt request. There is, therefore, a slight delay between the initial request and the time when the CPU is ready to process that request. We need some type of signal to tell the peripheral that generated the interrupt request when the CPU is ready to do business. The Z80 samples the $\overline{\text{INT}}$ line on the rising edge of the last clock pulse of the current instruction. If the $\overline{\text{INT}}$ line is LOW, the CPU responds by generating an IORQ (input/output request) signal during

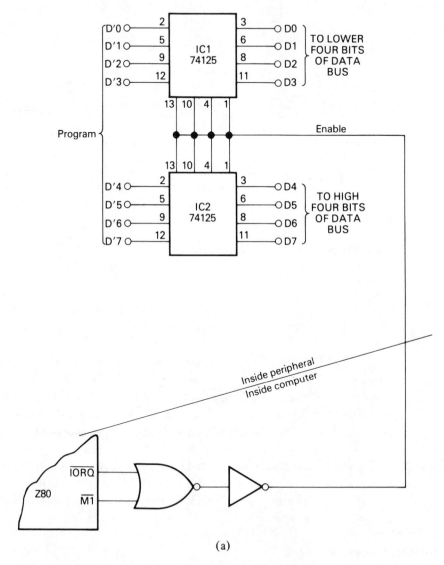

(a)

Figure 10-6   (a) Interrupt acknowledge circuit; (b) interrupt acknowledge for more than one device.

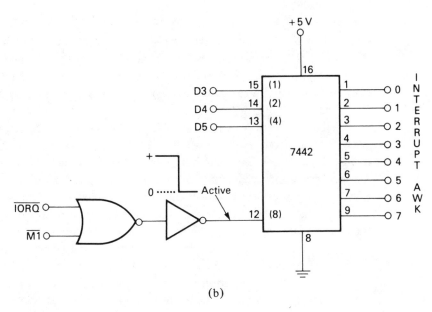

(b)

Figure 10-6 *(Continued)*

the next M1 machine cycle. We can, then, accept simultaneous existence of LOW conditions on $\overline{\text{IORQ}}$ or $\overline{\text{M1}}$ to form the interrupt acknowledge signal.

Figure 10-6a shows an interrupt acknowledge scheme that works for a single interrupt line. We assume that one of the interrupt request schemes of Figure 10-5 is also used. The 74125 (IC1/IC2) is a quad, tristate, TTL buffer. Each 74125 contains four noninverting buffer amplifiers that accept TTL inputs and provide TTL outputs. When a control line is HIGH, the associated buffer output will *float* in the high-impedance tristate mode. But if the control line is brought LOW, the buffer turns on and operates like any other TTL buffer. The control lines for all eight tristate buffers (four from each 74125) are tied together to form a single *enable* line. The 74125 devices are located inside the peripheral device.

The particular restart instruction designated to service a particular peripheral must be programmed onto the inputs of the 74125s. For example, if we want the peripheral to cause a jump to the RST 10 location (i.e., memory location 00 10), we must place D7 (hex), or 11010111 (binary), on the data bus following the acknowledgment of the interrupt request. We program this value by setting the D0, D1, D2, D4, D6, and D7 inputs of IC1/IC2 to HIGH (binary 1) and the D3 and D5 inputs to LOW (binary 0). This enable line is connected to the inverted output of the NOR gate that detects the interrupt acknowledge condition (i.e., the simultaneous LOW on $\overline{IORQ}$ and $\overline{M1}$). The enable line ordinarily remains HIGH, causing the 74125 outputs to float at high impedance. When the brief interrupt acknowledge pulse comes along, this line momentarily drops LOW, thereby transferring the word (D7 hex) at the 74125 inputs to the data bus. The CPU will decode this instruction and perform a restart jump to 00 10 (hex).

Although there is a practical limit to how many tri-state outputs one can easily float across the data bus, we find it quite easy to connect all eight allowed in mode 0, and a few more. But how do we differentiate between the peripherals? All will generate the same interrupt request, and these can be handled by using a multi-input NAND gate (see Figure 10-5 again). But how do we decode the restart instruction given and then send the interrupt acknowledgment to only the *correct* peripheral? Chaos would result if we sent the signal to all eight (or more) peripherals at the same time. It is very often to examine the range of *possible* binary words that are to be used in any given situation. For the mode 0 interrupt, we are going to use one of eight restart locations, each having its own unique RST op-code. These are listed in Table 10-2. Note that, for all possible states, only three bits change: D3, D4, and D5. The other bits (D0, D1, D2, D6, and D7) remain constant in all cases (in this particular example, they are all HIGH, but the *important* thing is that they remain at one level in all cases). We can, then, press the 7442 1-of-10 decoder into service once again (see Figure 10-6b). Recall that the 7442 is a 4-bit (BCD) to 1-of-10 decoder. The BCD inputs are weighted 1-2-4-8. The 1-2-4 inputs are connected to the D3-D4-D5 lines of the data bus. The 8 line of the 7442 is used as the control line and is connected to the interrupt acknowledge signal.

TABLE 10-2 RST *n* CODES FOR INTERRUPTS 0 to 7

Interrupt	RST n	Hexadecimal	Binary
0	00	C7	11000111
1	08	CF	11001111
2	10	D7	11010111
3	18	DF	11011111
4	20	E7	11100111
5	28	EF	11101111
6	30	F7	11110111
7	38	FF	11111111

In normal, noninterrupt operation, the 8-input of the 7442 is kept HIGH, so the lower eight outputs can never be LOW (when 8 is HIGH, only the 8 and 9 outputs can be active). But when the interrupt acknowledge signal is generated, the 7442 detects the condition of the D3-D5 lines of the data bus and issues the appropriate signal. The only problem that must be considered is the possibility that more than one peripheral will attempt to interrupt at one time. This could cause confusion, to say the least. In a moment we will consider methods for prioritizing the interrupts.

Figure 10-7 shows a decoding scheme that can be used inside the computer and will allow single line selection for up to eight interrupt lines in mode 0. We are using 74125 quad, tristate buffers in the same manner as in Figure 10-6. But notice in Table 10-2 that the least significant 4 bits of each restart instruction op-code are always either a 7 or F (both hex). Furthermore, the most significant 4 bits will be one of four possible states, C, D, E, or F. We can, then, create all eight possible op-codes by using only six 74125s and some gates, instead of 16 (as would be required if Figure 10-6 were implemented for all eight). The inputs of the 74125s are programmed as follows:

IC1	7
IC2	F
IC3	C
IC4	D
IC5	E
IC6	F

The key to our decoding scheme is to gate on the enable lines of only the appropriate 74125s. IC1 and IC2 form the code for the least significant half-byte of the op-code. There are four interrupt lines that should turn on IC1, and the other four should turn on IC2. We may use a 7420 four-input NAND gate to select which is turned on. If any input of a NAND gate goes LOW, then its output is HIGH. We connect the respective inputs of gate G1 to those interrupt

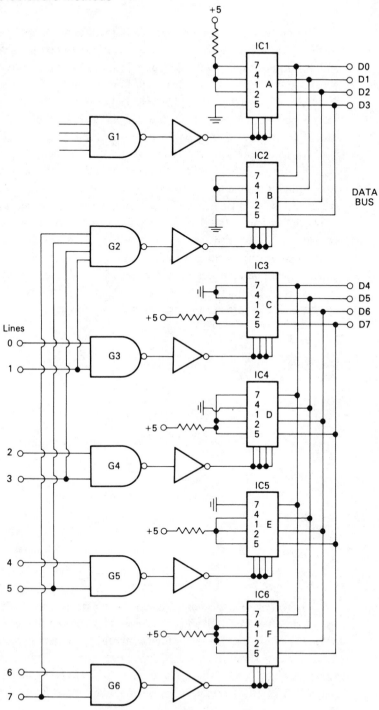

Figure 10-7 Generating RST codes for multiple-device interrupts.

lines that want a 7 in the least significant spot, that is, 0, 2, 4, and 6 (see Table 10-2). If any of these four interrupt lines goes LOW, then IC1 is turned on, and a hex 7 is output to the lower-order half-byte of the data bus. Similarly, gate G2 controls IC2. Its inputs are connected to the 1, 3, 5, and 7 interrupt lines. If any of these lines goes LOW, a hex F is output to the lower-order half-byte of the data bus.

A similar scheme is used to control the higher-order half-byte of the op-code. But in this case, we have four possibilities, each affecting two interrupt lines. IC3 to IC6 form the high-order half-byte of the op-code. Since each of these ICs affects only two interrupt lines, gates G3 to G6 need only two inputs. These are connected as follows:

Gate	Interrupt lines
G3	0, 1
G4	2, 3
G5	4, 5
G6	6, 7

If either interrupt 0 or 1 becomes active, that line will go LOW, causing the output of G_3 to go HIGH. This signal is inverted and applied to IC3, which outputs a hex C onto the data bus. Similarly, G4 to G6 will cause the appropriate 74125 to output the correct op-code when their interrupts become active.

The preceding schemes are all relatively simple, and involve the use of ordinary TTL support integrated circuits. But they all also suffer from a common malady. If more than one peripheral device decides to issue an interrupt request, chaos reigns. The logic to prioritize the interrupt response sequence is much more complex than the circuits shown thus far. Fortunately, there are special-purpose integrated circuits, designed for direct interfacing with microprocessor chips that will allow programming to prioritize and control the interrupts.

In the famous *Bugbook* series[1] a 74148 priority encoder and an Intel 8212 are used to prioritize interrupts for the 8080A. With little modification the same scheme should work on the Z80 in mode 0.

You are also permitted to use the Intel 8214 interrupt controller IC (with

---

[1]Rony, et al., *The 8080A Bugbook*, Howard W. Sams & Co., Inc., Indianapolis.

a little extra logic), even though it was designed for use with the 8080A. Both 8255 and 8257 devices are also useful in Z80 circuits.

Zilog and Mostek, the sources for the Z80, make a Z80-PIO device. This IC is an I/O controller that can handle interrupts.

SERVICING INTERRUPTS

Interrupts are a powerful tool on any programmable digital computer. The designers of the Z80 microprocessor chip, probably well aware of this fact, built into the device four ways to interrupt the CPU: nonmaskable, maskable mode 0, maskable mode 1, and maskable mode 2. Previously, we briefly discussed these interrupts and then concerned ourselves with the hardware aspects of the Z80 interrupt system. In this chapter, we will expand the topic of interrupts by considering the programming aspects of servicing the interrupt request.

Nonmaskable Interrupts

The nonmaskable interrupt is always recognized by the CPU, regardless of the programming being executed. The nonmaskable interrupt goes into effect following the completion of the instruction currently being executed, and is initiated by bringing the $\overline{\text{NMI}}$ terminal of the Z80 (i.e., pin 17) LOW. This terminal is sampled by the CPU during the last clock pulse (i.e., T period) of each machine cycle. If $\overline{\text{NMI}}$ is found to be LOW when this sample is taken, the CPU will automatically begin the interrupt sequence on the next clock pulse.

One principal difference between the nonmaskable interrupt and the maskable interrupts is that the maskables must be enabled by turning on the interrupt flip-flop (IFF1). The nonmaskable does not need to see IFF1 in a SET condition and, in fact, will cause IFF1 to RESEET in order to lock out the maskable interrupts ($\overline{\text{INT}}$).

The nonmaskable interrupt is very much like a "hardware restart" instruction. In fact, it is an RST 66 instruction (meaning that it will cause a restart instruction to be executed to location 00 66 hex). The nonmaskable interrupt cannot be disabled by software and is always recognized by bringing $\overline{\text{NMI}}$ LOW. Recall that the restart instructions caused program control to be transferred to one of eight locations in page 0. The principal difference between the eight software restart instructions and the nonmaskable interrupt are (1) $\overline{\text{NMI}}$ to a fixed location (address 00 66 hex), and (2) $\overline{\text{NMI}}$ is *hardware* implemented.

$\overline{\text{NMI}}$ is used in those situations where it is not prudent to ignore the interrupt. It may be that critical, but transitory, data may be ready to input. Or it may be an alarm condition. A program used to control the environment in a building, for example, probably would want to see no priority higher than the automatic fire alarm. One common application of $\overline{\text{NMI}}$ when the Z80 is used in a microcomputer is to guard against the problems consequent to a loss of ac mains power. A circuit is built that monitors the ac mains at the primary of the computer's dc power supply. If the ac power drops out for even a few cycles, the circuit generates an $\overline{\text{NMI}}$ signal to the CPU. The CPU will immediately honor the request and transfer program control to a power loss subroutine. This program is used to transfer all the data in the volatile (i.e., solid-state) memory and the CPU registers/flags into some form of nonvolatile memory (i.e., disk, magnetic tape, etc.). Computers that require this ability must have sufficient back-up power stored in batteries, or in the massive filter capacitors of the dc power supply, to execute the power loss subroutine before the energy gives out.

Figure 10-8 shows an example of a typical program sequence for the nonmaskable interrupt. We are executing a program in page 6 (i.e., locations from 60 00 hex). The interrupt service subroutine is stored in locations beginning at 80 00 hex. An interrupt occurs while the instruction at location 60 03 is being executed. The sequence of events is as follows:

1. $\overline{\text{NMI}}$ occurs while the CPU is executing the instruction located at 60 03.

2. Program counter (PC) is incremented from 60 03 to 60 04, and then its contents are pushed onto the external memory stack.

3. PC is then loaded with 00 66 hex, transferring program control to 00 66 hex.

Before we can service the interrupt, however, we must tend to some housekeeping chores that will allow us to reenter the main program at the point left off, and with no problems. We will want the main program to begin executing at the location that would have been called if the interrupt had not occurred (i.e., 60 04). The *address* of this next location was saved automatically in an external memory stack, but nothing has been done for the flags and other CPU registers. In order to save this environment for use when program control is returned to the main program, we must execute the two exchange instructions (EX and EXX). These are the instructions located at the restart location (00 66 and 00 67 hex). The EX instruction exchanges the contents of the AF and

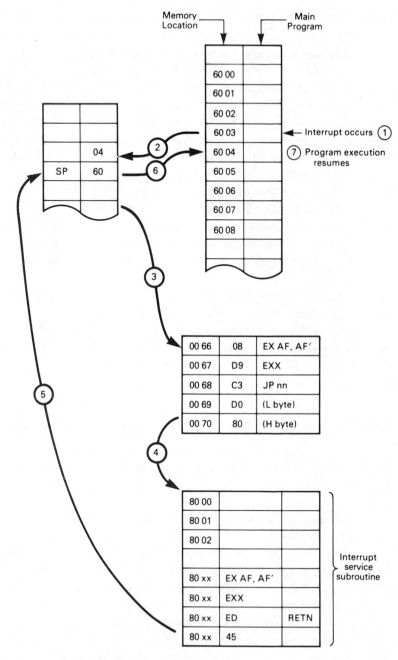

Figure 10-8   Operations in interrupt servicing.

A'F' registers, while the EXX instruction causes the other CPU registers to exchange with their alternates. (A', F', B', C', D', E', H', and L' are the alternate bank of CPU register in the Z80.) The environment (i.e., the contents of the main registers) is now saved in the alternate registers. This will free the main registers for use in the interrupt subroutine and will permit the main program to come back unscratched from the interrupt. Trying to figure out where the CPU was otherwise, without EX and EXX, would be very difficult.

In some cases, the interrupt service program is short enough that it can be located in the page 0 locations following 00 66 hex. We could, for example, make the first instruction of the service routine at 00 68 hex. But we usually want to save that part of memory for other housekeeping chores (i.e., other restart instructions). In the example shown in Figure 10-8, we execute EX and EXX to save the environment, and then jump immediately to location 80 00.

4. The interrupt service program is located higher in memory. In this example we have located it at 80 00. This program is not shown in detail, because its nature would depend on the type of interrupt being serviced.

5. The last instruction in any nonmaskable interrupt service program *must* be RETN (return from nonmaskable interrupt). This instruction tells the CPU to return control to the main program. RETN returns the contents of the external memory stack to the program counter. Since the PC now contains 60 04 hex, the program resumes at that location. This is the location immediately following the location that was executing when the $\overline{\text{NMI}}$ signal occurred. Note that, prior to the RETN instruction, we had to reexchange the registers by executing once again the EX and EXX instructions. This will regain the environment lost when the restart-66 occurred.

The nonmaskable interrupt is a hardware function of the Z80 CPU chip. It *cannot* be overridden by the programmer. The maskable interrupt, on the other hand, is designed so that it *can* be overridden by the programmer.

The Z80 contains two interrupt filp-flops, labeled IFF1 and IFF2. The first of these, IFF1, is the main interrupt flip-flop, whereas IFF2 is a secondary interrupt flip-flop used to store the condition of IFF1 when a nonmaskable interrupt occurs. We want the CPU restored to its previous state when the nonmaskable interrupt has been serviced. The contents of IFF1 are copied into IFF2 automatically when $\overline{\text{NMI}}$ is recongized. When RETN is executed, the contents of IFF2 are copied back to IFF1, restoring the condition of IFF1 to that existing when the interrupt occurred. This action completes the restoration of the CPU.

The $\overline{\text{NMI}}$ will automatically cause the state of IFF1 to be stored in IFF2 and then cause IFF1 to be RESET. This is done to prohibit any additional maskable interrupts during the period that $\overline{\text{NMI}}$ is being serviced.

Maskable Interrupts

Maskable interrupts can be software-controlled through the use of EI, DI, IM0, IM1, and IM2 instructions. The maskable interrupt is initiated by bringing the $\overline{\text{INT}}$ terminal on the Z80 (pin 16) LOW momentarily. This action is necessary, but not sufficient, to turn on the interrupt. Recall that IFF1 must be SET before a maskable interrupt is recognized by the CPU. If IFF1 is RESET, then the $\overline{\text{INT}}$ command is masked; that is, it is not seen by the CPU, it is ignored. IFF1 is SET by executing IM0, IM1, IM2, or EI instructions. It can RESET by applying a $\overline{\text{RESET}}$ pulse to pin 16 of the Z80 or by executing a DI (disable interrupt) instruction. There are, then, two ways to turn off the maskable interrupt capability of the CPU.

There are three types of maskable interrupts, designated mode 0, mode 1, and mode 2. Mode 0 is the *default* mode. Unless the programmer demands another mode, by causing the IM1 or IM2 instruction to be executed, mode 0 will be assumed. The CPU is placed in mode 0 as soon as a $\overline{\text{RESET}}$ signal is received at pin 26 of the Z80. It is usually the practice of designers to automatically apply a *power-on* $\overline{\text{RESET}}$ as soon as dc power is applied to the Z80.

Of course, setting any given interrupt mode does not allow the CPU to respond to interrupts. An EI (enable interrupt) instruction must be executed first. Once EI is executed, the interrupt flip-flop (IFF1) is SET, so the CPU will respond to $\overline{\text{INT}}$ requests (regardless of mode selected).

Mode 0

Mode 0 is used to make the Z80 think that it is an 8080A microprocessor. This was probably done because one of the objectives of Z80 design was to maintain as much software compatibility between Z80 and the older 8080A as possible. Although there are some differences where timing becomes important, it is a general rule of thumb that 8080A programs will execute on Z80 systems. But the reverse is not true; many Z80 instructions have no 8080A counterparts.

Mode 0 is automatically selected as soon as a $\overline{\text{RESET}}$ pulse is received. Mode 0 can also be selected through software. The IM0 instruction will cause the CPU to enter mode 0; it is used when the programmer has previously selected one of the other interrupt modes and then wants to return to mode 0 without resetting the CPU.

Like all the maskable interrupts, mode 0 cannot be recognized by the CPU unless the interrupt flip-flop is SET. This flip-flop will be set only if the enable interrupt (EI) instruction is executed. When this is done, the CPU will be ready to respond to maskable interrupt requests.

The mode 0 interrupt requires that the interrupting device place a valid Z80 instruction onto the 8-bit data bus as soon as the interrupt acknowledge signal is generated. In most cases, the instruction used is the 1-byte restart instruction. There are eight unique restart instructions in the Z80 instruction repertoire, and these cause immediate jumps in program control to eight different locations in page 0.

The interrupt service routine should be located at the location in memory where the restart transfers control. For example, if a keyboard causes an interrupt and then jams a restart-10 instruction onto the data bus, the CPU will transfer control to the instruction located at 00 10. If the interrupt service routine is short enough, it might be located in the memory spots immediately following 00 10 (as might well be the case in a simple keyboard input subroutine), or the instruction may be a jump immediate to some location higher in memory. It is very common for programmers to locate these service programs in the top end of the memory available in a particular computer.

Figure 10-9 shows a typical mode 0 response. For the sake of continuity, we are using the same locations as in the nonmaskable interrupt discussion earlier. The program is executing the instruction at location 60 03 when the $\overline{\text{INT}}$ signal is received by the CPU. The interrupt request is recognized following the completion of the instruction at 60 03, provided that IFF1 is SET. The sequence is as follows:

1. $\overline{\text{INT}}$ occurs during the execution of the instruction at location 60 03. This is recognized by the CPU during the last clock cycle of that instruction.

2. On the other clock pulse, the CPU acknowledges the interrupt request by causing $\overline{\text{IORQ}}$ and and $\overline{\text{M1}}$ to go LOW immediately.

3. When the interrupt acknowledges signal is received, the interrupting device places an RST 10 code on the CPU data bus.

4. The CPU executes the RST 10 by incrementing the PC to 60 04, storing the incremented contents in the external memory stack and then jumping immediately to location 00 10.

5. At location 00 10 the instruction is an immediate jump to location 80 00, where the interrupt service program is found.

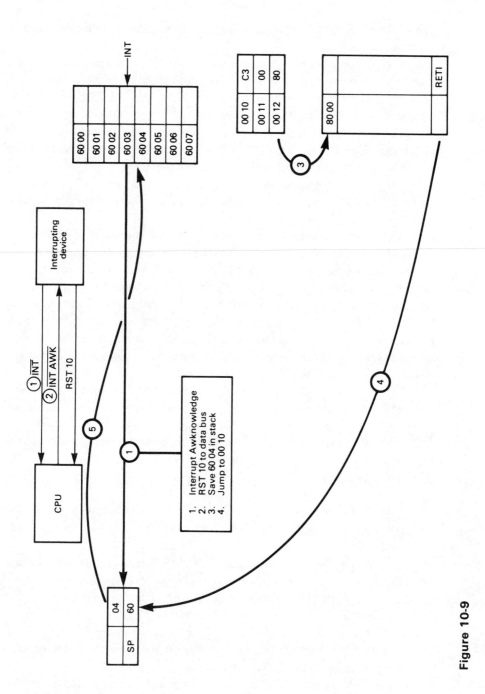

232

Figure 10-9

6. Again, the environment must be saved. There are two ways in which this can be done. One is to use the EX and EXX instructions of the previous example. Another is to use the PUSH instructions:

80 00	PUSH AF
80 01	PUSH BC
80 02	PUSH DE
80 03	PUSH HL
80 04	PUSH IY
80 05	PUSH IX

The next instructions would then be instructions of the interrupt service subroutine. When this program is completed, we must execute all of the POP instructions, to bring the contents of the registers back from the memory stack, and an RETI (return from maskable interrupt) instruction:

80 xx	POP AF
80 xx	POP BC
80 xx	POP DE
80 xx	POP HL
80 xx	POP IY
80 xx	POP IX
80 xx	RETI

7. After the RETN instruction, the CPU will replace the contents of PC with the data stored in the external stack (60 04). This is the address of the instruction in the main program that would have been executed *next* if the interrupt had not occurred.

8. Program execution resumes at location 60 04.

The mode 0 interrupt preserves some of the compatibility of the Z80 with the Intel 8080A microprocessor. But there is a limitation in this mode. The device will allow only eight interrupt devices, one for each of the eight restart locations.

Interrupt priority encoding is possible by using a priority controller, such as the Intel 8214 (or one of the related devices) or one of the Zilog Z80 peripheral chips.

Mode 1

Mode 1 is not similar to any function of the 8080A device, so it is unique to the Z80, in this respect. It is almost identical to the nonmaskable interrupt, except (1) it is maskable, and (2) it causes a restart jump to location 00 38 instead of 00 66.

The mode 1 interrupt is dependent upon the porgrammer's setting mode 1 by enabling interrupt flip-flop IFF1 (the EI instruction) and setting mode 1 by executing an IM1 instruction.

The use of mode 1 is similar to the nonmaskable interrupt, except that the priority would be lower than that of a nonmaskable interrupt. It has the advantage that no external logic is needed to cause the restart instruction. It is, then, somewhat faster than the mode 0 operation.

Refer back to the discussion of the nonmaskable interrupt for how this interrupt is serviced. Just be sure to replace in your mind the location 00 66 with 00 38.

Mode 2

The mode 2 interrupt is one of the most powerful microcomputer interrupts. It allows vectored interrupts of up to 128 levels, as opposed to only eight levels in mode 0 and one level in mode 1 and the nonmaskable interrupt.

Zilog has conveniently caused the Z80 peripheral control chips (Z80-PIO, Z80-SIO, and Z80-CTC) to allow prioritizing of the interrupts through a daisy-chaining scheme.

The key to the versatility of the mode 2 interrupt is that it is *vectored*. That is, it can use a single 8-bit word to point to any location in memory. The 1-bit address of the interrupt service program is stored in a table of interrupt addresses located somewhere in memory. The location of this table is pointed to by a 2-byte digital word formed from the contents of the interrupt (I) register and the 1-byte word supplied by the interrupting device. The upper 8 bits of this 16-bit pointer are supplied by the I register and must be preloaded by the program. The lower-order 8 bits of the pointer are supplied by the interrupting device.

There is one restriction on the addresses of the table, which is that they must begin on an even-numbered memory location. All the entries in this table will be 2 bytes in adjacent locations. The first byte of each entry in the table is the low-order byte of the desired address, while the second entry is the high-order byte. One consequence of this constraint is that the least significant bit of the 8-bit word supplied by the interrupting device must be 0.

Figure 10-10 shows an example of such a table. In this case, the programmer elected to locate the table in page 8, and it commences at 80 00 hex. The first entry is found at 80 00 and 80 01. These locations contain the low- and high-order bytes of the address where the first interrupt service program is located. The first part of this address (80 hex) is stored in the I register. The second part is supplied by the interrupting device. Notice that the binary equivalent of 00 ends in a 0.

Similarly, the other entries are found beginning at 80 02, 80 04, 80 06, and so on, all the way up to 80 FE (if 128 levels are required). Each of these table addresses contains the address of a location in memory where the CPU will find the program that serves that particular interrupting device.

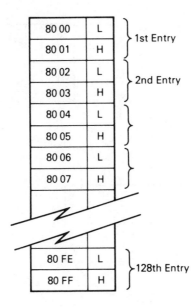

Figure 10-10

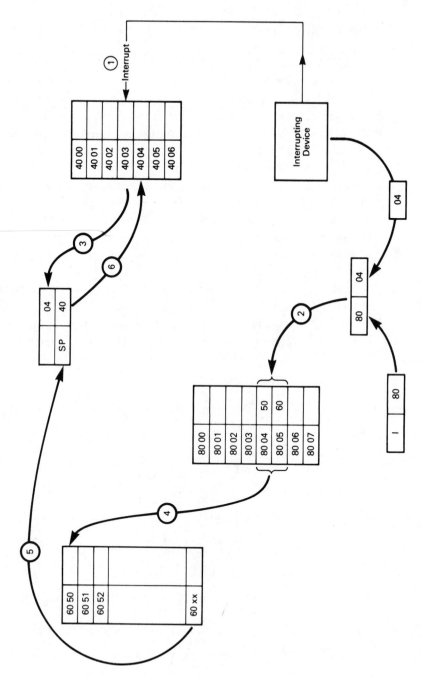

Figure 10-11

Figure 10-11 shows a typical mode 2 interrupt sequence. In this program, the main program is located in page 4 (i.e., beginning at 40 00), the vector table is located in page 8, and the interrupt subroutine for the device shown is in page 6 (begins at 60 50 hex). The I register contains 80 hex, and the interrupting device is programmed to enter 04 hex on the data bus when the interrupt acknowledge signal is received. The interrupt flip-flop IFF1 must be SET, and the bus request $\overline{BUSRQ}$ must be HIGH. The sequence of events is as follows:

1. The interrupting peripheral issues an $\overline{INT}$ signal to the CPU.

2. When the interrupt acknowledges signal is received, the peripheral jams 04 hex onto the data bus. This is merged with the 80 from the I register to form the address 80 04 hex. This address in memory will contain the address of the actual interrupt service program required by this peripheral.

3. The PC is incremented, and then its contents are pushed onto an external memory stack.

4. The PC is loaded with the address found at location 80 04. This address is 60 50 hex, so program control jumps to this location.

5. After the last instruction (RETI) of the service program, the PC data saved in the external stack are loaded back into the PC.

6. The main program resumes at location 40 04.

It is necessary to save the environment when the jump occurs, or the CPU will not necessarily be in the same state as before the interrupt occurred. These techniques were discussed earlier in this chapter.

11

Interfacing with the
Real World:
The Analog Subsystem

Many applications for microcomputers and microprocessors involve the analog world, which is to say the *real* world. Many of the signals and transducers that measure various physical parameters are either only available in an analog version, or the analog version is a lot less costly than a digital version. Medical, scientific, engineering, and industrial instrumentation, for example, uses many analog transducers. Human blood pressure is usually measured in a special transducer that is either piezoresistive or inductive Wheatstone bridges or a piezoelectric quartz transducer. Temperature is usually measured by thermistors, thermocouples, or PN junction sensors. Indeed, a wide variety of signal transducers is available that output an analog signal.

Amplifiers are also used in the analog subsystem. These amplifiers may be used only to build up the low-level transducer output signal so that it is compatible with the range of the analog-to-digital converter (see Chapter 12) used in the microcomputer. In other cases, we might actually do some signal processing in the analog subsystem. This statement might be pure heresy to the digitally oriented person, but it is often the case that analog processing is the better choice. One must remember that the engineer's job is not necessarily to use the most modern technology, but to get the job done in the most economic and efficient manner possible. There are times when that requirement means using a small amount of analog preprocessing. It is especially necessary when the computer memory size is limited by some other uncontrollable factor, or when the computer cycle time is too slow for the particular digital algorithm to be executed on the signal. In other cases, especially in 4- or 8-bit microcomputers, the word length limits resolution too much, yet such resolution is available in an analog subassembly. An engineer from Burr-Brown Research Corporation, a leading maker of both analog devices and data-acquisition products for computers, has stated that one of their analog signal-processing hybrid modules has the resolution to compete with a 20-bit computer. An 8-bit microcomputer would require three successive operations to obtain the triple precision needed to beat that specification.

However, the digital method is usually the best for any signal-processing application. For the most part, we will limit analog processing to the amplification (and possibly filtering) needed to make the signal compatible with the A/D converter at the input of the computer. One must, however, keep in mind that other applications may require analog processing.

Some may criticize the inclusion of operational amplifier and transducer information in a book on microcomputer interfacing. However, if the computer is to be interfaced to the real world of scientific, medical, engineering, and industrial signals (which is a major market for interface engineering), it is highly pertinent to include in our studies material on the transducers and signal processors suitable to that world.

OPERATIONAL AMPLIFIERS: AN INTRODUCTION

The operational amplifier has been in existence for several decades, but only in the last 15 or 20 years has it come into its own as an almost universal electronic building block. The term *operational* is derived from the fact that these devices were originally designed for use in analog computers to solve *mathematical operations*. The range of circuit applications today, however, has increased immensely, so the operational amplifier has survived and prospered, even though analog computers, in which they were once a principal constituent, are now almost in eclipse.

Keep in mind, however, that even though the programmable analog computer is no longer used extensively, many instruments are little more than a nonprogrammable, dedicated-to-one-chore analog computer with a numeric readout of some sort.

In this chapter we will examine the *gross,* or large-scale, properties of the basic operational amplifier, and we will learn to derive the transfer equations for most common operational amplifier circuits using only Ohm's law, Kirchhoff's law, and the basic properties of all operational amplifiers.

One of the profound beauties of the modern, integrated-circuit, operational amplifier is its simplicity when viewed from the outside world. Of course, the inner workings are complex, but they are of little interest in our discussion of the operational amplifier's gross properties. We will limit our discussion somewhat by considering the operational amplifier as a *black box*, and that allows for a very simple analysis in which we relate the performance to the universal transfer function for all electronic circuits: E_{out}/E_{in}.

PROPERTIES OF THE IDEAL OP-AMP

An *ideal* operational amplifier is a *gain block*, or black box if you prefer, that has the following general properties:

1. Infinite *open-loop* (i.e., no feedback) gain ($A_{vol} = \infty$).
2. Infinite input impedance ($Z_{in} = \infty$).
3. Zero output impedance ($Z_0 = 0$).
4. Infinite bandwidth ($f_0 = \infty$).
5. Zero noise generation.

Of course, it is not possible to obtain a real IC operational amplifier that meets these properties—they are *ideal*—but if we read "infinite" as "very, very high" and "zero" as "very, very low," then the approximations of the ideal situation are very accurate. Real IC operational amplifiers, for example, can have an open-loop voltage gain from 50,000 to over 1,000,000, so it can be classed as *relatively infinite*, and the equations work in most cases.

DIFFERENTIAL INPUTS

Figure 11-1 shows the basic symbol for the common operational amplifier, including power terminals. In many schematics of operational amplifier circuits, the V_{CC} and V_{EE} power terminals are deleted, so the drawing will be less "busy."

Note that there are two input terminals, labeled ($-$) and ($+$). The terminal labeled ($-$) is the *inverting* input. The output signal will be out of phase with signals applied to this input terminal (i.e., there will be a 180-degree phase shift). The terminal labeled ($+$) is the *noninverting* input, so output signals will be in phase with signals applied to this input. It is important to remember that these

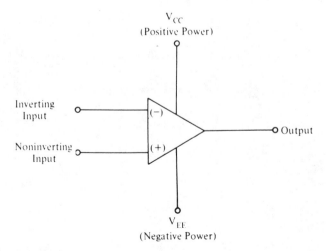

Figure 11-1 Symbol for an operational amplifier.

inputs look into *equal* open-loop gains, so they will have equal but opposite effects on the output voltage.

At this point let us add one further property to our list of ideal properties:

6. Differential inputs follow each other.

This property implies that the two inputs will behave as if they were at the same potential, especially under static conditions. In Figure 11-2 we see an inverting follower circuit in which the noninverting (+) input is grounded. The sixth property allows us, in fact requires us, to treat the inverting (−) input as if it were *also* grounded. Many textbooks and magazine articles like to call this phenomenon a "virtual" ground, but such a term serves only to confuse the reader. It is better to accept as a basic axiom of operational amplifier circuitry that, for purposes of calculation and voltage measurement, the (−) input will be grounded if the (+) input is actually grounded.

ANALYSIS USING KIRCHHOFF AND OHM

We know from Kirchhoff's current law that the algebraic sum of all currents entering and leaving a point in a circuit must be zero. The total current flow into and out of point A in Fig. 11-2, then, must be *zero*. Three possible currents exist at this point: input current $I1$, feedback current $I2$, and any currents flowing

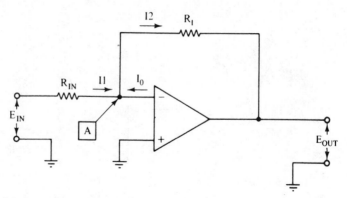

Figure 11-2 Inverting follower.

into or out of the $(-)$ input terminal of the operational amplifier, I_0. But according to ideal property 2, the input impedance of this type of device is infinite. Ohm's law tells us that by

$$I_0 = \frac{E}{Z_{in}} \qquad (11\text{-}1)$$

current I_0 is zero, because E/Z_{in} is zero. So if current I_0 is equal to zero, we conclude that $I1 + I2 = 0$ (Kirchhoff's law). Since this is true, then

$$I2 = -I1 \qquad (11\text{-}2)$$

We also know that

$$I1 = \frac{E_{in}}{R_{in}} \qquad (11\text{-}3)$$

and

$$I2 = \frac{E_{out}}{R_F} \qquad (11\text{-}4)$$

By substituting Eqs. (11-3) and (11-4) into Eq. (11-2), we obtain the result

$$\frac{E_{out}}{R_F} = \frac{-E_{in}}{R_{in}} \qquad (11\text{-}5)$$

Solving for E_{out} gives us the transfer function normally given in operational amplifier literature for an inverting amplifier:

$$E_{out} = -E_{in} \times \frac{R_F}{R_{in}} \qquad (11\text{-}6)$$

Example 11-1   Calculate the output voltage from an inverting operational amplifier circuit if the input signal is 100 mV, the feedback resistor is 100 kΩ, and the input resistor is 10 kΩ.

Solution

$$E_{out} = E_{in} \times \frac{R_F}{R_{in}} \qquad (11\text{-}6)$$

$$= 0.1 \text{ V} \frac{10^5 \text{ } \Omega}{10^4 \text{ } \Omega}$$

$$= (0.1 \text{ V})(10) = \mathbf{1 \text{ V}}$$

The term R_F/R_{in} is the voltage gain factor, and is usually designated by the symbol A_V, which is written as

$$A_V = \frac{-R_F}{R_{in}} \qquad (11\text{-}7)$$

We sometimes encounter Eq. (11-6) written using the left-hand side of Eq. (11-7):

$$E_{out} = -A_V E_{in} \qquad (11\text{-}8)$$

When designing simple inverting followers using operational amplifiers, use Eqs. (11-7) and (11-8). Let us look at a specific example. Suppose that we have a requirement for an amplifier with a gain of 50. We want to drive this amplifier from a source that has an output impedance of 1000 Ω. A standard rule of thumb for designers to follow is to make the input impedance not less than ten times the source impedance, so in this case the amplifier must have a source impedance that is equal to or greater than 10,000 Ω (10 kΩ). This requirement sets the value of the input resistor at 10 kΩ or higher, but in this example we select a 10-kΩ value for R_{in}.

$$A_V = \frac{R_F}{R_{in}} \qquad\qquad (11\text{-}9)$$

$$50 = \frac{R_F}{10{,}000 \ \Omega} \qquad\qquad (11\text{-}10)$$

$$R_F = 500{,}000 \ \Omega$$

Our gain-of-50 amplifier will look like Figure 11-3.

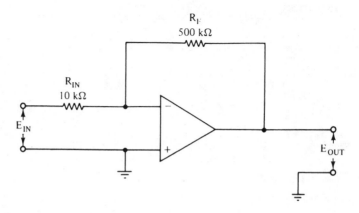

Figure 11-3   Gain-of-50 inverting follower.

NONINVERTING FOLLOWERS

The inverting follower circuits of Figures 11-2 and 11-3 suffer badly from low input impedance, especially at higher gains, because the input impedance is the value of R_{in}. This problem becomes especially acute when we attempt to obtain even moderately high gain figures from low-cost devices. Although some types of operational amplifier allow the use of 500-kΩ to 2-MΩ input resistors, they are costly and often uneconomical. The *noninverting follower* of Figure 11-4 solves this problem by using the input impedance problem very nicely, because the input impedance of the op-amp is typically very high (ideal property 2).

We may once again resort to Kirchhoff's law to derive the transfer equation from our basic ideal properties. By property 6 we know that the inputs tend to

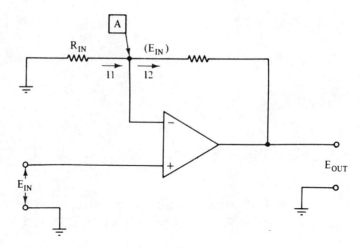

Figure 11-4   Noninverting follower with gain.

follow each other, so the inverting input can be treated as if it were at the same potential as the noninverting input, which is E_{in}, the input signal voltage. We know that

$$I1 = I2 \tag{11-11}$$

$$I1 = \frac{E_{in}}{R_{in}} \tag{11-12}$$

$$I2 = \frac{E_{out} - E_{in}}{R_F} \tag{11-13}$$

By substituting Eqs. (11-12) and (11-13) into Eq. (11-11), we obtain

$$I1 = I2 \tag{11-14}$$

$$\frac{E_{in}}{R_{in}} = \frac{E_{out} - E_{in}}{R_F} \tag{11-15}$$

Solving Eq. (11-15) for E_{out} results in the transfer equation for the noninverting follower amplifier circuit. Multiply both sides by R_F:

$$\frac{R_F E_{in}}{R_{in}} = E_{out} - E_{in} \tag{11-16}$$

Add E_{in} to both sides:

$$\frac{R_F E_{in}}{R_{in}} + E_{in} = E_{out} \qquad (11\text{-}17)$$

Factor out E_{in}:

$$E_{in} \times \left(\frac{R_F}{R_{in}} + 1\right) = E_{out} \qquad (11\text{-}18)$$

Example 11-2   Calculate the output voltage for 100-mV (i.e., 0.1 V) input in a noninverting follower amplifier if R_F is 100 kΩ and R_{in} is 10 kΩ.

Solution

$$E_{out} = E_{in}\left(\frac{R_F}{R_{in}} + 1\right) \qquad (11\text{-}18)$$

$$= 0.1 \text{ V} \left(\frac{10^5 \text{ Ω}}{10^4 \text{ Ω}} + 1\right)$$

$$= (0.1 \text{ V})(10 + 1)$$

$$= (0.1 \text{ V})(11) = \mathbf{1.1 \text{ V}}$$

In this discussion we have arrived at both of the transfer functions commonly used in operational amplifier design by using only the basic properties, Ohm's law, and Kirchhoff's current law. We may safely assume that the operational amplifier is merely a feedback device that generates a current that exactly cancels the input current. Figure 11-5 gives a synopsis of the characteristics of the most popular operational amplifier configurations. The unity gain noninverting follower of Figure 11-5c is a special case of the circuit in Figure 11-5b, in which $R_F/R_{in} = 0$. In this case, the transfer equation becomes

$$E_{out} = E_{in}(0 + 1) \qquad (11\text{-}19)$$

$$= E_{in}(1) \qquad (11\text{-}20)$$

$$= E_{in} \qquad (11\text{-}21)$$

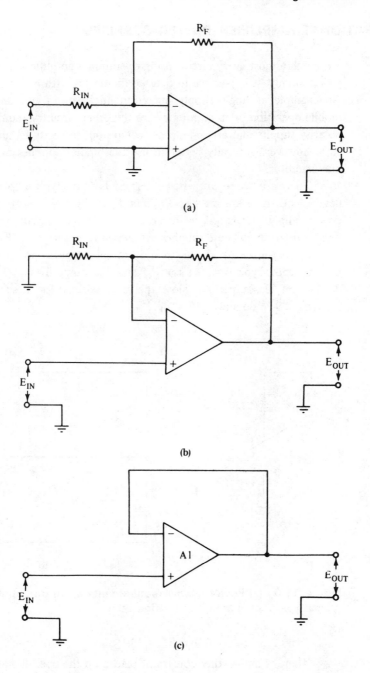

Figure 11-5 (a) Inverting follower; (b) noninverting gain follower; (c) unity gain noninverting follower.

OPERATIONAL AMPLIFIER POWER SUPPLIES

Although almost every circuit using operational amplifiers uses a dual polarity power supply, it is possible to operate the device with a single polarity supply. An example of single supply operation might be in equipment designed for mobile operation or in circuits where the other circuitry requires only a single polarity supply, and an op-amp or two are but minority features in the design. It is, however, generally better to use the bipolar supplies as intended by the manufacturer.

There are two separate power terminals on the typical operational amplifier device, and these are marked V_{CC} and V_{EE}. The V_{CC} supply is connected to a power supply that is *positive* to ground, while the V_{EE} supply is *negative* with respect to ground. These supplies are shown in Figure 11-6. Keep in mind that, although batteries are shown in the example, regular power supplies may be used instead. Typical values for V_{CC} and V_{EE} range from ± 3 V dc to ± 22 V dc. In many cases, perhaps most, the value selected for these potentials will be between ± 9 V dc and ± 15 V dc.

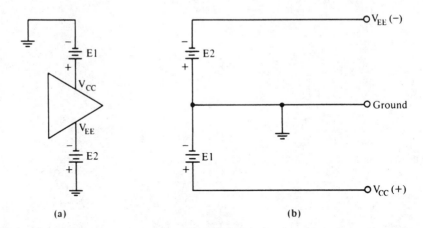

(a)   (b)

Figure 11-6 (a) Power supply requirements of an operational amplifier; (b) typical operational amplifier configuration.

There is one further constraint placed on the operational amplifier power supply: $V_{CC} - V_{EE}$ must be less than some specified voltage, usually 30 V. So if V_{CC} is $+18$ V dc, then V_{EE} must be not greater than $(30 - 18)$, or 12 V dc.

PRACTICAL DEVICES: SOME PROBLEMS

Before we can properly apply operational amplifiers in real equipment we must learn some of the limitations of real-world devices. The devices that we have considered up until now have been *ideal,* so they do not exist. Real IC operational amplifiers carry price tags of less than half a dollar up to several dozen dollars each. The lower the cost, generally, the less ideal the device.

Three main problems exist in real operational amplifiers: offset current, offset voltage, and frequency response. Of less importance in many cases is noise generation.

In real operational amplifier devices the input impedance is less than infinite, and this implies that a small input bias current exists. The input current may flow into or out of the input terminals of the operational amplifier. In other words, current I_0 of Figure 11-2 is *not* zero, so it will produce an output voltage equal to $-I_0 \times R_F$. The cure for this problem is shown in Figure 11-7, and involves placing a *compensation resistor* between the noninverting input terminal and ground. This tactic works because the currents in the respective inputs are approximately equal. Since resistor R_C is equal to the parallel combination of R_F and R_{in}, it will generate the same *voltage drop* that appears at the inverting input. The resultant output voltage, then, is zero, because the two inputs have equal but opposite polarity effect on the output.

Output offset voltage is the value of E_{out} that will exist if the input end of the R_{in} is grounded (i.e., $E_{in} = 0$). In the ideal device, E_{out} would be zero under this condition, but in real devices there may be some offset potential present.

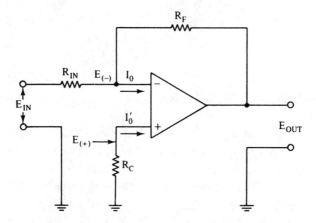

Figure 11-7 Use of a compensation resistor.

This output potential can be forced to zero by any of the circuits in Figure 11-8.

The circuit in Figure 11-8a uses a pair of *offset null* terminals found on many, but not all, operational amplifiers. Although many IC operational amplifiers use this technique, some do not. Alternatively, the offset range may be insufficient in some cases. In either event, we may use the circuit of Figure 11-8b to solve the problem.

The offset null circuit of Figure 11-8b creates a current flowing in resistor $R1$ to the summing junction of the operational amplifier. Since the offset current may flow either *into* or *out of* the input terminal, the null control circuit must be able to supply currents of both polarities. Because of this requirement, the ends of the potentiometer ($R1$) are connected to V_{CC} and V_{EE}.

In many cases, it is found that the offset is small compared with normally expected values of input signal voltage. This is especially true in low-gain applications, in which case the nominal offset current will create such a low output error that no action need be taken. In still other cases, the offset of each stage in a cascade chain of amplifiers may be small, but their cumulative effect may be a large offset error. In this type of situation, it is usually sufficient to null only one of the stages late in the chain (i.e., close to the output stage).

In those circuits where the offset is small, but critical, it may be useful to replace $R1$ and $R2$ of Figure 11-8b with one of the resistor networks of Figures 11-8c through 11-8e. These perform essentially the same function, but have superior resolution. That is, there is a smaller change in output voltage for a single turn of the potentiometer. This type of circuit will have a superior resolution in any event, but even further improvement is possible if a ten-turn (or more) potentiometer is used.

DC DIFFERENTIAL AMPLIFIERS

The fact that an IC operational amplifier has two complementary inputs, inverting and noninverting, makes it natural to use it for application as a *differential amplifier*. These circuits produce an output voltage that is proportional to the *difference* between two ground-referenced input voltages. Recall from our previous discussion that the two inputs of an operational amplifier have equal but opposite effect on the output voltage. If the same voltage or two equal voltages are applied to the two inputs (i.e., a *common-mode* voltage, $E3$ in Figure

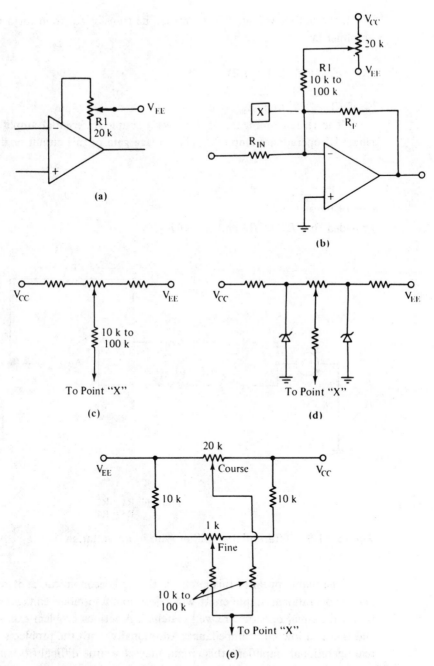

Figure 11-8 (a) Use of offset terminals to null output; (b) use of summing current to null output; (c), (d), and (e) high-resolution offset null circuits.

11-1), the output voltage will be zero. The transfer equation for a differential amplifier is

$$E_{out} = A_V(E1 - E2) \tag{11-22}$$

So if $E1 = E2$, then $E_{out} = 0$.

The circuit of Figure 11-9 shows a simple differential amplifier using a single IC operational amplifier. The voltage gain of this circuit is given by

$$A_V = \frac{R\,3}{R\,1} \tag{11-23}$$

provided that $R1 = R2$ and $R3 = R4$.

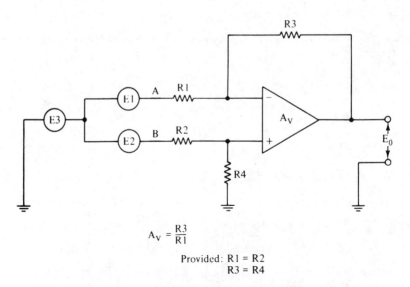

$$A_V = \frac{R3}{R1}$$

Provided: $R1 = R2$
$R3 = R4$

Figure 11-9   Differential amplifier with input voltages.

The main appeal of this circuit is that it is economical, as it requires but one IC operational amplifier. It will reject common-mode voltages reasonably well if the equal resistors are well matched. A serious problem exists, however, and that is a low input impedance. Additionally, with the problems existing in real operational amplifiers, this circuit may be a little difficult to tame in high-gain applications. As a result, designers frequently use an alternate circuit in these cases.

In recent years, the instrumentation amplifier (IA) of Figure 11-10 has become popular because it alleviates most of the problems associated with the circuit of Figure 11-9. The input stages are noninverting followers, so they will have a characteristically high input impedance. Typical values run to as much as 1000 MΩ.

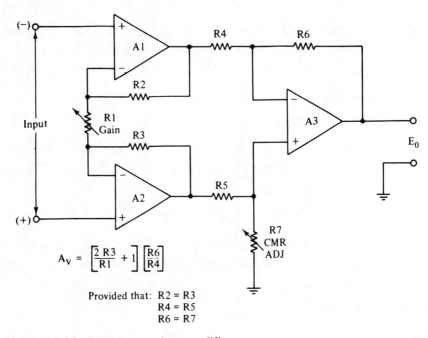

$$A_V = \left[\frac{2\,R3}{R1} + 1\right]\left[\frac{R6}{R4}\right]$$

Provided that: R2 = R3
R4 = R5
R6 = R7

Figure 11-10   Instrumentation amplifier.

The instrumentation amplifier is relatively tolerant of different resistor ratios used to create voltage gain. In the simplest case, the differential voltage gain is given by

$$A_V = \frac{2R\,3}{R\,1} + 1 \qquad\qquad (11\text{-}24)$$

provided that $R3 = R2$ and $R4 = R5 = R6 = R7$.

It is interesting to note that the common-mode rejection ratio is not seriously degraded by mismatch of resistors $R2$ and $R3$; only the gain is affected. If these resistors are mismatched, a differential voltage gain error will be introduced.

The situation created by Eq. (11-24) results in having the gain of $A3$ equal to unity (i.e., 1), which is a waste. If gain in $A3$ is desired, Eq. (11-24) must be rewritten into the form

$$A_V = \left(\frac{2R3}{R1} + 1\right)\frac{R7}{R5}$$ (11-25)

Example 11-3   Calculate the differential voltage gain of an instrumentation amplifier that uses the following resistor values: $R3 = 33$ kΩ, $R1 = 2.2$ kΩ, $R5 = 3.3$ kΩ, and $R7 = 15$ kΩ.

Solution

$$A_V = \left(\frac{2R3}{R1} + 1\right)\frac{R7}{R5}$$ (11-25)

$$= \left[\frac{(2)(33 \text{ k}\Omega)}{2.2 \text{ k}\Omega} + 1\right]\frac{15 \text{ k}\Omega}{3.3 \text{ k}\Omega}$$

$$= 141$$

One further equation that may be of interest is the general expression from which the other instrumentation amplifier transfer equations are derived:

$$A_V = \frac{R7(R1 + R2 + R3)}{R1R6}$$ (11-26)

which remains valid provided that the ratio $R7/R6 = R5/R4$.

Equation (11-26) is especially useful, since you need not be concerned with matched pairs of precision resistors, but only that their ratios be equal.

PRACTICAL CIRCUIT

In this section we will consider a practical design example using the instrumentation amplifier circuit. The particular problem requires a frequency response to 100 kHz, and that the input lines be shielded. But the latter requirement would also deteriorate the signal at high frequencies because of the shunt capacitance of the input cables. To overcome this problem, a *high-frequency compensation* control is built into the amplifier. Voltage gain is approximately 10.

The circuit to the preamplifier is shown in Figure 11-11. It is the instrumentation amplifier of Figure 11-10 with some modifications. When the frequency response is less than 10 kHz or so, we may use any of the 741-family devices (i.e., 741, 747, 1456, and 1458), but premium performance demands a better operational amplifier. In this case, one of the most economical is the RCA CA3140, although an L156 would also suffice.

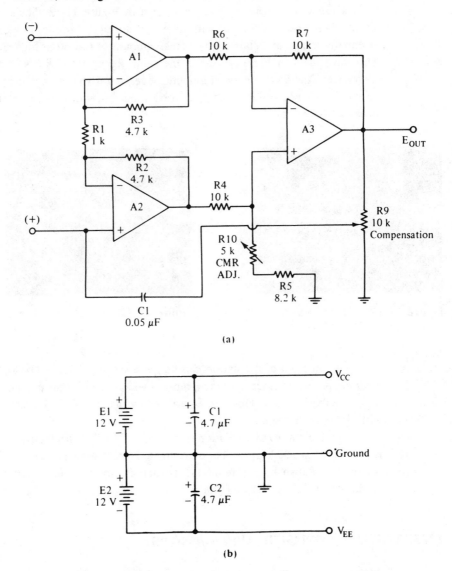

(a)

(b)

Figure 11-11 (a) Instrumentation amplifier with capacitance null; (b) power supply for (a).

Common-mode rejection can be adjusted to compensate for any mismatch in the resistors or IC devices by adjusting $R10$. This potentiometer is adjusted for zero output when the same signal is applied simultaneously to both inputs.

The frequency response characteristics of this preamplifier are shown in Figures 11-12 through 11-16. The input in each case is a 1000-Hz square wave from a function generator. The wave form in Figure 11-12 shows the output signal when resistor $R9$ is set with its wiper closest to ground. Notice that it is essentially square and shows only a small amount of roll-off of high frequencies. The wave form in Figure 11-13 is the same signal when $R9$ is at maximum resistance. This creates a small amount of regenerative (i.e., positive) feedback, although it is not sufficient to start oscillation, but will enhance amplification of high frequencies.

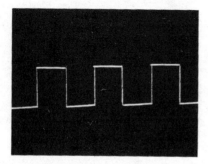

Figure 11-12   Square wave.

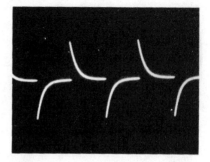

Figure 11-13   Differentiated square wave.

The problem of oscillation can be quite serious (Figure 11-15), however, if certain precautions are not taken, most of which involve limiting the amplitude of the feedback signal. This goal is realized by using a 2200-Ω resistor in series with the potentiometer.

Another source of oscillation is the value of $C1$. When a 0.001-μF capacitor is used at $C1$, an 80-kHz oscillation is created (see Figure 11-16). The frequency response is shown in Figure 11-14. To obtain any particular response curve, modify the values of $C1$ and $R9$.

DIFFERENTIAL AMPLIFIER APPLICATIONS

Differential amplifiers find application in many different instrumentation situations. Of course, it should be realized that they are required wherever a dif-

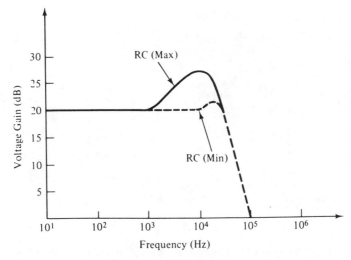

Figure 11-14 Voltage gain versus frequency.

ferential signal voltage is found. Less obvious, perhaps, is that they are used to acquire signals or to operate in control systems in the presence of large noise signals. Many medical applications, for example, use the differential amplifier, because they look for minute bipotentials in the presence of strong 60-Hz fields from the ac power mains.

Another class of applications is the amplification of the output signal from a Wheatstone bridge; this is shown in Figure 11-17. If one side of the bridge's excitation potential is grounded, the output voltage is a differential signal voltage. This signal can be applied to the inputs of a differential amplifier or instrumentation amplifier to create an amplified, single-ended, output voltage.

Figure 11-15 Ringing on square wave.

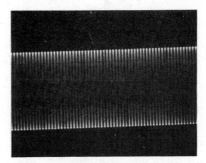

Figure 11-16 Eighty-kilohertz oscillation.

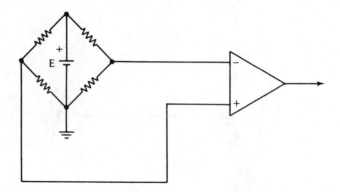

Figure 11-17 Differential amplifier used to amplify output of Wheatstone bridge.

A "rear end" stage suitable for many operational amplifier instrumentation projects is shown in Figure 11-18. This circuit consists of three low-cost operational amplifier ICs. Since they follow most of the circuit gain, we may use low-cost devices such as the 741 in this circuit. The gain of this circuit is given by $R2/10^4$.

INTEGRATORS

Figure 11-19 shows the basic operational amplifier *integrator* circuit. The transfer equation for this circuit may be derived in the same manner as before, with due consideration for $C1$.

$$I2 = -I1 \tag{11-27}$$

but

$$I1 = \frac{E_{in}}{R1} \tag{11-28}$$

and

$$I2 = C1 \frac{dE_0}{dt} \tag{11-29}$$

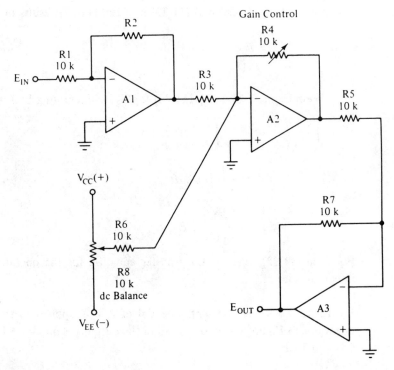

Figure 11-18 Universal rear end for instrumentation amplifiers and other purposes.

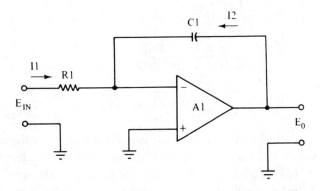

Figure 11-19 Integrator circuit.

Substituting Eqs. (11-28) and (11-29) into Eq. (11-27) results in

$$\frac{C1\,dE_0}{dt} = \frac{-E_{in}}{R1} \tag{11-30}$$

We may now solve Eq. (11-30) for E_0 by integrating both sides.

$$\int \frac{C1\,dE_0}{dt}\,dt = -\int \frac{E_{in}}{R1}\,dt \tag{11-31}$$

$$C1E_0 = \frac{-1}{R1}\int_0^t E_{in}\,dt \tag{11-32}$$

$$E_0 = \frac{-1}{R1C1}\int_0^t E_{in}\,dt \tag{11-33}$$

Equation (11-33), then, is the transfer equation for the operational amplifier integrator circuit.

Example 11-4 A constant potential of 2 V is applied to the input of the integrator in Figure 11-19 for 3 s. Find the output potential if $R1 = 1\ M\Omega$ and $C1 = 0.5\ \mu F$.

Solution

$$E_0 = \frac{-1}{R1C1}\int_0^t E_{in}\,dt \tag{11-33}$$

$$E_0 = \frac{-E_{in}}{R1C1}\int_0^3 dt$$

$$E_0 = \frac{(-2\ V)(t)}{(10^6\ \Omega)(5 \times 10^{27}\ F)}\Big|_0^3$$

$$E_0 = \frac{(-2\ V)(3\ s)}{(5 \times 10^{22}\ s)} - 0 = -12\ \textbf{volts}$$

Note that the *gain* of the integrator is given by the term $1/R1C1$. If small values of $R1$ and $C1$ are used, the gain can be very large. For example, if $R1 = 100\ k\Omega$ and $C1 = 0.001\ \mu F$, the gain is 10,000. A very small input voltage in that case will saturate the output very quickly. In general, the *time constant* $R1C1$ should be longer than the period of the input wave form.

DIFFERENTIATORS

An operational amplifier *differentiator* is formed by reversing the roles of $R1$ and $C1$ in the integrator, as shown in Figure 11-20. We know that

$$I2 = -I1 \tag{11-34}$$

$$I1 = \frac{C1\, dE_{in}}{dt} \tag{11-35}$$

and

$$I2 = \frac{E_0}{R1} \tag{11-36}$$

Substituting Eqs. (11-35) and (11-36) into Eq. (11-34) results in

$$\frac{E_0}{R1} = \frac{-C1\, dE_{in}}{dt} \tag{11-37}$$

Solving Eq. (11-37) for E_0 gives us the transfer equation for an operational amplifier differentiator circuit:

$$E_0 = -R1C1 \frac{dE_{in}}{dt} \tag{11-38}$$

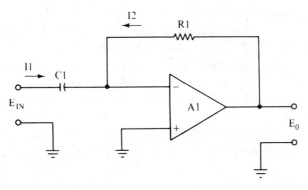

Figure 11-20 Differentiator circuit.

Example 11-5   A 12-V/s ramp function voltage is applied to the input of an operational amplifier differentiator, in which $R1 = 1\ M\Omega$ and $C1 = 0.2\ \mu F$. What is the output voltage?

Solution

$$E_0 = -R1\,C1\,\frac{dE_{in}}{dt} \tag{11-38}$$

$$= -(10^6\ \Omega)(2 \times 10^{-7}\,F)(12\ V/s)$$

$$= -(2 \times 10^{-1}\ s)(12\ V/s) = -2.4\ V$$

The differentiator time constant $R1C1$ should be set very short relative to the period of the wave form being differentiated, or in the case of square waves, triangle waves, and certain other signals, the time constant should be short compared with the *rise time* of the leading edge.

LOGARITHMIC AND ANTILOG AMPLIFIERS

Figure 11-21a shows an elementary *logarithmic amplifier* circuit using a bipolar transistor in the feedback loop. We know that the collector current bears a logarithmic relationship to the base-emitter potential, V_{be}:

$$V_{be} = \frac{KT}{q} \ln\left[\frac{I_c}{I_s}\right] \tag{11-39}$$

where V_{be} = base-emitter potential in volts (V)
  K = Boltzmann's constant, 1.38×10^{-23} joules/Kelvin (J/K)
  T = temperature in Kelvins (K)
  q = electronic charge, 1.6×10^{-19} coulombs (C)
  I_c = collector current in amperes (A)
  I_s = reverse saturation current for the transistor in amperes (A)

At 27°C (300K), that is, room temperature, the term KT/q evaluates to approximately 26 mV (i.e., 0.026 V), so Eq. (11-40) becomes

$$V_{be} = 26\ mV\ \ln\left(\frac{I_c}{I_s}\right) \tag{11-40}$$

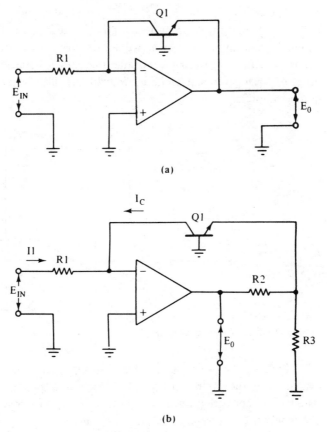

Figure 11-21   (a) Logarithmic amplifier; (b) improved logarithmic amplifier.

But $V_{be} = E_0$, and $I_c = E_{in}/R1$, so we may safely say that

$$E_0 = 26 \text{ m V } \ln \left(\frac{E_{in}}{I_s R 1} \right) \tag{11-41}$$

But I_s is a constant if the temperature is also constant, and $R1$ is constant under all conditions, so, by the rule that the logarithm of a constant is also a constant, we may state that Eq. (11-41) is the transfer function for the natural logarithmic amplifier. For base 10 logarithms,

$$E_0 = 60 \text{ m V } \log_{10} \left(\frac{E_{in}}{I_s R 1} \right) \tag{11-42}$$

The relationship of Eqs. (11-41) and (11-42) allows us to construct amplifiers with logarithmic properties. If $Q1$ is in the feedback loop of an operational amplifier, the output voltage E_o will be proportional to the logarithm of input voltage E_{in}. If, on the other hand, the transistor is connected in series with the input of the operational amplifier (see Figure 11-22), the circuit becomes an antilog amplifier.

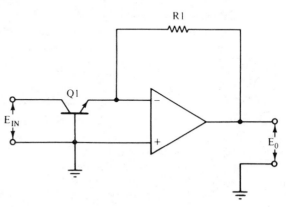

Figure 11-22   Antilog amplifier.

Both of these circuits exhibit a strong dependence on temperature, as evidenced by the T term in Eq. (11-39). In actual practice, then, some form of temperature correction must be used. Two forms of temperature correction are commonly used: *compensation* and *stabilization.*

The compensation method uses temperature-dependent resistors, or, *thermistors,* to regulate the gain of the circuit with changes in temperature. For example, it is common practice to make $R3$ in Figure 11-21b a thermistor.

The stabilization method requires that the temperature of $Q1$, and preferably the op-amp also, be held constant. In the past, this has meant that the components must be kept inside an electrically heated oven, but today other techniques are used. One manufacturer builds a temperature-controlled hybrid logarithmic amplifier by nesting the op-amp and transistor on the same substrate as a class-A amplifier. Such an amplifier, under zero-signal conditions, dissipates very nearly constant heat. After the chip comes to equilibrium, the temperature will remain constant.

In the case of the antilog amplifier,

$$I_c = \frac{E_0}{R\,1} \tag{11-43}$$

and

$$E_{in} = V_{be} \tag{11-44}$$

$$= 26 \text{ m V } \ln \left(\frac{E_0}{R\, 1I_s} \right) \tag{11-45}$$

CURRENT-TO-VOLTAGE CONVERTERS

Most analog recording devices, such as oscilloscopes or graphic recorders, are voltage-input devices. That is, they require a *voltage* for an input signal. When measuring or recording a current, however, they require some sort of *voltage-to-current converter* circuit.

Two examples of operational amplifier versions are shown in Figure 11-23. In the first example, Figure 11-23a, a small-value resistor R is placed in

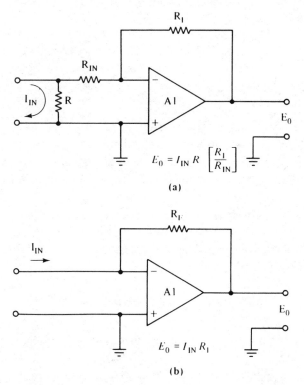

$$E_0 = I_{IN} R \left[\frac{R_1}{R_{IN}} \right]$$

(a)

$$E_0 = I_{IN} R_1$$

(b)

Figure 11-23   (a) Current-to-voltage converter; (b) current-to-voltage converter for small currents.

series with the current I, which produces a voltage equal to IR. This potential is seen by the operational amplifier as a valid input voltage. The output voltage is

$$E_0 = \frac{-IRR_F}{R_{in}}$$

provided that

$$R \ll R_{in}$$

$$R \ll R_F$$

The circuit shown in Figure 11-23b is used for small currents. The output voltage in that circuit is given by

$$E_0 = -I_{in}R_F \tag{11-46}$$

CHOPPER AMPLIFIERS

DC amplifiers have a certain inherent *drift* and tend to be *noisy*. These factors are not too important in low- and medium-gain applications (i.e., gains less than 1000), but loom very large indeed at high gain. For example, a 50-μV/°C drift figure in a $\times 100$ amplifier produces an output voltage of

$$(50 \ \mu V/°C) \times 100 = 5 \ mV/°C \tag{11-47}$$

which is tolerable in most cases. But in a $\times 100{,}000$ amplifier, the output voltage would be

$$(50 \ \mu V/°C) \times 10^5 = 5 \ V/°C$$

and that amount of drift will probably obscure any real signals in a very short time.

Similarly, noise can be a problem in high-gain applications, where it had been negligible in most low- to medium-gain applications. Operational amplifier noise is usually specified in terms of *nanovolts per square root* hertz [i.e., noise$_{rms}$

= nV(Hz)$^{1/2}$]. A typical low-cost operational amplifier has a noise specification of 100 nV(Hz)$^{1/2}$, so at a bandwidth of 10 kHz the noise amplitude will be

$$\text{Noise}_{rms} = 100 \text{ nV } (10^4 \text{ Hz})^{1/2}$$
$$= 100 \text{ nV } (10^2)$$
$$= 10^4 \text{ nV} = 10^{-5} \text{ V}$$

In a × 100 amplifier, without low-pass filtering, the output amplitude will be only 1 mV, but in a × 100,000 amplifier it will be 1 V.

A circuit called a *chopper amplifier* will solve both problems, because it makes use of an ac-coupled amplifier.

The drift problem is cured because of two properties of ac amplifiers; one is the inability to pass low-frequency (i.e., near-dc) changes such as those caused by drift, and the other is the ability to regulate the stage through the use of heavy doses of negative feedback.

But many low analog signals are very low frequency (i.e., in the dc to 30-Hz range) and will not pass through such an amplifier. The answer to this problem is to *chop* the signal so that it passes through the ac amplifier and then

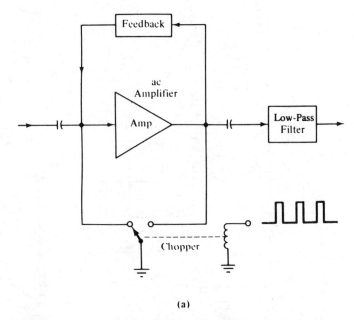

(a)

Figure 11-24 (a) Chopper amplifier; (b) differential chopper amplifier; (c) continuous versus sampled analog wave forms.

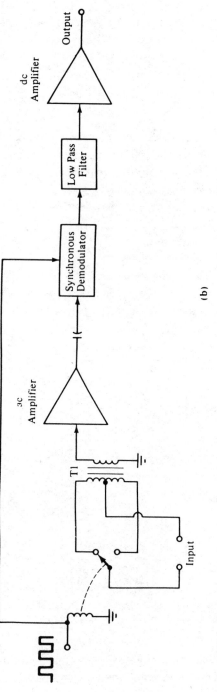

Figure 11-24 *(Continued)*

268

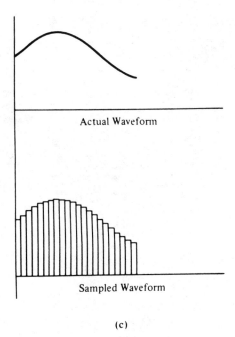

(c)

Figure 11-24 *(Continued)*

to demodulate the amplifier output signal to recover the original wave shape, but at a higher amplitude.

Figure 11-24a shows the basic chopper circuit. The traditional chopper is a vibrator-driven SPDT switch (S1) connected so that it alternately grounds first the input and then the output of the ac amplifier. An example of a chopped wave form is shown in Figure 11-24c. A low-pass filter following the amplifier filters out any residual chopper hash and any miscellaneous noise signals that may be present.

Most of these mechanical choppers use a chop rate of 400 Hz, although 60-, 100-, 200-, and 500-Hz choppers are also known. The main criterion for the chop rate is that it be twice the highest component frequency that is present in the input wave form. In other words, it must obey Nyquist's criterion.

A differential chopper amplifier is shown in Figure 11-24b. In this circuit an input transformer with a center-tapped primary is used. One input terminal is connected to the transformer center tap, while the other input terminal is switched back and forth between the two ends of the primary winding.

A synchronous demodulator following the ac amplifier detects the signal, and restores the original, but now amplified, wave shape. Again, a low-pass filter smoothes out the signal.

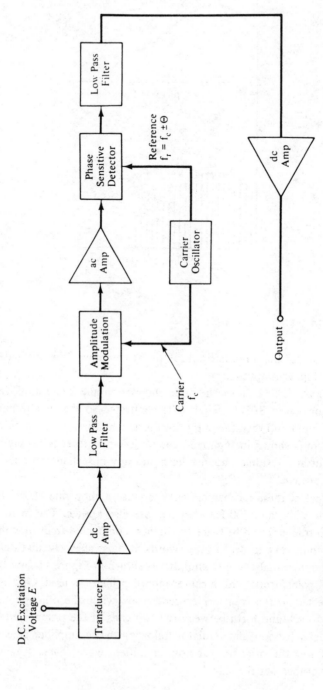

Figure 11-25 DC-excited carrier amplifier.

The modern chopper amplifier may not use mechanical vibrator switches as the chopper. A pair of CMOS or JFET electronic switches driven out of phase with each other will perform the same job. Some monolithic or hybrid function module chopper amplifiers use a varactor switching bridge for the chopper.

The chopper amplifier limits noise because of the low-pass filter and because the amplifier can have a narrow bandpass centered around the chopper frequency.

CARRIER AMPLIFIERS

A *carrier amplifier* is any type of signal-processing amplifier in which the signal carrying the desired information is modulated onto another signal (i.e., a *carrier*). The chopper amplifier is considered by many to fit this definition, but it is usually regarded as a type in its own right. The two principal carrier amplifiers are the dc-excited and ac-excited varieties.

Figure 11-25 shows a dc-excited carrier amplifier. The Wheatstone bridge transducer is excited by dc potential E. The output of the transducer, then, is a small dc voltage that varies with the value of the stimulating parameter. The transducer signal is usually of very low amplitude and is noisy. An amplifier builds up the amplitude, and a low-pass filter removes much of the noise. In some models the first stage is actually a composite of these two functions, being a filter with gain.

The signal at the output of the amplifier-filter section is used to amplitude-modulate a carrier signal. Typical carrier frequencies range from 400 Hz to 25 kHz, with 1 kHz and 2.5 kHz being very common. The signal frequency response of a carrier amplifier is a function of the carrier frequency and is usually considered to be one-fourth of the carrier frequency. A carrier or 400 Hz, then, is capable of signal frequency response to 100 Hz, while the 25-kHz carrier will support a frequency response of 6.25 kHz. Further amplification of the signal is provided by an ac amplifier.

The key to the performance of any carrier amplifier worthy of the name is the phase sensitive detector (PSD) that demodulates the amplified ac signal. Envelope detectors, while very simple and of low cost, suffer from an inability to discriminate between the real signal and spurious signals.

Figure 11-26 shows a simplified PSD circuit. Transistors $Q1$ and $Q2$ provide a return path to ground for the opposite ends of the secondary winding of input transformer $T1$. These transistors are alternately switched into an out of conduction by the reference signal in such a way that $Q1$ is off when $Q2$ is on, and

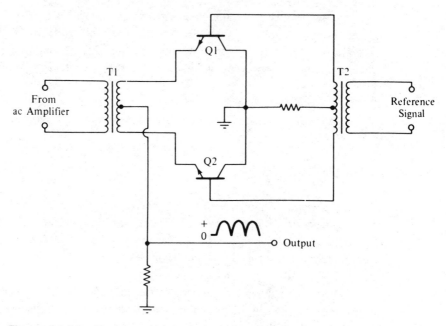

Figure 11-26   Phase-sensitive detector.

vice versa. The output wave form of the PSD is a full-wave rectified version of the input signal.

Other electronic switching circuits are also used in PSD design. All systems are designed using the fact that a PSD is essentially an electronic DPDT switch. The digital PSD circuit most often seen uses a CMOS electronic IC switch such as the CD4016/CD4066. These switches are toggled by the reference frequency in such a way that the output is always positive going, regardless of the phase of the input signal.

The advantages of the PSD include the fact that it rejects signals not of the carrier frequency and certain signals that *are* of the carrier frequency. The PSD, for example, will reject even harmonics of the carrier frequency and those components that are out of phase with the reference signal. The PSD will, however, respond to odd harmonics of the carrier frequency. Some carrier amplifiers seem to neglect this problem altogether. But in some cases, manufacturers will design the ac amplifier section to be a bandpass amplifier with a response limited to $F_c \pm (F_c/4)$. This response will eliminate any third, or higher-order, odd harmonics of the carrier frequency before they reach the PSD. It is then necessary only to assure the purity of the reference signal.

An alternate, but very common, form of carrier amplifier is the ac-excited circuit shown in Figure 11-27. In this circuit the transducer is ac excited by the

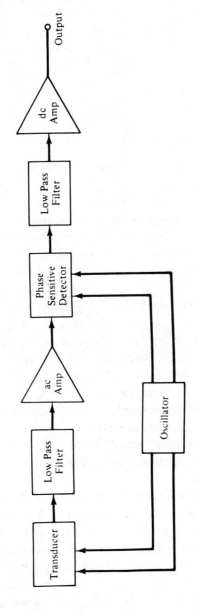

Figure 11-27 AC-excited carrier amplifier.

273

carrier signal, eliminating the need for the amplitude modulator. The small ac signal from the transducer is amplified and filtered before being applied to the PSD circuit. Again, some designs use a bandpass ac amplifier to eliminate odd-harmonic response. This circuit allows adjustment of transducer offset errors in the PSD circuit instead of in the transducer by varying the phase of the reference signal.

LOCK-IN AMPLIFIERS

The amplifiers discussed so far in this chapter produce relatively large amounts of noise and will respond to noise present in the input signal. They suffer from shot noise, thermal noise, H-field noise, E-field noise, ground loop noise, and so forth. The noise voltage or power at the output is directly proportional to the square root of the circuit bandwidth. The *lock-in amplifier* is a special case of the carrier amplifier idea in which the bandwidth is very narrow. Some lock-in amplifiers use the carrier amplifier circuit of Figure 11-27, but use an input amplifier with a very high Q bandpass. The carrier frequency may be anything between 1 Hz and 200 kHz. The lock-in principle works because the information signal is made to contain the carrier frequency in a way that is easy to demodulate and interpret. The ac amplifier accepts only a narrow band of frequencies centered about the carrier frequency. The narrowness of the bandwidth, which makes possible the improved signal-to-noise ratio, also limits the lock-in amplifier to very low frequency input signals. Even then, it is sometimes necessary to time average the signal for several seconds to obtain the needed data.

Lock-in amplifiers are capable of thinning out the noise and retrieving signals that are otherwise "buried" in the noise level. Improvements of up to 85 decibels (dB) are relatively easily obtained, and up to 100 dB is possible if the cost is no factor.

There are actually several different forms of lock-in amplifier. The type discussed here is perhaps the simplest type. It is merely a narrow-band version of the ac-excited carrier amplifier. The lock-in amplifier of Figure 11-28, however, uses a slightly different technique. It is called an autocorrelation amplifier. The carrier is modulated by the input signal and then integrated (i.e., time averaged). The output of the integrator is demodulated in a product detector circuit. The circuit in Figure 11-28 produces very low output voltages for input signals that are not in phase with the reference signals, but produces a relatively high output at the proper frequency.

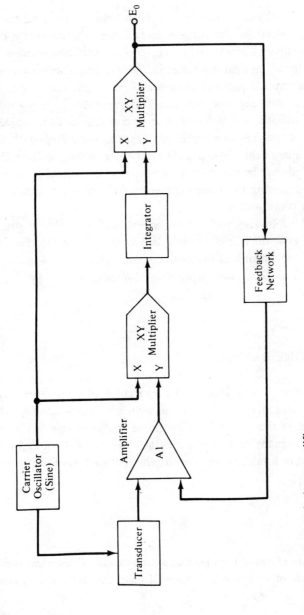

Figure 11-28 Autocorrelation amplifier.

TRANSDUCERS AND TRANSDUCTION

Not all the physical variables that must be measured lend themselves to direct input into electronic instruments and circuits. Unfortunately, electronic circuits operate only with inputs that are currents and voltages. So, when one is measuring nonelectrical physical quantities it becomes necessary to provide a device that converts physical parameters such as *force, displacement,* and *temperature,* into proportional voltages or currents. The transducer is such a device.

A *transducer* is a device or apparatus that converts nonelectrical physical parameters into electrical signals (i.e., currents or voltages), that are proportional to the value of the physical parameter being measured. Transducers take many forms and may be based on a wide variety of physical phenomena. Even when one is measuring the *same* parameter, different instruments may use different types of transducer.

The following will not be an exhaustive catalog treatment covering all transducers—the manufacturer's data sheets may be used for that purpose—but we will discuss some of the more common *types* of transducer used in scientific, industrial, medical, and engineering applications.

THE WHEATSTONE BRIDGE

Many forms of transducer create a variation in an electrical resistance, inductance, or capacitance in response to some physical parameter. These transducers are often in the form of a Wheatstone bridge or one of the related ac bridge circuits. In many cases where the transducer itself is not in the form of a bridge, it is used in a bridge circuit with other components forming the other arms of the bridge.

Strain Gages

All electrical conductors possess some amount of electrical resistance. A bar or wire made of such a conductor will have an electrical resistance that is given by

$$R = \rho \frac{L}{A} \tag{11-48}$$

where R = resistance in ohms (Ω)

ρ = *resistivity constant*, a property specific to the conductor material, given in units of ohm-centimeters (Ω-cm)

L = length in centimeters (cm)

A = cross-sectional area in square centimeters (cm²)

Example 11-6 A constantan (a 55 percent copper, 45 percent nickel alloy) round wire is 10 cm long and has a radius of 0.01 mm. Find the electrical resistance in ohms. (*Hint:* The resistivity of constantan is 44.2 $\times$ 10^{-6} Ω-cm).

Solution

$$R = \rho \frac{L}{A} \tag{11-48}$$

$$= \frac{(44.2 \times 10^{-6} \ \Omega\text{-cm})(10 \ \text{cm})}{\pi \left(0.01 \ \text{mm} \times \dfrac{1 \ \text{cm}}{10 \ \text{mm}}\right)^2}$$

$$= \frac{4.42 \times 10^{-4} \ \Omega\text{-cm}^2}{\pi (0.001 \ \text{cm})^2}$$

$$= \frac{4.42 \times 10^{-4} \ \Omega\text{-cm}^2}{\pi \ 10^{-6} \ \text{cm}^2} = \mathbf{141 \ \Omega}$$

Note that the resistivity factor (ρ) in Eq. (11-48) is a constant, so if length L or area A can be made to vary under the influence of an outside parameter, then the electrical resistance of the wire will change. This phenomenon is called *piezoresistivity,* and is an example of a transducible property of a material. *Piezoresistivity* is the change in the electrical resistance of a conductor due to changes in length and cross-sectional area. In piezoresistive materials mechanical deformation of the material produces changes in electrical resistance.

Figure 11-29 shows how an electrical conductor can use the piezoresistivity property to measure *strain,* that is, *forces* applied to it in *compression* or *tension.* In 11-29(a) we have a conductor at rest, in which no forces are acting. The length is given as L_0 and the cross-sectional area as A_0. The resistance of this conductor, from Eq. (11-48), is

$$R_0 = \rho \left(\frac{L_0}{A_0}\right) \tag{11-49}$$

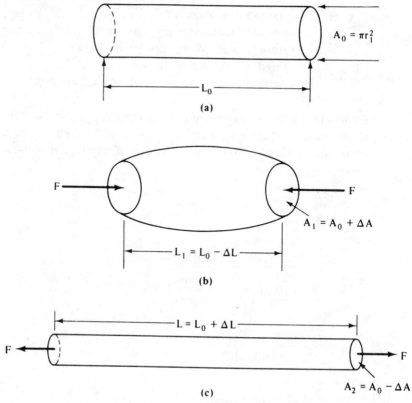

Figure 11-29 (a) Unstrained metal bar; (b) metal bar in compression; (c) metal bar in tension.

where ρ = resistivity as defined previously

R_0 = resistance in ohms (Ω) when no forces are applied

L_0 = resting (i.e., no force) length (cm)

A_0 = resting cross-sectional area (cm^2)

But in Figure 11-29(b) we see the situation where a compression force of magnitude F is applied along the axis in the inward direction. The conductor will deform, causing the length L_1 to decrease to $(L_0 - \Delta L)$ and the cross-sectional area to increase to $(A_0 + \Delta A)$. The electrical resistance decreases to $(R_0 - \Delta R)$:

$$R_1 = (R_0 - \Delta R) \propto \frac{L_0 - \Delta L}{A_0 + \Delta A} \tag{11-50}$$

Similarly, when a tension force of the same magnitude (i.e., F) is applied (i.e., a force that is directed outward along the axis), the length increases to ($L_0 + \Delta L$), and the cross-sectional area decreases to ($A_0 - \Delta A$). The resistance will increase to

$$R_2 = (R_0 - \Delta R) \propto \frac{L_0 + \Delta L}{A_0 + \Delta A} \tag{11-50}$$

The *sensitivity* of the strain gage is expressed in terms of unit change of electrical resistance for a unit change in length and is given in the form of a *gage factor S:*

$$S = \frac{\Delta R / R}{\Delta L / L} \tag{11-51}$$

where $S =$ gage factor (dimensionless)
$R =$ unstrained resistance of the conductor
$\Delta R =$ change in resistance due to strain
$L =$ unstrained length of the conductor
$\Delta L =$ change in length due to strain

Example 11-7   Find the gage factor of a 128-Ω conductor that is 24 mm long if the resistance changes 13.3 Ω and the length changes 1.6 mm under a tension force.

Solution

$$S = \frac{\Delta R / R}{\Delta L / L} \tag{11-51}$$

$$= \frac{13.3 \ \Omega / 128 \ \Omega}{1.6 \ \text{mm} / 24 \ \text{mm}}$$

$$= \frac{1.04 \times 10^{-1}}{6.67 \times 10^{-2}} = \mathbf{1.56}$$

We may also express the gage factor in terms of the length and diameter of the conductor. Recall that the diameter is related to the cross-sectional area (i.e., $A = \pi d^2 / 4 = \pi r^2$), so the relationship between the gage factor S and these other factors is given by

$$S = 1 + 2 \frac{\Delta d / d}{\Delta L / L} \tag{11-52}$$

Example 11-8 Calculate the gage factor S if a 1.5-mm-diameter conductor that is 24 mm long changes length by 1 mm and diameter by 0.02 mm under a compression force.

Solution

$$S = 1 + 2\, \frac{\Delta d/d}{\Delta d/d} \tag{11-52}$$

$$= 1 + \frac{2[(0.02 \text{ mm})/(1.5 \text{ mm})]}{(1 \text{ mm})/(24 \text{ mm})}$$

$$= 1 + \frac{(2)(1.3 \times 10^{-2})}{4.2 \times 10^{-2}}$$

$$= 1 + (2)(0.31) = \mathbf{1.62}$$

Note that the expression $(\Delta L/L)$ is sometimes denoted by the Greek letter ϵ, so Eqs. (11-51) and (11-52) become

$$S = 1 + \frac{2(\Delta d/d)}{\epsilon}$$

$$= \frac{\Delta R/R}{\epsilon}$$

Gage factors for various metals vary considerably. Constantan, for example, has a gage factor of approximately 2, while certain other common alloys have gage factors between 1 and 2. At least one alloy (92 percent platinum, 8 percent tungsten) has a gage factor of 4. Semiconductor materials such as germanium and silicon can be doped with impurities to provide custom gage factors between 50 and 250. The problem with semiconductor strain gages, however, is that they exhibit a marked sensitivity to temperature changes. Where semiconductor strain gages are used, either a thermally controlled environment or temperature compensating circuitry must be provided.

Bonded and Unbonded Strain Gages

Strain gages can be classified as *unbonded* or *bonded*. These categories refer to the method of construction. Figure 11-30 shows both methods of construction.

The unbonded type of strain gage is shown in Figure 11-30a and consists of a wire resistance element stretched taut between two flexible supports. These

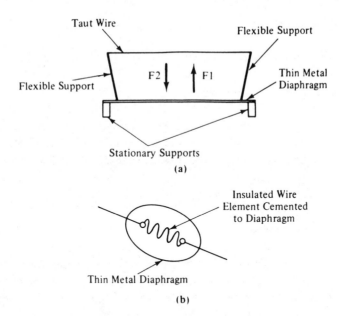

Taut Wire

Flexible Support

F2 ↓   ↑ F1

Flexible Support

Thin Metal
Diaphragm

Stationary Supports

(a)

Insulated Wire
Element Cemented
to Diaphragm

Thin Metal Diaphragm

(b)

Figure 11-30   (a) Unbonded strain gage; (b) bonded strain gage.

supports are configured in such a way as to place tension or compression forces on the taut wire when external forces are applied. In the particular example shown, the supports are mounted on a thin metal diaphragm that flexes when a force is applied. Force $F1$ will cause the flexible supports to spread apart, placing a tension force on the wire and increasing its resistance. Alternatively, when force $F2$ is applied, the ends of the flexible supports tend to move closer together, effectively placing a compression force on the wire element and thereby reducing its resistance. In actuality, the wire's resting condition is *tautness,* which implies a tension force. So $F1$ increases the tension force from normal, and $F2$ decreases the normal tension.

The bonded strain gage is shown in Figure 11-30b. In this type of device a wire or semiconductor element is cemented to a thin metal diaphragm. When the diaphragm is flexed, the element deforms to produce a resistance change.

The linearity of both types can be quite good, provided that the elastic limits of the diaphragm and the element are not exceeded. It is also necessary to ensure that the ΔL term is only a very small percentage of L.

In the past it has been "standard wisdom" that bonded strain gages are more rugged, but less linear, than unbonded models. Although this may have been true at one time, recent experience has shown that modern manufacturing techniques produce linear, reliable instruments of both types.

Strain Gage Circuitry

Before a strain gage can be useful, it must be connected into a circuit that will convert its resistance changes to a current or voltage output. Most applications are voltage output circuits.

Figure 11-31a shows the *half-bridge* (so called because it is actually half of a Wheatstone bridge circurit) or *voltage-divider* circuit. The strain gage element of resistance R is placed in series with a fixed resistance $R1$ across a stable and well-regulated voltage source E. The output voltage E_0 is found from the voltage-divider equation

$$E_0 = \frac{ER}{R + R\,1} \tag{11-53}$$

Equation (11-53) describes the output voltage E_0 when the transducer is at rest (i.e., nothing is stimulating the strain gage element). When the element is stimulated, however, its resistance changes a small amount ΔR. To simplify our discussion we will adopt the standard convention used in many texts of letting $h = \Delta R$.

$$E_0 = \frac{E(R + h)}{(R \pm h) + R\,1} \tag{11-54}$$

Another half-bridge is shown in Figure 11-31b, but in this case the strain gage is in series with a *constant current source* (CCS), which will maintain current I at a constant level regardless of changes in strain gage resistance. The normal output voltage E_0 is

$$E_0 = IR \tag{11-55}$$

$$E_0 = I(R \pm h) \tag{11-56}$$

under stimulated conditions.

The half-bridge circuits suffer from one major defect: Output voltage E_0 will always be present regardless of the stimulus. Ideally, in any transducer system, we want E_0 to be zero when the stimulus is also zero and take a value proportional to the stimulus when the stimulus value is nonzero. A Wheatstone bridge circuit in which one or more strain gage elements form the bridge arms has this property.

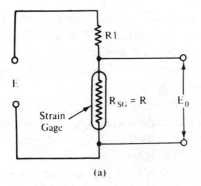

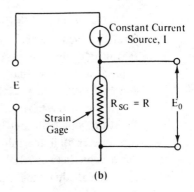

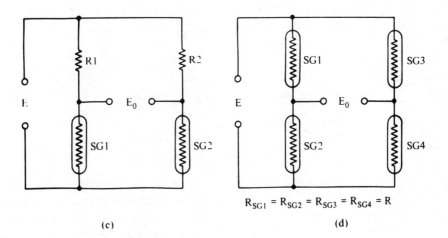

Figure 11-31 (a) Constant-voltage strain gage circuit, half-bridge type; (b) constant-current strain gage circuit, half-bridge type; (c) two strain gage elements in Wheatstone bridge; (d) four-active-element strain gage Wheatstone bridge.

Figure 11-31c shows a circuit in which strain gage elements *SG*1 and *SG*2 form two bridge arms and fixed resistors *R*1 and *R*2 form the other two arms. It is usually the case that *SG*1 and *SG*2 will be configured so that their actions oppose each other; that is, under stimulus, *SG*1 will have a resistance $R + h$ and *SG*2 will have a resistance $R - h$, or vice versa.

One of the most linear forms of transducer bridge is the circuit of Figure 11-31d in which all four bridge arms contain strain gage elements. In most such transducers all four strain gage elements have the same resistance (i.e., *R*), which has a value between 100 and 1000Ω in most cases.

Recall that the output voltage from a Wheatstone bridge is the difference between the voltages across the two half-bridge dividers. The following equations hold true for bridges in which one, two, or four equal active elements are used. For one active element,

$$E_0 = \frac{E}{4} \frac{h}{R} \tag{11-57}$$

(accurate to $\pm$ 5 percent, provided that $h \leq 0.1$). For two active elements,

$$E_0 = \frac{E}{2} \frac{h}{R} \tag{11-58}$$

For four active elements,

$$E_0 = \frac{Eh}{R} \tag{11-59}$$

where, for all three equations, E_0 = output potential in volts (V)
E = excitation potential in volts (V)
R = resistance of all bridge arms
h = quantity ΔR, the change in resistance of a bridge arm under stimulus

(These equations apply only for the case where all the bridge arms have equal resistances under zero stimulus conditions.)

Example 11-9 A transducer that measures force has a nominal resting resistance of 300 Ω and is excited by +7.5 V dc. When a 980-dyne force is applied, all four equal-resistance bridge elements change resistance by 5.2 Ω. Find the output voltage E_0.

Solution

$$E_0 = E \frac{h}{R} \tag{11-59}$$

$$= 7.5 \text{ V} \frac{5.2 \ \Omega}{300 \ \Omega}$$

$$= \frac{(7.5 \text{ V})(5.2)}{300} = \mathbf{0.13 \text{ V}}$$

Transducer Sensitivity

When designing electronic instrumentation systems involving strain gage transducers, it is convenient to use the *sensitivity factor* (denoted by the Greek letter psi, ψ), which relates the output voltage in terms of the excitation voltage and the applied stimulus. In most cases, we see a specification giving the number of microvolts or millivolts output per volt of excitation potential per unit of applied stimulus (i.e., $\mu V/V/Q_0$ or $mV/V/Q_0$).

$$\psi = E_0/V/Q_0 \tag{11-60a}$$

and

$$\psi = \frac{E_0'}{V \times Q_0} \tag{11-60b}$$

where E_0' = output potential
V = one unit of potential (i.e., 1 V)
Q_0 = one unit of stimulus

The sensitivity is often given as a specification by the transducer manufacturer. From it we can predict output voltage for any level of stimulus and excitation potential. The output voltage, then, is found from

$$E_0 = \psi E Q \tag{11-61}$$

where E_0 = output potential in volts (V)
ψ = sensitivity in $\mu V/V/Q_0$
E = excitation potential in volts (V)
Q = stimulus parameter

Example 11-10 A well-known medical arterial blood pressure transducer uses a four-element piezoresistive Wheatstone bridge with a sensitivity of 5 μV per volt of excitation per torr of pressure, that is 5 $\mu V/V/T$ (*Note*: 1 torr = 1 mm Hg). Find the output voltage if the bridge is excited by 5 V dc and 120 torr of pressure is applied.

Solution

$$E_0 = \psi E Q \tag{11-61}$$

$$= \frac{5\,\mu V}{V - T} \times (5\ V) \times (120\ T)$$

$$= (5 \times 5 \times 120)\ \mu V = \mathbf{3000\ \boldsymbol{\mu} V}$$

Balancing and Calibrating the Bridge

Few, if any, Wheatstone bridge strain gages meet the ideal condition in which all four arms have exactly equal resistances. In fact, the bridge resistance specified by the manufacturer is a *nominal* value only. There will inevitably be an *offset voltage* (i.e., $E_0 \neq 0$) when $Q = 0$. Figure 11-32 shows a circuit that will balance the bridge when the stimulus is zero. Potentiometer $R1$, usually a type with ten or more turns of operation, is used to inject a balancing current I into the bridge circuit at one of the nodes. $R1$ is adjusted, with the stimulus at zero, for zero output voltage.

The best calibration method is to apply a precisely known value of stimulus to the transducer and adjust the amplifier following the transducer for the output proper for that level of stimulus. But that may prove unreasonably difficult in some cases, so an *artificial* calibrator is needed to simulate the stimulus. This function is provided by $R3$ and $S1$ in Figure 11-32. When $S1$ is open, the transducer is able to operate normally, but when $S1$ is closed it *unbalances* the

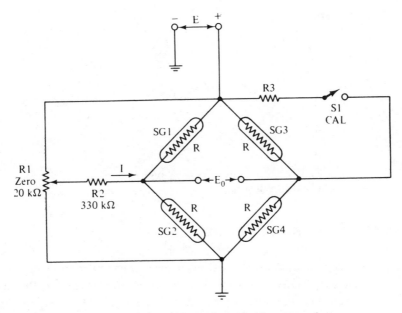

Figure 11-32 Circuit for using Wheatstone bridge transducer.

bridge and produces an output voltage E_0 that simulates some standard value of the stimulus. The value of $R3$ is given by

$$R3 = \frac{R}{4Q\psi} - \frac{R}{2} \tag{11-62}$$

where $R3$ = resistance of $R3$ (Ω)
     R = nominal resistance of the bridge arms (Ω)
     Q = calibrated stimulus parameter
     ψ = sensitivity factor (μV/V/Q); *note* the difference in the units of ψ: V instead of μV

Example 11-11 An arterial blood pressure transducer has a sensitivity of 10 μV/V/torr, and a nominal bridge arm resistance of 200 Ω. Find a value for $R3$ in Figure 11-32 if we want the calibration to simulate an arterial pressure of 200 mm Hg (i.e., 200 torr).

Solution

$$R3 = \frac{R}{4Q\psi} - \frac{R}{2} \tag{11-62}$$

$$= \frac{200 \ \Omega}{4 \times \dfrac{10^{-5} \ V}{V - T} \times 200T} - \frac{200 \ \Omega}{2}$$

$$= \frac{200 \ \Omega}{(4)(10^{-5})(200)} - 100 \ \Omega = \mathbf{24{,}900 \ \Omega}$$

TEMPERATURE TRANSDUCERS

A large number of physical phenomena are temperature dependent, so we find quite a variety of electrical temperature transducers on the market. In this discussion, however, we will discuss only three basic types: *thermistor, thermocouple,* and *semiconductor pn junctions.*

Thermistors

Metals and most other conductors are temperature sensitive and will change electrical resistance with changes in temperature, as follows:

$$R_t = R_0 \left[1 + \alpha(T - T_0) \right] \tag{11-63}$$

where R_t = resistance in ohms at temperature T
  R_0 = resistance in ohms at temperature T_0 (often a standard reference temperature)
  T = temperature of the conductor
  T_0 = a previous temperature of the conductor at which R_0 was determined
  α = *temperature coefficient* of the material, a property of the conductor (°C^{-1})

The temperature coefficients of most metals are positive, as are the coefficients for most semiconductors (e.g., gold has a value of +0.004/°C). Ceramic semiconductors used to make *thermistors* (i.e., thermal resistors) can have either negative or positive temperature coefficients depending upon their composition.

The resistance of a thermistor is given by

$$R_t = R_0 \exp \beta \left(\frac{1}{T} - \frac{1}{T_0} \right)$$

where R_t = resistance of the thermistor at temperature T

R_0 = resistance of the thermistor at a reference temperature (usually the ice point, 0°C, or room temperature, 25°C)

e = base of the natural logarithms

T = thermistor temperature in Kelvins (K)

T_0 = reference temperature in Kelvins (K)

β = a property of the material used to make the thermistor

(*Note*: β will usually have a value between 1500 and 7000 K.)

Example 11-12   Calculate the resistance of a thermistor at 100°C if the resistance at 0°C was 18 kΩ. The material of the thermistor has a value of 2200 K. (*Note*: 0°C = 273 K, so 100°C = 373 K.)

Solution

$$R_t = R_0 \exp \beta \left(\frac{1}{T} - \frac{1}{T_0} \right) \tag{11-64}$$

$$= (1.8 \times 10^4 \ \Omega) \exp \left[(2200 \ \text{K}) \left(\frac{1}{373 \ \text{K}} - \frac{1}{273 \ \text{K}} \right) \right]$$

$$= 1.8 \times 10^4 \ \Omega \ e^{-2.15} = \mathbf{2089 \ \Omega}$$

Equation (11-64) demonstrates that the response of a thermistor is exponential, as shown in Figure 11-33. Note that both curves are nearly linear over a portion of their ranges, but become decidedly nonlinear in the remainder of the region. If a wide measurement range is needed, a linearization network will be required.

Thermistor transducers will be used in any of the circuits in Figure 11-31. They will also be found using many packaging arrangements. Figure 11-34 shows a bead thermistor used in medical instruments to continuously monitor a patient's rectal temperature.

The equations governing thermistors usually apply if there is little *self-heating* of the thermistor, although there are applications where self-heating is used. But in straight temperature measurements it is to be avoided. To minimize self-heating it is necessary to control the power dissipation of the thermistor.

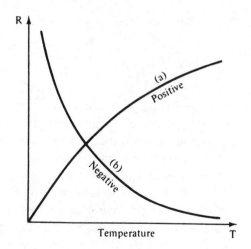

Figure 11-33 Thermistor temperature versus resistance curves.

Also of concern in some applications is the *time constant* of the thermistor. The resistance does not jump immediately to the new value when the temperature changes, but requires a small amount of time to stabilize at the new resistance value. This is expressed in terms of the time constant of the thermistor in a manner that is reminiscent of capacitors charging in *RC* circuits.

Thermocouples

When two dissimilar metals are joined together to form a "vee" as in Figure 11-35a, it is possible to generate an electrical potential merely by heating the

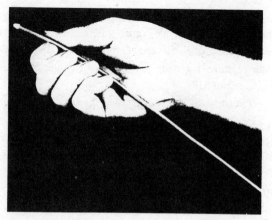

Figure 11-34 Thermistor in a medical rectal probe. (*Courtesy of Electronics-for-Medicine.*)

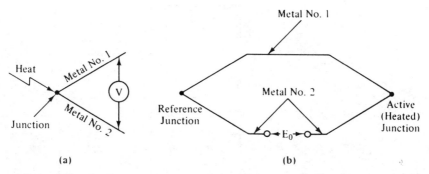

Figure 11-35   (a) Thermocouple junction; (b) two-thermocouple temperature transducer.

junction. This phenomenon, first noted by Seebeck in 1823, is due to different *work functions* for the two metals. Such a junction is called a *thermocouple*. Seebeck emf generated by the junction is proportional to the junction temperature and is reasonably linear over wide temperature ranges.

A simple thermocouple is shown in Figure 11-35b; it uses two junctions. One junction is the measurement junction, and it is used as the thermometry probe. The other junction is a reference and is kept at a reference temperature, such as the ice point (0°C) or room temperature.

Interestingly, there is an inverse thermocouple phenomenon, called the *Peltier effect,* in which an electrical potential applied across A-B in Figure 11-35b will cause one junction to absorb heat (i.e., get hot) and the other to lose heat (i.e., get cold). Semiconductor thermocouples have been used in small-scale environmental temperature chambers, and it is reported that one company researched the possibility of using Peltier devices to cool submarine equipment. Ordinary air conditioning equipment proves too noisy in submarines desirous of "silent running."

Semiconductor Temperature Transducers

Ordinary pn junction diodes exhibit a strong dependence upon temperature. This effect can be easily demonstrated by using an ohmmeter and an ordinary rectifier diode such as the 1N4000-series devices. Connect the ohmmeter so that it forward biases the diode and note the resistance at room temperature. Next hold a soldering iron or other heat source close to the diode's body and watch the electrical resistance change. In a circuit such as Figure 11-36 the current is held constant, so output voltage E_0 will change with temperature-caused changes in diode resistance.

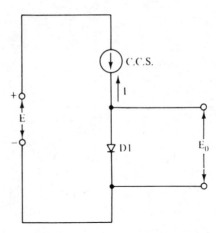

Figure 11-36   PN junction diode as a temperature transducer.

Another solid-state temperature transducer is shown in Figure 11-37. In this version, the temperature sensor device is a pair of diode-connected transistors. In any transistor the base–emitter voltage V_{be} is

$$V_{be} = \frac{kT}{q} \ln \left(\frac{I_c}{I_s} \right)$$

(11-65)

where V_{be} = base–emitter potential in volts (V)
       k = Boltzmann's constant (1.38×10^{-23} J/K)
       T = temperature in Kelvins (K)
      Q = electronic charge, 1.6×10^{-19} coulomb (C)
      ln denotes the natural logarithms
      I_C = collector current in amperes (A)
      I_S = reverse saturation current in amperes (A)

Note that the k and q terms in Eq. (11-65) are constants, and both currents can be made to be constant. The only variable, then, is *temperature.*

In the circuit of Figure 11-37, we use two transistors connected to provide a differential output voltage ΔV_{be} that is the difference between $V_{be(Q1)}$ and $V_{be(Q2)}$. Combining the expressions for V_{be} for both transistors yields the expression

$$\Delta V_{be} = \frac{kT}{q} \ln \left(\frac{I1}{I2} \right)$$

(11-66)

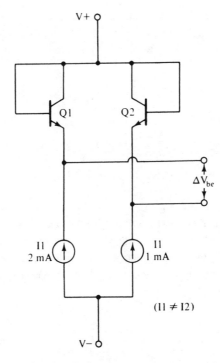

Figure 11-37   Two transistors connected as diodes from a temperature transducer if I1 = I2.

Note that, since ln 1 = 0, currents $I1$ and $I2$ *must not be equal.* In general, designers set a ratio of 2:1; for example, $I1 = 2$ mA and $I2 = 1$ mA. Since currents $I1$ and $I2$ are supplied from constant current sources, the ratio $I1/I2$ is a constant. Also, it is true that the logarithm of a constant is a constant. Therefore, all terms in Eq. (11-66) are constants, except temperature T. Equation (11-66), therefore, may be written in the form

$$\Delta V_{be} = KT \qquad\qquad (11\text{-}67)$$

where $K = (k/q) \ln (I1/I2)$
$= (1.38 \times 10^{-23})/(1.6 \times 10^{-19}) \ln (2/1)$
$= 5.98 \times 10^{-5}$ V/K $= 59.8$ μV/K

We may now rewrite Eq. (11-67) in the form

$$\Delta V_{be} = 59.8 \ \mu V/K$$

Example 11-13 Calculate the output voltage from a circuit such as Figure 11-37 if the temperature is 35°C (*Hint:* K = °C + 273).

Solution

$$\Delta V_{be} = KT \qquad (11\text{-}67)$$

$$= \frac{59.8 \ \mu V}{K} \times (35 + 273) \ K$$

$$= (59.8)(308) \ \mu V = 18{,}418 \ \mu V = \textbf{0.0184 V}$$

In most thermometers using the circuit of Figure 11-37 an amplifier increases the output voltage to a level that is numerically the same as a unit of temperature, so the temperature may be easily read from a digital voltmeter. The most common scale factor is 10 mV/K, so for our transducer the postamplifier requires a gain of

$$A_V = \frac{10 \ \text{mV/K}}{59.8 \ \mu V \times (1 \ \text{m V} / 10^3 \ \mu \ V)} = 167$$

INDUCTIVE TRANSDUCERS

Inductance L and inductive reactance X_L are transducible properties, because they can be *varied* by certain mechanical methods.

Figure 11-38a shows an example of an inductive Wheatstone bridge. Resistors $R1$ and $R2$ form two fixed arms of the bridge, while coils $L1$ and $L2$ form variable arms. Since inductors are used, the excitation voltage must be ac. In most cases, the ac excitation source will have a frequency between 400 and 5000 Hz and an rms amplitude of 5 to 10 V.

The inductors are constructed coaxially, as shown in Figure 11-38b, with a common core. It is a fundamental property of any inductor that a ferrous core increases its inductance. In the rest condition (i.e., zero stimulus), the core will be positioned equally inside of both coils. If the stimulus moves the core in the direction shown in Figure 11-38b, the core tends to move out of $L1$ and further into $L2$. This action reduces the inductive reactance of $L1$ and increases that of $L2$, unbalancing the bridge.

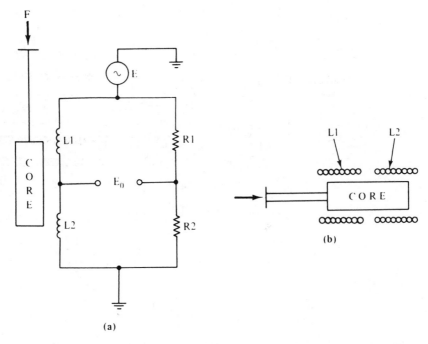

Figure 11-38 (a) Inductive Wheatstone bridge transducer; (b) mechanical form.

LINEAR VARIABLE DIFFERENTIAL TRANSFORMERS

Another form of inductive transformer is the *linear variable differential transformer* (LVDT) shown in Figure 11-39. The construction of the LVDT is similar to that of the inductive bridge, except that it also contains a primary winding.

One advantage of the LVDT over the bridge-type transducer is that it provides higher output voltages for small changes in core position. Several commercial models are available that produce 50 to 300 mV/mm. In the latter case, this means that a 1-mm displacement of the core produces a voltage output of 300 mV.

In normal operation, the core is equally inside both secondary coils, *L2A* and *L2B,* and an ac carrier is applied to the primary winding. This carrier typically has a frequency between 40 Hz and 20 kHz and an amplitude in the range from 1 to 10 V rms.

Under rest conditions the coupling between the primary and each secondary is equal. The currents flowing in each secondary, then, are equal to each other.

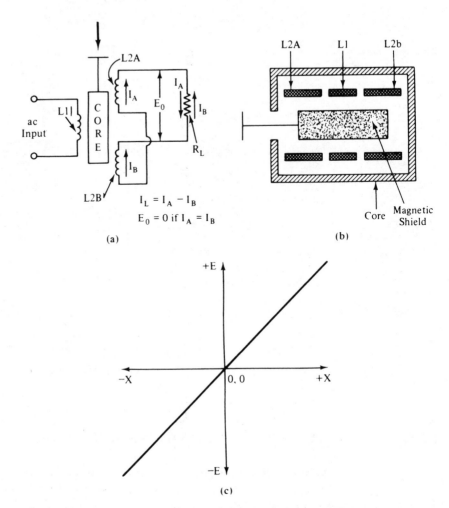

Figure 11-39 (a) LVDT; (b) LVDT construction; (c) output transfer function.

Note in Figure 11-39a that the secondary windings are connected in series opposing, so if the secondary winding currents are equal, they will exactly cancel each other in the load. The ac voltage appearing across the load, therefore, is *zero* ($I_A = I_B$).

But when the core is moved so that it is more inside *L2B* and less inside *L2A*, the coupling between the primary and *L2B* is greater than the coupling between the primary and *L2A*. Since this fact makes the two secondary currents no longer equal, the cancellation is not complete. The current in the load I_L is no longer zero. The output voltage appearing across load resistor R_L is proportional to the core displacement, as shown in Figure 11-39c. The *magnitude* of the output voltage is proportional to the *amount* of core displacement, while the *phase* of the output voltage is determined by the *direction* of the displacement.

POSITION-DISPLACEMENT TRANSDUCERS

A position transducer will create an output signal that is proportional to the position of some object along a given axis. For very small position ranges we could use a strain gage (i.e., Figure 11-40), but note that the range of such transducers is necessarily very small. Most strain gages either are nonlinear for large displacements or are damaged by large displacements.

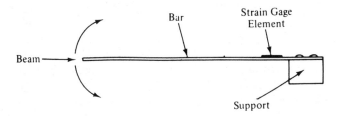

Figure 11-40   Beam transducer using a strain gage element.

The LVDT can be used as a position transducer. Recall that the output polarity indicates the direction of movement from a zero-reference position, and the amplitude indicates the magnitude of the displacement. Although the LVDT will accommodate larger displacements than the strain gage, it is still limited in range.

The most common form of position transducer is the potentiometer. For applications that are not too critical, it is often the case that ordinary linear taper potentiometers are sufficient. Rotary models are used for curvilinear motion, and slide models for rectilinear motion.

In precision applications designers use either regular precision potentiometers or special potentiometers designed specifically as position transducers.

Figure 11-41 shows two possible circuits using potentiometers as position transducers. In Figure 11-41a we see a single-quadrant circuit for use where the zero point (i.e., starting reference) is at one end of the scale. The pointer will always be at some point such that $0 \leq x \leq X_m$. The potentiometer is connected so that one end is grounded and the other is connected to a precision, regulated

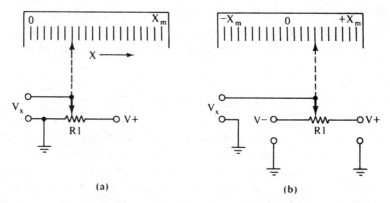

(a)   (b)

Figure 11-41   (a) Position transducer using a potentiometer (one quadrant); (b) position transducer using a potentiometer (two quadrants).

voltage source $V+$. The value of V_x represents X, and will be $0 \le V_x \le V+$, such that $V_x = 0$ when $X = 0$, and $V_x = V+$ when $X = X_m$.

A two-quadrant system is shown in Figure 11-41b and is similar to the previous circuit except that, instead of grounding one end of the potentiometer, it is connected to a precision, regulated *negative*-to-ground power source, $V-$. Figure 11-42 shows the output functions of these two transducers. Figure 11-42a represents the circuit of Figure 11-41a, while Figure 11-42b represents the circuit of Figure 11-41b.

A four-quadrant transducer can be made by placing two circuits such as Figure 11-41b at right angles to each other and arranging linkage so that the output signal varies appropriately.

VELOCITY AND ACCELERATION TRANSDUCERS

Velocity can be defined as displacement per unit of time, and acceleration is the time rate of change of velocity. Since both velocity (v) and acceleration (a) can be related back to position (s), we often find position transducers used to *derive* velocity and acceleration signals. The relationships are

$$v = \frac{ds}{dt} \tag{11-68}$$

$$a = \frac{dv}{dt} \tag{11-69}$$

$$a = \frac{d^2s}{dt^2} \tag{11-70}$$

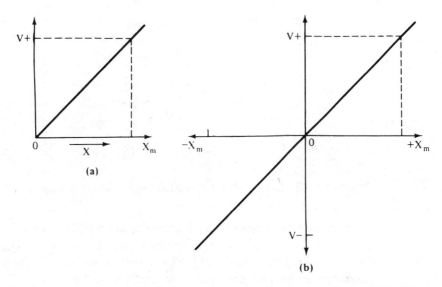

Figure 11-42 (a) $V+$ versus X for Figure 11-41(a); (b) V versus X for Figure 11-41(b).

Velocity and acceleration are the first and second time derivatives of displacement (i.e., change of position), respectively. We may derive electrical signals proportional to v and a by using an operational amplifier differentiator circuit (see Figure 11-43). The output of the transducer is a time-dependent function of position (i.e., displacement). This signal is differentiated by the stages following to produce the velocity and acceleration signals.

TACHOMETERS

Alternating- and direct-current generators are also used as velocity transducers. In their basic form they will transduce rotary motion (i.e., produce an angular velocity signal), but with appropriate mechanical linkage will also indicate rectilinear motion.

In the case of a dc generator, the output signal is a dc voltage with a magnitude that is proportional to the angular velocity of the armature shaft.

The ac generator, or *alternator,* maintains a relatively constant output voltage, but its ac *frequency* is proportional to the angular velocity of the armature shaft.

If a dc output is desired, instead of an ac signal, a circuit similar to Figure 11-44 is used. The ac output of the tachometer is fed to a trigger circuit (either

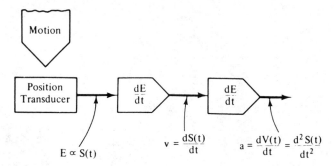

$E \propto S(t)$ $v = \dfrac{dS(t)}{dt}$ $a = \dfrac{dV(t)}{dt} = \dfrac{d^2 S(t)}{dt^2}$

Figure 11-43   Example of derived signals using integration or differentiation.

a comparator or Schmitt trigger) so that squared-off pulses are created. These pulses are then differentiated to produce spikelike pulses to trigger the monostable multivibrator (one-shot). The output of the one-shot is integrated to produce a dc level proportional to the tachometer frequency.

The reason for using the one-shot stage is to produce output pulses that have a *constant amplitude* and *duration*. Only the pulse repetition rate (i.e., number of pulses per unit of time) varies with the input frequency. This fact allows us to integrate the one-shot output to obtain our needed dc signal. If either duration or amplitude varied, the integrator output would be meaningless. This technique is widespread in electronic instruments, so it should be understood well.

FORCE AND PRESSURE TRANSDUCERS

Force transducers can be made by using strain gages or either LVDT or potentiometer displacement transducers. In the case of the displacement transducer

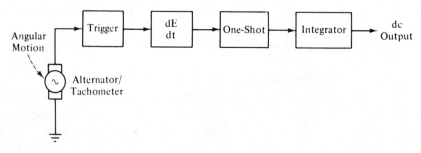

Figure 11-44   Alternator tachometer.

(Figure 11-45a) it becomes a force transducer by causing a power spring to either compress or stretch. Recall Hooke's law, which tells us that the force required to compress or stretch a spring is proportional to a *constant* and the *displacement* caused by the compression or tension force applied to the spring. So by using a displacement transducer and a calibrated spring, we are able to measure force.

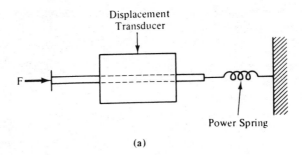

(a)

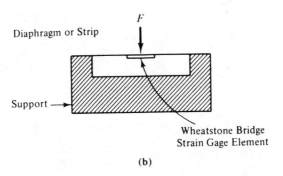

(b)

Figure 11-45 (a) Force from a displacement transducer; (b) force–pressure transducer.

Strain gages connected to flexible metal bars are also used to measure force, because it requires a certain amount of force to deflect the bar any given amount. Several transducers on the market use this technique; they are advertised as "force-displacement" transducers. Such transducers form the basis of the digital bathroom scales now on the market.

Do not be surprised to see such transducers, especially the smaller types, calibrated in *grams.* We know that the gram is a unit of *mass*, not force, so what this usage refers to is the gravitational force on 1 gram at the earth's surface, roughly 980 dynes. A 1-g weight suspended from the end of the bar in Figure 11-40 will represent a force of 980 dynes.

A side view of a cantilever force transducer is shown in Figure 11-45b. In this device a flexible strip is supported by mounts at either end, and a piezoresistive strain gage is mounted to the under side of the strip. Flexing the strip unbalances the gage's Wheatstone bridge, producing an output voltage.

A related device uses a cup- or barrel-shaped support and a circular diaphragm instead of the strip. Such a device will measure force or pressure, that is, *force per unit of area.*

FLUID PRESSURE TRANSDUCERS

Fluid pressures are measured in a variety of ways, but the most common involve a transducer such as those shown in Figures 11-46 and 11-47.

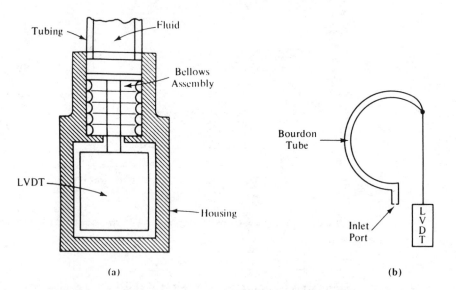

(a)   (b)

Figure 11-46   (a) Fluid pressure transducer; (b) Bourdon tube fluid pressure transducer.

In the example of Figure 11-46a, a strain gage or LVDT is mounted inside a housing that has a bellows or aneroid assembly exposed to the fluid. More force is applied to the LVDT or gage assembly as the bellows compresses. The compression of the bellows is proportional to the fluid pressure.

An example of the *Bourdon tube* pressure transducer is shown in Figure 11-46b. Such a tube is hollow and curved, but flexible. When a pressure is applied through the inlet port, the tube tends to straighten out. If the end tip is connected to a position/displacement transducer, the transducer output will be proportional to the applied pressure.

Figure 11-47a shows another popular form of fluid transducer. In this version, a diaphragm is mounted on a cylindrical support similar to Figure 11-46. In some cases, a bonded strain gage is attached to the under side of the diaphragm, or flexible supports to an unbonded type are used. In the example shown, the diaphragm is connected to the core drive bar of an inductive transducer or LVDT.

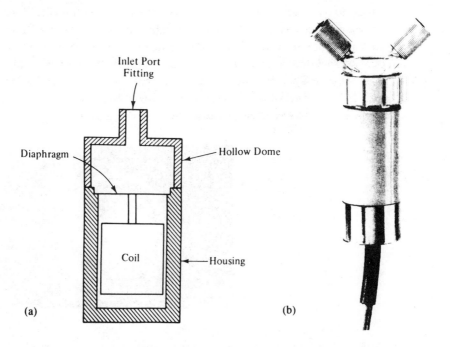

Figure 11-47   (a) Dome-type fluid pressure transducer; (b) commercial dome-type transducer. (*Courtesy of Hewlett-Packard.*)

Figure 11-47b shows the Hewlett-Packard type 1280 transducer used in medical electronics to measure human blood pressure. In this device, the hollow fluid-filled dome is fitted with *Luer-lock* fittings, standards in medical apparatus.

The fluid transducers shown so far will measure gage pressure (i.e., pressure above atmospheric pressure) because one side of the diaphragm is open to air.

A *differential* pressure transducer will measure the difference between pressures applied to the two sides of the diaphragm. Such devices will have two ports marked, such as $P1$ and $P2$, or something similar.

LIGHT TRANSDUCERS

There are several different phenomena for measuring light, and they create different types of transducer. We will limit the discussion to *photoresistors, photovoltaic cells, photodiodes,* and *phototransistors.*

A photoresistor can be made because certain semiconductor elements show a marked decrease in electrical resistance when exposed to light. Most materials do not change linearly with increased light intensity, but certain combinations such as cadmium sulfide (CdS) and cadmium selenide (CdSe) are effective. These cells operate over a spectrum from "near-infrared" through most of the visible light range, and can be made to operate at light levels of 10^{-3} to 10^{+3} footcandles (i.e., 10^{-3} to 70 mW/cm^2). Figure 11-48a shows the photoresistor circuit symbol, while Figure 11-48b shows an example of a photoresistor.

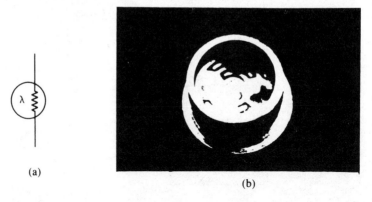

(a)

(b)

Figure 11-48   (a) Symbol for photoresistor cell; (b) actual photoresistor cell.

A photovoltaic cell, or "solar cell" as it is sometimes called, will produce an electrical current when connected to a load. Both silicon (Si) and selenium (Se) types are known. The Si type covers the visible and near-infrared spectrum, at intensities between 10^{-3} and 10^{+3} mW/cm^2. The selenium cell, on the other hand, operates at intensities of 10^{-1} to 10^2 mW/cm^2, but accepts a spectrum of near-infrared to the ultraviolet.

Semiconductor pn junctions under sufficient illumination will respond to light. They tend to be photoconductive when heavily reverse biased, and photovoltaic when forward biased. These phenomena have led to a whole family of photodiodes and phototransistors.

CAPACITIVE TRANSDUCERS

A parallel plate capacitor can be made by positioning two conductive planes parallel to each other. The capacitance is given by

$$C = \frac{kKA}{d} \tag{11-71}$$

where $C =$ capacitance in *farads* (F) or a subunit (μF, pF, etc.)
$k =$ a units constant
$K =$ dielectric constant of the material used in the space between the plates (K for air is 1)
$A =$ area of the plates "shading" each other
$d =$ the distance between the plates

Figure 11-49 shows several forms of capacitance transducer. In Figure 11-49a we see a rotary plate capacitor that is not unlike the variable capacitors used to tune radio transmitters and receivers. The capacitance of this unit is proportional to the amount of area on the fixed plate that is covered (i.e., "shaded") by the moving plate. This type of transducer will give signals proportional to curvilinear displacement or angular velocity.

A rectilinear capacitance transducer is shown in Figure 11-49b; it consists of a fixed cylinder and a moving cylinder. These pieces are configured so that the moving piece fits inside the fixed piece, but is insulated from it.

The two types of capacitive transducer discussed so far vary capacitance by changing the shaded area of two conductive surfaces. Figure 11-49c, on the other hand, shows a transducer that varies the *spacing* between surfaces, that is the *d* term in Eq. (11-71). In this device, the metal surfaces are a fixed plate and a thin diaphragm. The dielectric is either air or a vacuum. Such devices are often used as capacitance microphones.

Capacitance transducers can be used in several ways. One method is to use the varying capacitance to frequency modulate an RF oscillator. This is the

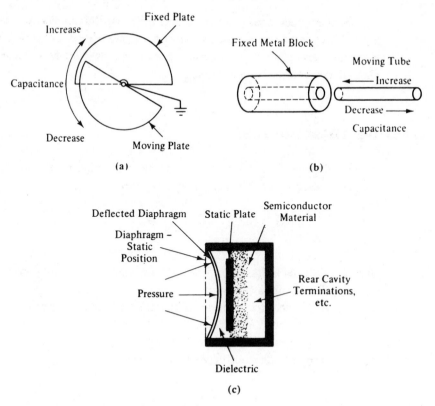

Figure 11-49 Capacitance transducers. (Source: Harry Thomas, *Handbook of Biomedical Instrumentation and Measurement,* Figure 1-6, p. 13, Reston Publishing Co., Reston, Va.)

method employed with capacitance microphones (those built like Figure 11-49c, not the electrotet type). Another method is to use the capacitance transducer in an ac bridge circuit.

REFERENCE SOURCES

Reference voltage sources are used in data acquisition for two main purposes: transducer excitation and in analog-to-digital or digital-to-analog data converters (Chapter 12). In this section we will consider some basic forms of reference voltage source that will suit most applications for which an 8-bit microcomputer is suitable. Computers with longer word lengths will require somewhat greater precision (unless you want the longer word length to be little more than a joke) than these circuits can supply. The principles, however, are the same.

The basic voltage reference in most electronics is the zener diode, as shown in Figure 11-50a. The zener diode uses a controlled avalanche point to maintain a constant voltage.

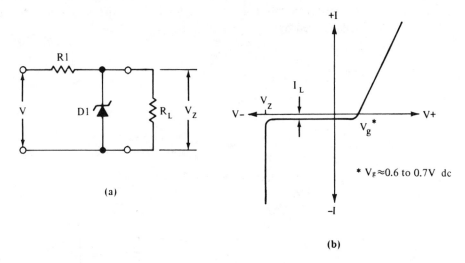

(a)

(b)

* $V_g \approx 0.6$ to $0.7V$ dc

Figure 11-50 (a) Zener diode circuit; (b) I versus V curve for zener diodes.

The I *versus* V *curve* for a zener diode is shown in Figure 11-50b. At applied voltages from V_z to V_g, the current through the zener diode is merely a tiny reverse leakage current, I_L. At voltages above V_g, which is usually 0.6 to 0.7 V in silicon diodes, the zener operates in exactly the same manner as any other silicon rectifier diode. The current increases rapidly with applied forward voltage.

It is in the area of V_z, however, that the zener diode is unique: the voltage across the diode (which is a reverse bias) remains constant despite increases in the applied voltage. The result is a reasonably reliable reference voltage.

Unfortunately, zener diodes are not too precise (V_z is merely nominal) and may tend to vary with temperature. Some manufacturers, such as Ferranti Semiconductor and National Semiconductor, offer band-gap zeners that are an improvement. National also offers the LM-199 device, which contains an on-chip heater that keeps the embedded zener element at a constant temperature, thereby providing superior temperature performance.

Figure 11-51 shows an operational amplifier circuit that can be used to buffer the zener diode and provide precision control over the output voltage. It also allows us to provide any output voltage (within the output range of the operational amplifier) from any zener diode. This fact allows us to use the 6.2-V LM-199 device, or the 1.26- and 2.45-V band-gap devices to produce 2.56-, 5.00-, or 10.00-V reference supplies. In essence, the circuit is a noninverting follower with gain with the zener potential (V_z) as the input voltage. The output potential is given by

$$V_0 = V_z \left(\frac{R1+R2}{R3} + 1 \right) \tag{11-72}$$

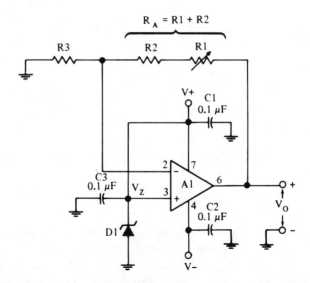

Figure 11-51 Reference voltage circuit using operational amplifier and zener diode.

The potentiometer ($R1$) should be a quality 10- to 20-turn trimmer type in order to adjust the output voltage to a precise value. It should be of high quality so that temperature variations and mechanical shock do not cause its value to change. The other resistors in the circuit should be precision wirewound resistors in order to obtain the low temperature coefficient of such resistors. We may use either an ordinary zener diode, a band-gap zener, a reference-grade zener, or an LM-199-type device.

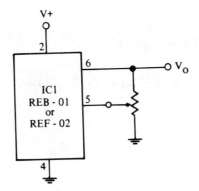

Figure 11-52   Precision Monolithics, Inc., REF-01 and REF-02 reference voltage ICs.

The last alternative is to use an IC reference voltage source, of which there are many now on the market. Perhaps the oldest is the Precision Monolithics, Inc., type REF-01 (10 V) or REF-02 (5 V), as shown in Figure 11-52. These devices can be adjusted to a very precise value close to their rated voltages. As in the circuit previously given, the potentiometer should be a 10- or 20-turn trimmer potentiometer of good quality.

12
Data Conversion:
Techniques and Interfacing

Many of the control and data reduction chores performed by small microprocessor-based computers involve data values taken from the real world. Signals that are proportional to some physical parameter or another are said to be analogs of that parameter and are used extensively in electronic instrumentation and data-collection systems.

For example, let's suppose that a resistive strain-gage Wheatstone bridge is used to measure human blood pressure in medical electronics. The output of the transducer will be a voltage that is proportional to the pressure applied to the strain gage diaphragm. Typically, in 0- to 10-V systems, the voltage analog is 10 millivolts per millimeter of mercury pressure (10 mV/mm Hg) or 10 mV/torr in modern units, which are used very little in clinical medicine. The output will, therefore, be 1200, or 1.2 V, when the patient's blood pressure is 120 mm Hg. But this is of little interest to the computer because it cannot interpret voltage levels. A computer will want to see a binary number that represents the blood pressure, not a voltage analog.

The *data converter* is a circuit or device that converts data to or from the binary and analog worlds. An *analog-to-digital converter* (ADC), for example, could look at the 1.2-V signal and produce a representative binary word that the computer could understand. Similarly, a *digital-to-analog converter* (DAC) produces either a current or voltage output that is proportional to some binary word applied to its inputs. A DAC can be used in a computer system to drive an oscilloscope or strip chart (i.e., paper recorder) so that the user can see the shape of the wave form that produced the data.

Returning to our medical example, suppose we wanted to make a micro-processor-based blood pressure monitor that would display the diastolic (i.e., lowest) and systolic (i.e., highest) values on the patient's blood pressure wave form and the wave form itself. We would create a system in which the amplified transducer output would be applied to the analog-to-digital converter to make a binary word that can be interpreted by the computer. The computer would then apply a bubble sort or some similar routine to find the peak maxima and minima values and then display them on either LED readouts or a video monitor. The computer could also sequentially output the binary values to a DAC, which would reconstruct the wave shape. While it is true that the analog signal could be directly displayed, there are sometimes good reasons why the DAC version might be used (e.g., when the data have to be transmitted over great distances that would be difficult for the analog wave form but not for the digital, or when the doctor wanted to compare a previous wave form with the real-time wave form, which is sometimes done by a coronary care unit or anesthesiology doctors who wish to see the effect of some drug or treatment on the wave form).

WHAT ARE DATA CONVERTERS?

Analog circuits and digital instruments occupy mutually exclusive realms. In the analog world, a signal may vary between upper and low limits and may assume any value within the range. Analog signals are continuous between limits. But the signals in digital circuits may assume only one of two discrete voltage levels (i.e., one each for the two binary digits, 0 and 1). A *data converter* is a circuit or device that examines a signal from one of these realms and then converts it to a proportional signal from the other.

A *digital-to-analog (D/A) converter* (DAC), for example, converts a digital (i.e., binary) "word" consisting of a certain number of *bits* into a *voltage* or *current* that represents the binary number value of the digital word. An 8-bit DAC, for example, may produce an output signal of 0 V when the binary word applied to its digital inputs is 00000000_2, and, say, 2.56 V when the digital inputs see a word of 11111111_2. For binary words applied to the inputs, then, a proportional output voltage is created.

In the case of an *analog-to-digital (A/D) converter* (ADC), an analog voltage or current produces a proportional binary word output. If an 8-bit ADC has a 0 to 2.56-V input signal range, then 0-V input could produce an output word of 00000000_2, while the +2.56-V level seen at the input would produce an output word of 11111111_2.

Data converters are used primarily to interface transducers (most of which produce analog output signals) to digital instruments or computer inputs, and to interface digital instrument outputs to analog-world devices such as meter movements, chart recorders, and motors.

In this chapter we will consider common DAC circuits, and the following ADC circuits: *servo* (also called the *binary counter* or *ramp* ADC), *successive approximation, parallel converter, voltage-to-frequency converter,* and *integrating types.*

DAC CIRCUITS

Figure 12-1 shows a *binary weighted resistance ladder* and operational amplifier used as a binary DAC. The resistors in the ladder are said to be *binary weighted* because their values are related to each other by powers of 2. If the lowest-value resistor is given the value R, then the next in the sequence will have a value of

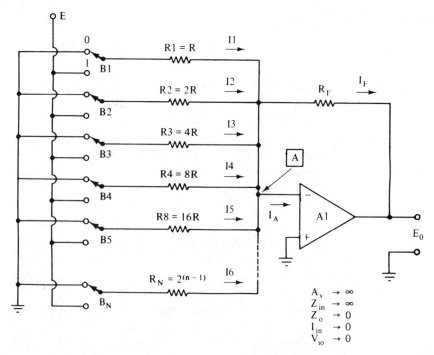

Figure 12-1 Binary weighted resistor ladder DAC circuit.

$2R$, followed by $4R$, $8R$, $16R$, all the way up to the nth resistor (last one in the chain), which has a value of $(2^{n-1})R$.

The switches $B1$ through B_n represent the input bits of the digital word. Although shown here as mechanical switches, they would be transistor switches in actual practice. The switches are used to connect the input resistors to either ground, or voltage source E, to represent binary states 0 to 1, respectively. Switches $B1$ through B_n create currents $I1$ through I_n, respectively, when they are set to the 1 position.

We know from Ohm's law that each current $I1$ through I_n is equal to the quotient of E and the value of the associated resistor; that is,

$$I1 = \frac{E}{R1} = \frac{E}{R}$$

$$I2 = \frac{E}{R2} = \frac{E}{2R}$$

$$I3 = \frac{E}{R3} = \frac{E}{4R}$$

$$\cdot \quad \cdot \quad \cdot$$
$$\cdot \quad \cdot \quad \cdot$$
$$\cdot \quad \cdot \quad \cdot$$

$$I_n = \frac{E}{R_n} = \frac{E}{(2^{n-1})R}$$

The total current into the junction (point A in Figure 12-1) is expressed by the summation of current $I1$ through I_n:

$$I_A = \sum_{i=1}^{n} \frac{a_i E}{2^{i-1}R} \tag{12-1}$$

where I_A = current into the junction (point A) in amperes (A)
E = reference potential in volts (V)
R = resistance of $R1$ in ohms (Ω)
a_1 = either 1 or 0, depending on whether the input bit is 1 or 0
n = number of bits (i.e., the number of switches)

From operational amplifier theory we know that

$$I_A = -I_F \tag{12-2}$$

and

$$E_0 = I_F R_F \qquad (12\text{-}3)$$

So, by substituting Eq. (12-2) into Eq. (12-3), we obtain

$$E_0 = -I_A R_F \qquad (12\text{-}4)$$

and substituting Eq. (12-1) into Eq. (12-4) yields

$$E_0 = -R_F \sum_{i=1}^{n} \frac{a_i E}{2^{i-1} R} \qquad (12\text{-}5)$$

Since E and R are constants, we usually write Eq. (12-5) in the form

$$E_0 = \frac{-E R_F}{R} \sum \frac{a_i}{2^{i-1} R} \qquad (12\text{-}6)$$

Example 12-1   A 4-bit (i.e., $n = 4$) DAC using a binary weighted resistor ladder has a reference source of 10 V dc, and $R_F = R$. Find the output voltage E_0 for the input word 1011_2. (*Hint*: For input 1011, $a_1 = 1$, $a_2 = 0$, $a_3 = 1$, and $a_4 = 1$.)

Solution

$$E_0 = \frac{-E R_F}{R} \sum \frac{a_i}{2^{i-1} R} \qquad (12\text{-}6)$$

$$= \frac{-10 \text{ V}(R)}{R} \left(\frac{1}{2^{1-1}} + \frac{0}{2^{2-1}} + \frac{1}{2^{3-1}} + \frac{1}{2^{4-1}} \right)$$

$$= -10 \text{ V} \left(\frac{1}{2^0} + \frac{1}{2^2} + \frac{1}{2^3} \right)$$

$$= -10 \text{ V} \left(\frac{1}{1} + \frac{1}{4} + \frac{1}{8} \right)$$

$$= -10 \text{ V} \left(\frac{1}{1.375} \right) = -7.27 \text{ V}$$

Although not revealed by the idealized equations, the binary weighted resistance ladder suffers from a serious drawback in actual practice. The values of the input resistors tend to become very large and very small at the ends of the range as the bit length of the input word becomes longer. If R is set to 10 kΩ (a popular value), then $R8$ will be 1.28 MΩ. If we assume a reference potential E of 10.00 V dc, then $I8$ will be only 7.8 μA. Most common non-premium-grade operational amplifiers will not be able to resolve signals that low from the inherent noise. As a result, the bit length of the binary weighted ladder is severely limited. Few of these types of converters are found with more than 6- or 8-bit word lengths.

In commercial DACs, all the resistors have a value of either R or $2R$. The gain of the amplifier is unity, so E_0 can be expressed as

$$E_0 = E \sum_{i=1}^{n} \frac{a_i}{2_i} \qquad (12\text{-}7)$$

(provided that $R_L >> R$ so that the voltage-divider effect between the ladder and R_L can safely be neglected).

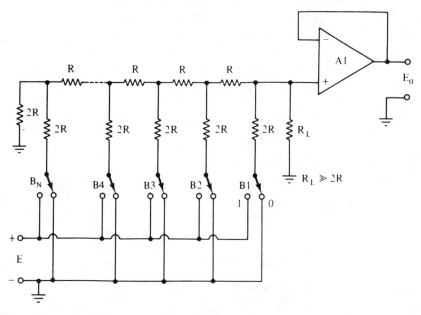

Figure 12-2 R-2R resistor ladder DAC circuit.

Example 12-2   A 4-bit DAC using the R-$2R$ technique has a 5.00-V dc reference potential. Calculate E_0 for the input word $101 1_2$.

Solution

$$E_0 = E \sum_{i=1}^{n} \frac{a_i}{2^i} \qquad (12\text{-}7)$$

$$= 5 \text{ V} \left(\frac{1}{2^1} + \frac{0}{2^2} + \frac{1}{2^3} + \frac{1}{2^4} \right)$$

$$= 5 \text{ V} \left(\frac{1}{2} + 0 + \frac{1}{8} + \frac{1}{16} \right)$$

$$= 5 \text{ V} \ (0.688) = \mathbf{3.44 \ V}$$

The full-scale output voltage for any DAC using the R-$2R$ resistor ladder is given by

$$E_{fs} = \frac{E(2^n - 1)}{2^n} \qquad (12\text{-}8)$$

where E_{fs} = full-scale output potential in volts (V)
$\quad\quad\quad E$ = reference potential in volts (V)
$\quad\quad\quad n$ = bit length of the digital input word

Example 12-3   Find the full-scale output potential for an 8-bit DAC with a reference potential of 10.00 V dc.

Solution

$$E_{fs} = \frac{E(2^n - 1)}{2^n} \qquad (12\text{-}8)$$

$$= \frac{10 \text{ V} \ (2^8 - 1)}{2^8}$$

$$= \frac{10 \text{ V} \ (2^7)}{(2^8)}$$

$$= \frac{10 \text{ V} \ (255)}{(256)} = \mathbf{9.96 \ V}$$

The output of a DAC cannot change in a continuous manner, because the input is a digital word (i.e., it can exist only in certain discrete states). Each successive binary number changes the output an amount equal to the change created by the least significant bit (LSB), which is expressed by

$$\Delta E_0 = \frac{E}{2^n} \qquad (12\text{-}9)$$

So, for the DAC in Example 12-3, E_0 would be

$$\Delta E_0 = \frac{10 \text{ V}}{2^8}$$

$$= \frac{10 \text{ V}}{256} = 40 \text{ mV}$$

ΔE_0 is often called the 1 LSB value of E_0 and is the smallest change in output voltage that can occur. It is interesting that, if we let 0 V represent 00000000_2 in our 8-bit system, the maximum value of E_0 at 11111111_2 will be 1 LSB less than E (confirmed by the result of Example 12-3).

There are numerous commercial DACs on the market in IC, function module block, and equipment form. The reader should consult manufacturer's catalogs for appropriate types in any given application.

SERVO ADC CIRCUITS

The *servo* ADC circuit (also called *binary counter* or *ramp* ADC circuit) uses a binary counter to drive the digital inputs of a DAC. A voltage comparator keeps the clock gate to the counter open as long as $E_0 \neq E_{in}$.

An example of such a circuit is the 8-bit ADC in Figure 12-3a, while the relationship of E_0 and E_{in} relative to time is shown in Figure 12-3b.

Two things happen when a *start* pulse is received by the control logic circuits: the binary counter is reset to 00000000_2, and the gate is opened to allow clock pulses into the counter. This will permit the counter to begin incrementing, thereby causing the DAC output voltage E_0 to begin rising (Figure 12-3b). E_0 will continue to rise until $E_0 = E_{in}$. When this condition is met, the output of the comparator drops *low*, turning off the gate. The binary number appearing on the counter output at this time is proportional to E_{in}.

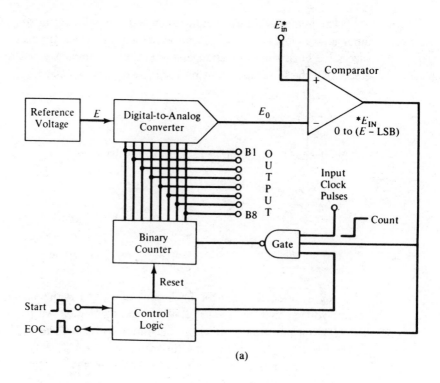

(a)

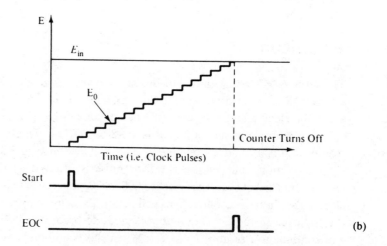

(b)

Figure 12-3   (a) Servo ADC circuit; (b) operation of the servo-type ADC circuit.

The control logic section senses the change in comparator output level and uses it to issue an *end-of-conversion* (EOC) pulse. This EOC pulse is used by instruments of circuitry connected to the ADC to verify that the output data are valid.

The *conversion time* T_c of an ADC such as this depends upon the value of E_{in}, so when E_{in} is maximum (i.e., full scale), so is T_c. Conversion time for this type of ADC is on the order of 2^n clock pulses for a full-scale conversion.

SUCCESSIVE APPROXIMATION ADC CIRCUITS

The conversion time of the servo ADC is too long for some applications. The successive approximation (SA) ADC is much faster for the same clock speed; it takes $(n + 1)$ clock pulses instead of 2^n. For the 8-bit ADC that has been our example, the SA type of ADC is 28 times *faster* than the *servo* ADC.

The basic concept of the SA ADC circuit can be represented by a platform balance, such as Figure 12-4, in which a full-scale weight W will deflect the pointer all the way to the left when pan 2 is empty.

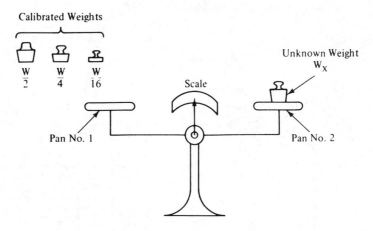

Figure 12-4 Successive approximation ADC circuits are like a platform balance.

Our calibrated weight set consists of many separate pieces, which weigh $W/2$, $W/4$, $W/8$, $W/16$, and so on. When an unknown weight W_x is placed on pan 2, the scale will deflect to the right. To make our measurement, we start with $W/2$ and place it on pan 1. Three conditions are now possible:

$$\frac{W}{2} = W_x \qquad \text{(scale is at zero)}$$

$$\frac{W}{2} > W_x \qquad \text{(scale is to the left of zero)}$$

$$\frac{W}{2} < W_x \qquad \text{(scale is to the right of zero)}$$

If $W/2 = W_x$, the measurement is finished, and no additional trials are necessary. But if $W/2$ is less than W_x, we must add more weights in succession ($W/4$, then $W/8$, etc.) until we find a combination equal to W_x.

If, on the other hand, $W/2$ is greater than W_x, we must *remove* the $W/2$ weight and in the second trial start again with $W/4$. This procedure will continue until a combination equal to W_x is found.

In the SA ADC circuit we do not use a scale, but a shift register, as in Figure 12-5. A successive approximation register (SAR) contains the control logic, a shift register, and a set of output latches, one for each register section. The outputs of the latches drive a DAC.

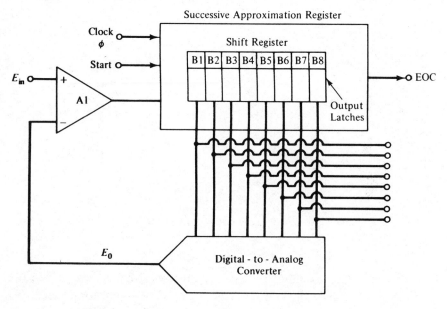

Figure 12-5 Successive approximation ADC circuit.

A *start* pulse sets the first bit of the shift register *high*, so the DAC will see the word 10000000_2 and therefore produce an output voltage equal to one-half of the full-scale output voltage. If the input voltage is greater than $\frac{1}{2}E_{fs}$, the *B*1 latch is set *high*. On the next clock pulse, register *B*2 is set high for trial 2. The output of the DAC is now $\frac{3}{4}$-scale. If, on any trial, it is found that $E_{in} < E_0$, that bit is reset *low*.

Let us follow a 3-bit SAR through a sample conversion. In our example, let us say that the full-scale potential is 1 V, and E_{in} is 0.625 V. Consider Figure 12-6.

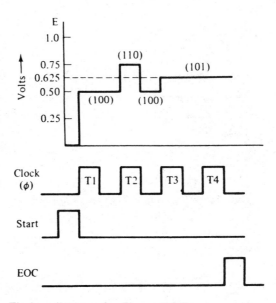

Figure 12-6   Timing diagram for Figure 12-5.

1. Time t_1: The *start* is received, so register *B*1 goes *high*. The output word is now 100_2, so $E_0 = 0.5$ V. Since E_0 is less than E_{in}, latch *B*1 is set to 1, so at the end of the trial, the output word remains 100_2.

2. Time t_2: On this trial (which starts upon receiving the next clock pulse), register *B*2 is set *high*, so the output word is 110_2. Voltage E_0 is now 0.75 V. Since E_{in} is less than E_0, the *B*2 latch is set to 0, and the output word reverts to 100_2.

3. Time t_3: Register *B*3 is set *high*, marking the output word 101_2. The value of E_0 is now 0.625 V, so $E_{in} = E_0$. The *B*3 register is latched to 1, and the output word remains 101_2.

4. Time t_4: Overflow occurs, telling the control logic to issue an EOC pulse. In some cases the overflow pulse *is* the EOC pulse.

Note that in the example we had a 3-bit SAR, so by our $(n + 1)$ rule, we required four clock pulses to complete the conversion. The SA type of ADC was once regarded as difficult to design because of the logic required. But today, IC and function blocks are available that use this technique, so the design job is reduced considerably. The SA technique can be implemented in software under computer control using only an external DAC and comparator. All register functions are handled in the software (program).

PARALLEL CONVERTERS

The parallel ADC circuit (Figure 12-7) is probably the fastest type of ADC known. In fact, some texts call it the "flash" converter in testimony to its speed. It consists of a bank of $(2^n - 1)$ voltage comparators biased by reference potential E through a resistor network that keeps the individual comparators 1 LSB apart. Since the input voltage is applied to all the comparators simultaneously, the speed of conversion is essentially the slewing speed of the *slowest* comparator in the bank and the decoder propagation time (if logic is used). The decoder converts the output code to binary code, or possibly BDC in some cases.

VOLTAGE-TO-FREQUENCY CONVERTERS

A voltage-to-frequency (V/F) converter is a voltage-controlled oscillator (VCO) in which an input voltage E_{in} is represented by an output frequency F. An ADC using the V/F converter is shown in Figure 12-8. It consists of no more than the VCO and a frequency counter. The display, or output states, on the counter gives us the value of E_{in}.

Voltage-to-frequency converters are used mainly where economics dictate serial transmission of data from a remote collection point to the instrument. Such data can be transmitted by wire or radio communications channels. Another application is the tape recording of analog data that are themselves too low in frequency to be recorded.

The inverse procedure, F/V conversion, is a form of DAC, in which an input *frequency* is converted to an output *voltage.*

The type of V/F converter shown in Figure 12-8 is somewhat archaic and is not used extensively today. A somewhat better circuit method is shown in

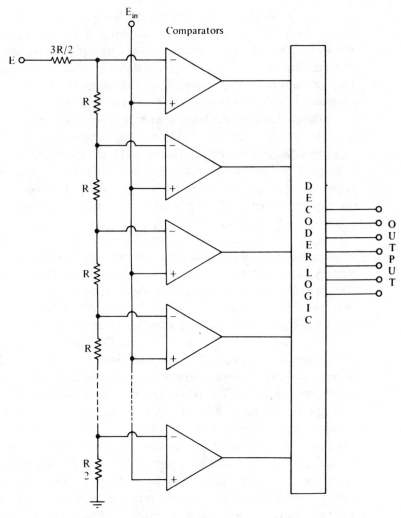

Figure 12-7 Parallel or "flash" ADC circuit.

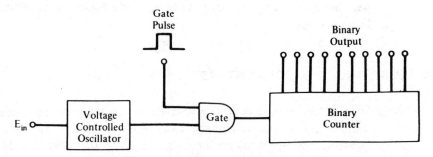

Figure 12-8 Voltage-to-frequency converter ADC.

Figure 12-9a, with the timing wave forms shown in Figure 12-9b. The operation of this circuit is dependent upon the charging of a capacitor, although not an *RC* network as is the case in some timers. The input voltage signal is amplified by input amplifier *A*1, if necessary, and then converted to a proportional current value in the *V-to-I converter stage*. If the voltage applied to the input, V_{in}, remains constant, so will the output of the *V-to-I* converter (I).

The current from the *V-to-I* converter is used to charge the timing capacitor (C). The voltage appearing across this capacitor will vary with time as the capacitor charges (see wave form in Figure 12-9b). The precision discharge circuit is designed to discharge the capacitor to a certain level ($V2$) whenever the voltage across the capacitor reaches a predetermined value ($V1$). When the voltage across the capacitor reaches $V2$, a Schmitt trigger circuit is fired that turns on the precision discharge circuit. The precision discharge circuit, in its turn, will cause the capacitor to discharge rapidly but in a controlled manner to value $V1$. The output pulse snaps HIGH when the Schmitt trigger fires (i.e., at the instant V_c reaches $V1$) and drops LOW again when the value of V_c has discharged to $V2$. The result is a train of output pulses whose repetition rate is exactly dependent upon the capacitor charging current, which, in turn, is dependent upon the applied voltage. Hence, we have a voltage-to-frequency converter.

There are several ways in which the V/F converter can be used with a microcomputer to input data. One method is to use a binary or decade counter to count the output frequency (or at least the number of pulses) during a known-length sample period. The binary or BCD outputs of the counters are then applied (in a manner like Figure 12-8) to the input port of a microcomputer. An alternative version of this same method is to feed the pulses from the V/F output to the timer or counter input of a microprocessor support chip such as the Z80-CTC or the 6522 that is used with the 6502-series devices. Our second method is to apply the pulses to 1 bit of the input port of the microcomputer and then write a program that will measure the time between pulses. This is the basis for the *frequency-counter* programs that some people use; frequency is, after all, the reciprocal of period. In either case, we will input some representation to the computer that can be used as a binary analog of the parameter being measured.

INTEGRATING A/D CONVERTERS

Some of the lowest-cost A/D converters are the integrating converters that are often used in digital voltmeters. These A/D converters are slow, but that is often an advantage when the input signal is noisy. In other cases, the slow speed

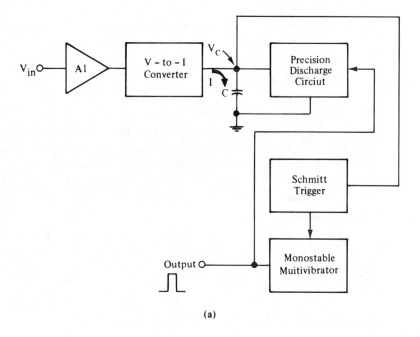

(a)

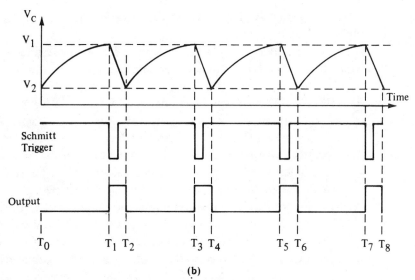

(b)

Figure 12-9   (a) Voltage-to-frequency converter block diagram; (b) timing wave forms.

of conversion is of little practical concern if the parameter being measured is also slow changing. The temperature of a large pot of metal, for example, is not going to change in microseconds, milliseconds, or even seconds; minutes or hours are more reasonable units of measure. It makes little difference in such a case whether the design engineer uses a 50-ms converter instead of a 10-μs version.

There are several different designs for the integrating A/D converter, but perhaps the most common are the *single-slope integrator* and the *dual-slope integrator;* of these, the latter is considered the better for most applications.

An example of the single-slope integrator is shown in Figure 12-10. The principal components of this circuit are the input amplifier (A1), which is optional, a Miller integrator (I), a comparator (COMP), a main gate (G1), and a binary counter.

The input amplifier may or may not be used in any given single-slope integrator. It is optional and is merely used to scale the input signal to a level that optimizes the operation of the integrator circuit. Obviously, a too-small signal would take a long time to charge the integrator capacitor.

The Miller integrator uses an operational amplifier and a resistor–capacitor combination to produce an output voltage ($V1$) that is proportional to the integral (i.e., *time-average* of the applied input signal). For purposes of discussion, we will assume that A1 has a gain of unity, so the input to the integrator is the unknown input voltage V_x.

A comparator (COMP) is sometimes called an amplifier with too much gain. Indeed, we can make a comparator using an operational amplifier with an open feedback loop. This makes the amplifier gain 50,000 in cheap models to well over 1,000,000 in premium devices. Obviously, a few millivolts of input signal will saturate such an amplifier. This is the way a comparator operates. It produces an output level that indicates when the two input voltages are equal (i.e., output zero) or which of the two is highest. In the limited case shown here, one input of the comparator is grounded (at a 0-V potential), so the output will be zero when $V1$ is zero and HIGH when $V1$ is more than a few millivolts higher than ground. When the output of the comparator is HIGH, gate G1 is enabled and can pass pulses (provided that the START pulse is also HIGH).

The counter will have either binary or BCD formats (the BCD format is used in digital voltmeter converters) and thus can be connected either to a display device (like the readout on the DVM) or to a microcomputer input port. An overflow indicator is used to denote when the input voltage is overrange.

When a start pulse is received (it may be internally generated), switch S1 is closed briefly in order to discharge capacitor C so that no accumulated charge will foul the results. Switch S1 is opened again almost immediately, thereby

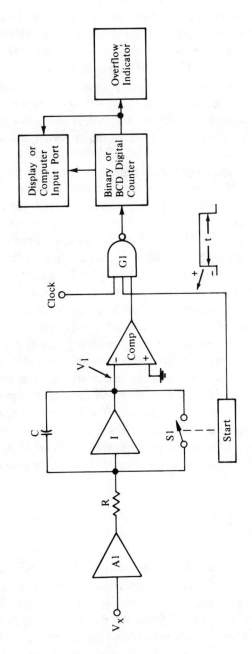

Figure 12-10 Single-slope integrator.

allowing C to begin charging at a rate that is determined by the input voltage V_x. As soon as the integrator output voltage is more than a few millivolts higher than ground, the output of the comparator will snap HIGH, thereby allowing pulses to flow into the counter. A third signal applied to G1 is the timing signal from the *start* section. This pulse stays on for a period t and prevents the integrator from continuing to charge until the counter overflows. The count at the end of the timing period is proportional to the applied voltage.

One major problem with the single-slope integrator is that it is sensitive to noise riding on the input signal. A noisy signal will usually produce an erroneous result.

The dual-slope integrator of Figure 12-11a solves the noise problem. The circuit is shown in Figure 12-11a and its timing diagram in Figure 12-11b. The principal difference between the two converters is that the dual-slope converter makes the conversion in two steps. During the first step, period t_0 to t_1 in Figure 12-11b, the integrator is charged from the unknown input signal V_x. The output voltage of the integrator continues to rise as long as the input switch S2 is connected to the input circuit. The binary/BCD counter is allowed to overflow (at time t_1), and this overflow signal tells the control logic circuits to switch S2 to position B, the output of a fixed precision reference voltage supply. The polarity of this voltage source is such that it will cause the integrator to discharge at a fixed rate. The counter state at the instant this switch is changed is 0000 and begins incrementing from there. The counter will continue to increment until the reference source completely discharges the integrator capacitor. At that instant, the output of the comparator will drop LOW again, thereby stopping the flow of clock pulses to the counter. The state of the counter output at that instant is proportional to the input voltage V_x. Since the counter state occurred as the result of a *constant* integrator output discharge slope, it will not contain noise errors. The noise errors are integrated out of the data by the action of the integrator.

A/D CONVERTER SIGNALS

There are two basic methods of providing A/D converter control systems. Most A/D converters have a *start* line, which will cause the converter to initiate the conversion process when it is made active. It is in the signal that tells the outside world when the data are valid that the various converters differ. Figure 12-12 shows both systems. In Figure 12-12a we see the timing diagram for the system that uses an *end-of-conversion* (EOC) pulse. The data output lines (B0–B7) may contain invalid data after the initiation of the *start* pulse, and these data cannot

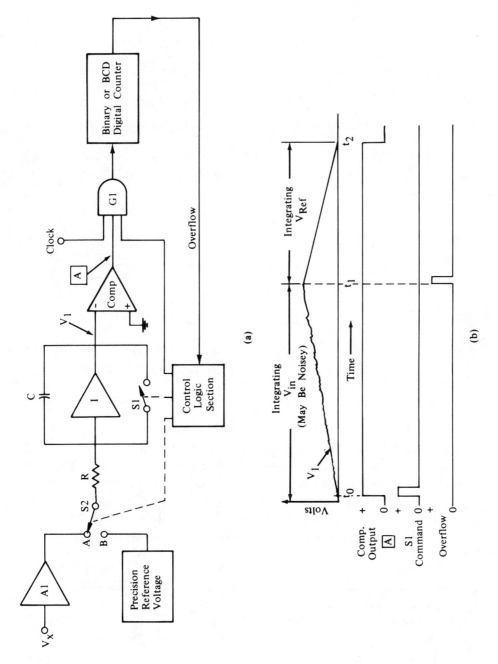

Figure 12-11 (a) Dual-slope integrator; (b) timing wave form.

329

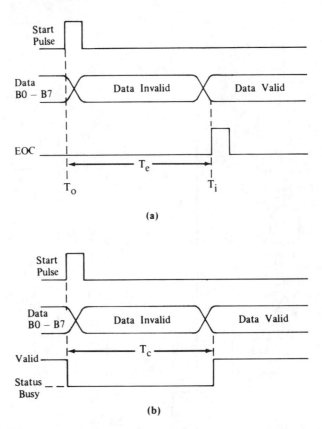

Figure 12-12   Timing wave forms.

be used. When the conversion process is completed, however, the data on B0 to B7 are valid, so an EOC pulse is issued. The period between EOC pulses (t_1 to t_0) is the *conversion time, T_c.*

The second method uses a *status* signal as shown in Figure 12-12b. The status line may also be called the *busy* signal. It will be HIGH when the data are valid and drop LOW when the conversion is being made and the data are invalid.

Figure 12-13 shows a method for converting an EOC pulse system to a status line system. This conversion may be required in some cases where an A/D converter is being interfaced to an existing computer that uses software that wants to see a status signal.

The basis of this circuit is an R–S (reset–set) flip-flop that is made from a pair of cross-connected NAND gates. When the start pulse is received, the status line will drop LOW. The start pulse need only be momentarily present,

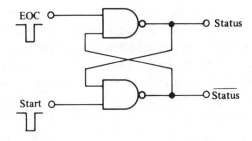

Figure 12-13 RS flip-flop used as a status indicator from EOC and start signals.

so the circuit is ideal for "catching" that temporary pulse. Similarly, when the EOC pulse is received, the status line goes HIGH again.

Another problem is that the A/D converter will be dormant between conversions. The device must be "tickled" by the start pulse, which is generated by the computer, before it can begin its work. But suppose we want the A/D converter to make continuous conversions, that is, to operate asynchronously. In that case (see Figure 12-14) we can connect the EOC output to the START input. When the EOC pulse occurs, it automatically tells the A/D converter to begin again the conversion process.

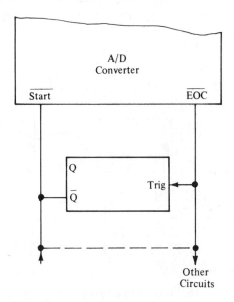

Figure 12-14 Continuous conversion circuit.

A problem that is sometimes experienced with asynchronous conversion, however, is that the data are valid for only one clock pulse. If that period is too fast, some data may be lost because the computer cannot input them fast enough. A solution to this problem (also shown in Figure 12-14) is to connect a monostable multivibrator (one-shot) stage between the EOC output and START input. The one-shot will insert a delay equal to its period between the two events.

INTERFACING DACs

The digital-to-analog converter (DAC) is a device that will convert a binary word applied to its inputs to a proportional voltage or current at the output. Both voltage- and current-output DACs exist. There are two basic methods for interfacing DACs: *I/O based* and *memory mapped*.

The I/O-based method is shown in Figure 12-15. Since several aspects of DAC interfacing are common to both methods, we will show them only in this figure. One facet is *current-to-voltage conversion;* another is *low-pass filtering*. The *I*-to-*V* conversion is used to produce a voltage output (which is what is needed by oscilloscopes and most strip-chart paper recorders) from the output of the current type of DAC. In Figure 12-15, the DAC output current (I_0) is converted to a voltage by passing it through a fixed precision resistor R. The output voltage will be, according to Ohm's law;

$$V_0 = I_0 R$$

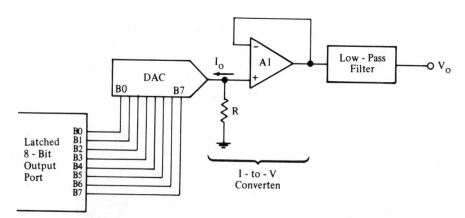

Figure 12-15   Digital-to-analog converter (DAC) to create analog output voltage.

The low-pass filter is used to smooth the output wave form. The DAC can produce only certain discrete output levels, so instead of a ramp function it would produce an "equivalent" staircase function. The low-pass filter will smooth the staircase to make it look more like a ramp.

The interfacing method shown in Figure 12-15 is used when there is an output port available that is latched (as are most); that is, the output port will contain the last valid data even after the computer has gone on to other chores. In that case, it is merely necessary to connect the output port bits to the DAC input bits on a one-for-one basis.

In a memory-mapped system, the DAC (or other peripheral; the method is not limited to data converters) is treated as a memory location and is assigned an address. Figure 12-16 shows the basic memory-mapped system. The OUT n signal is an output device-select pulse (see Chapter 4). For the case of a micro-computer that uses such a system, the elements that go into forming the OUT n signal are those that form a memory write operation. When the computer executes a write to the memory location defined in the OUT n signal, data on the data bus are transferred to the output of the 74100 dual quad-latch TTL IC. The outputs of the 74100 are used to drive the inputs of the DAC and are

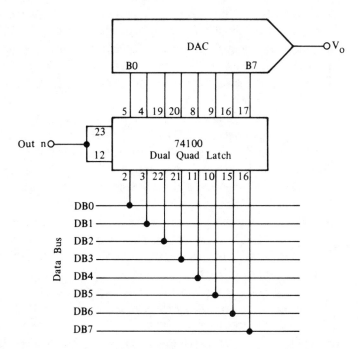

Figure 12-16   Data latching for output DAC.

updated whenever the computer writes a new value to the memory location defined by the OUT n operation. Several IC devices other than the 74100 will do the same job.

The circuits shown thus far in this section are fine when used with 8-bit DACs connected to 8-bit computers. But how do we connect a DAC that uses more than 8 bits? The 8-bit computer can easily handle greater than 8-bit input words because it can use double-precision programming techniques. Machines based on the Z80 microprocessor chip even have the ability to use 8-bit register pairs in single-instruction operations. We will, therefore, occasionally see the need for interfacing a larger than 8-bit DAC to an 8-bit microcomputer.

Figure 12-17a shows the method for connecting the large-length DAC to an 8-bit output port or data bus (which, of course, depends upon whether memory-mapping is used); it is called the double-buffered method. For any word greater than 8-bits in length, we can output the entire word using more than one output operation. For example, up to 16 bits can be handled by two successive output operations. If we wanted to output, say, a 12-bit word, we could output the lower-order 8 bits on the first operation and the high-order 4 bits on the second operation. This is the basis for operation of Figure 12-17a.

Let's assume that the circuit is in the memory-mapped mode, as shown in Figure 12-17a. The OUT1, OUT2, and OUT3 signals are device-select pulses as discussed in Chapter 4. The lower-order 8 bits of the 12-bit data word are output on the 8-bit data bus, and an OUT1 signal is generated by the CPU. This signal will cause IC1, a 74100 eight-bit data latch, to input and hold the signal. Thus the lower-order 8 bits of the required 12 will be stored at the output of IC1 after the OUT1 signal disappears. On the next operation, the high-order 4 bits of the 12-bit data word will appear on the lower 4 bits of the data bus, while simultaneously an OUT2 signal is generated. The effect of the OUT2 signal is to cause IC3 to input and hold the lower-order 4 bits; only 4 of the 8 bits are used on this operation. Hence, after the OUT2 signal disappears, we will have the lower-order 8 bits stored in IC1 and the higher-order 4 bits of the 12-bit data word stored in IC3. The DAC is now ready to receive the entire 12 bits. If an attempt had been made to apply any of the data to the DAC prior to this time, the DAC would temporarily see an incorrect data word for part of the operation. Now that the entire 12 bits are available at the outputs of IC1 and IC3, we can crank the data into the 12-bit DAC-driver register consisting of IC2 and IC4. An OUT3 pulse will turn on both IC2 and IC4 and thereby transfer the data that are on the outputs of IC1 and IC3 to the DAC inputs. The DAC will now have an entire 12-bit data word on its inputs.

The specific circuit shown in Figure 12-17a will accommodate up to 16 bits because each 74100 device is essentially an 8-bit latch (actually, it is a dual

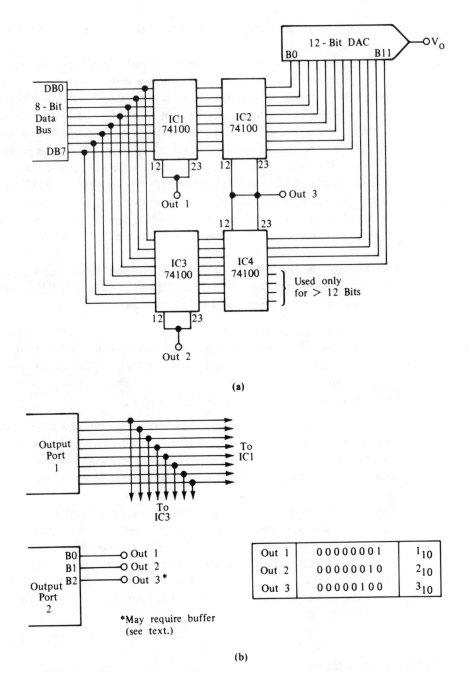

(a)

(b)

Figure 12-17 (a) Circuit for interfacing longer DACs with 8-bit ports; (b) alternate scheme.

quad latch, but it is effectively an 8-bit latch if the two strobe lines, pins 12 and 23, are tied together).

Figure 12-17b shows a variation of the basic circuit that allows interfacing with a pair of 8-bit output ports. If you are using a commercially available computer or intend to use one of the commercial "no frills" SBCs that are frequently sold as "controllers," it may be more cost-effective to use extra I/O ports for this application rather than design a memory-mapped add-on. Two output ports are needed, here designated at ports 1 and 2 (any designation could be used). The output lines from port 1 are connected to the input lines of the 74100s designated IC1 and IC3 in Figure 12-17a. The OUT1, OUT2, and OUT3 signals are taken from 3 bits of a second output port, here designated as port 2. To generate a device-select pulse on the output port, we must write an appropriate data word to that port that will cause the correct bit to go HIGH for a short period and then drop LOW again. For example, the line for the OUT1 signal is connected to bit B0. This situation means that we must write a number to port 2 that will make B0 HIGH and all others LOW (i.e., 00000001). A typical program sequence will follow these steps:

1. Write 01 hex to port 2.
2. Jump to a timer subroutine that will provide a short delay (1 ms is usually a good selection, and the 74100 devices will react to much faster pulses).
3. Clear OUT2 by writing 00 hex to port 2.

In the initialization section of the main program, it will be necessary to ensure that port 2 is reset (i.e., 00000000) or there may be unwanted HIGH conditions on some of the lines at certain times following power up. The binary words needed to create the three select signals are given in the inset table in Figure 12-17b.

Because of the limitation of output port drive current, it may be that bit B2 of port 2, which drives the OUT3 signal, will require a high-current buffer stage. This is because there are four TTL inputs connected to this line (i.e., pins 12 and 23 on IC2 and IC4), and many microcomputer output devices are limited to 3.6 mA, which will support only two TTL inputs. This extra buffer will not be used if the output port device used in some particular application will support four TTL lines.

INTERFACING ADCs

Perhaps the simplest method for interfacing an A/D converter to a microcomputer is shown in Figure 12-18; Figure 12-18a shows the method used when the operation is synchronized under program control, and Figure 12-18b shows the method used when the A/D converter operates asynchronously. In both cases, the eight data lines from the A/D converter are connected directly to the eight lines of an 8-bit parallel input port.

Figure 12-18a shows the circuit for the case when the A/D converter is under direct program control (i.e., the program issues the start pulse that begins the conversion process). The start line of the A/D converter is connected to 1 bit (B0 selected here) of output port 1. Any bit or port could be selected, and the unused bit remaining can be used for other applications.

The EOC (end of conversion) pulse is applied to 1 bit of a second input port (other than the data input port). A typical program sequence would be as follows:

1. Write 01 hex to port 2. This step causes B0 of port 2 to be HIGH.
2. Reset port 2 by writing 00 hex to port 2.
3. Loop until bit B0 of input port 1 is made HIGH.
4. Input data on port 1.

The method shown in Figure 12-18a is wasteful of one output port (i.e., the port used for the start pulse) and requires the program to be continuously dedicated to that task. The method of Figure 12-18b is asynchronous and will free up the computer somewhat, provided that the A/D converter uses a latched output stage and the conversion time is sufficiently long. The asynchronism is gained by the simple expedient of connecting the EOC and start lines together. The EOC pulse becomes the start pulse for the next conversion cycle. The computer will loop until it sees the EOC pulse on bit B0 of input port 2. Again, the assumption is made that the A/D converter has a latched output stage.

We can add a latched output stage to an A/D converter that lacks such capability by using the circuit of Figure 12-18c. The data latch is a 74100 dual quad latch (or some similar chip). The two halves of the latch are each activated by a separate strobe terminal (pins 12 and 23), which are here wired together in order to accommodate the 8-bit word length. When the EOC/start pulse is generated, indicating that the data on the output of the A/D converter are valid, the data will be transferred from the inputs of the 74100 to the respective outputs.

We can both gain freedom from keeping the computer tied up looking for the A/D converter data and free up one input port by adding a few components to the basic circuit (see Figure 12-19). The 8-bit input port is driven by IC2, a tristate 8-bit buffer, and tristate inverter G2, which is connected to only one bit of the port (bit B7). The reason for the tristate components is to permit them to be floated at high impedance when not in use. Otherwise, any LOW on the

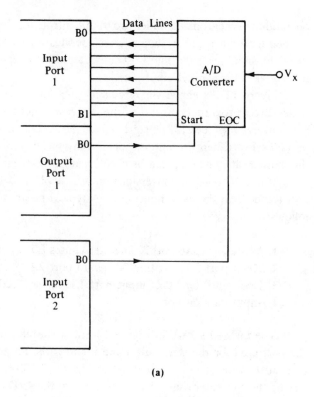

(a)

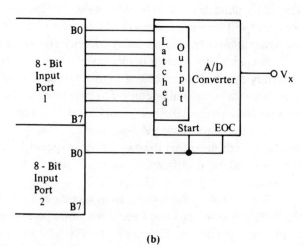

(b)

Figure 12-18 (a) A/D converter interfacing; (b) alternate method; (c) use of 74100 to interface ADC.

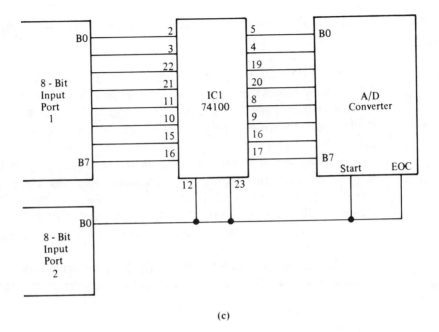

(c)

Figure 12-18 *(Continued)*

specific line affected would automatically affect the other devices connected to the line. For example, in the case of Figure 12-19, a LOW on the output of G2 would short to ground the B7 output of IC2.

The transient nature of the EOC pulse requires the computer in our previous examples to loop while searching for the HIGH EOC pulse; this is very wasteful of CPU time. Although the use of the interrupt capability of the CPU is a better selection, this method allows interfacing with an existing computer I/O port without the necessity of gaining access to the interrupt terminals. Flip-flop FF1 is used to store the EOC pulse, thereby making it essentially a status signal.

The control signals for the A/D converter circuit of Figure 12-19 are designated OUT1, OUT2 (and its inverse $\overline{OUT2}$), and OUT3. These signals are generated by making specific bits of the output port HIGH for a short period of time. A typical operation consists of making the appropriate bit HIGH for a specified period of time and then resetting it LOW. Such a program that will, for example, generate OUT1 will have to do the following:

1. Write 80 hex (i.e., 10000000_2) to the output port.
2. Jump to a timer subroutine, if necessary, to generate a delay during which B7 is HIGH. This step sets the duration of the OUT1 pulse.

3. Write 00 hex to the output port thereby resetting it and canceling the OUT1 signal.

The A/D converter must have either latched output lines or incorporate IC1 in order to store the output data temporarily. The purpose of IC2 is to provide a tristate buffer between the TTL outputs of IC1 and the input lines of the I/O port. Otherwise, we would not be allowed to bus the output of inverter G2 to B7 of the I/O port.

The first step in the program sequence will be to generate the OUT2 signal in order to ensure that flip-flop FF1 is cleared. This step will be performed when the computer is first turned on or, alternatively, when the A/D converter program is first invoked. When the NOT-Q output of FF1 is LOW (i.e., the FF is in the *set* state), inverter G2 is turned on and a LOW is applied to bit B7 of the input port.

When the program calls for the A/D converter to begin a conversion cycle, it will generate the OUT1 signal. This pulse is connected to the start input of

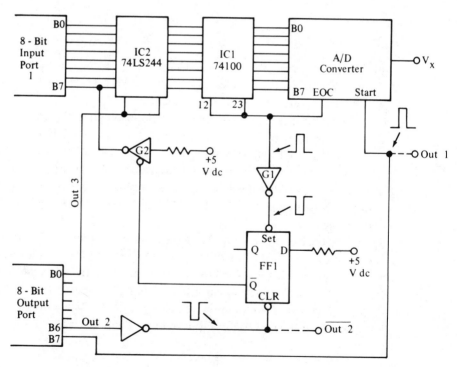

Figure 12-19 A/D interfacing scheme.

the A/D converter and so will initiate the conversion process. The computer is then free to perform other chores while the conversion is taking place. In most applications the computer program will have to inspect B7 of the input port every few milliseconds (this depends upon the conversion time of the A/D) to see if a LOW is present. When the EOC pulse is generated by the A/D converter, it will cause the A/D output data to be stored in IC1, and the pulse is also inverted (in G1) and used to set FF1. The NOT-Q output of FF1 thereby goes LOW and turns on G2. Since the input of inverter G2 is HIGH, its output will be LOW. When the computer program returns to check B7, it will jump to the A/D input subroutine when it sees B7 LOW. An appropriate program will then issue an OUT2 signal to reset FF1, followed by an OUT3 signal that turns on IC2 and thereby gates the A/D converter data input to the input port. The sequence will be as follows:

1. Ensure FF1 is reset by generating an OUT2 signal during program initialization when the computer is first turned on or when the A/D program is first invoked. Alternatively, a system power-on reset pulse could be used by adding an OR gate to the circuit.
2. Generate a start pulse by generating signal OUT1.
3. Periodically check bit B7 of the input port for a LOW.
4. When the LOW is sensed at B7, generate an OUT2 pulse to reset FF1.
5. Generate an OUT3 signal to gate the contents of IC1 onto the input port lines. Hold this signal until the data are input.
6. Read the input port data and store it at the memory location required.
7. Reset OUT3 signal.

A similar system can also be used for memory-mapped A/D converter applications. In those cases, however, we might also want to consider a simpler system that makes use of genuine device-select pulses (see Chapter 4). Figure 12-20 shows such a method in which OUT1 and IN1 signals are used to control the A/D converter.

In a memory-mapped system, the A/D converter is equipped with its own dedicated *input port,* which in Figure 12-20a consists of the 74100 data latch (IC1) and the 74LS244 tristate 8-bit buffer (IC2). The output lines of IC2 are connected to the data bus lines. Since the lines from IC2 are tristate, they will not load down the data bus lines when IC2 is in the inactive state. But when an IN2 signal is generated, it will gate the contents of the 74100 latch onto the data bus.

The conversion sequence is initiated by generating the OUT1 device select

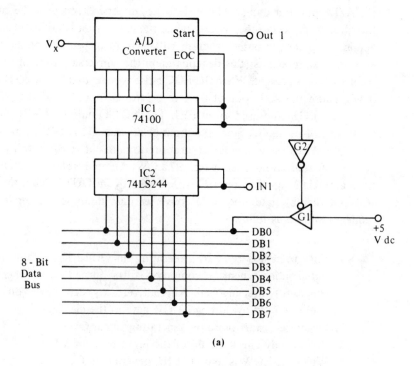

(a)

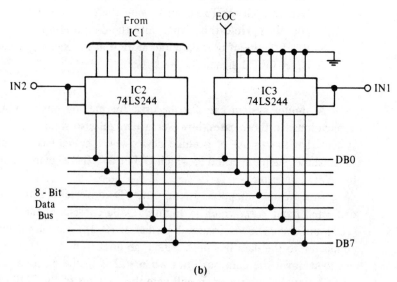

(b)

Figure 12-20 (a) A/D interfacing with microprocessor data bus; (b) alternate scheme.

pulse, which is applied to the start input of the A/D converter. When the conversion process is completed, the EOC pulse will be generated. This pulse has two effects; one is to latch the A/D data, while the other is to turn on G1 (the EOC pulse is inverted by G2 before being applied to the enable terminal on G1). When G1 is enabled, a HIGH is placed on bit DB0 of the data bus. This signal tells the program that the A/D converter data are ready. The program will generate an IN1 device-select signal, thereby gating the data from the 74100 outputs onto the data bus. Figure 12-20b shows a method for using one section of a second 74LS244 to form gate G1. Although this illustration shows the unused inputs of the 74LS244 as grounded, they could be used for other applications if the need arose.

The A/D converter interfacing techniques presented thus far have limited applications. The method of Figure 12-20, for example, requires the program to occasionally check for the EOC signal, and such an arrangement is at best clumsy. A somewhat better approach that is open to those who can access the interrupt line(s) of the computer is shown in Figure 12-21. In this circuit, a J-K flip-flop (FF1) is used to send an interrupt signal to the CPU.

Again, we require either an A/D converter that has latched outputs or a 74100 arrangement as in the previous cases. Also, once again we are using an

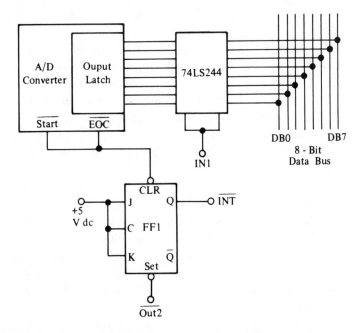

Figure 12-21   Use of interrupt line to interface A/D converters.

8-bit tristate buffer to control entry of the A/D output data onto the data bus. This buffer is actuated by the IN1 device-select signal. In the circuit of Figure 12-21 the A/D converter is connected in the asynchronous mode, so the EOC pulse becomes the start pulse for the next conversion cycle. The A/D converter, therefore, will continuously convert the input signal. Every time the data are ready anew, the EOC pulse will cause the latest value to be input to the data latch. This same EOC pulse also clears FF1, thereby making the Q output LOW. The Q output of FF1 is connected to the active-low interrupt line to the CPU, so this action will cause the CPU to be interrupted.

The CPU will not respond to the interrupt immediately, but will wait until the execution of the current instruction is completed. In most microprocessor CPUs, the interrupt line is examined during the last clock pulse of the execution cycle. If the interrupt line is active (i.e., LOW in this case), the address of the next instruction to be executed in the normal program sequence is stored on an external stack somewhere in memory and the program control jumps to an interrupt service subroutine. In this case, the service program will be the A/D data input routine. Such a subroutine must accomplish the following:

1. Generate an $\overline{OUT2}$ signal to reset the interrupt flip-flop (FF1).
2. Generate an IN1 signal to gate the A/D data onto the data bus.
3. Store the A/D data at some appropriate point in memory.

The principal advantage of this arrangement is that the computer can be used for other chores while awaiting the A/D converter data. Except for a few really high speed A/D converters, most A/D converters have conversion times that are very long compared with the clock period of the computer. Some A/D converters will perform an 8-bit conversion in 5 to 10 μs, but there are many that have 50- to 100-ms conversion times. Of course, we could always specify the speedy versions, but that would be wasteful of both money and CPU time.

The conversion time should be related to the maximum frequency component in the analog input signal that is considered significant. For example, the human ECG wave form has a 0.05- to 100-Hz bandwidth. According to a well-known criterion, we must sample this signal at a rate that is equal to at least twice the highest frequency, so a 200 sample/second rate is sufficient; many experts would select a rate five times faster than the minimum required, so we would sample at 1000/s. This rate means that the A/D converter should be capable of 1-ms conversion time.

We can get an idea of the scale of time involved by comparing the rate of operations with the time that the CPU would idle uselessly while awaiting the EOC signal. In one model, the CPU can execute 400,000 operations/second, so the CPU could perform 400 operations during the 1 ms required for the A/D converter to do its job. Most applications where an A/D converter is needed will require some signal processing or further data massage other than a simple storage operation. We could use that 1-ms "lost time" to perform some of these operations.

An example is the evoked potentials computer used in medical and physiological studies to examine the component of the electroencephalograph (EEG) brain wave form that is due to some specific stimulus. This type of computer will either sum or average successive input data in a coherent manner, thereby processing out the randomness and leaving only the desired data. For the 30-Hz EEG wave form, we could sample at 200/s (5-ms conversion time) and then use the lost time to either sum or average previous data. The A/D converter will interrupt the signal processing any time that new data are available.

Many computers allow more than one device to interrupt the CPU, but have only a single general interrupt line or a single interrupt and one nonmaskable interrupt. The Z80 chip allows eight different devices to be used in a *vectored interrupt* mode.[1] In a vectored interrupt on the Z80, all eight devices will drive the $\overline{INT}$ line, but will also place onto the data bus an 8-bit *RST n* code that tells the program counter where to jump to find the interrupt service routine; the term *n* directs the CPU to a specific memory location. An RST 3, for example, causes an automatic jump to location 00 18 hex. According to the Z80 instructions, we must place the hex code DF (11011111_2) on the data bus during the time when the $\overline{INT}$ line is active. In Figure 12-22 we see the previous circuit modified to add this capability.

The $\overline{INT}^*$ signal in this circuit is the same as the $\overline{INT}$ signal in Figure 12-21. Since more than one device may interrupt the computer, we use the $\overline{INT}^*$ signal to drive one input of a 7430 NAND gate (G2). We invert the output of G2 in order to form the $\overline{INT}$ signal that is actually connected to the computer interrupt line.

The INTAWK (interrupt acknowledge) signal turns on IC2, a 74LS244 8-bit tristate buffer. The input lines of IC2 are connected either HIGH or LOW as required for the specific *n* code, in this case 11011111. When the INTAWK signal is generated by the CPU, the data word 11011111 is applied to the data bus and tells the CPU to jump to the beginning of the service subroutine.

---

[1]See Joseph J. Carr, *Z80 Users Manual,* Reston Publishing Co., Reston, Va., 1981.

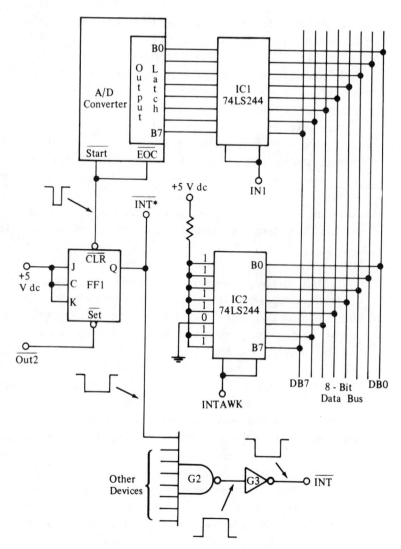

Figure 12-22 Complete scheme.

MISCELLANEOUS TOPICS

Figure 12-23a shows a simple circuit that can be used to implement a software A/D converter. Both ramp and successive approximation methods can be accommodated by this arrangement. The elements of the circuit are a digital-to-analog converter (DAC) and a voltage comparator. The comparator output will

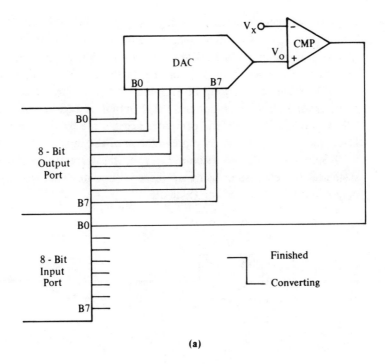

(a)

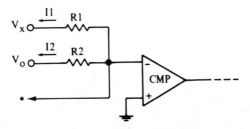

*Alternate DAC connection if
DAC is current - output type.

$$I_1 = \frac{V_x}{R_1}$$

$$I_2 = \frac{V_o}{R_2}$$

(b)

Figure 12-23 (a) Interface circuit needed for software implementation of data conversion; (b) current-mode connection.

be LOW whenever the input voltage is higher than the DAC output voltage (V_0). When $V_x = V_0$, the comparator output snaps HIGH. The output of the comparator is applied to 1 bit of an input port. The program will vary the data applied to the DAC inputs according to the specific method and algorithm selected (either binary ramp or SA), and then examine the comparator output to determine whether or not the DAC output voltage matches the unknown. When a match is found, the computer accepts the binary word applied to the DAC via the output port as representative of the input voltage value.

Software A/D conversion reduces the hardware overhead of the computer system at the expense of using up more CPU time. The designer will have to determine the validity of the trade-off.

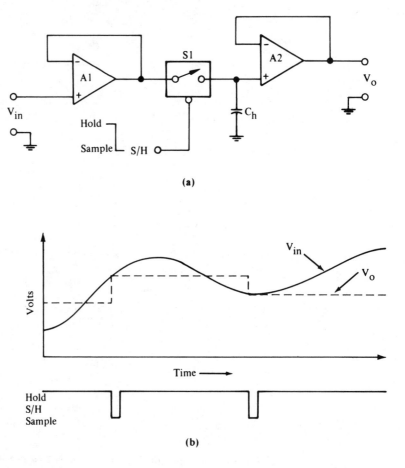

(a)

(b)

Figure 12-24 Sample and hold.

A variation on the theme is shown in Figure 12-23b. In this circuit we are using the comparator in the current mode, a tactic that will make the operation a little faster for many forms of comparator. It is the comparator settling time that limits many of these circuits, and that time is less for current-mode operation. In current-mode operation, the two voltages are applied to the comparator inverting input through resistors that convert the voltages to currents. The noninverting input of the comparator is grounded, so output transition occurs when $I1 = I2$. We can reduce the component count by one resistor if a current-output DAC (1408, DAC-08, etc.) is used instead of a voltage-output model.

Our last topic involves the sample and hold (S&H) circuit of Figure 12-24. There are times when we want to sample the signal prior to conversion. In some cases, for example, the A/D output will contain substantial error terms if the input analog signal varies during the conversion period. The S&H circuit will hold that signal constant for the brief period required to make the conversion. In other cases, we may wish to convert simultaneous instantaneous values (i.e., values that are related to each other in time), but use only one converter to do the job. While this requirement may be met by using parallel A/D converters that operate from the same start pulse, such use is uneconomical even in this era of low-cost A/D converters. The answer is to use a separate S&H circuit for each signal and drive them from the same sample line. The A/D converter can then make the conversions in sequence while retaining the simultaneity of the data.

The elements of the S&H are an input amplifier (A1), an electronic switch (S1), a hold capacitor (C_h) and an output buffer amplifier (A2). Both amplifiers are unity gain noninverting types and act to isolate the switch and the hold capacitor from the outside world. The tightest restrictions are applied to A2, which must have an extremely high input impedance in order to avoid discharging capacitor C_h while the signal is supposedly being held; amplifier A2 is usually specified as a BiFET or BiMOS type. Figure 12-24b shows the sampling pulse signal and the relationship to the input and output voltages.

13
Controlling External Circuits

Control of external circuitry by the microcomputer has made it much more useful. Certain calculation or signal-processing chores can be performed in the machine and then used to control external circuits. The simplest forms of external control are on–off switches that are controlled by a single bit of the computer's output port. More complex control applications use devices such as amplifiers, digital-to-analog converters (DACs), and so forth. Extremely complex feedback control systems have been implemented using computers. The availability of microcomputers has accelerated the process, and has, in an interesting way, made the design of computerized control circuits less a problem for arcane areas of engineering and more a game for all.

Some external control circuits have already been discussed in Chapter 6. In that chapter we showed methods for connecting the computer to digital display devices such as the seven-segment LED decimal display. Some of the same methods are also used to interface other devices. For example, Figure 13-1 shows methods of interfacing electromechanical relays.

Why would one want to interface an electromechanical relay, which is a century-old device, to a modern space-age device like a microcomputer? The old relay may well be the best solution to many problems, especially where a certain degree of isolation is needed between the computer and the controlled circuit. An example might be 115-V ac applications, especially those that may require heavy current loads. A typical homeowner application might be turning on and off 115-V ac lamps around the house. The computer can be used as a timer and will turn on and off the lights according to a programmed schedule, such as when you are away. Another application might be to use the computer to monitor burglar alarm sensors and then turn on a lamp if one of them senses a break-in.

Figure 13-3 shows two basic methods for connecting the relay to the computer. Control over the relay is maintained by using 1 bit of the computer output port, in this case B0. Since only 1 bit is used, the other 7 bits are available for other applications, which may be displays, other relays, or certain other devices.

Most microcomputer outputs are not capable of driving heavy loads. Some devices will have a fan-out of 10 (i.e., will drive 18 mA at +5 V), while others have a low fan-out, typically 2 (3.6 mA). To increase the drive capacity and to provide a mechanism for control, we use an open-collector TTL inverter stage, U1. One end of relay coil K1 is connected to the inverter output, and the other end of the coil is connected to the V+ supply. Some TTL devices (7406, 7407, 7416, and 7417) will operate with potentials greater than +5 V dc on the output, so we can use 6-, 12-, or 28-V relays. The package dc potential applied to the inverter is still the normal +5 V required by all TTL devices. These inverters are actually hex inverters and so will contain six individual inverter circuits in each package. All six inverters can be operated independently of each other.

The operation of the circuit revolves around the fact that the relay (K1) coil is grounded when the inverter output is LOW and ungrounded when the inverter output is HIGH. As a result, we can control the on–off states of the relay by applying a HIGH or LOW level to the input of the inverter. If the

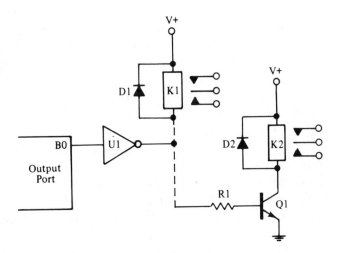

Figure 13-1 Interfacing relays.

inverter input is LOW, for example, the output is HIGH, so the relay coil is not grounded. In that case, the relay coil is not energized because both ends are at the same electrical potential. When a HIGH is applied to the input of the inverter (i.e., when B0 of the output port is HIGH), the inverter output is LOW, which makes the "cold" end of the relay coil grounded. The relay will be energized, which closes the contacts. We may turn the relay on, then, by writing a HIGH (logical 1) to bit B0 of the output port, and turn if off by writing a LOW (logical 0) to the output port.

The inverter devices cited previously have greater output current capability than some TTL devices, but it is still low compared with the current requirements of some relays. High-current relays, for example, may have coil current requirements of 1 to 5 A. If we want to increase the drive capability of the circuit, we may connect a transistor driver such as Q1 in Figure 13-1.

In the case of relay K2, the "cold" end of the coil is grounded or kept high by the action of transistor Q1. This relay driver will ground the coil when the transistor is turned on (i.e., saturated) and will unground the coil when the transistor is turned off. As a result, we must design a method by which the transistor will be cut off when we want the relay off, and saturated when we want the relay on.

For circuits such as K2, the TTL interface with the computer output port (U1) may be an inverter or a noninverting TTL buffer. The on–off protocol will be different for the two. Also, we need not use an open-collector inverter for U1, as was the case in the preceding. If we want to use an open-collector device, however, we supply a 2.2-kΩ pull-up resistor from the inverter output to the +5-V dc power supply. The idea in this circuit is to use the inverter or buffer output to provide a bias current to transistor Q1. The value of the base resistor (R1) is a function of the Q1 collector current and the beta of Q1. This resistor should be selected to safely turn on the transistor all the way to saturation when the output of U1 is HIGH.

The relay will be energized when the output of Q1 is HIGH. Therefore, the B0 control signal should also be HIGH if U1 is a noninverting buffer and LOW if U1 is an inverter.

Both relays K1 and K2 in Figure 13-1 use a diode in parallel with the relay coil. This diode is used to suppress the inductive kick spike created when the relay is de-energized. The magnetic field surrounding the coil contains energy. When the current flow is interrupted, the field collapses, which causes that energy to be dumped back into the circuit. The result is a high-voltage counter-emf spike that will possibly burn out the semiconductor devices or, in the case of digital circuits, create *glitches* (pulses that should not occur). The diode should be a rectifier type with a peak inverse voltage rating of 1000 V and a current of 500 mA or more. The 1N4007 diode has a 1000 PIV rating at 1 A. This diode will suffice for all but the heaviest relay currents.

Figure 13-2 shows a method for driving a relay from a low fan-out output port bit without the use of the inverter. The transistor driver is a pair of transistors connected in the Darlington amplifier configuration. Such a circuit connects the two collectors together; the base of Q1 becomes the base for the pair; the emitter of Q2 becomes the emitter for the pair. The advantage of the Darlington amplifier is that the current gain is greatly magnified. Current gain, *beta,* is defined as the ratio of the collector current to base current (I_c/I_b). For the Darlington amplifier, the beta of the pair is the product of the individual beta ratings:

$$\beta_{1\text{-}2} = \beta_{Q1} \times \beta_{Q2} \tag{13-1}$$

or

$$\beta_{1\text{-}2} = \beta^2 \tag{13-2}$$

Equation 13-2 is used when the two transistors are identical. Since the total beta is the product of the individual beta ratings, when two identical transistors are used this figure is the beta squared.

You can use either a pair of discrete transistors to make the Darlington pair or one of the newer Darlington devices that houses both transistors inside one TO-5, TO-66, or TO-3 power transistor case.

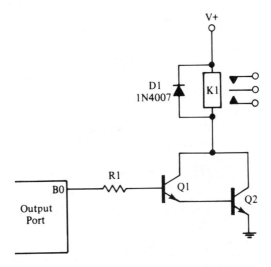

Figure 13-2   Use of Darlington transistor to interface with relays.

Another method for isolating dangerous or heavy-duty loads from the microcomputer output port is shown in Figure 13-3. In this case we use an optoisolator as the interface media. The optoisolator uses light flux between a light-emitting diode (LED) and a phototransistor to couple the on–off signal from input to output. The LED produces light when a current is caused to flow in it, while the phototransistor is turned on (saturated) when light falls on the base and is off when the base is dark (LED off). The transistor and LED are housed together, usually in a six-pin DIP package.

The LED in the optoisolator is connected to the output of an open-collector TTL inverter (see Chapter 6 also). The cathode end of the LED is grounded and the LED thereby turned on whenever the output of the inverter is LOW. Thus, the LED is turned on whenever bit B0 of the output port is HIGH. At the instant that the LED is turned on, transistor Q1 comes saturated, so collector–emitter current flows in resistor R4, thereby causing a voltage drop that can be used for control purposes.

The voltage drop across resistor R4 can be used to drive another NPN transistor that actually controls the load. Or we can create an RC differentiator (R2/C1) and use the leading edge of the voltage across R4 (as it turns on) to trigger some other device. In Figure 13-3, for example, we are using a triac to control the ac load. A triac is basically a full-wave silicon-controlled rectifier (SCR) and will gate on when a pulse is received at the gate (G) terminal. Most triacs or SCRs will not turn off with gate signals, so some means must be

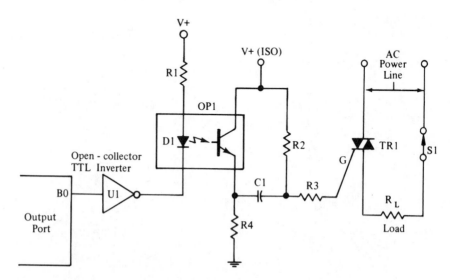

Figure 13-3 Isolation method of interfacing to 115-V ac line.

provided to reduce the cathode–anode current to near zero when we want to turn off the device. That is the purpose of switch S1. When we want to turn the circuit off, switch S1 is opened long enough to allow the triac/SCR to revert to its off condition. Some devices allow turn off as well as turn on by external pulses.

A method for interfacing the microcomputer with display devices such as an oscilloscope or a strip-chart paper recorder is shown in Figure 13-4. There are instances when these devices are the most appropriate means of display, so we will want to provide some means to convert binary data to analog voltages for the oscilloscope or recorder. In Figure 13-4, the conversion is made by a digital-to-analog converter (DAC), which is covered in detail in Chapter 12. The DAC produces an output potential V_0 that is proportional to the binary output. Various coding schemes are available (they will not be discussed here). We will assume for the purposes of our discussion that straight binary coding is used in which the 0-V state is represented by a binary word of 00000000, and full-scale output is represented by the binary word 11111111. States in between zero and full scale are represented by proportional binary words; half-scale, for example, is represented by 10000000.

We will want to be able to scale the output potential V_{ot} to some value that is compatible with the display device. Not all oscilloscopes or paper recorders will accept any potential we apply, so some order must be introduced. Some oscilloscopes used in special medical, scientific, or industrial monitor applica-

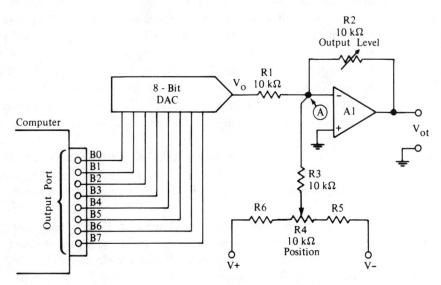

Figure 13-4 Interfacing circuit for oscilloscope or strip-chart/XY recorders.

tions, for example, come with fixed 1-V inputs. These instruments are often the most likely to be selected for applications involving a computer, yet they lack the multivoltage input selector of engineering models. For these we must select a DAC output voltage V_0 that will match the oscilloscope input requirements. If the DAC output is somewhat higher (0 to 2.56 V is common), some form of output attenuation is needed. The operational amplifier used in Figure 13-4 provides that attenuation.

The voltage gain of an ordinary operational amplifier connected in the inverting follower configuration, as in the case of A1 in Figure 13-4, is set by the ratio of feedback to input resistances (i.e., R2 and R1). For this circuit, the gain is $(-R2/R1)$; the minus sign indicates polarity inversion. The inversion means that we must design either the DAC output or the oscilloscope/recorder input to be negative. We can reinvert the signal by following the amplifier with another circuit that is identical except that R2 is a fixed resistor rather than a potentiometer. In that case, R1 = R2 = 10 kΩ (or any other value that is convenient). The product of two inversions is the same as if none had taken place; V_{ot} will be in-phase with V_0.

A position control is provided by potentiometer R4. In this circuit, we are producing an intentional output offset potential around which the wave form V_0 will vary. The effect of this potential is to position the wave form on the oscilloscope screen or chart paper where we want it. Sometimes the base-line (i.e., zero-signal) position will be in the center of the display screen or paper; in other cases it will be at one limit or the other.

An alternative system that would allow positioning of the base line under program control is to connect a second DAC (with its own R1) to point A, which is the operational amplifier summing junction. The program can output a binary word to this other DAC that represents the desired position on the display. That position can be controlled automatically by the program or manually in response to some keyboard action by the operator. This approach requires the investment of one additional DAC, but IC DACs are relatively cheap these days.

If the dc load driven by the DAC–computer combination is somewhat more significant than an oscilloscope input, the simple op-amp method of Figure 13-4 may not suffice. For such applications we may need a power amplifier to drive the load.

A power amplifier is shown in Figure 13-5. Here we have a *complementary symmetry* class B power amplifier. A *complementary pair* of power transistors is a pair, one NPN and the other PNP, that are electrically identical except for polarity. When these transistors are connected with their respective bases in parallel and their collector-emitter paths in series, the result is a simple push-

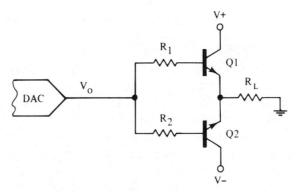

Figure 13-5 Increasing output power of DAC.

pull class B amplifier. When the DAC output voltage V_o goes positive, transistor Q1 will tend to turn on, and current flowing through Q1 under the influence of V+ will drive the load also positive. If, on the other hand, the output voltage of the DAC is negative, PNP transistor Q2 will turn on and the load will be driven by current from the V− power supply. Since each transistor turns on only on one-half of the input signal, the result is full wave power amplification when the two signals are combined in the load.

The load in Figure 13-5 can be any of several different devices. If it is an electrical motor, for example, the DAC output voltage will vary the speed of the dc motor; hence the computer will control the speed because it controls V_o. If we provide some means for measuring the speed of the motor, the computer can be used in a negative feedback loop to keep the speed constant or change it to some specific value at will.

There is also a method by which the motor can be controlled without the DAC. If we use a transistor driver to turn the motor on and off, we can effectively control its speed by controlling the relative duty cycle of the motor current. By using a form of pulse-width modulation, we can set the motor speed as desired.

Pulse-width modulation of the motor current works by setting the total percentage of unit time that the motor is energized. The current will always be either all on or all off, never at some intermediate value. If we vary the length of time during each second that current is applied, we control the total energy applied to the motor and hence its speed. If we want the motor to turn very slowly, we arrange to output very narrow pulses through the output port to U1 to the motor control transistor. If, however, we want the motor speed to be very fast, long-duration pulses, or a constant level, is applied to the output port.

Can you spot the most common programming error that will be made when you actually try to implement this circuit? It occurs at turn on. The dc motor has a certain amount of inertia that keeps it from wanting to start moving when it is off. As a result, if we want to start the motor at a slow speed, the pulse width may not be great enough to overcome inertia, and the motor will just sit there dormant. The solution is to apply a quick, one-time, long-duration pulse to get the motor in motion anytime we want it to turn on from a dead stop. After this initial pulse, the normal pulse coding will apply.

If we want to actively control the speed of the motor, we will need a sensor that converts angular rotation into a pulse train. On some motors this problem is made less of a nuisance because the motor is mechanically linked with an ac alternator housed in the same case. A pair of output terminals will exhibit an ac sinewave signal whenever the motor shaft is rotating. If we apply this ac signal to a voltage comparator (such as the LM-311 device), we will produce a TTL-compatible output signal from the comparator that has the same frequency

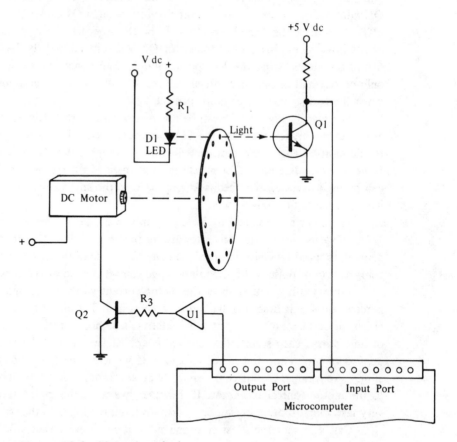

Figure 13-6 Motor interfacing.

as the ac from the motor. A typical case uses the inverting input of the comparator to look at the ac signal, and the noninverting input of the comparator is at ground potential. Under this condition, there will be an output pulse generated every time the ac signal crosses the 0-V base line. Such a circuit is called a *zero-crossing detector,* appropriately enough.

If there is no alternator, some other means of providing the signal must be designed. One popular system is shown in Figure 13-6. A wheel with holes in the outer rim is connected to the motor output shaft. An LED and photo-transistor are positioned such that light from the LED will fall on the photo-transistor whenever a hole in the wheel is in the path; otherwise, the light path is interrupted. Flashes of light produced when the wheel rotates trigger the transistor to produce a signal that is in turn applied to the input port bit, as shown. A program can then be written to sample this input port bit and determine the motor speed from the frequency of the pulses or, as is more likely with some microprocessors, the time between successive pulses.

The sensor shown in Figure 13-6 may be constructed from discrete components, if desired, but several companies make such sensors already built into a plastic housing. A slot is provided to admit the rim of the wheel to interfere with the light path.

The methods shown in this chapter are intended to be used as guides only, and you may well come up with others that are a lot more clever. The computer does not need much in the way of sophisticated interfacing in most cases, as can be seen from some of the foregoing examples.

APPENDIX A

DC Power Supply for Computers

Most texts on microcomputer/microprocessor interfacing assume that the reader has available some form of microcomputer or trainer on which to try out the methods taught either as part of a classroom situation for students or on the bench for a working journeyman engineer. It is usually assumed in such texts that the reader's microcomputer is ready-made and of the "plug and chug" variety. Unfortunately, many machines on the market lack a power supply and you might not read the fine print in the advertisement until it is too late. In other cases, you might have an extensive collection of used or scrap components on which to base a microcomputer power supply. In still other cases, you might be using either a custom designed or "standard" single-board computer such as the Pro-Log series and may well want to design your own power supply. A shortcoming of some books in this field is the lack of instructions on what to do for a power supply.

The circuit for a basic power supply is shown in Figure A-1, while a photograph of the completed project is shown in Figure A-2. There is nothing special in the circuit of Figure A-1; it is based on well-known principles and easily available components.

The heart of any dc power supply is the transformer. The purpose of the transformer in the power supply is to adjust the voltage from the ac power mains down (or up) to the voltage levels required by electronic circuits. In the case of the typical small single-board trainer computer, the required voltages are $+5$ V at a current rating of 3 to 6 A, and ± 12 V dc at a current rating of 1 A for each potential (total of 2 A). The 5-V potential is obtained from a 6.3-

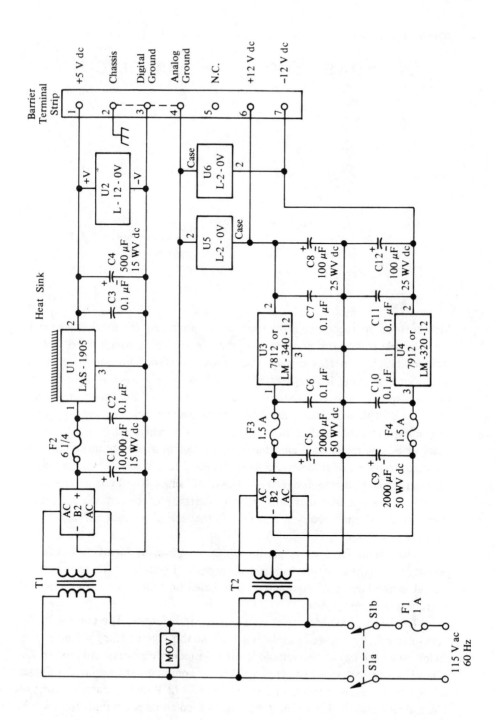

Figure A-1 Power supply with +5 V dc at 5 A, ±12 V at 1 V.

V ac filament transformer of appropriate rating. The extra voltage (which rectifies to +8 V dc on peaks) is needed because the regulator input voltage must be 2.5 V, or more, greater than the rated output voltage. For a 5-V regulator, therefore, we would require at least 7.5 V dc into the voltage regulator.

A suitable transformer for this project is the triad-type F24U, which is rated at 6.3/7.5 V rms at 8 A of secondary current. The 6.3/7.5 designation for the secondary voltage comes from the fact that the transformer has a tapped primary that will cause the secondary potential to be either 6.3 V ac rms or 7.5 V ac rms, depending upon which tap is connected to the hot side of the 115-V ac power mains. The current rating for this transformer technically should be 10 A for a 5-A power supply in order not to exceed the primary VA rating. This rating is needed because the transformer is used in the bridge-rectified configuration shown in Figure A-1. The power supply has run at 5 A for many months, however, and no problems have occurred. But be aware that, technically, running the full 5 A is "pushing it."

The transformer for the ± 12-V dc supply can be any type with a secondary rating of 25 to 28 V ac rms (25.6 V is common) with a current rating of 2 A or more (there are several 2.8-A models on the market). The absolute necessity, however, is a center tap on the secondary winding. There are only a few models that have the required center tap, without which the circuit will not work.

The rectifiers are standard bridge-rectifier stacks. The rectifier for the

Figure A-2 Typical power supply built from Figure A-1.

± 12-V supply is any 50 PIV at 1 A model. Most builders will use one of the printed circuit models that have radial leads.

The rectifier for the +5-V supply, however, is a little heavier and must be rated at 5 A or more. The PIV rating can be anything over 25 V. The use of a chassis-mounted 25-A bridge is recommended if you obtain the rectifier from a prepackaged source, and a 12-A model if from an industrial supplier. The reason for the difference in apparent rating for what seems to be the same rectifier is that some distributers of prepackaged items seem to overrate their products. This is not so much a reflection of dishonesty as a realization that amateur and hobby applications are intermittent in nature.

The three different power supplies in Figure A-1 are essentially the same, so only one description will be needed. The filter capacitors are selected according to a 1000-μF/A rule for the 12-V supplies and 2000 μF/A for the +5-V supply. The difference is due to the large dynamic current changes that can be expected from digital circuits. The 0.1-μF capacitors (C2, C3, C6, C7, C10 and C11) at the inputs and outputs of the voltage regulators are meant to provide bypassing for noise transients. To be effective, these capacitors must be mounted as close as possible to the body of the regulators. Most builders prefer to mount these capacitors *on* the body of the regulators, despite the fact that this method may be esthetically less appealing than some other methods. The output capacitors (C4, C8, and C12) are selected according to a 100-μF/A rule and are intended to improve the transient response of the circuit. In the case of a large, short-duration transient current demand the excess current can be taken from the capacitor while the regulator catches up.

The voltage regulators used in these projects are three-terminal IC regulators. The 12-V power supplies use either 7812 or LM-340-12 (either T or K styles) for the +12-V supply and either 7912 or LM-320-12 (either T or K) for the −12-V dc supply. Note the difference in pinouts for these two regulators. Failure to recognize this can be fatal for the regulator.

The 5-A regulator for the +5-V dc supply is a special type in a TO-3 transistor case and is made by Lambda Electronics (515 Broad Hollow Road, Melville, NY, 11747). In this application the use of a finned heat sink (see Figure A-2) for the regulator is recommended; it will cause it to run a lot cooler, which means potentially longer and more reliable operation of the device (as is true of any semiconductor power device).

Overvoltage protection is an absolute necessity for any dc power supply used with computers. The regulator input voltage is higher than the rated output voltage by at least 2.5 V. If something happens to the regulator (and it often does), the higher voltage at the input may appear at the output and *will* (not may) damage the circuits of the computer. TTL electronic devices, after all, can withstand only potentials of less than +5.25 V. There are several methods for supplying protection against the possibility of overvoltage damage, but in this case we must use two more Lambda products, the L-12-OV and L-2-OV overvoltage protection modules. The 2-A L-2-OV device must be operated with reverse polarity for the −12-V dc supply (note the diagram). On this device, the case is the same as the TO-66 diamond-shaped power transistor case. The V− is the case, while the V+ is pin 2 (which would correspond to the emitter on a transistor).

The MOV device across the primaries of the transformers is used to suppress high-voltage transients appearing on the ac power line. These transients occur frequently, especially in industrial environments. They will cause the computer to run amuck if they hit at the wrong time.

There are three grounds in this circuit: chassis, digital, and analog. In most cases, these grounds will be joined together at the power supply, so terminals 2, 3, and 4 will be shorted together. In other cases, separate grounds must be maintained to prevent ground loops.

Fast Fourier Transform Program for Apple II Users

The fast Fourier transform (FFT) has revolutionized certain instrumentation chores because it allows more rapid determination of frequency components than was previously possible. In previous times, the engineer who needed to know the constituent frequency components of a wave form had to use either a mammoth analog filter system (which was both expensive and unreliable) or a gigantic mainframe computer to calculate the Fourier components. The FFT is a relatively recent development that, when coupled with microcomputer technology, has made possible a large number of new and improved instruments, as well as allowing laboratory scientists to perform experiments that were previously impossible for all but the wealthy and well equipped.

The FFT program in this appendix was developed by C. E. McCullough, a personal friend of the author, from earlier published sources and his own ingenuity. The original project was to permit FFT analysis of electroencephalograph (EEG) real-time and evoked potentials in the Anesthesiology Research Laboratory of the George Washington University School of Medicine. McCullough holds BSEE and MSEE degrees and works for the GWU Medical Center Bioelectronics Laboratory. The program was developed under the direction and auspices of Michael Shaffer, Director of the Bioelectronics Laboratory and assistant professor of anesthesiology.

The assembly language program published in this appendix is configured to run on the Apple II 6502-based microcomputer equipped with Applesoft and DOS 3.2. It may be rewritten for other 6502 systems.

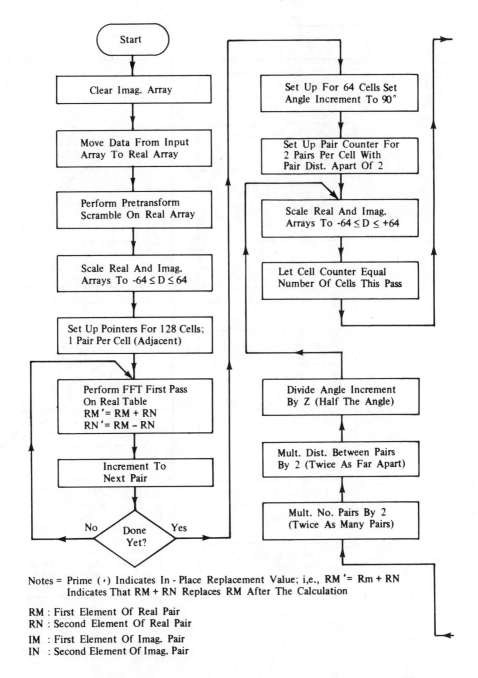

Notes = Prime (') Indicates In - Place Replacement Value; i,e., RM '= Rm + RN
Indicates That RM + RN Replaces RM After The Calculation

RM : First Element Of Real Pair
RN : Second Element Of Real Pair

IM : First Element Of Imag. Pair
IN : Second Element Of Imag. Pair

Figure B-1 FFT flow chart. *(Copyright 1979 by C. E. McCullough. Used by permission)*

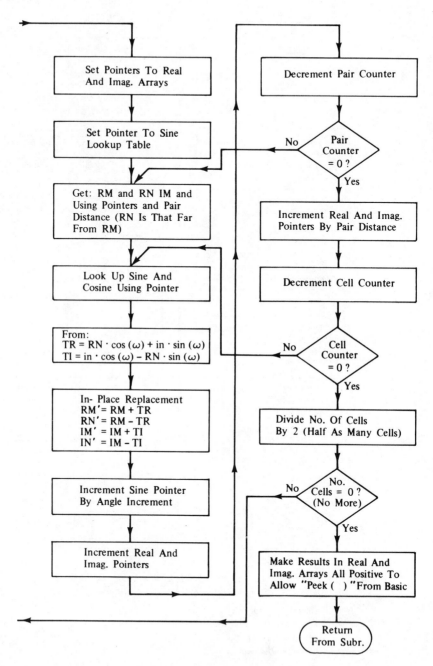

Figure B-1 *Continued* **FFT flow chart.** *(Copyright 1979 by C. E. McCullough. Used by permission)*

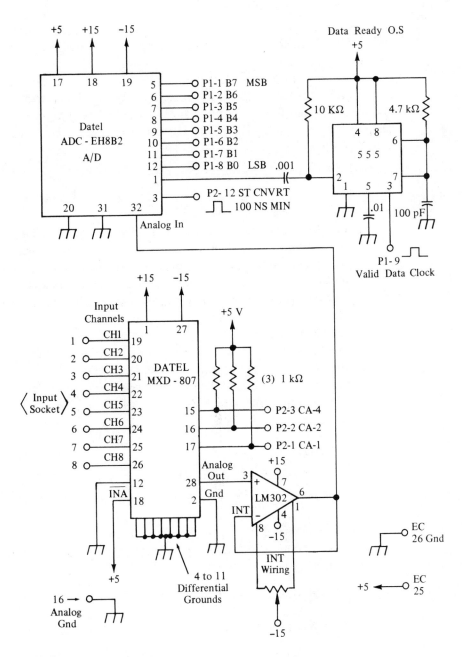

Figure B-2 A/D converter with 8-channel MUX, for Apple II computers.

Figure B-1 shows the flow chart for the FFT program. This chart is included to facilitate understanding the program and modifying it for other systems.

An eight-channel A/D converter designed for use on Apple II to supply input data for the FFT is shown in Figure B-2. The circuit is extremely simple, and it (or its equivalent) may be built on a standard plug-in interfacing–prototyping card designed to fit Apple II (several companies make these cards, including Vector Electronics).

FFT NOTES

1. For A/D conversion, an 8-bit A/D converter must input 256 *two's complement* numbers into the input sample area. To design the A/D sampling hardware and software, you need to consider the maximum frequency component of the input signal and the desired resolution between spectral lines. You are constrained by the fact that you need 256 samples, so this and the other factors will set the record length (sampling book).[1]

2. The output will be found in the two areas of memory designated REAL and IMAG. The theory of the FFT and the in-place algorithm are such that the first and last 128 points are redundant. The power spectrum is calculated as the sum of the squares of the corresponding 128 reals and imaginaries. In BASIC,

> FOR I = 0 to 127
>
> FFT(I) + PEEK (REAL + I) $\wedge$ 2 + PEEK (IMAG + I) $\wedge$ 2
>
> NEXT I

will fill and array FFT ( ) with the power spectrum.

3. As an example of the design process, the FFT A/D sampler program included is set up as follows:

> Sample rate: 127.5 Hz
>
> Sample period: 2 s
>
> Samples: 256

---

[1]See Frank Stanley, *Digital Signal Processing,* Reston Publishing Co., Reston, Va., p. 284.

These specifications will result in a spectral resolution of ½ s or 0.5 Hz between lines. Since the FFT power spectrum is based on 128 pairs from the real and imaginary arrays (the other 128 being redundant), the system will display 128 × 0.5 Hz, or a spectral display of dc to 64 Hz. This is adequate for real-time EEG and evoked potentials work, but may not be adequate for other signal-processing applications.

4. The FFT program is a machine-language subroutine that may be called by another machine-language program or by a high-level language. Control is returned to the main program by executing an RTS instruction.[2]

5. This FFT program and driver software for the A/D converter was written to run on Apple II, DOS 3.2, and fits into the memory space between Applesoft and the DOS. The A/D routine is completely hardware dependent, so the A/D circuit is provided in Figure B-2.

6. The whole program can be reassembled to run anywhere in memory on any 6502 system, but keep in mind the following:

a. The input data, sine look-up, REAL, and IMAG areas must be located on page boundaries and contiguously in memory.

b. Note that the sine look-up table (see program listing) must be resident in memory at all times; it is not generated by the FFT program listing.

7. Note that a routine was added after the FFT was calculated that makes all the resulting data positive, since Applesoft's PEEK statement can only interpret straight binary words (0–255), not two's complement. You square these numbers and add to calculate the power spectrum.

---

[2]Based on Lord, R.H.: "Fast Fourier for 6800; *Byte* (Feb. 1979).

```
            1000 *      6502 ASSEMBLY LANGUAGE
            1010 *      FAST FOURIER TRANSFORM SUBROUTINE
            1020 *      VERSION 1.41  10/22/79
            1030 *
            1040 *
            1050 *
            1060 * *    H I M E M :   3 6 3 5 2   T O   M A K E   R O O M
                                                   F O R   F F T  * * *
            1070 *
            1080 *
            1090 *
            1100 *
            1110 *    M E M O R Y    M A P
            1120 *
            1130 *    HEX ADDRESS     USE
            1140 *    -----------     ---
            1150 *    8E01 - 8EFF     POINTER AND SCRATCHPAD AREA
            1160 *    8F00 - 8FFF     INPUT DATA TABLE
            1170 *    9000 - 90FF     SINE LOOKUP TABLE
            1180 *    9100 - 91FF     REAL DATA TABLE
            1190 *    9200 - 92FF     IMAG DATA TABLE
            1200 *    9300 - 95FF     SUBROUTINE CODING
            1210 *
            1220 *
            1230 *    JSR $9300 OR CALL 37632 TO RUN FFT OF INPUT DATA
            1240 *
            1250 *    JSR $8E1A OR CALL 36378 TO SAMPLE INPUT
            1260 *
            1270 *    LDA $C0B1 WITH 0 THRU 7 TO SELECT CHANNEL
            1280 *    OR POKE 49329,CHAN    WHERE CHAN= 0 THRU 7
            1290 *
            1300 *
            1310 *    DATA AREAS
            1320 *
            1330 INPT .EQ $8F00      INPUT DATA TABLE
            1340 RELT .EQ $9100      REAL DATA TABLE
            1350 IMGT .EQ $9200      IMAG DATA TABLE
            1360 SINT .EQ $9000      SINE LOOKUP TABLE
            1370 *
            1380 *
            1390 *
            1400 *    POINTER AREA
            1410 *
            1420      .OR $8E01
            1430      .TA $0801
8E01- 00 00 1440 RPT1 .DA *-*        "REAL" DATA POINTERS
8E03- 00 00 1450 RPT2 .DA *-*
8E05- 00 00 1460 IPT1 .DA *-*        "IMAG" DATA POINTERS
8E07- 00 00 1470 IPT2 .DA *-*
8E09- 00 00 1480 SNPT .DA *-*        SINE TABLE POINTER
```

```
8E0B- 00        1490 CLNM .DA #*-*      CELLS FOR THIS PASS
8E0C- 00        1500 CLCT .DA #*-*      CELL COUNTER FOR PASS
8E0D- 00        1510 PRNM .DA #*-*      PAIRS/CELL
8E0E- 00        1520 CLDS .DA #*-*      CELL OFFSET (DISTANCE)
8E0F- 00        1530 DLTA .DA #*-*      ANGLE INCREMENT
8E10- 00        1540 SCFT .DA #*-*      SCALE FACTOR COUNTER
8E11- 00        1550 COSA .DA #*-*      TEMPORARY COSINE
8E12- 00        1560 SINA .DA #*-*      TEMPORARY SINE
8E13- 00        1570 TREL .DA #*-*      TEMP. REAL DATA
8E14- 00        1580 TMAG .DA #*-*      TEMP. IMAG DATA
8E15- 00        1590 LSBY .DA #*-*      PRODUCT LSBY
8E16- 00        1600 MSBY .DA #*-*      PRODUCT MSBY
8E17- 00        1610 CAND .DA #*-*      MULTIPLICAND
8E18- 00        1620 PLYR .DA #*-*      MULTIPLIER
8E19- 00        1630 DEC  .DA #*-*      DECIMAL MODE FLAG
                1640 *
                1650 *
                1660 *
                1670 *    A-D SAMPLING SUBROUTINE
                1680 *    2 SECONDS AT 127.5 HERTZ
                1690 *    OR 256 SAMPLES TAKEN.
                1700 *
                1710 CVRT .EQ $C0B4      START CONVERT STROBE
                1720 IPRT .EQ $C0B0      INPUT PORT ADDRESS
                1730 CHAN .EQ $C0B1      CHAN. SELECT PORT
                1740 *
8E1A- A2 00     1750 SMPL LDX #$00
8E1C- 8D B4 C0  1760 SPL  STA CVRT      FIRE START CONVERT ONE SHOT
8E1F- A9 04     1770      LDA #$04      DELAY 7.84 MSEC
8E21- A0 66     1780 POT  LDY #$66
8E23- EA        1790 INS  NOP
8E24- EA        1800      NOP
8E25- EA        1810      NOP
8E26- EA        1820      NOP
8E27- EA        1830      NOP
8E28- EA        1840      NOP
8E29- EA        1850      NOP
8E2A- 88        1860      DEY
8E2B- D0 F6     1870      BNE INS
8E2D- 38        1880      SEC
8E2E- E9 01     1890      SBC #$01
8E30- EA        1900      NOP
8E31- EA        1910      NOP
8E32- EA        1920      NOP
8E33- EA        1930      NOP
8E34- EA        1940      NOP
8E35- D0 EA     1950      BNE POT       END OF DELAY
8E37- AD B0 C0  1960      LDA IPRT      READ A/D
8E3A- EA        1970      NOP
8E3B- 9D 00 8F  1980      STA INPT,X    PUT IN INPUT TABLE
```

```
8E3E- E8        1990        INX             NEXT SAMPLE
8E3F- E0 00     2000        CPX #$00        DONE?
8E41- D0 D9     2010        BNE SPL         NO, GET ANOTHER
8E43- 60        2020        RTS             RETURN TO PROG.
                2030 *
                2040 *
                2050 *
                2060 *
                2070 *
                2080 *    START OF TRANSFORM
                2090 *
                2100        .OR $9300
                2110        .TA $0D00
9300- 08        2120        PHP             PUSH PSW
9301- 68        2130        PLA             PULL PSW
9302- 29 08     2140        AND #$08        MASK OFF DECI. FLAG
9304- 8D 19 8E  2150        STA DEC
9307- D8        2160        CLD             CLEAR DEC. MODE
9308- 4C 13 93  2170        JMP STRT        JUMP AROUND PARAMETERS
                2180 *
                2190 *
                2200 *
                2210 *    ADDRESS LOOKUP TABLE
                2220 *
930B- 00 8F     2230 INPD .DA INPT     SET UP DATA AREAS
930D- 00 91     2240 REAL .DA RELT
930F- 00 92     2250 IMAG .DA IMGT
9311- 00 90     2260 SINE .DA SINT
                2270 *
                2280 *
                2290 *
                2300 *    INPUT DATA SET UP
                2310 *
9313- A9 00     2320 STRT LDA #00
9315- 8D 10 8E  2330        STA SCFT
9318- A2 00     2340 CLER LDX #00
931A- 9D 00 92  2350 CLR1 STA IMGT,X     CLEAR IMAG AREA
931D- CA        2360        DEX
931E- D0 FA     2370        BNE CLR1
9320- A2 00     2380        LDX #00        MOVE INPUT DATA
9322- BD 00 8F  2390 MOV1 LDA INPT,X     TO REAL ARRAY
9325- 9D 00 91  2400        STA RELT,X
9328- CA        2410        DEX
9329- D0 F7     2420        BNE MOV1
                2430 *
                2440 *
                2450 *
                2460 *    PRE-TRANSFORM SCRAMBLER ROUTINE
                2470 *
932B- AD 0D 93  2480        LDA REAL        SET UP DATA POINTERS
932E- 8D 01 8E  2490        STA RPT1
```

```
9331- 8D 03 8E   2500        STA RPT2
9334- AD 0E 93   2510        LDA REAL+1
9337- 8D 02 8E   2520        STA RPT1+1
933A- 8D 04 8E   2530        STA RPT2+1
933D- A0 08      2540 BREV LDY #8        SET BIT COUNTER
933F- AD 01 8E   2550        LDA RPT1     GET POINTER 1
9342- 6A         2560 BRV1 ROR           REVERSE BIT ORDER
9343- 2E 03 8E   2570        ROL RPT2     FOR SECOND POINTER
9346- 88         2580        DEY          COUNT BITS
9347- D0 F9      2590        BNE BRV1
9349- AD 03 8E   2600        LDA RPT2     GET REVERSED BYTE
934C- CD 01 8E   2610        CMP RPT1     COMPARE WITH #1
934F- 90 16      2620        BCC SWP1     BRANCH IF SWAPPED
9351- AE 01 8E   2630 SWAP LDX RPT1      GET POINTER 1
9354- BD 00 91   2640        LDA RELT,X   GET VAL 1
9357- AE 03 8E   2650        LDX RPT2     GET POINTER 2
935A- BC 00 91   2660        LDY RELT,X   GET VAL 2
935D- 9D 00 91   2670        STA RELT,X   REPLACE WITH VAL 1
9360- AE 01 8E   2680        LDX RPT1     GET FIRST POINTER
9363- 98         2690        TYA          COMPLETE THE
9364- 9D 00 91   2700        STA RELT,X   SWAP.
9367- EE 01 8E   2710 SWP1 INC RPT1      DO NEXT POINT PAIR
936A- D0 D1      2720        BNE BREV     UNLESS ALL ARE DONE
                 2730 *
                 2740 *
                 2750 *
                 2760 *   FFT FIRST PASS
                 2770 *
936C- 20 E4 94   2780 PAS1 JSR SCAL      SCALE IF ANY OVER-RANGE DATA
936F- AE 0D 93   2790        LDX REAL     GET REAL POINTER
9372- BD 00 91   2800 PA1 LDA RELT,X     GET RM
9375- A8         2810        TAY          HOLD RM
9376- 18         2820        CLC
9377- 7D 01 91   2830        ADC RELT+1,X LET RM'=RM+RN
937A- 9D 00 91   2840        STA RELT,X   STORE RM'
937D- 98         2850        TYA          GET OLD RM
937E- 38         2860        SEC
937F- FD 01 91   2870        SBC RELT+1,X LET RN'=RM-RN
9382- 9D 01 91   2880        STA RELT+1,X STORE RN'
9385- E8         2890        INX          MOVE TO
9386- E8         2900        INX          NEXT PAIR
9387- D0 E9      2910        BNE PA1      KEEP GOING TILL DONE
                 2920 *
                 2930 *
                 2940 *
                 2950 *   FFT COMPUTATION: PASS 2 THRU N
                 2960 *
9389- A9 40      2970 FPAS LDA #64       SET UP PARAMETERS
938B- 8D 0B 8E   2980        STA CLNM     FOR CELL COUNT
938E- 8D 0F 8E   2990        STA DLTA     AND ANGLE
9391- A9 02      3000        LDA #2       AND FOR
```

```
9393- 8D 0D 8E 3010        STA PRNM       PAIRS/CELL
9396- 8D 0E 8E 3020        STA CLDS       DIST. BETWEEN PAIRS
9399- 20 E4 94 3030 NPAS JSR SCAL         KEEP DATA IN RANGE
939C- AD 0B 8E 3040        LDA CLNM       GET NUMBER OF CELLS
939F- 8D 0C 8E 3050        STA CLCT       PUT IN COUNTER
93A2- AD 0D 93 3060        LDA REAL       SET UP POINTERS
93A5- 8D 01 8E 3070        STA RPT1
93A8- 8D 03 8E 3080        STA RPT2
93AB- AD 0E 93 3090        LDA REAL+1
93AE- 8D 02 8E 3100        STA RPT1+1
93B1- 8D 04 8E 3110        STA RPT2+1
93B4- AD 0F 93 3120        LDA IMAG
93B7- 8D 05 8E 3130        STA IPT1
93BA- 8D 07 8E 3140        STA IPT2
93BD- AD 10 93 3150        LDA IMAG+1
93C0- 8D 06 8E 3160        STA IPT1+1
93C3- 8D 08 8E 3170        STA IPT2+1
93C6- AD 11 93 3180 NCEL LDA SINE
93C9- 8D 09 8E 3190        STA SNPT
93CC- AD 12 93 3200        LDA SINE+1
93CF- 8D 0A 8E 3210        STA SNPT+1
93D2- AC 0D 8E 3220        LDY PRNM       GET PAIRS/CELL COUNTER
93D5- AD 01 8E 3230 NC1  LDA RPT1         GET POINTER 1 LSBY
93D8- 18       3240        CLC
93D9- 6D 0E 8E 3250        ADC CLDS       ADD PAIR OFFSET
93DC- 8D 03 8E 3260        STA RPT2       SET BOTH POINTER 2'S
93DF- 8D 07 8E 3270        STA IPT2
93E2- 98       3280        TYA            SAVE PAIR COUNTER
93E3- 48       3290        PHA
93E4- AE 09 8E 3300        LDX SNPT       SET UP SINE LOOKUP
93E7- BD 00 90 3310        LDA SINT,X     GET COS OF ANGLE
93EA- 8D 11 8E 3320        STA COSA       SAVE COS
93ED- BD 40 90 3330        LDA SINT+64,X  GET SINE
93F0- 8D 12 8E 3340        STA SINA       SAVE SINE
93F3- AE 03 8E 3350        LDX RPT2       GET REAL POINTER 2
93F6- BD 00 91 3360        LDA RELT,X     GET RN
93F9- 48       3370        PHA            SAVE IT
93FA- AC 11 8E 3380        LDY COSA       GET COS
93FD- 20 17 95 3390        JSR MPY        MAKE RN*COS(A)
9400- 8D 13 8E 3400        STA TREL       SAVE IT
9403- 68       3410        PLA            RESTORE RN
9404- AC 12 8E 3420        LDY SINA       GET SINE
9407- 20 17 95 3430        JSR MPY        RN*SIN(A)
940A- 8D 14 8E 3440        STA TMAG
940D- AE 07 8E 3450        LDX IPT2       GET IMAG POINTER 2
9410- BD 00 92 3460        LDA IMGT,X     GET IN
9413- 48       3470        PHA            SAVE IT
9414- AC 12 8E 3480        LDY SINA       GET SINE
9417- 20 17 95 3490        JSR MPY        IN*SIN(A)
941A- 18       3500        CLC
941B- 6D 13 8E 3510        ADC TREL       TR=RN*COS+IN*SINE
```

```
941E- 8D 13 8E   3520        STA TREL
9421- 68         3530        PLA              RESTORE IN
9422- AC 11 8E   3540        LDY COSA         GET COS
9425- 20 17 95   3550        JSR MPY          IN*COS(A)
9428- 38         3560        SEC
9429- ED 14 8E   3570        SBC TMAG         TI=IN*COS-RN*SINE
942C- 8D 14 8E   3580        STA TMAG
942F- AE 01 8E   3590        LDX RPT1
9432- BD 00 91   3600        LDA RELT,X       GET RM
9435- A8         3610        TAY              SAVE IT
9436- 18         3620        CLC
9437- 6D 13 8E   3630        ADC TREL         RM'=RM+TR
943A- 9D 00 91   3640        STA RELT,X
943D- AE 03 8E   3650        LDX RPT2
9440- 98         3660        TYA
9441- 38         3670        SEC
9442- ED 13 8E   3680        SBC TREL         RN'=RM-TREL
9445- 9D 00 91   3690        STA RELT,X
9448- AE 05 8E   3700        LDX IPT1
944B- BD 00 92   3710        LDA IMGT,X       GET IM
944E- A8         3720        TAY              SAVE IT
944F- 18         3730        CLC
9450- 6D 14 8E   3740        ADC TMAG         IM'=IM+TI
9453- 9D 00 92   3750        STA IMGT,X
9456- AE 07 8E   3760        LDX IPT2
9459- 98         3770        TYA
945A- 38         3780        SEC
945B- ED 14 8E   3790        SBC TMAG         IN'=IM-TI
945E- 9D 00 92   3800        STA IMGT,X
9461- AD 09 8E   3810        LDA SNPT         INCREMENT ANGLE
9464- 18         3820        CLC
9465- 6D 0F 8E   3830        ADC DLTA
9468- 8D 09 8E   3840        STA SNPT
946B- EE 01 8E   3850        INC RPT1         INCREMENT POINTERS
946E- EE 05 8E   3860        INC IPT1
9471- 68         3870        PLA              GET PAIR COUNTER
9472- A8         3880        TAY              AND
9473- 88         3890        DEY              DECREMENT IT
9474- F0 03      3900        BEQ NOPE
9476- 4C D5 93   3910        JMP NC1          DO NEXT PAIR
9479- AD 01 8E   3920 NOPE LDA RPT1           GET POINTERS
947C- 18         3930        CLC
947D- 6D 0E 8E   3940        ADC CLDS         ADD CELL OFFSET
9480- 8D 01 8E   3950        STA RPT1
9483- 8D 05 8E   3960        STA IPT1
9486- CE 0C 8E   3970        DEC CLCT         DECREMENT CELL COUNTER
9489- F0 03      3980        BEQ NP1          NEXT PASS?
948B- 4C C6 93   3990        JMP NCEL         NO, DO NEXT CELL
                 4000 *
                 4010 *
                 4020 *
```

```
                        4030 *     CHANGE PARAMETERS FOR NEXT PASS
                        4040 *
948E- 4E 0B 8E 4050 NP1 LSR CLNM        HALF AS MANY CELLS
9491- F0 0C      4060     BEQ ABSO      NO MORE CELLS
9493- 0E 0D 8E 4070     ASL PRNM        TWICE AS MANY PAIRS
9496- 0E 0E 8E 4080     ASL CLDS        TWICE AS FAR APART
9499- 4E 0F 8E 4090     LSR DLTA        HALF THE ANGLE
949C- 4C 99 93 4100     JMP NPAS        DO NEXT PASS
                        4110 *
                        4120 *
                        4130 *
                        4140 *     END OF FFT ROUTINE
                        4150 *
                        4160 *
                        4170 *
                        4180 *     MAKE OUTPUT DATA ALL POSITIVE
                        4190 *
                        4200 *
949F- A2 00      4210 ABSO LDX #00
94A1- BD 00 92 4220 ONE  LDA IMGT,X     CHECK IMAG AREA
94A4- C9 00      4230     CMP #00       IS IT NEG?
94A6- 30 06      4240     BMI PLUS      IF SO, MAKE POS.
94A8- CA         4250     DEX
94A9- D0 F6      4260     BNE ONE       NEXT POINT
94AB- 4C BD 94 4270     JMP DOWN        DO REALS NEXT
94AE- 38         4280 PLUS SEC
94AF- A9 FF      4290     LDA #255      COMPLEMENT THE NUMBER
94B1- FD 00 92 4300     SBC IMGT,X
94B4- A8         4310     TAY
94B5- C8         4320     INY           ADD ONE
94B6- 98         4330     TYA
94B7- 9D 00 92 4340     STA IMGT,X      STORE THE POS. #
94BA- CA         4350     DEX
94BB- D0 E4      4360     BNE ONE       NEXT POINT
94BD- A2 00      4370 DOWN LDX #00      CHECK REAL AREA
94BF- BD 00 91 4380 TWO  LDA RELT,X
94C2- C9 00      4390     CMP #00       IS IT NEG?
94C4- 30 06      4400     BMI POS       IF SO, MAKE POS.
94C6- CA         4410     DEX
94C7- D0 F6      4420     BNE TWO       NEXT POINT
94C9- 4C DB 94 4430     JMP MDST        DONE, GO RESTORE DEC. MODE
94CC- 38         4440 POS  SEC
94CD- A9 FF      4450     LDA #255      COMPLEMENT THE NUMBER
94CF- FD 00 91 4460     SBC RELT,X
94D2- A8         4470     TAY
94D3- C8         4480     INY           ADD ONE
94D4- 98         4490     TYA
94D5- 9D 00 91 4500     STA RELT,X      STORE THE POS. NUMBER
94D8- CA         4510     DEX
94D9- D0 E4      4520     BNE TWO       NEXT POINT
94DB- AD 19 8E 4530 MDST LDA DEC        GET DEC. FLAG
```

```
94DE- C9 00    4540         CMP #00      IF ZERO
94E0- F0 01    4550         BEQ DONE     LEAVE ALONE
94E2- F8       4560         SED          OTHERWISE, SET IT
94E3- 60       4570 DONE RTS             RETURN TO PROGRAM
               4580 *
               4590 *
               4600 *
               4610 *    OVER RANGE DATA SCALING ROUTINE
               4620 *    BY D. MACINTOSH
               4630 *
94E4- A2 00    4640 SCAL LDX #00         INIT INDEX
94E6- BD 00 91 4650 TEST LDA RELT,X      GET AN ARRAY VALUE
94E9- 18       4660         CLC          TEST FOR OUT OF RANGE
94EA- 69 40    4670         ADC #$40     MOVE C0-3F TO 00-7F
94EC- 30 0C    4680         BMI DIV      OUT OF RANGE VALUES NOW 80-FF
94EE- BD 00 92 4690         LDA IMGT,X   DO THE
94F1- 18       4700         CLC          SAME TEST ON AN
94F2- 69 40    4710         ADC #$40     IMAG ARRAY
94F4- 30 04    4720         BMI DIV      VALUE
94F6- E8       4730         INX          POINT TO NEXT VALUE
94F7- D0 ED    4740         BNE TEST     MORE? YES:  LOOP
94F9- 60       4750         RTS          NO:  RETURN
94FA- A2 00    4760 DIV  LDX #00         BOTTOM OF TABLE
94FC- BD 00 91 4770 DIV1 LDA RELT,X      GET AN ARRAY VALUE
94FF- 18       4780         CLC          ASSUME POSITIVE:  SIGN EXTEND=0
9500- 10 01    4790         BPL DIV2     TEST IT: POS: YES,GO
9502- 38       4800         SEC          NEG: SIGN EXTEND=1
9503- 7E 00 91 4810 DIV2 ROR RELT,X      SCALE IT
9506- BD 00 92 4820         LDA IMGT,X   NOW DO
9509- 18       4830         CLC          THE SAME
950A- 10 01    4840         BPL DIV3     FOR
950C- 38       4850         SEC          IMAG
950D- 7E 00 92 4860 DIV3 ROR IMGT,X      ARRAY
9510- E8       4870         INX          POINT TO NEXT VALUE
9511- D0 E9    4880         BNE DIV1     MORE:  YES, LOOP
9513- EE 10 8E 4890         INC SCFT     NO....
9516- 60       4900         RTS          DONE SCALING.
               4910 *
               4920 *
               4930 *
               4940 *    TWO'S COMPLEMENT MULTIPLY SUBROUTINE
               4950 *    ROUTINE FROM EDN MAGAZINE 9/5/79
               4960 *    BY A. D. ROBISON
               4970 *
9517- 8D 18 8E 4980 MPY  STA PLYR        STORE A AT MULTIPLIER
951A- 8C 17 8E 4990         STY CAND     STORE Y AT MULTIPLICAND
951D- 4A       5000         LSR          SHIFT OUT FIRST BIT OF MULTIPLIER
951E- 8D 15 8E 5010         STA LSBY     STORE IN LOW BYTE IF PROD.
9521- A9 00    5020         LDA #$00     CLEAR HIGH BYTE OF PROD.
9523- A2 07    5030         LDX #$07     INITIALIZE LOOP
9525- 90 04    5040 CHEK BCC SHFT        TEST MULTIPLIER
```

```
9527- 18           5050      CLC          IF 1, ADD MULTIPLICAND
9528- 6D 17 8E     5060      ADC CAND       TO PARTIAL PROD.
952B- 6A           5070 SHFT ROR          SHIFT PROD. AND SHIFT IN POSSIBLE
952C- 6E 15 8E     5080      ROR LSBY       CARRY FROM MULTIPLICAND ADDITION
952F- CA           5090      DEX          REPEAT LOOP UNITIL ALL 7 LOWER BITS
9530- D0 F3        5100      BNE CHEK       OF MULTIPLIER
9532- 90 07        5110      BCC ADJ      TEST LAST BIT OF MULTIPLIER.
9534- ED 17 8E     5120      SBC CAND     IF 1, SUBTRACT MULTIPLICAND
9537- 6A           5130      ROR          COMPLEMENT CARRY, SINCE THE 6502
9538- 49 80        5140      EOR #$80       DEFINES BORROW AS THE COMPLEMENT
953A- 2A           5150      ROL            OF THE CARRY FLAG.
953B- 6A           5160 ADJ  ROR          SHIFT PRODUCT ONCE MORE AND SHIFT IN
953C- 6E 15 8E     5170      ROR LSBY       POSSIBLE BORRPW FROM SUBTRACTION
953F- AE 17 8E     5180      LDX CAND     TEST SIGN OF MULTIPLICAND.
9542- 10 04        5190      BPL EXIT     IF MULTIPLICAND IS NEGATIVE,
9544- 38           5200      SEC            THEN SUBTRACT MULTIPLIER FROM
9545- ED 18 8E     5210      SBC PLYR       HIGH BYTE OF PRODUCT
9548- 8D 16 8E     5220 EXIT STA MSBY    STORE PRODUCT MSB
954B- 2E 15 8E     5230      ROL LSBY     SCALE IT UP
954E- 2A           5240      ROL
954F- 60           5250      RTS          RETURN WITH PRODUCT IN A.
                   5260 *********** E N D **************
                   5270      .EN
```

SYMBOL TABLE

INPT	8F00	RELT	9100	IMGT	9200
SINT	9000	RPT1	8E01	RPT2	8E03
IPT1	8E05	IPT2	8E07	SNPT	8E09
CLNM	8E0B	CLCT	8E0C	PRNM	8E0D
CLDS	8E0E	DLTA	8E0F	SCFT	8E10
COSA	8E11	SINA	8E12	TREL	8E13
TMAG	8E14	LSBY	8E15	MSBY	8E16
CAND	8E17	PLYR	8E18	DEC	8E19
CVRT	C0B4	IPRT	C0B0	CHAN	C0B1
SMPL	8E1A	SPL	8E1C	POT	8E21
INS	8E23	INPD	930B	REAL	930D
IMAG	930F	SINE	9311	STRT	9313
CLER	9318	CLR1	931A	MOV1	9322
BREV	933D	BRV1	9342	SWAP	9351
SWP1	9367	PAS1	936C	PA1	9372
FPAS	9389	NPAS	9399	NCEL	93C6
NC1	93D5	NOPE	9479	NP1	948E
ABSO	949F	ONE	94A1	PLUS	94AE
DOWN	94BD	TWO	94BF	POS	94CC
MDST	94DB	DONE	94E3	SCAL	94E4
TEST	94E6	DIV	94FA	DIV1	94FC
DIV2	9503	DIV3	950D	MPY	9517
CHEK	9525	SHFT	952B	ADJ	953B
EXIT	9548				

;a hex dump of the sine lookup follows:

9000.90FF

```
9000- 7F 7F 7F 7F 7F 7F 7E 7E
9008- 7D 7D 7C 7B 7A 79 78 77
9010- 76 75 73 72 71 6F 6D 6C
9018- 6A 68 66 65 63 61 5E 5C
9020- 5A 58 56 53 51 4E 4C 49
9028- 47 44 41 3F 3C 39 36 33
9030- 31 2E 2B 28 25 22 1F 1C
9038- 19 16 12 0F 0C 09 06 03
9040- 00 FD FA F7 F4 F1 EE EA
9048- E7 E4 E1 DE DB D8 D5 D2
9050- CF CD CA C7 C4 C1 BF BC
9058- B9 B7 B4 B2 AF AD AA A8
9060- A6 A4 A2 9F 9D 9B 9A 98
9068- 96 94 93 91 8F 8E 8D 8B
9070- 8A 89 88 87 86 85 84 83
9078- 83 82 82 81 81 81 81 81
9080- 81 81 81 81 81 81 82 82
9088- 83 83 84 85 86 87 88 89
9090- 8A 8B 8D 8E 8F 91 93 94
9098- 96 98 9A 9B 9D 9F A2 A4
90A0- A6 A8 AA AD AF B2 B4 B7
90A8- B9 BC BF C1 C4 C7 CA CD
90B0- CF D2 D5 D8 DB DE E1 E4
90B8- E7 EA EE F1 F4 F7 FA FD
90C0- 00 03 06 09 0C 0F 12 16
90C8- 19 1C 1F 22 25 28 2B 2E
90D0- 31 33 36 39 3C 3F 41 44
90D8- 47 49 4C 4E 51 53 56 58
90E0- 5A 5C 5E 61 63 65 66 68
90E8- 6A 6C 6D 6F 71 72 73 75
90F0- 76 77 78 79 7A 7B 7C 7D
90F8- 7D 7E 7E 7F 7F 7F 7F 4C
```
*

Index